Britain and European Integration Since 1945

This book provi̶d̶e̶s̶ ̶a̶ ̶c̶o̶m̶p̶r̶e̶h̶e̶n̶s̶i̶v̶e̶ introductio̶n̶ ̶a̶n̶d̶ ̶s̶y̶s̶t̶e̶m̶a̶t̶i̶c̶ examination of Britain's relatio̶n̶s̶ ̶w̶i̶t̶h̶ ̶t̶h̶e̶ ̶E̶uropean Community and the European Union since 1945, combining an historical account with political analysis to illustrate the changing and multifaceted nature of British and European politics.

Few issues in British politics since 1945 have generated such heated controversy as Britain's approach to the process of European integration associated with the European Union. The long-running debate on the subject has not only played a major part in the downfall of prime ministers and other leading political figures but has also exposed major fault-lines within governments and caused deep and rancorous divisions within and between the major political parties. This highly contested issue has given rise to bitter campaigning in the press and between pressure groups, and it has bemused, confused and divided the public at large.

Key questions addressed include:

- Why has Europe had such an explosive impact on British politics?
- What impelled British policymakers to join the European Community and to undertake one of the radical, if not the most radical, changes in modern British history?
- What have been the perceived advantages and disadvantages of British membership of the European Union?
- Why has British membership of the European Union rarely attracted a national consensus?

Engaging with both academic and public debates about Britain and the European Union, this volume is essential reading for all students of British history, British politics, and European politics.

David Gowland was the founder and first director of the School of Contemporary European Studies at the University of Dundee where he was also head of the History Department. He has written extensively about the history of European integration and especially about Britain and the European Union.

Arthur Turner was a lecturer at the University of Dundee from 1968–2005. He has written a number of books and articles on different aspects of British foreign policy and international relations in the twentieth century.

Alex Wright lectures on European Union, UK and Scottish politics at the University of Dundee where he has written extensively on devolution and the European Union. He was a member of the Scottish Consumer Council and acted as an Assessor for the Commissioner for Public Appointments Scotland.

Britain and European Integration Since 1945

On the sidelines

David Gowland, Arthur Turner and Alex Wright

 Routledge
Taylor & Francis Group

LONDON AND NEW YORK

First published 2010
by Routledge
2 Park Square, Milton Park, Abingdon, Oxon, OX14 4RN

Simultaneously published in the USA and Canada
by Routledge
270 Madison Avenue, New York, NY 10016

Routledge is an imprint of the Taylor & Francis Group, an informa business

© 2010 David Gowland, Arthur Turner and Alex Wright

Typeset in Times New Roman by Taylor & Francis Books
Printed and bound in Great Britain by CPI Antony Rowe

British Library Cataloguing in Publication Data
A catalogue record for this book is available from the British Library

Library of Congress Cataloging in Publication Data
Gowland, David.
Britain and European integration since 1945 : on the sidelines / David Gowland, Arthur Turner & Alex Wright.
  p. cm.
1. European Union–Great Britain. 2. Great Britain–Politics and government–1945- 3. Europe–Economic integration. I. Turner, Arthur, 1941- II. Wright, Alex, 1952- III. Title.
   HC240.25.G7G68 2009
   341.24'2–dc22
                        2009007753

ISBN10 0-415-32212-X
ISBN10 0-415-32213-8
ISBN10 0-203-3990-6

ISBN13: 978-0-415-32212-6 (hbk)
ISBN13: 978-0-415-32213-3 (pbk)
ISBN13: 978-0-203-29990-6 (ebk)

For Deryck, Chris and Susan

'No man is an island, entire of itself; every man is a piece of the continent, a part of the main; if a clod be washed away by the sea, Europe is the less … '

(John Donne, 'Meditation XVII', 1624)

'Europe, because of its very disorder, has need of Britain; and wretched as this continent may seem, it is certain that Britain will not find salvation apart from Europe … The facts affirm that, for better or worse, Britain and Europe are bound up together. It may seem an unfortunate marriage. But as one of our moralists said: marriage may sometimes be good but never delightful. As our marriage is not a delightful one, let us try at least to make it a good one, since divorce is out of the question.'

(Albert Camus, The Listener, vol. 36, no. 1186, November 22 1951)

Contents

List of Abbreviations

ACP	African, Caribbean and Pacific States
APEX	Association of Professional, Executive, Clerical and Computer Staff
ASTMS	Association of Scientific, Technical and Managerial Staffs
BSE	Bovine Spongiform Encephalopathy
BTO	Brussels Treaty Organisation
CAP	Common Agricultural Policy
CBI	Confederation of British Industry
CFP	Common Fisheries Policy
CJD	Creutzfeldt-Jakob disease
CLPD	Campaign for Labour Party Democracy
CoR	Committee of the Regions
COSAC	Conference of Community and European Affairs Committees of Parliaments of the European Union
COSLA	Convention of Scottish Local Authorities
EAEC	European Atomic Energy Community
EC	European Community/ies
ECA	Economic Cooperation Administration
ECB	European Central Bank
ECJ	European Court of Justice
ECOFIN	EU Council of Finance Ministers
ECSC	European Coal and Steel Community
ECU	European Currency Unit
EDC	European Defence Community
EEC	European Economic Community
EERC	European and External Relations Committee of the Scottish Parliament
EFTA	European Free Trade Association
EMS	European Monetary System
EMU	Economic and Monetary Union
EP	European Parliament
EPC	European Political Cooperation
EPU	European Payments Union

ERDF	European Regional Development Fund
ERM	Exchange Rate Mechanism
ERP	European Recovery Programme
ETUC	European Trade Union Confederation
EU	European Union
FDP	Free Democratic Party (Federal Republic of Germany)
FTA	Free Trade Area
GATT	General Agreement on Tariffs and Trade
GDP	Gross Domestic Product
GNP	Gross National Product
IGC	Intergovernmental Conference
IMF	International Monetary Fund
IRA	Irish Republican Army
JMC	Joint Ministerial Committee
LA	Legislative Assembly of Northern Ireland
MAFF	Ministry of Agriculture, Fisheries and Food
MEP	Member of European Parliament
MINECOR	Ministerial European Co-ordination Committee
MRP	Mouvement Républicain Populaire
MSP	Member of the Scottish Parliament
NATO	North Atlantic Treaty Organisation
NEC	National Executive Committee
NFU	National Farmers Union
NICE	Northern Ireland Centre in Europe
NOP	National Opinion Polls
NRC	National Referendum Campaign
NUR	National Union of Railwaymen
OECD	Organisation for Economic Cooperation and Development
OEEC	Organisation for European Economic Cooperation
OPEC	Organisation of Petroleum Exporting Countries
PLP	Parliamentary Labour Party
PSBR	Public Sector Borrowing Requirement
QMV	Qualified Majority Voting
RegLeG	Regions with Legislative Power
SDP	Social Democratic Party
SEA	Single European Act
SFE	Scottish Financial Enterprise
SNE	Belgian Sub-National Entities
SNP	Scottish National Party
SPD	Social Democratic Party of Germany (Federal Republic of Germany)
TEU	Treaty on European Union
TGWU	Transport and General Workers' Union
TUC	Trades Union Congress
UKRep	United Kingdom Permanent Representation

UPW	Union of Post Office Workers
USDAW	Union of Shop, Distributive and Allied Workers
VAT	Value Added Tax
WEU	Western European Union

Introduction

This book provides a study of British policy and attitudes towards the process of European integration associated with the European Union (EU), formerly European Communities (EC). It covers the period from the end of the Second World War in 1945 down to the present day.

Few aspects of British politics during the past sixty years have attracted as much continuing attention and intense debate as British involvement in European integration. This highly contested issue has frequently exposed major faultlines within governments; it has wreaked havoc with the political careers and reputations of prime ministers and other government ministers; it has caused rancorous disputes within and between the major political parties and their leaderships; it has given rise to bitter polemics in the press and between pressure groups; it has produced different explanations from historians, political scientists and a variety of commentators; and it has bemused, confused and divided the public at large. The subject has also given rise to some colourful journalese. The British press is often thick with martial language, Churchillian rhetoric, and banner headlines proclaiming victory, surrender, defeat or unwarranted interference whenever Brussels and EU matters are in the news. A sample of the views of politicians and commentators conveys similar high drama. For example, Britain's involvement in European integration has been variously portrayed as the end of a thousand years of history, as a thorn in the side of British politics, as a matter triggering the most visceral reactions in the British psyche, as the cause of a nervous breakdown in the political class, as a suitable case for treatment by psychotherapists as much as by historians and political scientists, and as an issue guaranteed to reduce politicians and the press to a pantomime routine of foot-stamping, finger wagging and name-calling.

There is little disputing, then, that Britain's strange relationship with European integration is one of the persistently neuralgic issues in the country's politics. The often heated controversy is understandable, if only because the decisions taken by British governments on this subject over the past fifty years amount to one of the radical, if not the most radical, changes in the country's domestic and foreign affairs during this period. Why involvement in European integration has caused such an uproar and has often appeared as a disagreeable necessity rather than a positive benefit, why the role and functions of European integration have rarely attracted a national consensus, why a period of relative peace occasionally descends on this battlefield, and why policymaking has frequently consisted of a set of tactical adjustments to suit the needs of the moment and to preserve a 'wait and see' position towards plans for further integration, are among some of the key questions addressed in this study.

At the outset it should be noted what this book is and is not about. The subject matter is approached with a view to providing an historical understanding of the changing nature, scope and significance of British policy and attitudes towards European integration. The emphasis throughout is on presenting an interpretation of past events that attempts to make sense of British policy and attitudes towards the EU. The analysis also offers both a basis for understanding current events, problems and issues and for scrutinizing myths and prejudices that have gathered around the subject. This is not to suggest that an historical approach to the subject is sufficient in itself to illuminate contemporary problems. It is to say, however, that an understanding of long-term trends and developments and an awareness of the haunting of the present by the past, can shed light on how the past informs the present and may shape the future.

A major feature of the book centres on the determination of policy and attitudes. The main focus of attention in this respect is on the significance of national government and party politics in shaping the nature and extent of British involvement in European integration and on the influence and interplay of principles, policies and personalities. This approach, one among many, means that particular attention is paid to the role and interaction of internal and external factors in accounting for the stance of successive governments towards European integration. Themes of particular interest in this context are the interrelationship between domestic and foreign policy, the changing mixture of real or perceived constraints, opportunities and threats that faced and continue to face policymakers, and the British contribution to the course of European integration. The analysis deals to a more limited extent with the impact of European integration on British politics and economic performance. It does, however, consider the 'Europeanization' of policymaking on matters previously under exclusively national control and jurisdiction. The analysis also provides rare coverage in this type of work of the concepts of Europeanization and regionalization in relation to Northern Ireland, Scotland and Wales.

Throughout the book we have tried to avoid making judgements about whether, how far and on what terms Britain should be involved in the process of European integration, and also about how fast or how slowly British governments have responded to this process. The making of some general judgements about Britain's performance as a member state of the EC/EU does in any case require comparative treatment that is beyond the scope of this book. We alighted on the sub-title 'On the sidelines' because the nature and extent of Britain's involvement in both the origins and early leadership of the EC (nil) and in the current range of EU policies (limited) can be demonstrated by objective criteria. The sub-title also has significance in terms of the role played by Northern Ireland, Scotland and Wales in the making of British policy towards the EU. Sixty years ago in May 1948, the British Labour government of the time boycotted The Hague Congress of Europe on the grounds that it was too closely associated with the idea of a federal Europe and with the mainland European political leaders who were to the fore in the origins of the EC from which Britain excluded itself in the 1950s. Since then, Britain has become a full member of the EC/EU. At present, however, Britain is not a member of the euro zone, which is the centrepiece of the EU. Robin Cook, the former British Foreign Secretary, observed that Britain cannot be at the core of Europe if it is outside the single currency that increasingly defines that core (Cook: 2003). At the very least, therefore, it is difficult for any British government to pretend to be a key player in the EU while excluded from this major project. It is also the case that Britain does not belong to the group of EU states subscribing to the Schengen Agreements on the abolition of internal border controls. Furthermore, Britain holds opt outs on particular measures such as the EU's working time directive limiting the working week to 48 hours and also has United Kingdom (UK)-specific protocols on the Charter of Fundamental Rights of the European Union.[1] Certainly, British governments have played a leading role in some spheres, notably in pressing for reform of the Common Agricultural Policy (CAP), in advocating the creation of the single market, and in developing European foreign and defence policy where the principle of intergovernmental cooperation is much more to the liking of British governments. But the general record, studded with a history of showdowns, boycotts, opt outs and 'red lines', has frequently given rise to the view of Britain as a semi-detached or associate member of the EU. Reflecting on this record, Chris Patten, a former member of the European Commission, once commented that Britain has never actually 'joined Europe'.

The principal objects of the book are threefold. First, it attempts within the limits imposed by space to provide a comprehensive and up-to-date study of the nature, influence and interaction of internal and external factors that have shaped policy and attitudes towards European integration. Coverage of the often-multidimensional character of British policy and attitudes includes the choices and dilemmas confronting policymakers and the character of the debate within and between political parties. Such matters are considered in the context of the changing configuration of the international system and of particular responses to the dynamics of European integration. Second, the book aims to highlight several themes that are closely linked to the question of Britain and European integration. For example, the treatment deals with the loss of empire and of great power status, the management of relative economic decline and the modernization of the British economy, elitist and popular attitudes towards European integration, the strains in Britain's relationship with the EU as well as the tensions between the territorial components of the UK concerning EU membership, and the 'special relationship' between Britain and the USA. Finally, the book examines the degree of continuity and change in British policy and attitudes towards European integration over the past sixty years. In particular, it discusses both the nature and extent of change and also the recurring features in the British approach to European integration.

There are several reasons for undertaking a general study of the subject at this stage, some of which are worth mentioning here to illustrate the general scope and importance of the subject. First, few, if any, broad-based studies of Britain and European integration have emerged since the turn of the century when a clutch of books appeared on the subject (H. Young 1998, J.W. Young 2000, Gowland and Turner 2000a, Pilkington 2001). British policy and attitudes towards the EU since 1997 have therefore received limited treatment in this type of literature. This book also takes account of some of the large volume of published research on the subject in the past ten years. Furthermore, during this recent period some of the major trends in the EU have proved markedly different from the tone, texture and character of EC/EU developments in the 1980s and 1990s. During this latter period, there were major changes and significant advances in the character of European integration, and at the very least the vestigial remains of the earlier momentum, vision and inspiration underlying the formation and early development of the EC were still in evidence. The first decade of this century, however, has witnessed few landmark events in the EU landscape, while stalled attempts at institutional reform have raised questions about the limits of further integration.

Second, British membership of the EC/EU has had a pervasive influence on many aspects of Britain's political and economic life. It has had a major impact on British political institutions as well as on a wide range of policy fields and on the standing and supremacy of domestic law. At least 10 per cent of all UK laws originate in the EU, while approximately 50 per cent of the legislation affecting British business is currently determined at the EU level. Furthermore, varying estimates suggest that between 60 per cent and 90 per cent of national legislation is affected by EU decisions. At the time of writing, for example, the Brown government's bailout package for the Northern Rock building society has to demonstrate compatibility with EU rules on state restructuring aid. Meanwhile, attempts in some quarters to impose quotas on the number of non-national footballers in British professional club sides fall foul of EU law on the free movement of workers (MacShane 2005: 2; Forster and Blair 2002: 2). EC/EU membership has had a particularly profound effect on the law making powers of the UK Parliament, especially in recent decades with the widening of EU competencies and the ongoing march of European integration. This process is so far advanced that in the view of some observers the House of Commons has become little more than a provincial assembly progressively relegated to what Walter Bagehot, the Victorian constitutional authority, called 'the dignified part of the constitution'.[2] Other no less significant effects of EU membership are evident in relation to the status of EU law in several important respects. Especially notable is the fact that EU law is capable of conferring rights on individuals which British courts are obliged to uphold (direct effect), and furthermore that EU law takes precedence over conflicting provisions of British law, regardless of whether these were made before or after the EU law in question (Giddings and Drewry 2004: 37).

It is a commonplace that British membership of the EU has not put Britain at the heart of Europe but it has put Europe at the heart of Britain. Certainly, EU membership has figured as the elephant in the room of British politics, sometimes dormant, usually stirring and rarely passing unnoticed for long, and this for at least two reasons.

First, Britain's EU membership raises fundamental questions that have bedevilled British politics for sixty years and that have centred on the country's post-imperial role and identity in the wider world and in particular its relationship with mainland Europe. Some of the key questions focus on whether Britain should primarily engage militarily, politically and financially with Europe or concentrate on the world beyond Europe. There are also questions about whether the country is politically and psychologically part of Europe or is in some way an island apart. Such questions are scarcely novel. Indeed, they figure in a recent study of the rise and fall of the first British empire as precisely the sort of questions that were at the heart of eighteenth-century British politics, so much so that the British debate about European integration since 1945 'would have struck an informed eighteenth-century observer as remarkably familiar' (Simms 2007: 2).

Second, major global and European developments invariably pose questions about the nature of Britain's membership of the EU. For example, at the time of writing, the tumultuous events since August 2007 and especially during the period October–December 2008 in the financial markets included the plummeting value of sterling as it rapidly closed in on parity with the euro and added the year 2008 to the series of periodic major devaluations of sterling: 1949, 1967, 1976 and 1992. These developments brought in their train very different judgements about the meaning of events for the EU at large and for Britain's relationship with the EU in particular. There was much speculation on the question of British membership of the euro zone, and some rustling sounds in the undergrowth of British politics around an issue that had scarcely attracted attention during the preceding five years. In December 2008, José Manuel Barroso, President of the European Commission, claimed that 'the people who matter in Britain' (but evidently not the electorate) were currently thinking about the possibility of joining the euro zone.[3] Some commentators suggested that Britain might now have to enter the euro zone in order to secure the necessary financial power to deal with the crisis, while recognizing that such a course of action was political poison even as its logic became more compelling. Others insisted, however, that this was no time to contemplate joining the euro zone.[4] At the same time, one long-standing view in some British circles received yet another airing. In short, the euro zone was almost certain to disintegrate, as it was an unstable halfway house to a political union. According to this view, it could easily unravel under the impact of the crisis and in the absence of a consistent euro zone policy and a large-scale central or federal spending authority. The issue entered so much into the public domain by late 2008 that Gordon Brown publicly denied that there were any plans to scrap the pound and he insisted that it would remain in being 'this year, and next year and beyond'.[5] Shortly afterwards, William Hague, the Conservative Party Shadow Foreign Secretary, criticized the Brown government's handling of the matter, possibly fearing the loss of votes to the UK Independence Party and the British National Party in the European parliamentary elections (June 2009). In any event, Hague declared that a Conservative government under the leadership of David Cameron would never join the euro zone.[6] Meanwhile, an ICM poll carried out in December 2008 reported that 71 per cent of Britons questioned would vote to keep the pound while 23 per cent would vote to join the euro.[7] It is not the validity of these views or the significance of the polling data that are relevant here. Rather it is the extent to which the vexed question of Britain's relationship with the euro zone is so easily resurrected by events and becomes an issue in party politics once again.

Third, a general study of Britain and European integration can help to convey knowledge of a subject that attracts many opinions, some of which are based on slender evidence or outright prejudice. Certainly, there is a large amount of ignorance about Britain and Europe among the public at large and among holders of political office in particular. According to one well-informed observer, the lack of knowledge of, or empathy for, the history of Europe and of Britain's complex role within it extends across much of the British political elite (Wallace 2005). As Leader of the House of Commons, Robin Cook concluded that the Commons had not recognized the extent to which what happened within the EU had such a big bearing on what happened in domestic politics.[8] Denis MacShane, a former Europe minister in the Foreign and Commonwealth Office (hereafter FCO), claimed that Britain and Europe was a subject that all too clearly demonstrated the poor level of policy discussion and debate in British political parties. MacShane further maintained that ignorance weakened British influence and masked the real question of how Britain could extract maximum advantage from EU membership (MacShane 2005: 2, 13–14). Public knowledge about the EU is in short supply. At best the EU is regarded as remote, complex, interfering or boring in so far as it attracts any attention. In the biggest survey of British public opinion carried out by the EU's Commission, well over 50 per cent of the respondents said they knew only a bit about the EU, while 30 per cent of respondents said that they knew nothing.[9] Such limited knowledge has often meant that distortions, simplistic and demonizing narratives, deeply ingrained prejudices and stereotypes easily creep into British media representations of the EU and acquire status as immutable historical truths. As a highly politicized issue, moreover, Britain's past relationship with the process of European integration is frequently plundered for partisan purposes. Politicians, in particular, sometimes place a one-sided, unnuanced construction on past events in the form of self-serving, unreliable memoirs. These are written with the benefit of hindsight and are often designed to demonstrate the strengths or limitations of past or present policies and attitudes. In fact, political debate about the EU in Britain often appears to be determined to remain entrenched in the past with the history of the past sixty years weighing heavily on the present. This extended British version of coming to terms with the past, or of failing to do so and thereby becoming imprisoned by the past, found eloquent expression in Hugo Young's arresting opening sentence to his stimulating study of Britain and Europe since 1945: 'This is the story of fifty years in which Britain struggled to reconcile the past she could not forget with the future she could not avoid' (H. Young 1998: 1). The combination of the historical and the polemical in this single sentence is illustrative of some of the literature on the subject that involves historical scholarship and political values.

The historiography of this subject is still in its infancy partly because of the huge gaps in the availability of primary source material, especially in the form of government papers for the second half of the period covered by this study, and partly because of the close proximity to the events discussed in this book. Much of the published work of historians has so far concentrated on the period 1945–73 and has made extensive use of government papers in the National Archives that are available under the 30-year rule. British policy towards the origins and early development of the EEC in this period has received contrasting treatment at the hands of historians and commentators. Some of the early studies of the subject portray British governments as short-sighted and unimaginative in their response to the Schuman plan of 1950 that resulted in the formation of the ESCS and to the Messina initiative of 1955 that culminated in the formation of the EEC and EAEC. According to this version of events, the leadership of Europe was Britain's for the taking. British governments, however, failed to take opportunities as they occurred in 1950 and 1955 and thus left a legacy of 'lost opportunities', a failure portrayed in the literature as Britain missing the European bus or never missing an opportunity to miss an opportunity. Anthony Nutting offered one of the most powerful, contemporary expressions of this view in his polemical book *Europe Will Not Wait* (1960), arguing that the Schuman plan, in particular, was the most critical of the lost opportunities for Britain to lead Europe. The classic exposition of this view appeared shortly afterwards in Miriam Camps' book, *Britain and the European Community 1955–63* (1964). In this account, the British withdrawal (November 1955) from the negotiations resulting in the formation of the EEC was the major lost opportunity. Camps argued that the policymakers lacked vision and failed to recognize the value of the Community method of European integration. A recent biographical sketch of one senior Foreign Office official of this period, Roger Makins, perhaps summed up the lack of vision that Camps and others perceived in British policymakers of the time; Makins was described as a man 'for whom security outbid futurity and the purposive crowded out the imaginative'.[10] Later accounts based on primary source material echo some of the criticisms of British policy associated with this explanation. But they do so while seeking only to explain why Britain was not a founder member of the EEC and without making unhistorical comments or judgements based on hindsight about whether any British government could or should have acted differently in this period. At the same time, the 'lost opportunities' account remained a potent force, at least in political circles; Tony Blair as Prime Minister, for example, subscribed to this version of events in some of his major pro-European speeches.[11]

This explanation was increasingly challenged as government papers for the 1950s were released in the 1980s. Historians were now more inclined to view Britain's European policy in a more positive and constructive light, especially citing the willingness of British governments to participate in intergovernmental organizations and to support the origins of the EC by guarantees and forms of association. Such accounts judged British policy on its merits in the context of the domestic and international situation then prevailing and without any polemical undertones. It was generally agreed that 1955 rather than 1950 represented the crucial parting of the ways between Britain and the founder member states of the EC, though in both cases the choices open to decision makers were considered far less clear cut than in earlier studies of the subject. The overworked metaphor of Britain missing the European bus was now employed only for the purpose of demonstrating its unhistorical features. In particular, for example, it was argued that that there was no guarantee that the bus was roadworthy. Furthermore, British leaders did not really miss the bus as fail to realize that it was there to be caught, and even if Britain had boarded the bus it was unlikely that the other passengers would have allowed Britain to act as driver and determine the destination. Besides which, as one of the leading historians of Britain's European policy has put it, Britain could not have had the leadership of Europe on its own terms because, unlike the founders of the EC, Britain saw no need to abandon its sovereignty to common institutions (J. W. Young 2000).

Some of the more recent work on the subject suggests the makings of a new school of thought, at least according to one path-breaking, historiographical work which discerns the familiar model of traditional, revisionist and post-revisionist accounts in studies of the subject (Daddow 2004). Some recent studies generally tend to view British policy as a messy, improvised process of muddling through. This approach dismisses the name, blame and shame accounts of the 'lost opportunities' explanation. It also rejects the neat and tidy explanations offered by earlier studies as either misguided or simplistic, and instead it claims to provide a more nuanced, sophisticated analysis. For example, it emphasizes the rapidly changing views of key individuals and government departments, the complex interplay of events, and the contradictions, ambiguities, divided opinions and unintended consequences at the heart of policymaking, all of which account for what is sometimes viewed as the incoherence and disorganization in the making of Britain's European policy. The absence of underlying patterns, the emphasis on the contingent and the accidental, and the concentration on numerous, intricate interactions in multilayered organizations, occasionally suggest a combination of the workings of chaos theory and H. A. L. Fisher's view of history as 'one damned thing after another' (Fisher 1935: 2).

Few of the emphases or main features in recent accounts are novel. In many respects, they correspond to the view that politicians often react to developments in a much more contradictory, confused and apprehensive way than is sometimes allowed for in some historical accounts or political theories. In short, as A. J. P. Taylor reminded a generation of historians, politicians stumble forward like military generals in the fog of war and where they emerge when the fog lifts is often a complete surprise to them, though they will quickly claim the credit for a successful outcome. The unexpected turn of events has occurred at various stages in the evolution of British policy and attitudes towards European integration. For example, most British political leaders, government officials and the public at large for at least a decade or so after the Second World War believed that a Franco-German reconciliation advanced by means of a common market was inconceivable. Similarly, neither Harold Macmillan nor Harold Wilson following their success in the general elections of 1959 and 1964 respectively expected to be filing applications for EEC membership within less than three years of their electoral victories. Likewise, Margaret Thatcher supported the Single European Act of 1986, but soon recoiled in horror at the previously unimaginable economic and monetary union implications of the Act. In 1990 she undertook a sudden about-turn by agreeing to include sterling in the Exchange Rate Mechanism (ERM), after strongly resisting such a move since coming to power in 1979. Her comment at her last Cabinet meeting – 'It's a funny old world' – in many respects applied as much to her EC policy in the period 1986–90 as to any other aspect of her prime ministerial career. Thatcher's successor, John Major, shepherded sterling into the ERM as Chancellor of the Exchequer in 1990, only to be faced by its unexpected and unceremonious exit from the ERM two years later. A similar unanticipated turn of events in the Blair premiership occurred when Blair decided to hold a referendum on the EU's Constitutional Treaty. He had strenuously and lengthily argued against such a proposal and only six months earlier he had boasted that he had no reverse gear. It is fair to say, therefore, that British policy towards the process of European integration has rarely lost its capacity to surprise. It has often validated Macmillan's celebrated answer to a journalist's question about what can most easily steer a government off course: 'Events, dear boy, events.'[12]

Throughout the story of Britain's engagement with the process of European integration, it is evident that there is no single driving force or monocausal explanation for a particular policy or attitude but rather an intermingling of factors. In his recent reflections on life as Britain's ambassador to the EU and later as Blair's EU adviser, Stephen Wall observes that as opposed to the view of government decision-making as ordered, logical, rational and predictable, the reality was altogether more complex and messy. In short, a changing mixture of factors is at work, ranging from an inherited view of national interest, partisanship and circumstance to public pressures and luck, or what he later describes as a rich mixture of the systematic, logical, instinctive, personal reasonable and unreasonable in the shaping of negotiating positions (Wall 2008: 185, 201). For our own part, we have endeavoured to stick to the always impossible undertaking of not reading history backwards, of avoiding the benefit of hindsight, and of remaining alert to the ways in which individual contributions to the debate about Britain's relations with the EC/EU have been influenced by considerations which were not necessarily at the heart of the matter in dispute. We have sought to remember, as one author has put it, that 'Every important decision is taken with inadequate knowledge by imperfect men and women whom the future will confound' (Bobbit 2008). It is against this background, for example, that one of the key questions during the early period of this study is not whether Britain 'missed the European bus' in the 1950s but rather how far governments of the day addressed the counterfactuals with any degree of rigour and seriousness.

There are several problems in tackling a subject of this kind in a general text. There is, for example, the difficulty of determining the weighting and influence of a number of perspectives in the shaping of policy and attitudes whether from the insular and the European to the Atlantic and the global or from grand designs concerning Britain's role and status in the wider world to low calculations of party or personal advantage. Then, too, studies of this subject have reflected the particular interests and expertise of the historian and have thus drawn on different branches of historical scholarship such as international, diplomatic, economic, political, cultural and financial history. There are problems, too, in terms of the availability of evidence. For example, the period covered in this book includes publicly accessible and voluminous primary source material for the first half of the period under the operation of the 30-year rule concerning access to British government papers. Any study of the second half of the period, however, still has to rely mainly on secondary source material. This is not to say that primary source material should have privileged status. It is to note, however, that material for the later period often takes the form of political memoirs which are written with hindsight and with an eye to the historical record and may differ significantly from what the subject thought at the time or thought was happening at the time.

The character, aims, and identity of the EC/EU require some introductory comment. First, and to avoid any confusing nomenclature, it should be noted that for the period 1957–72 we often use the title European Economic Community (EEC) or Common Market as it was popularly called in Britain until the late 1970s. The legally correct title throughout this period and until 1992 was the 'European Communities' (EC), comprising the European Coal and

Steel Community (ECSC), based on the Treaty of Paris (1951), and the European Economic Community (EEC) and the European Atomic Energy Community (EAEC), founded on the Treaties of Rome (1957). For the post-1992 period, we have used the EU title derived from the (Maastricht) Treaty on European Union (1992). Occasionally, we employ the shorthand expression 'Europe' which, unless otherwise specified, refers to the EC/EU. We also use the acronym EU, as in the next few paragraphs, as an umbrella term where it is not strictly accurate legally and historically.[13] 'Britain' and 'UK' are synonymous terms, and 'America', 'US' and 'USA' are similarly treated throughout the text. Needless to say, we apologize for resorting to the forest of acronyms that litters the post-1945 international landscape.

We deal with the particular origins and development of the EU as and where appropriate in the text. Here it is sufficient to note some of the key features of the history and dynamics of European integration as associated with the EU. Integration and enlargement have figured as two of the main processes in the history of the EU. The principal landmarks in the field of integration are fourfold. First, the supranational principle and the idea of sector integration found expression in the ECSC Treaty of Paris, the only EU treaty to employ the term 'supranational'. Second, the Treaty of Rome establishing the EEC was designed to create a common market for the free movement of goods, capital, labour and services. Third, the Single European Act (SEA) of 1986 committed the EEC states to the creation of a single market by 1992. Finally, the Maastricht Treaty introduced institutional changes and laid out a programme for economic and monetary union including a single currency and a European Central Bank. Eleven of the 15 EU member states eventually adopted the euro as their single currency in January 1999 with euro notes and coins in circulation as from January 1 2002. On the tenth anniversary (January 2009) of the launching of the euro zone, 16 EU countries, including Slovakia which joined in January 2009, were within the euro zone. Nine of the remaining EU states are obliged to join the euro zone in due course, while Britain and Denmark obtained special derogations (opt outs) in the Maastricht Treaty negotiations.

The enlargement of the EU represents one of the massive changes in its history over the past thirty years. The original membership of six states (Belgium, France, Italy, Luxembourg, the Netherlands and West Germany) has increased to 27 states, comprising a population of 495 million (2008). Enlargement has occurred in four major waves, the first involving Denmark, Ireland and the UK (1973), the second taking in the former military dictatorships of Greece (1981), Portugal and Spain (1986), the third extending to Austria, Finland and Sweden (1995), and the fourth incorporating many of the former eastern Europe communist states: the Czech Republic, Estonia, Hungary, Latvia, Lithuania, Poland, Slovakia and Slovenia (2004) together with Bulgaria and Roumania (2007). In addition, East Germany joined the EU as part of a united Germany (1990), and the island states of Cyprus and Malta secured membership in 2004.

The relationship between integration and enlargement in the history of the EU has varied over time and in different cases. In the 1970s the implications of the first enlargement generally overshadowed the process of integration. During the 1980s, however, the EU expanded at the same time as it embarked upon the single market programme, and in the 1990s the decision to form the euro zone preceded the enlargement of 1995. During the current decade, enlargement has acted as a spur to belated and still incomplete institutional reform that failed to materialize in the Constitutional Treaty (2004) and is currently taking the form of the Treaty of Lisbon, the future of which is uncertain at the time of writing following Ireland's referendum result against the treaty. Such mishaps as the French and Dutch rejections of the Constitutional Treaty and earlier reservations about the Maastricht Treaty, which was initially rejected by Denmark, suggest that the European project has run out of steam. It appears to lack a contemporary and compelling narrative and rationale comparable in vision, strength and impact to that of the founding fathers of the EC in the 1950s.

The combination of integration and enlargement has produced an organization that is a formidable economic, commercial and monetary bloc on the global scene. On its formation in 1957, the EEC was a relatively small unit in the global trading and monetary system, with primarily European-focused trading patterns and with a set of national rather than international currencies. At the time, it was clearly overshadowed by the strength and scale of the US economy that had so recently supported the post-war recovery efforts of the EEC member states through dollar aid. By 2002, however, the EU with an economy of more than $9 trillion was larger than that of the USA. By 2008, it accounted for about 31 per cent of the world's total economic output. In addition, it has become the world's biggest trader with the largest share (18 per cent in 2005) of the world market for internationally traded goods.[14] Meanwhile, since its launch in January 1999, the euro has become the world's second major currency, thereby defying some of the initial predictions that it would be a non-starter or a 'toilet currency' in the parlance of some foreign exchange dealers. Over the past 50 years, the proportion of total British trade accounted for by the EC/EU has increased from 12 per cent to nearly 60 per cent. British companies export about £150 billion worth of goods to EU countries (2006), and at least three million British jobs are estimated to depend on EU membership.[15]

European integration as a process or as a means has attracted a wide variety of theories, explanations and aspirations concerning its nature, course and direction.[16] The collective existence, experience and aims of the EU states have often been portrayed in terms of interchangeable words like 'unity', 'unification' and 'union'. The underlying purpose of the EU, as specified in the preamble to the Treaty of Rome of 1957 establishing the EEC and endorsed by the Maastricht Treaty, is 'to create an ever closer union among the peoples of Europe'. This declaration has proved sufficiently imprecise to accommodate some polarized visions of the EU's potential in terms of federal

and confederal systems of government or supranational and intergovernmental forms of decision-making. This reaches to the heart of the uniqueness
of the EU as a political system in that it defies classification either as a conventional international organization or as a sovereign state.

One of the underlying features of the EU since its origins has been the
fluctuating balance between supranationalism and intergovernmentalism
which in turn has a bearing on the changing position of the EC/EU on the
spectrum between confederal and federal forms of government. Support for a
federal Europe in the first decade or so after the Second World War was severely
checked by Gaullist France in the 1960s. By the 1970s the EC resembled a
traditional international organization, with a strong emphasis on intergovernmental cooperation and a form of decision-making based on the lowest
common denominator. During the 1980s and 1990s, however, the relationship
between the EU and its constituent states changed yet again as the SEA
greatly undermined the exercise of a national veto by a single member state in
the EC's decision-making system. The Maastricht Treaty subsequently shifted
the balance even further towards the federal end of the spectrum, especially in
its provisions for economic and monetary union and for a European Central
Bank.

The EU is in fact a hybrid creation both in terms of its policy range and its
institutional character. The euro zone, for example, is very much a halfway
house in that it constitutes a monetary union but not a political union with a
full range of fiscal powers. This much is evident at the time of writing as
individual member states of the euro zone initially responded unilaterally to
banking crises in their states, as if it remains the case that the comradely
rhetoric of the single market counts for little as 'national dog still eats
national dog' (Patten 1998: 99–100). In this, as in other respects, the EU is an
organization still delicately poised between a confederation of states and a
federal state. The populations of its member states are EU citizens. Yet the
EU still falls far short of possessing the competences of a state, whether
organized on federal or unitary lines. It has no independent powers to tax its
citizens. Furthermore, it has neither the right nor the resources to exercise the
legitimate use of force within and beyond its borders. The EU still does not
'do' war, as Joschka Fischer, a former German foreign minister, expressed the
matter. In recent years, the concept of a 'multi-speed' Europe with some
member states more willing and able than others to advance towards common
objectives has further clouded the identity and future development of the EU
as an undifferentiated entity.

Another aspect of the mixed character of the EU is evident in the way it
has been commonly represented as an economic giant but a political dwarf.
There is a marked contrast between the economic clout of the EU and its
lightweight political and diplomatic standing in foreign and security policy.
The collective responses of the EU states to the international crises in the
1990s and most notably to the military conflicts surrounding the decaying
corpse of Yugoslavia scarcely changed this image or gave much expression to

the Common Foreign and Security Policy (CFSP) earlier enshrined in the Maastricht Treaty. Furthermore, the deep divisions exposed before, during and after the US-led invasion of Iraq (April 2003) indicated all too clearly that the EU was far from speaking with one voice on major issues. More recently still, in an episode that echoed the initial disarray of the EU states over the recognition of Croatia as an independent state in 1992, the EU states were divided in their response to the declaration of independence in Kosovo (February 2008). They were also at odds over their initial response to the banking crisis of 2008, most notably, for example, in the different reactions of Germany and Ireland.

The mixed character of the EU is also evident in institutional terms. EU institutions are normally classified as either supranational or intergovernmental. Neither of these terms is precisely defined in the treaties but they have emerged to indicate differences in the membership and representative functions of the EU institutions. Two of the six main institutions, the European Council and the Council of the European Union, are intergovernmental and comprise official representatives of the member states, principally heads of state or government in the former and government ministers in the latter. They pursue the preferences of member state governments and represent the interests of the individual member states in the EU decision-making process. The other institutions are supranational and consist of personnel either appointed or elected to serve and represent the collective 'European' interest. The European Commission and the European Court of Justice are supranational institutions that play an important regulatory role in settling disputes between member states or between parties within and across member states. In the absence of these institutions, such disputes would remain unresolved or be determined by *force majeure*. This supranational function is often misunderstood or overlooked by British politicians and the public, for whom the concept of supranationality elicits almost as much distaste as the idea of a federal Europe. While the European Parliament (EP) is directly elected, judges are appointed to work in the European Court of Justice (ECJ), bankers are appointed to make monetary policy in the ECB (European Central Bank), and officials are appointed to develop and oversee the policies in the European Commission. The terms 'intergovernmental' and 'supranational' also describe different decision-making procedures in the Council of the European Union. Intergovernmental procedures mean that member state governments can exercise the right to veto unwanted decisions. In contrast, supranational decision rules, such as QMV (Qualified Majority Voting), are procedures by which member states accept surrendering their veto.

Some of the particular features of the institutional character and range of policies of the EC/EU are evident in relation to regions and stateless nations. This subject receives detailed coverage in Chapters 5 and 7 of this book. The separate treatment of Northern Ireland, Scotland and Wales in this context is one of the distinctive features of this book and represents an important departure from the largely English or nominally British analysis of the subject. Here, it is sufficient to note some of the key developments and questions raised by the regionalization of the EU. As far as the EEC's regions and stateless nations were concerned (sometimes referred to as territories hereafter), the EEC was potentially a problem. That was because in its early years at least, the EEC was essentially an intergovernmental organization, albeit that it possessed supranational characteristics, where its treaties so allowed. During the first thirty years of the EEC's existence, the member states treated EEC relations as foreign policy, and consequently this fell within the competence of state governments, with virtually no substantive role for their territorial or sub-state administrations. That began to change, following the Single European Act (SEA) when the EEC embarked upon the completion of the single market. By 1987, it was difficult to avoid the impression that some territorial administrations, especially those with the most political authority, stood to be the net losers when competence was transferred to the EEC. In effect, areas of policy which were the sole competence of territorial administrations, or which they shared with their state government, were decided at the European level, with the Council of Ministers (until the Treaty on European Union in 1992) acting as a de facto legislature. For the most part, ministers from the governments of the member states represented the interests of their territorial administrations in the Council. Consequently the regions were one step removed from decision-making in the EEC. That began to change during the 1990s. The Treaty on European Union tacitly acknowledged that its territories had a role to play in EU policy making where the treaties so allowed. Depending on their national constitutional arrangements, ministers from sub-state governments could vote in the Council. The principle of subsidiarity portended that where possible decisions in the EU should be taken at the lowest level where appropriate. Last, a Committee of the Regions (CoR) was set up. Although it did not have decision-making status it was at least recognition that the EU's regions and stateless nations should have a formal role in the policy process where appropriate. The regions which capitalized on the new arrangements and which were the driving force for regional empowerment were the Belgian Sub-national Entities and the German Länder. But even they subsequently secured new inter-governmental arrangements within their respective countries, which potentially provided them with a greater influence internally over EU matters (Gerstenlauer 1985 and 1995; Hooghe 1995; Jeffery 1997a; Kerremans and Beyers 1997; Kerremans 2000).

The regionalization of the EU would have a number of consequences for the UK. In the first place the Conservative governments of Thatcher (1979–90) and Major (1990–97) were opposed to the principle of subsidiarity, save that it should be used to protect UK sovereignty. More particularly after 1992 the Conservatives were losing ground in Scotland. The SNP's (Scottish National Party) 'Independence in Europe' campaign, though potentially defective (the EU's Common Fisheries Policy – CFP – was not popular in parts of Scotland), did have a resonance at a time when the legitimacy of the Conservatives in Scotland was open to question. In addition the EU posed a particular problem for the UK and its territorial administrations in Northern Ireland, Scotland and Wales. First, the system of government varied from territory to territory. So far as Northern Ireland was concerned, devolution was suspended in March 1972. Thereafter until the Good Friday Agreement it was governed directly by Westminster albeit that it retained its own civil service at the Northern Ireland Office. Wales also had its own administration at the Welsh Office and a team of ministers. Scotland was not dissimilar to Wales, though the Scottish Office enjoyed rather more administrative devolution. Prior to the UK's membership of the EEC, in one way or another the interests of these territories were directly represented within the UK government (e.g. they each had their own Secretary of State who was a member of the UK Cabinet – a body which was chaired by the Prime Minister). The EEC posed something of a challenge as from 1973 onwards it rested with the UK government to promote and defend their respective interests in the EEC.

For its part the UK was a unitary state prior to the inception of constitutional change during 1999. Whilst there was the possibility that Scotland and Wales would have devolved governments at the end of the 1970s, that came to nought in 1979. Thereafter the issue was laid to rest temporarily. But by the mid-1980s, the issue began to climb up the agenda once more. Consequently as time went by the UK government found itself squeezed from above and below. At the EC/EU level each successive treaty transferred more power to the EC/EU. If devolution came to fruition then additional powers would be transferred to the territorial administrations. The 1997 general election proved to be a watershed. The Conservatives were routed and Tony Blair became Prime Minister of a Labour government. Blair led a party that for some years had been committed to devolution, which he viewed as but one facet of his programme to modernize how the UK was governed. He also took a personal interest in Northern Ireland. Although the initial move to secure a peace settlement lay with his predecessor, John Major, the Conservative Prime Minister, Blair devoted considerable energy to restoring devolution to Northern Ireland which eventually came to fruition but did not stabilize until 2007.

In some respects the inception of devolution during the Blair years created something of a paradox. The devolved legislatures had a greater (i.e. Northern Ireland and Scotland) or lesser (i.e. Wales) degree of autonomy over domestic matters. But to no small degree the EU was involved in a swathe of policies that fell within their competence. As the EU's authority was paramount in such instances, it called into question just how much power the new administrations really possessed. In addition, they had no alternative but to use the UK government as their link to the Council of Ministers (subsequently renamed the Council of the European Union).[17] However, that was not the whole picture, as the new administrations as well as the legislatures could forge their own links with the EU and its territorial governments. That coincided with RegLeg, which aimed to raise the collective influence of the EU's regions with legislative powers. Northern Ireland did not participate as devolution was suspended off and on until 2007.

In effect, the period 1999–2008 was one of challenges and opportunities for the devolved administrations as far as the EU was concerned. But the issue remained, how much autonomy did they really possess with regard to EU matters both in the context of the UK and of the EU more generally. Allied to which there is a number of issues. Did devolution provide them with additional channels of influence to the EU? Did the EU undergo regionalization during this period and if so what were the consequences for the devolved administrations? These questions will be addressed in greater detail in Chapters 5 and 7.

1 Limited liability, 1945–55

This chapter focuses on key episodes in the evolution of British policy and attitudes towards the idea of European unity in the first decade after the Second World War. The analysis concentrates on three periods that were of critical importance in determining the nature and extent of British involvement in the formative stages of post-war European organizations. The first period, January 1948–January 1949, began with a ringing endorsement of an expansive view of European unity expressed by British Foreign Secretary Ernest Bevin in his Western Union speech of January 1948. It terminated, however, with a more circumscribed, official definition of the limits of British involvement in the post-war reconstruction and organization of western Europe. The second period, May–June 1950, included the unveiling of a plan for a coal and steel community by Robert Schuman, the French foreign minister, and subsequent British aloofness from the negotiations resulting in the formation of the European Coal and Steel Community (ECSC), comprising Belgium, France, Italy, Luxembourg, the Netherlands and West Germany (thereafter known as 'the Six'). The third period, June–November 1955, opened with a decision by the Six to consider plans for a common market. It ended with the British refusal to participate in negotiations resulting in the signing of the Treaties of Rome (March 1957) and the creation of the European Economic Community (EEC) and the European Atomic Energy Community (EAEC).

The principal aims of this chapter are to identify the distinctive features of the British approach to these developments, to assess the main and especially long-standing determinants of policy, and to identify, where appropriate, different explanations for the course of events in the immediate post-war decade. The concept of limited liability, frequently employed to characterize Britain's minimal military commitment to the defence of Europe in the inter-war period, gradually emerged as the benchmark of British policy towards the reconstruction and integration of mainland Europe in the immediate post-war decade. It first figured prominently in January 1949 among the conclusions of a paper by senior Whitehall officials. Their advice on the essentials of Britain's European policy was subsequently endorsed by the Cabinet of the Labour government under the leadership of Clement Attlee:

Our policy should be to assist Europe to recover as far as we can … But the concept must be one of limited liability. In no circumstances must we assist them [the Europeans] beyond the point at which the assistance leaves us too weak to be a worth-while ally for U.S.A. if Europe collapses … Nor can we embark upon measures of "cooperation" which surrender our sovereignty and which lead us down paths along which there is no return.

(Cairncross 1982: 209)

This general conclusion was most immediately shaped by wartime experiences and early post-war conditions.

The Second World War had a profound and lasting impact on the post-war attitudes of British policymakers and public towards involvement in mainland Europe. Wartime experiences reinforced a deep-seated sense of insularity and detachment from the continent. This experience was famously captured in the David Low cartoon of 1940 with a British Tommy waving his fist at German bombers and yelling defiantly 'Very well, alone!'. It was also equally well conveyed by the no doubt apocryphal comment of the London taxi driver who, on hearing news of the defeat of France by Nazi Germany (June 1940), commented: 'Thank God we're playing the final at home'. Popular and entrenched British perceptions of Europe as a source of war, disorder and undemocratic politics together with contempt for the weaknesses of individual European countries and widespread Germanophobia, created a pathological distrust of Europe and strengthened the case against mainland European entanglements. Furthermore, Britain had escaped the mainland European wartime trauma of invasion, defeat and occupation. There was thus a far greater inclination in Britain than among the mainland European states to regard the wartime record, especially the landmark events of 1940 like the Dunkirk evacuation and the Battle of Britain, as a matter of perpetual celebration maintained by a memory bank of wartime exploits, myths and prejudices; Britain's future seemed to lie in its past.

This wartime record was viewed as affirming rather than calling into question the strength of British national culture, institutions and sovereignty. In addition, the 'standing alone' imagery of Britain as the sole bulwark against Nazi Germany in 1940 instilled into policymakers and public alike a strong sense of moral superiority and of unequalled leadership qualities in Europe. Meanwhile, Britain's status as one of the three major victorious allies alongside the USA and the USSR combined with its widespread overseas ties through the Commonwealth and Empire seemed, outwardly at least, to confirm the country's position as a global power. There was limited appreciation, in effect, of the extent to which, since the deceptive independence of 1940–41, Britain had entered a phase displaying the characteristics of a second class power: military dependence on a powerful ally, persistent economic vulnerability, imperial overstretch and a narrowing range of options in international affairs. This condition was further underlined by the extent to which, as compared with the USA and the USSR, Britain emerged from the war with few material rewards for its sacrifice and virtual bankruptcy

The impact of the war and of immediate post-war conditions on Britain's global standing and resources also greatly influenced the handling of mainland European affairs. Several factors shaped British policy towards mainland Europe in the early post-war years and eventually determined how and why policymakers alighted upon the concept of limited liability, which in turn governed policy towards post-war European organizations. One important factor was the marked difference in resources between Britain and much of mainland Europe in the early post-war years. Britain had its own post-war national strategy or 'special' path to post-war recovery that was assisted by assets and short-term advantages denied to or only partially available to most European states. The list of assets most immediately included such advantages as Commonwealth markets, colonial resources, London's position as a financial centre and large armed forces, all of which were soon to be joined by a close peacetime alliance with the US and the acquisition of nuclear weapons.[1] These advantages indicated that Britain's standing as a world power had substance and also meant that Europe was not a crucial or necessary element in Britain's post-war economic recovery. This position was highlighted by British involvement in the European response to the US (Marshall) offer of aid in 1947. Ideally, the British government wanted dollar aid without any strings attached in terms of European cooperation by all recipients of this aid. The government also wanted recognition by the Americans of Britain's special global standing as compared with the position of the other states. US policymakers rejected both views from the outset. British policymakers, however, continued to impress on the US Truman administration the distinctive features of Britain's standing as a major player in the world economy.

A further defining and recurring factor in the making of British policy was the belief that Europe could not be separated from the global dimensions of British foreign policy and that the European continent did not represent the major, exclusive area of British strategic interest. The complex interaction and changing importance of a number of factors that shaped British policy towards Europe in the early post-war years first became apparent in the making and outcome of the Western Union initiative. This project was formally launched by Bevin in January 1948 with a call for some form of union in Western Europe including Britain. During the next two years, however, and in a way that was to be characteristic of the tortuous course of British policy towards European integration over the next sixty years, this positive endorsement of the principle of west European union was relegated in importance. By April 1950 Bevin was convinced that it was necessary 'to get away from talk about Europe', to recognize that Europe did not constitute a separate self-contained unit, and to accept that the original conception of Western Union had to give way to the wider conception of the Atlantic Community.[2]

The origins and significance of this initiative have attracted different assessments at the hands of historians and commentators ever since. Some have viewed it as an integral part of Bevin's effort to lure the USA into giving military backing to western Europe in the face of deteriorating relations between the Western Powers and the USSR (Cold War) with heightened west European fears about Soviet intentions in Europe. According to this explanation, the Western Union was primarily designed to demonstrate that the west European states were prepared to make collective defence arrangements but clearly required US backing to make these effective. Bevin's underlying purpose was thus fulfilled in the Atlantic Pact of 1949 and the subsequent formation of the North Atlantic Treaty Organization (NATO), the crowning achievement of his foreign secretaryship according to this account. Other commentators, however, have argued that Western Union was not initially conceived as a first step in this direction but was in fact part of a general, long-term design to reassert British power and influence via a British-led western Europe extending to and utilizing western Europe's overseas colonies and links. In effect, Bevin aimed to organize the 'middle of the planet' and thus create a 'Third Force' in the international system that was on a par with, and independent of, the USA and the USSR. Still other commentators have maintained that this idea of Britain organizing the 'middle of the planet' was a fanciful notion reflecting illusions of grandeur and offering an insubstantial basis for dealing with the pressing problems of western Europe's economic weakness and defencelessness.[3]

In the wake of the Western Union initiative, the nature and extent of British interest in some form of union in western Europe was tested in the military, economic and political fields. The most immediate consequence of the initiative was the signing of the Brussels Treaty (March 1948) by Britain, France and the Benelux states (Belgium, Luxembourg and The Netherlands). By this mutual assistance pact, the five states agreed to provide military and other aid in the event of a military attack on a member state and to collaborate in economic, social and cultural matters via the Brussels Treaty Organisation (BTO). In its origins and early workings the BTO suggested a well-considered, positive British approach to the idea of European unity in the form of a west European bloc under British leadership. Several features of this undertaking soon became clearly defined and reflected both the immediate and longer-term limits of British interest in the organization of western Europe.

First, there was a strong determination to ensure that the Brussels Treaty commitment did not involve the commitment of British military forces to mainland Europe: 'We do not want any more Dunkirks', declared Bevin. At this time the main pillars of British defence policy, were the defence of the UK mainland, control of the lines of sea communication and defence commitments in the Middle East. These took priority over any possible peacetime undertaking to the defence of mainland Europe.[4]

Second, British policymakers, as in the inter-war period, were intent on resisting French requests for a strong British military commitment to the continent and for the closest possible form of military cooperation between

London and Paris. Such resistance was symptomatic of the ambivalent attitudes of the policymakers towards France in these early post-war years. They believed that any form of west European cooperation had to be based on a UK/France axis, and yet they feared that France's political, economic and military weaknesses offered no sound basis for cooperation.

Third, it became clear shortly after the signing of the Brussels Treaty that the BTO in the British view was not an instrument for furthering European unity as an end in itself. It was instead a staging post to the Atlantic Alliance and the revival of the wartime 'special relationship' between Britain and the USA. This process was set in motion by the Pentagon talks involving Britain, Canada and the USA (22 March–1 April 1948) which raised the possibility of involvement by the USA in a Western defence system and culminated in the signing of the North Atlantic Treaty (April 1949). If the growing involvement of the USA in western Europe at this time was a case of 'empire by invitation', Britain was to the fore in issuing the invitation. Thereafter, Cold War politics and the acquisition of nuclear weapons became the dominant elements in British foreign and defence policy and reinforced the illusion of British power and influence at the top table of international politics. Most importantly and significantly in the European context, these developments further sealed in British eyes at least the so-called 'special relationship' with the USA. In particular, they gave practical expression to the idea of using US power, as a wartime Foreign Office paper presciently summarized the ideal 'special relationship' in peacetime, 'for purposes which we regard as good' or what has been described as 'power-by-proxy'.[5]

The alliance with the USA now became the sheet anchor of British foreign policy. It served several manifest and latent functions in the immediate and longer term. British political leaders perceived a wide variety of advantages in cultivating the idea of a 'special relationship'. Most immediately, and in the face of the Soviet presence in eastern Europe, it protected post-war British governments from a repetition of the fearful pre-war charge of appeasement. In the longer term, the 'special relationship' helped to obscure Britain's declining role and status; it offered an emotional comfort blanket for a declining power; it concealed the imbalance of power between Britain and the USA; it provided privileged contacts with the US government especially for example in the intelligence-gathering field, on the money markets as a support for sterling, and (later) for gaining preferential access to US military technology; it sought to harness US power to serve British interests within and beyond Europe;[6] and finally it perpetuated the image of Britain as a bridge or pivot in relations between Europe and the USA. All in all, it was assumed that the US government could be persuaded to act in Britain's best interests, partly because the USA required the experience, knowledge and moral support of a worldly-wise guide like Britain in international affairs and partly because, as in the 'bases for destroyers deal' of 1941, Britain could trade military bases at home and abroad for material assistance from the USA.[7] A particularly important implication of the British view of this 'special relationship' was that this relationship became the single major external stumbling block to closer relations between Britain and the Six in the 1950s. Any suggestion of a closer relationship with the Six, that went beyond forms of association between Britain and the emerging EEC, invariably collapsed in the face of the prevailing argument that such moves would jeopardize or undermine relations with the US. It was in this European context that the British-manufactured myth of a special relationship was most in evidence, particularly since the USA was a keen supporter of full British involvement in the process of European integration.[8]

The second and eventually more significant gauge of British interest in west European union was in the field of economic cooperation. The particular litmus test of British policy in this respect was the question of whether to participate in the formation of a west European customs union. A customs union was to be the centrepiece of the EEC established by the Six ten years later. This issue had come to prominence following the US offer of aid to Europe in June 1947, commonly known as Marshall Aid and formally as the European Recovery Programme (ERP). It was following the announcement of this offer of aid that there was mounting US support for a single market in western Europe and the prospective recipients of US aid including Britain established an intergovernmental study group to consider the subject (November 1947). This matter received exhaustive consideration in Whitehall where there emerged the beginnings of a longer-term division of opinion between the Foreign Office, which was receptive to the political and strategic case for British involvement in European integration, and the Treasury which took an altogether more cautious, and in this case hostile, attitude towards the idea. Why, then, as one senior British diplomat expressed the matter, did the 'mere words "customs union" produce a shudder in the Treasury and nausea in the Board of Trade?'[9]

The Treasury case against participation in a customs union ultimately prevailed on the back of several arguments that held the high ground long into the 1950s. Much emphasis was placed on the far greater importance of Britain's trading and financial interests beyond rather than within Europe. An overriding priority in this respect was to ensure that the economic, commercial and financial ties associated with the British Empire and Commonwealth were not adversely affected by any of Britain's European commitments. The Commonwealth, as it came to be known after 1949, though a very important distinction remained between colonies under direct rule from London and the self-governing Dominions, was viewed as a highly prized asset. It still extended to a quarter of the world's land mass and symbolized British power and independence in the world. What became increasingly unclear in the post-war years was how far the mixture of tradition, sentiment and interest that held this enterprise together clouded judgements about the precise economic, commercial and financial value of the body to Britain. In the early post-war years, the Commonwealth and Empire attracted a disparate set of supporters ranging from enthusiasts for the Raj in India and believers in the

Commonwealth ideal to adherents of the kith and kin lobby in Africa and supporters of Britain's global strategic role (S. Howe 1993: 324). Its existence was undoubtedly of more concern to politicians and the press than to the general public whose knowledge of the subject was often limited to a general grasp of the imperial inheritance and of empire as an integral part of Britain's status as a world power; an opinion poll in 1947 found that 75 per cent of the respondents did not know the difference between a dominion and a colony while 50 per cent could not name a single colony, and one respondent nominated Lincolnshire as a possible colony (Sandbrook 2005: 252).[10]

In the early post-war years of shortages of raw materials, at least, the Commonwealth provided access to scarce resources through a stranglehold on some of the colonies that amounted to unqualified economic imperialism. It also offered an assured market for British goods via the operation of the protectionist imperial preference system. At this time 50 per cent of British trade was with the rest of the Commonwealth, whereas the whole of Europe accounted for only 20 per cent of British trade. Furthermore, much of the Commonwealth made up the sterling area for which Britain acted as the central banker and thus played a prominent role in the world's financial system as some 50 per cent of all international payments were in sterling. In the light of these considerations, British membership of a European customs union was regarded as unacceptable on a number of counts. Most notably, it would undermine the British preference for a 'one world' trading system including the Commonwealth, North America and Europe.[11] Furthermore, it would be incompatible with British involvement in the imperial preference system, while any attempt to merge this protectionist system with a European customs union would entail a net loss for British exporters and for British management of the sterling area. It was also argued that membership of a customs union would result in a loss of British trade with the rest of the Commonwealth that could not be offset by comparable gains in the more competitive European markets. It was, and remained the case through the 1950s, that the precise impact of the Commonwealth on the making of British policy towards the emerging EC was immeasurable. Certainly, the impact was far less clear-cut than was often suggested by some politicians for whom the existence of the Commonwealth was a ready-made excuse for pursuing a European policy that would have been adopted regardless of the existence of the Commonwealth

The dramatic downturn in Britain's economic fortunes in 1947 lent further weight to the argument against membership of a European customs union. The ballooning trade and payments deficit with the dollar area (the 'dollar gap'), the short-lived and disastrous attempt in July–August to make sterling convertible and the rapid exhaustion of the US loan of 1945, all combined to confront the Labour government with the gravest crisis in its period of office (1945–51). In these circumstances and under the forceful leadership of Stafford Cripps as Chancellor of the Exchequer from November 1947, the Treasury was determined to address the dollar deficit by increasing dollar-earning exports and reducing dollar-costing imports. Given these priorities, a European customs union was viewed as at best irrelevant and at worst an obstacle to reducing the dollar deficit. In short, membership of a European customs union would simply encourage British production for the dollar-starved European market rather than for the dollar area or for other markets in the Commonwealth where payment was to be had in dollars. On these grounds alone, Foreign Office and in particular Bevin's initial support for close economic relations with France buckled under the weight of the Treasury's opposition to any suggestion of a British and French-inspired west European customs union; in the Treasury view exporting to France reduced Britain's dollar-earning capacity, while importing from France scarcely contributed to Britain's dollar-saving programme.

A further set of considerations also weighed heavily against membership of a customs union and focused on questions of national economic management and sovereignty. For example, it was widely believed that a customs union would curtail the government's freedom to pursue its own budgetary, planning and exchange policies. Besides this unwelcome prospect for a Labour government favouring national controls, part of the subtext of this objection was a protectionist argument, most forcefully expressed by the Board of Trade, that a customs union would have an extremely damaging effect on some key British industries. In London, in contrast to opinion associated with some of the founders of the EEC, there was little or no interest until much later in the idea of undertaking national economic planning and modernization by means of a European customs union. Finally, a clinching argument against British membership of a customs union concerned the functions and potential of a customs union. Treasury thinking was dominated by two views of the likely evolution of a customs union, neither of which held out any attractions. One view was that a union confined to eliminating only import duties and to establishing a common external tariff between its member states was a bogus creation in that the member states would still be free to use quotas, which would have the same effect as tariffs. The other view was that customs unions had invariably been only impermanent and often inherently unstable halfway houses which either dissolved or proceeded towards economic union and political union. Given these stark alternatives, it was therefore necessary, as Cripps put the matter in a Cabinet paper of September 1948, to choose between abandoning the customs union idea or moving towards some complete form of European federation.[12] By this time a preference for the former course of action was becoming clear, partly as a result of increasing dismay with efforts to develop some form of west European political unity and partly in view of international developments.

The third test of Bevin's original support for some form of union in western Europe centred on the idea of creating political institutions expressing the collective identity and unity of the West European states. France took the lead in July 1948 with a proposal for a European Assembly which the BTO powers agreed to consider. What eventually emerged after six months of negotiations within the BTO was the Council of Europe, comprising a Committee of Ministers and a purely consultative Assembly with a greatly circumscribed agenda. Although this outcome was satisfactory to the British, the negotiations clearly revealed their distaste for the idea of institutionalizing political union and their preference for a gradual, pragmatic, step-by-step approach based on intergovernmental cooperation. It was in this context especially that British policymakers were first thrown onto the defensive, where they were to remain long afterwards, in their support for limited forms of European cooperation. Bevin himself was determined to ensure that any organization caused minimum embarrassment, while support for a federalist Europe on the continent was a source of much concern to him: 'When you open that Pandora's box you'll find it full of Trojan horses.' By this time, Bevin's earlier interest in European union was far more muted and qualified than at the time of the Western Union initiative. He thus became the first of a long procession of post-war British political figures who came to power with early strong professions of support for European unity that were not sustained in office (Bullock 1985: 659).

Bevin's views chimed in with growing antipathy towards the European unity movement within the ranks of the Parliamentary Labour Party (PLP). At the time of the launching of his Western Union initiative there was considerable support in the PLP for British leadership of a 'Third Force' European union between the USA and the USSR: in March 1948 a parliamentary motion advocating a democratic federation in Europe received the backing of some 100 Labour MPs. This tide of opinion rapidly receded, however, against the background of a fast-changing international landscape during the first half of 1948. The Communist coup in Czechoslovakia (February 1948), the Congressional approval of aid to western Europe under the ERP, the creation of the Organisation for European Economic Cooperation (OEEC) comprising the states in receipt of this aid (April 1948) and the beginnings of the Berlin blockade (June 1948), all intensified the Cold War, sealed the division of Europe and foreshadowed the partition of Germany. At the same time the Labour government and party indicated their unwillingness to proceed any further towards European political and economic union when they boycotted the unofficial Congress of Europe at The Hague (May 1948), the first of many occasions since 1945 when 'Europe' became a pawn in inter-party conflict as the Conservatives under Churchill's leadership supported the Congress. Opinion about European unity on the British side was also coloured by a deeply pessimistic view of the condition of the mainland European states. This attitude was increasingly shaped by constant dealings with such states at close quarters in the newly-formed organizations of the BTO and the OEEC; the head of the British delegation to the OEEC expressed a widespread view in British circles when he warned ministers: 'Do not put all your eggs in the European basket. It is a pretty shoddy contraption and there are no signs yet that the essential repairs are going to be made'.[13]

The varied mixture of arrogance, condescension, complacency and indifference that shot through the attitudes of British policymakers towards the mainland European states was combined with what policymakers regarded as a hard-headed appreciation of the liabilities rather than assets represented by these states. In the external environment, moreover, the key factor that influenced British policy towards European unity was the evolution of US policy. The commitment of US economic aid and subsequently the emergence of the US-led Atlantic Alliance ensured that more British resources could be devoted to maintaining positions beyond Europe. This development also meant that Britain could pose as a North Atlantic power with a 'special relationship' with the US rather than as a primarily European regional power. To be sure, heavy US pressure on Britain in 1948–49 to orchestrate moves towards a more integrated Europe was resisted. At the same time British policymakers aimed to secure maximum US economic and military aid whether by taking the lead in the formation of organizations like the BTO and the OEEC or by ensuring that certain projects like the European customs union idea continued to be aired long after the Labour government had decided against participation.

By the Spring of 1949, the limits of British involvement in the process of European integration were far more clearly established than had been the case when Bevin first called for some form of union in Western Europe. In policymaking circles a consensus was emerging that Britain must not compromise its independence or dilute its strength by integrating too closely with Western Europe. This conclusion first emerged in the Whitehall paper of January 1949 on limited liability mentioned earlier. A paper by Bevin and Cripps, supporting this view, was approved by the Cabinet's Economic Policy Committee in the same month, and a further paper on the economic implications of this assessment was endorsed by the Cabinet the following October.[14] A line was thus drawn under a wide-ranging debate in official circles. The concept of limited liability established the benchmark against which to judge the merits of any new schemes for European integration. What exactly limited liability meant in practice became evident following the emergence of the Schuman Plan (9 May 1950).

The Schuman Plan proposed to place all Franco-German coal and steel production under a common High Authority in an organization open to the participation of the other countries of Europe. The most distinctive feature of this plan, which was primarily devised by Jean Monnet, the head of France's post-war Modernization and Re-equipment Plan, was a proposed supranational High Authority with powers independent of the governments of the member states. The declared political purposes of this ostensibly economic organization, as expressed in Schuman's original announcement, were to overcome the deep, long-standing conflicts in Franco-German relations and to take the first steps towards the creation of a European federation. In the event, the immediate result in the history of the EC/EU was the signing of the Treaty of Paris by the Six (18 April 1951) establishing the ECSC.

Britain was a conspicuous absentee. The supranational dimension of the plan was ultimately the formal major obstacle to British membership, predictably so in view of the Cabinet's decisions on European integration in the previous year. The politics and diplomacy of this brief episode, however, involved more than the mechanical application of recently-established criteria. There were basic differences of perspective, priority and policy between Britain and France that surfaced in the period down to 3 June 1950, when it became clear that Britain would not be involved in formal negotiations concerning the plan.

Surprise and incredulity characterized the immediate response of British ministers and officials to this plan. This initial reaction soon gave way to a more considered and also widespread view which was expressed by Roger Makins, a senior Foreign Office official and one of the closest advisers to the ailing Bevin at this time. Shortly after the announcement of the plan Makins commented to Monnet: 'We are not ready and you will not succeed' (Charlton 1983:122). From the outset, there were strong doubts in Whitehall about the seriousness of French intentions. Memories of pre-war French 'Europeanism' in the form of the Briand memorandum of 1929 on a federal Europe were revived in the Foreign Office where the memorandum had been regarded as nebulous in content, suspect in motive, middling among the priorities of French policy, and unlikely to come to much (White 1995). More recent experience suggested that the plan was the latest in a series of post-war ambitious French schemes for European unity that were symptomatic of the internal weaknesses of France rather than viable, well-conceived projects; French interest in a European customs union and in a European Assembly were so categorized. Doubts about French intentions were further reinforced by hitherto stubborn French resistance to the recovery of post-war Germany and also by the implication that French fears of a revived Germany could not be allayed without a British commitment. Furthermore, when Monnet informed British ministers (14–19 May 1950) that Schuman's announcement contained all the information on the plan, he confirmed British suspicions that the plan had been hastily conceived for largely political, window dressing purposes and especially to convince the US that France was prepared to take the lead in a form of European integration including West Germany.[15]

This pessimistic view of the plan, however, was not allowed to stand in the way of a full Whitehall consideration of its strategic, economic and political merits. There was a mixed response. The Foreign Office viewed the plan as a French attempt to take the initiative in determining the pace of West Germany's political and economic recovery. It feared, however, that the plan might encourage a neutralist, third-force federated Europe between the two superpowers, thereby challenging the strong British preference for west European organizations to be anchored in or linked to the newly-formed Atlantic Alliance. The Chiefs of Staff welcomed the possibility of a Franco-German rapprochement as a contribution to the defence of Europe and as a means of facilitating some form of West German rearmament which they regarded as a necessity in the longer term. Meanwhile, the economics ministries were particularly concerned to defend the value of a global, 'one world', multilateral approach to economic problems rather than the narrow, regional European approach of the Schuman Plan, a continuing feature of British policy down to the present day.[16]

From the outset, French policymakers were determined to emphasize three aspects of the plan: that West Germany *had* to be involved while other states could join if they wished; that all member states had to surrender control of their coal and steel industries to the High Authority; and that all prospective member states had to make a prior commitment to the supranational principle of the plan before entering into formal negotiations about its details. Whether or not Britain entered into such negotiations was not uppermost in the minds of Schuman or Monnet, for whom West German participation was of vital importance while Britain's was at best desirable. Monnet's overriding concern was to ensure that the British did not negotiate away the fundamental principles of the plan by the sort of hedging and delaying tactics that they had successfully employed within the OEEC, in particular on the question of a European customs union. Furthermore, Monnet's discussions with British officials in the previous year had convinced him that the British had little understanding of, and even less sympathy for, his commitment to a single European economy and economic planning.[17] British officials did not approach the subject of post-war economic recovery in the same frame of mind as Monnet. Among other things, Monnet was determined to forge a link between the modernization of the French economy and the idea of an economically integrated Western Europe, a recurring theme of France's European policy in later years. The Labour government's declared interest in economic planning scarcely advanced much beyond the maintenance of wartime controls, the programme of nationalization and the creation of an Economic Planning Board (1947). At this time and throughout the next decade under Conservative governments, officials took it for granted that there was no economic planning, partly explaining why in the early 1950s there were no more than 10–15 economists working for the government and why there was often much complacency in official quarters about the performance of the British economy (Park 1997).

Besides such antipathy to economic planning, the grim economic conditions of the time invariably meant that the requirements of long-term economic planning were swept aside by the imperatives of day-to-day crisis management. In effect, a preoccupation with the needs of the moment and short-term complexities tended to overshadow what, in theory, were often acknowledged as the long-term advantages of British involvement in closer economic integration within Western Europe.[18]

Whatever its doubts about the underlying intentions and likely outcome of the Schuman Plan, the Labour government had good reason to support the initiative in so far as it signified a more constructive French attitude towards Germany. It was also important to demonstrate a positive interest in the plan in view of the fact that the US quickly backed it and thereafter played a key role in ensuring its success. Any suggestion of lukewarm British support for the plan or, worse still, efforts to sabotage it would have had a damaging effect on UK–USA relations and invited the now familiar American charge that the British were foot-dragging on European integration. Moreover, given that US pressure on Britain to take the lead in furthering European integration had recently relaxed in favour of US support for France as the most likely pacemaker, the British could not be seen to undermine a French response to such pressure.[19]

There was a marked difference between publicly welcoming the plan and supporting full British involvement. The government ideally wished to be associated with any Franco-German talks, while reserving its position pending a detailed study of the plan. The idea of association without commitment, which was to be a characteristic feature of British policy towards the emerging EC in the 1950s, was endorsed by the Cabinet's Economic Policy Committee (23 May) on the assumption that any substantial progress was likely to be slow.[20] Two days later, however, British calculations were upset by a French proposal to hold a conference on the plan comprising those states prepared to make a prior commitment to its supranational principle. France had managed to obtain West German agreement to the plan, and this decisive breakthrough meant that the French were determined to press ahead with or without British participation. This hardening in the French position became evident in the course of diplomatic exchanges between Paris and London (25 May–3 June), all of which failed to reconcile French insistence on prior commitment to the supranational principle with the British case for a preliminary meeting of interested states to obtain more details of the likely workings of the plan. The imposition of a French deadline – an ultimatum in the British view – brought matters to a head on 3 June when, following its rejection of a British proposal for a meeting of British and French ministers, France announced that the Six would hold a conference on the plan.[21]

There is much substance to the view that this procedural wrangle was a case of two governments which were either unwilling to discuss the question with each other or talking at cross purposes. From the British point of view, the idea of prior commitment to a principle in the absence of detailed information was comparable to signing a blank cheque. Some of the government's critics maintained that this obstacle might have been overcome by adopting the same escape clause as the Dutch, namely to accept the plan's principles while reserving the right to retract this acceptance if it proved impossible to apply these principles in practice. But this did not address the official British position of wishing to avoid either acceptance or rejection of the plan's principles in advance of detailed discussions. It was also argued that there would be far more damaging consequences for the project if Britain entered negotiations and subsequently withdrew than if the Dutch were to do so.[22]

Some contemporary observers like Oliver Harvey, the British ambassador to France, viewed this episode as indicative of a wide difference between

British and French modes of thought and diplomatic methods: 'a classic case of the difficulty of reconciling French cartesianism with British empiricism, the French habit of proposing lofty aims and then thinking out the methods of achieving them with the British habit of only advancing step by step'.[23] Furthermore, some British policymakers evidently felt uncomfortable with their French counterparts; Kenneth Younger, a junior minister at the Foreign Office who was primarily responsible for day-to-day handling of communications with the French at this time, described Schuman as too mystical and as a devout Catholic said to be under the influence of the priests (Warner 2005: 13). But whatever the validity of Harvey's rumination and the significance or otherwise of Younger's prejudices, which were widely shared by a Protestant country that often perceived the Europe of the Six as a black Vatican-inspired construction, the fact of the matter was that British and French national interests were very dissimilar at this stage. The lack of common ground between them was most strikingly demonstrated by their contrasting policies and attitudes towards the recovery of Germany, and also by their assessments of the needs and interests of their own heavy industries. In many respects the Schuman Plan exposed a major, and what proved to be an enduring, difference of outlook between Britain and France on the value of European integration in serving domestic interests and also in addressing the economic and security implications of a revived Germany. The British did not share the same compelling reasons as the French for viewing European integration on the Schuman model as an acceptable or necessary price for controlling or accommodating Germany within a new, tightly-knit European system. Nor did they see the latter as a means of revitalizing the war-ravaged British economy.

The evolution of British and French policies towards Germany in the early post-war years reflected these very different priorities and emphases. British policy towards Germany in the period of military occupation (1945–49) was greatly influenced by strategic and financial considerations favouring the political and economic recovery of the three western occupation zones. It was recognized that any attempt to maintain long-term occupation controls over a weakened German economy would have adverse consequences for the European economy at large and was likely to assist the further expansion of Soviet power and influence on the continent. Eventually, the heavy cost of maintaining the British occupation zone in Germany cleared the way for a more systematic commitment to Germany's recovery, first via the economic merger of the UK and US zones (January 1947) and subsequently through largely US-driven plans for the economic recovery of this Bizone. UK–US cooperation in occupied Germany, together with the making of the Atlantic Pact, strengthened British support for a particular approach towards accommodating the new West German state (1949) in the international system. By 1950, in effect, the British were convinced that the western alliance system offered the best way to supervise the recovery of West Germany. It was further maintained that this 'Atlantic solution', as Bevin described it, would also serve to allay French fears about a revanchist Germany. At the time of the launching of the Schuman Plan, therefore, British policymakers saw little or no need to devise a new European mechanism or organization to control a potentially strong West German state. Existing organizations were sufficient for this purpose, the more so as West Germany became a full member of the OEEC and an associate member of the Council of Europe in 1950.

By contrast, the French were not only more fearful than the British of a resurgent Germany, but far less convinced of the value of a western alliance solution. Against the background of three German invasions of France (1870, 1914, 1940) and on the defeat of Germany in 1945, French policymakers aimed to maintain a weak, divided Germany through dismemberment, heavy reparations and stringent controls. These plans, however, failed to come to fruition as the onset of the Cold War determined the more limited partition of Germany into two states and also intensified American and British determination to hasten the recovery of the western occupation zones. By 1947 and increasingly so thereafter, France had perforce to align itself more closely with American and British moves towards the formation of a West German state, particularly in view of its heavy dependence on US aid. At the same time, France sought to maintain as many restrictions as possible on the West German economy, especially over the operations of the Ruhr heavy industries. By 1950, therefore, French policymakers faced a critical choice between continuing to mount rearguard actions in the face of heavy American and British pressure to lift restrictions or taking matters into their own hands by proposing a direct Franco-German link. The French wanted European or more precisely French controls over Germany's recovery. The Schuman Plan offered a new, positive approach to achieving this objective.

The very different interests and resources of Britain and France in the heavy industrial sector also greatly contributed to dissimilar policies. Throughout the early post-war years, French governments were greatly exercised about the production and allocation arrangements for the coal, coke and steel output of Germany's heavy industrial arsenal in the Ruhr. By 1950, the progressive lifting of economic restrictions on West Germany greatly alarmed French policymakers. This process threatened both much-needed French access to German coal and also France's heavy post-war investment in the steel industry in view of rising German competition. It was out of such material considerations that the Schuman Plan was born.[24] None of these considerations amounted to overriding priorities in the case of Britain, as was evident from some of the main conclusions of the government's official working party on the implications of the Schuman Plan. Britain enjoyed a dominant position in coal and steel production as compared with the Six, accounting for 48.9 per cent of the total coal production of Britain and the Six combined and for 35.5 per cent of total steel production in that area (1949). The working party concluded that Britain might suffer some, but not intolerable, disadvantage over a continuing period by staying out of the plan. It conceded that there was a case for some form of international cooperation but not for a supranational authority, and it believed that the long-term prospects for the British coal and steel industries were good.[25] While the French were concerned about guaranteed access to German coal, the British were primarily intent on ensuring the maintenance of national controls over the distribution of British coal, particularly in the face of US pressure to export more British coal to assist the European recovery. Similarly, Britain did not share the same concerns as France about steel and the impact of increased German production and competition on the European market; approximately 60 per cent of total British exports went to the Commonwealth, while Western Europe accounted for only 5 per cent of total British steel exports.

These considerations found expression in British domestic politics surrounding the reception given to the plan. In the first major parliamentary debate (26 June 1950) both major parties expounded the same conventional wisdom. Cripps for the government and Churchill for the Opposition acknowledged that membership of a federal Europe was out of the question, not least because it was incompatible with ties and obligations beyond Europe. The Conservatives criticized the government's handling of the diplomatic exchanges with France and also tabled an amendment supporting the idea of participating in international consideration of the plan. But such reservations were swept aside by two main factors. First, electoral considerations entered into play. Labour's parliamentary majority of 146 in the 1945 general election had melted away to five as a result of the February 1950 election. Another election appeared imminent and was eventually held in October 1951. In these circumstances, Labour was quite prepared to capitalize on any suggestion of Conservative willingness to surrender national sovereignty and the Conservative leadership recognized the dangers of being portrayed as the party prepared to do so. Second, international conditions completely overshadowed the Schuman Plan in importance following the outbreak of the Korean War on the day before Parliament debated the plan. This major event intensified the Cold War, ushered into being NATO, and meant, as the Labour minister Kenneth Younger recorded in his diary, that 'The Korean situation has now knocked Schuman right into the background of public consciousness' (Warner 2005: 25). Fearful of Soviet intentions, British government interest in mainland European affairs was now increasingly confined to the issue of defence and, in particular, the question of rearmament.

The government's handling of the Schuman Plan was widely supported by the Labour party at large. The party's National Executive Committee (NEC) fairly reflected this opinion in a pamphlet entitled *European Unity* that appeared some ten days after the conclusion of diplomatic exchanges with France. The pamphlet stridently opposed the prospect of Britain being corralled into a European supranational authority with a permanent anti-socialist majority. The pamphlet's reference to retaining national controls over the coal and steel industries had a strong emotional appeal, as no other pair of industries was more likely to arouse Labour party passions than coal and steel. Both industries were central to the party's nationalization programme; the nationalization of the coal industry in 1946 was followed by the nationalization of the steel industry three years later. There was thus unquestioning support for the view that Labour had not assaulted 'the commanding heights of the economy' in order to hand over control of coal and steel to a supranational body.

Some accounts of this episode have charged the Labour government with a short-sighted, ill-considered view of the possibilities.[26] It was noted, for example, that the formal decision not to participate in the negotiations on the plan on French terms was taken at a Cabinet meeting in the absence of three of its leading figures: Attlee, Bevin and Cripps.[27] Yet their ministerial underlings were acting in accordance with their instructions and these, in turn, were ultimately based on a well-formulated, strategic view of the positive aspects and limits of British policy towards Western Europe. Policymakers may have lacked vision as ailing or tired ministers battered by the wartime and post-war experience of office, but even junior ministers like Younger, who was acting for Bevin at this stage and who greatly regretted that Britain was 'out on a limb' as usual, was nevertheless certain that 'we really had no choice' (Warner 2005: 25). The importance of the decision was not lost on some of the key actors; William Strang, the most senior official at the Foreign Office, observed at the time that this was a decision of fundamental importance which would have far-reaching consequences.[28] In any case, the Labour government's absence from the subsequent negotiations on the plan did not amount to the parting of the ways between Britain and the Six, while the chequered history of the ECSC itself scarcely suggested that Britain had missed out on a opportunity.

In conclusion, there was no compelling imperative for the Labour government to enter into negotiations on French terms. By 1950, the key features of Britain's claim to great power status in the post-war world were either in place like the sterling area and the maintenance of sterling as a global currency or were shortly to materialize like the acquisition of the atomic bomb in 1952. Furthermore, the government believed that the western international system had developed along satisfactory lines by this time through the emergence of the Atlantic Alliance, the revival of close UK/US relations, and the model of Britain as the centre of three interlocking circles: Europe, the Commonwealth, North America. There was little reason to expect or to encourage any new West European organization beyond the OEEC, the BTO and the Council of Europe. By 1950, in effect, Britain was a status quo rather than a revisionist power in Western Europe, endorsing change only in so far as West European organizations were subordinated to and meshed with the Atlantic framework. More precisely from a British perspective, the merits of intergovernmental cooperation, the weaknesses of idealistic schemes for European federation, the desirable balance between European and extra-European interests, and the restricted economic interest in Western Europe, all demonstrated the meaning of the concept of limited liability. Certainly, there was a basic miscalculation in Whitehall about the prospects for the original plan. Yet there was no subsequent British attempt to sabotage the Six's negotiations by stalling or wrecking tactics and no disclosure of an alternative British plan that was approved by ministers (28 June) and that abandoned the idea of a supranational High Authority for an intergovernmental council. In some respects, therefore, Britain contributed to the successful efforts of the Six through its absence from and refusal to interfere in the negotiations, the first of several occasions on which British aloofness or opting out indirectly helped to deepen the process of European integration. The eventual signing of a treaty of association between Britain and the ESCS in December 1954 was also a British vote of confidence in and a morale booster for the new organization. At the same time, of course, Britain was increasingly walled off from negotiations and discussions between the Six that helped to shape a strong sense of collective endeavour and identity.[29]

In the following year, the British response to a major initiative by the Six tested yet again the nature and extent of British interest in deepening the process of integration. In 1955 the Six set in motion a process that resulted in the signing of the Treaties of Rome and the creation of the EEC and the EAEC. This initiative was taken by a meeting of the foreign ministers of the Six at Messina (1–2 June 1955) on the basis of a Benelux memorandum containing both a general plan for a common European market and particular schemes for applying the ECSC model of sector integration to communications and power (including nuclear power). At Messina it was also agreed to appoint a preparatory committee which was to meet in Brussels under the chairmanship of Paul-Henri Spaak, the Belgian foreign minister, to consider these different approaches and to report back to governments.

Britain was invited to participate in this exercise without any of the preconditions that had been attached to the Schuman Plan. From the outset, however, there was no great expectation among the Six that Britain was likely to join any new organization. There was no British representation at Messina. Messina was 'a devilishly awkward place to get to' as one Foreign Office official observed. This view of mainland European travel was widely shared in the country at large. The English football governing authorities at this time, for example, barred English clubs from the newly-created (April 1955) European Cup competition on the grounds that they would not arrive back from the continent in time to play Saturday matches. Matt Busby, the visionary Scottish manager of Manchester United who believed Europe was the future, defied the ban, and the club entered the competition in two consecutive seasons but lost many of its finest players in the Munich air crash (February 1958), an event which to some people demonstrated that foreign competition was not worth it (Weight 2002: 263).

The response of the British government to the Messina initiative was largely determined by general notions of Britain's role in the wider world. It was also influenced by a set of assumptions about both the British ability to influence European developments and the Six's capacity to pursue further integration without Britain. These assumptions gave rise to miscalculations which became evident in the making of the key decision to withdraw from any further involvement in Spaak's preparatory committee in November 1955. The reactions of British policymakers were shaped by the prevailing view that Britain was still one of the three great powers in the world and occupied a pivotal position in the interlocking circles of Europe, the Commonwealth and North America. Certainly, the value of this type of world power/role rhetoric in masking Britain's diminishing international status was recognized by its practitioners in Whitehall, though there was still some substance to this British-centred view of the world. In addition, there was a widespread opinion that British leadership in Europe, which was considered the least important of these circles, was assured and that the Six's efforts to pursue European integration scarcely merited serious consideration. Under the newly-installed Conservative government of Anthony Eden following the general election of April 1955, Harold Macmillan made his first major parliamentary speech as Foreign Secretary, placing much emphasis on Britain's 'triple partnership' between the USA, the Commonwealth and Western Europe but without reference to the Messina conference.[30] This omission was symptomatic of the extent to which Messina was perceived in official British circles as an inconsequential undertaking. A deep sense of complacency permeated the reactions of British officials; Gladwyn Jebb, the British ambassador to France, advised London that no very spectacular developments were to be expected as a result of the Messina conference.[31] Why, then, was this the case?

One immediate influence partly accounting for this mentality concerned the unsuccessful attempt in the period 1950–54 to apply the Schuman model of European integration to the military field in the form of a plan for a European Defence Community (EDC) comprising the Six.[32] The collapse of this plan in August 1954 appeared to justify British scepticism about such grandiose designs. It also provided the British government with an opportunity to reassert its leadership in Western Europe. It did so by devising a scheme whereby a rearmed West Germany was ushered into being through an enlarged BTO, thereafter known as the Western European Union (WEU). This organization operated in accordance with British wishes on the principle of intergovernmental cooperation. Britain appeared to be back in the driving seat of European cooperation. The failure of the EDC project undoubtedly strengthened the British impression that the Six were unlikely to embark upon or to succeed in more adventurous schemes for integration. In particular, British policymakers confidently believed that divisions within and between the Six would thwart any successful outcome to the Messina initiative. This view owed much to British perceptions of French and West German attitudes. According to Whitehall assessments, France was in no fit state politically or economically to consider membership of a common market, especially in view of widespread fears about Germany, about loss of national sovereignty, and about exposing the highly protectionist French economy to the fast-growing West German economy. It seemed equally clear to British officials that conflicting views in the upper reaches of the West German government would in all likelihood hamper further integration of the Six; while Chancellor Konrad Adenauer was a strong supporter of Six-based integration for strategic and political reasons, Ludwig Erhard, his Economics Minister and Deputy Chancellor, was opposed, as he himself put it, to European inbreeding in the form of a tightly-knit, centrally directed economic grouping of the Six.

There were some fatal flaws in these British views of the Six's unpreparedness for further integration. Some of the initial impressions of policymakers were rooted in a tendency to perceive what they wanted or expected to perceive. This approach was reinforced by political and social attitudes which often reflected a high degree of consensus and satisfaction with the *status quo*. In this particular case, there was a limited appreciation of the political will and community of interests propelling the Messina initiative. The failure of the EDC plan was a misleading guide to the future. In fact, the removal of this issue allowed the Six to return to the process of economic integration at the centre of the Schuman Plan as a means towards political ends. Furthermore, there was a failure to appreciate that France and West Germany might eventually forge an agreement, especially if France was able to negotiate satisfactory concessions in return for agreeing to join a common market. One of the most mistaken underlying assumptions on the British side was the view that the Messina agenda was primarily an economic affair raising issues that were best considered in the OEEC forum. What the British did not fully grasp was that their leadership of the OEEC strengthened the Six's determination to pursue their own form of economic integration, in much the same way as Britain's positive but nonetheless modest ambitions for the BTO had convinced Monnet and others of the need to by-pass that British-led organization. By the mid-1950s the British had effectively reduced the OEEC to a nullity as far as further exclusively European economic cooperation was concerned. They had successfully kept the tariff issue off the agenda and had smothered several plans in this forum, each of which aimed for closer economic integration.[33] Following the end of the ERP in 1952, moreover, there was clearly little British interest in revitalizing the OEEC. Key questions of British foreign economic policy like sterling's convertibility were viewed as matters for discussion with the USA and the Commonwealth and not fit subjects for airing in a subordinate European organization like the OEEC. Time and again British political leaders insisted that trade and payments issues had to be addressed at the global (or 'one world') level rather than in a regional European body, a continuing emphasis albeit in different forms ever since.

The initial formal British response to the Messina initiative amounted to a holding operation, governed by the view that Britain should associate with the Six but avoid positive commitment to any schemes that might emerge from the Spaak committee. It was on this basis that Russell Bretherton, an

Under-Secretary at the Board of Trade, participated in the Spaak committee during the period July–November 1955. By the end of this period, the committee clearly favoured the formation of two new communities, an atomic energy community and a common market with a customs union as its centre-piece, in preference to the idea of a free trade area. Meanwhile, Bretherton performed the difficult role of participant without commitment. At an early stage he concluded that Britain had the power to guide the committee's conclusions in almost any direction, which was a very questionable view, but that nobody in London took any notice, which was nearer to the truth (Charlton 1983: 184).

The decision to withdraw from the Spaak committee was taken on 11 November 1955 by the Cabinet's Economic Policy Committee.[34] The advice of Whitehall officials was conveyed via the interdepartmental Mutual Aid Committee, which had established a working party on a Common Market, chaired by Burke Trend. Significantly, Trend was a senior Treasury official and his appointment symbolized Treasury rather than Foreign Office pre-eminence in responding to the Messina initiative. In support of its general recommendation against membership of a common market, the Trend Report identified four decisive considerations: the adverse impact on Britain's relationship with the rest of the Commonwealth including the colonies; the detrimental effect on the global approach to international trade and payments; the likelihood of further integration and perhaps political federation unacceptable to British public opinion; and the removal of protection from British industry against European competition. The report contained many finely-balanced arguments. There was much uncertainty about the weight to be given to imponderable considerations which seemed to multiply as the report sought to gauge the impact of two different scenarios, one of British membership of a common market and the other of British abstention from it. For example, it was acknowledged that the imperial preference system was declining in importance. There was, however, a marked difference between recognizing the diminishing value of imperial preference and accepting that British entry into a European customs union would involve the introduction of reverse preferences or discriminatory trading measures against other Commonwealth producers. A telling consideration against this latter possibility was the fact that the value of British trade with the Commonwealth was approximately double the value of that with the Six. In fact, the volume of British trade with the rest of the Commonwealth had peaked in the early 1950s as the early post-war conditions encouraging such trade, most notably sterling inconvertibility, the dollar shortage and the absence of Germany and Japan from international markets, were far less evident by the later 1950s. In the event, the stock argument about the political value of the Commonwealth carried all before it, especially when contrasted with mainland Europe. Lord Home, the Commonwealth Secretary, counselled Macmillan to follow an order of priorities with UK producer first, Commonwealth producer second and foreigner last.[35] Meanwhile, James Stuart at the Scottish Office typified mainstream opinion in the Conservative Party when he warned Eden of disastrous repercussions of any suggestion that the Conservative government was departing from the principle of the unity of the English speaking peoples in favour of a 'mixed collection of Europeans, who have not all been our friends in the past … ' (Griffiths 1995).

The Trend Report confirmed the conventional wisdom about Britain's European policy and scarcely amounted to the type of major strategic review undertaken in the 1947–49 period. There was no reframing of the problem, no strong or close ministerial direction, little advance on earlier findings and no consultation with interested parties such as British industry. To some extent, therefore, there were some traces of groupthink at work, not least, for example, in failing to reappraise initially rejected alternatives and in working out contingency plans.[36] The Report largely followed a track laid down in the different circumstances of the Schuman Plan, almost suggesting that working papers and reports from a few years earlier had simply been dusted down and updated without much regard for changing conditions.[37] There was little appreciation of, and even less interest, in the idea that European economic integration could help to modernize the British economy and promote faster economic growth. Officialdom still remained profoundly complacent about the weaknesses of the British economy. Meanwhile, both major political parties were deeply suspicious of a strong, positive role by government in the management of the economy; the belief in non-intervention was predominant and the government was viewed as 'an entity out to avoid trouble rather than to promote positive economic ends' (Park 1997). The principal concerns of government economic policy throughout the 1950s – the balance of payments and the status of sterling – were viewed in a global rather than a European context.

At the official level, the prevailing climate of opinion in the two key departments, the Foreign Office and the Treasury, opposed British membership of a common market. Edward Bridges, the Treasury's Permanent Secretary, argued that even a British presence at the Spaak committee was a mistake, and his opposite number at the Foreign Office, Ivone Kirkpatrick, maintained that any European institution founded on a Franco-German axis was bound to collapse. Indeed, the Trend Report's assessment of the political objections to membership of a common market was limited in its scope, largely because the Foreign Office judged it unnecessary to consider the eventuality of a common market project proceeding without Britain. The Foreign Office believed that proper handling of the matter would be sufficient to avoid such an outcome. All that needed to be done was to shunt the Messina initiative into the OEEC, a tactical response that Gladwyn Jebb, the UK ambassador to France, described as being to 'embrace destructively' (Horne 1988: 351 and 363).[38]

At Cabinet level, the decision to withdraw from the Spaak committee was taken almost as a matter of course with no division of opinion and little or no sense of a significant parting of the ways between Britain and the Six.

According to recently released government papers, the general opinion at the first Cabinet meeting following the Messina conference was almost uniformly negative on at least two counts, namely that the Six's plans did not coincide with British interests and that they were unlikely to succeed. True, the so-called 'pro-Europeanists' in the Cabinet pressed the case for some involvement in the Spaak committee; one of their number (Duncan Sandys) argued that Britain could not possibly join a common market but by attending the Spaak committee could 'bring it round the right way – or stop it'.[39]

During the next few months, Eden was scarcely involved in any discussions of the Six's plans, except to confirm that the right policy was to lean towards supporting the OEEC while trying to keep out of the Six's more far-reaching schemes. He lacked experience of, or interest in, economic affairs, and in any case his attention was principally focused on the larger stage of relations between the Western Powers and the USSR and the Geneva 'Summit' of July 1955, the first such meeting since the Potsdam Conference of 1945. R.A. Butler, the Chancellor of the Exchequer, was an intransigent opponent of any shift in policy. He detected little unity among the Six and saw no merit at all in their plans. Harold Macmillan, the Foreign Secretary, demonstrated from the outset a more tactically flexible approach than that of either Butler or Eden in pressing the case for participating in the Spaak committee, yet he did not demur when the decision was taken to withdraw from the committee.

In conclusion, there is little dispute in the various accounts of this episode that the preferred position of the British government on the question of the Six's plans for European integration by 1955 was one of paralysis or immobilism, which among other things relieved the government of having to take a major decision. A strong inclination to avoid taking such an irreversible decision was to be a recurring feature of British policy towards the process of European integration. Mainland European politicians, and especially the so-called godfathers of the EC like Monnet and Schuman, well-appreciated this British position at the time. One of their number remarked, when describing the attitudes of the British government towards the Messina initiative, that 'their profound wish was that nothing should happen' (Marjolin 1989: 282).

The often repeated claim of British leaders at the time that the mainland European states were eagerly awaiting, needed or required British leadership was based on a mixture of arrogance, ignorance and delusion. Equally indisputable is the view that the new movement towards European integration following the Messina conference had far more serious and lasting consequences for the British than their earlier aloofness from the Schuman Plan. By its withdrawal from the Spaak committee and thus exclusion from the negotiations resulting in the Treaties of Rome, Britain effectively lost the battle for proprietary rights over the concept of European unity, and it also enhanced the European leadership credentials of France. Furthermore, the

British absence from the negotiations allowed the Six to shape the EEC in accordance with their own requirements and with understandably no regard at all for British interests. At the same time the British idea of association with the Six became so increasingly outmoded and ultimately unsuccessful that it forced a major reappraisal and eventually a reversal of British policy towards the EEC.

2 Agonizing reappraisal, 1956–72

In September 1955, Macmillan as Foreign Secretary commented on the proceedings of the Spaak committee: 'This is our second string – we may need it. The "one world approach" isn't going with a swing at the moment. It may even bankrupt us.'[1] Six years later, and as Prime Minister, Macmillan pursued the 'second string' and applied for EEC membership. The failure of this attempt and also of the second application by the Wilson Labour government of 1966–70 was followed by the third and successful application undertaken by the Heath Conservative government of 1970–74.

This chapter focuses on the diminishing appeal of alternatives to EEC membership under both the Conservative and Labour governments. It examines the reappraisal of British policy towards the EEC including the assumptions, expectations and actual policies pursued by the government of the day and the particular reasons for seeking membership. It also highlights some of the features of the successful application for membership that were to leave a lasting legacy. Three common expressions may be said to capture the change of mood among those political leaders who came to espouse the idea of British membership of the EEC over the period 1956–72. These were in order of timing: the panic-ridden 'We've been caught out', the galvanizing 'We must do something', the fatalist 'There is no alternative'.

The Eden government had no sooner decided to withdraw from the Spaak committee than doubts, fears and anxieties began to creep into Whitehall assessments of the implications of the Six's plans for Britain. Within a matter of months, in fact, Treasury officials speculated that on a longer view the question might become not whether Britain should go into Europe to save Europe but whether Britain might have to move closer to Europe in order to save itself.[2] Here was an early indication of an important tipping point in official opinion away from the popular view of Britain helping to rescue Europe during and after the Second World War to the increasingly common view in the 1960s that EEC membership was the panacea for Britain's political and economic ills.

More immediately, however, British policymakers believed that they were increasingly on the horns of an acute dilemma in the wake of the Six's decision to forge ahead with the common market idea. Peter Thorneycroft,

President of the Board of Trade, succinctly described the dilemma: 'On any analysis it seems clear that we cannot afford that the Common Market should either succeed, or fail, without us.'[3] In effect, a common market without Britain would immediately have damaging effects on Britain's trading ties with the Six. It would also put at risk the preferred British approach to trade negotiations via the GATT. In the longer run, such a prospect presented the threat of a narrow, regional, German-dominated power bloc. Furthermore, a common market without Britain would seriously undermine the country's traditional role and influence in Europe whether in maintaining a balance of power or in mediating in Franco-German conflicts. Such a project would also jeopardize Britain's standing in the US and in the western system at large. On these grounds alone, Britain could not join the Eisenhower Administration in Washington in positively encouraging the Six's efforts. However, it was also reckoned to be the case that the collapse of the common market project would have dire consequences. It would weaken west European unity, resulting in an isolationist France and German revanchiste adventures in Eastern Europe. It would divide the western alliance and possibly realize the worst security fears of the British in the form of the withdrawal of the US from Europe, while also leaving Britain exposed to European and US criticism for jeopardizing the project.[4] On these grounds, British policy could never actively or passively encourage the disruption of the Six's unity. Nor could Britain remain completely isolated from this process, for the further European integration advanced the less Britain could afford to be excluded from it. How to overcome this dilemma was one of the main problems confronting policymakers over the next few years. The opening period 1956–59 was to demonstrate how this dilemma could not be resolved by pursuing the policy of association between Britain and the Six which, as noted earlier, was established at the time of the Schuman Plan. This period also served as the prelude to the major reappraisal of Britain's European policy in 1960–61.

Any assessment of the main thrust of British policy towards the Six during this period bristles with problems, some confined to the period while others have continuing significance as evidence of a deep-seated British ambivalence towards the Six's model of European integration. It is important to emphasize several general points before tracing the rise and fall of a British proposal for a European free trade area (FTA) during this period.

First, the political landscape of European integration underwent rapid change. The Spaak report favouring the creation of a common market was published in March 1956. The report was approved by the foreign ministers of the Six in May 1956. It was then subjected to intense intergovernmental negotiations in February of the following year resulting in the Treaties of Rome (March 1957). These treaties came into force in January 1958 and established the European Economic Community (EEC) and the European Atomic Energy Community (EAEC). The EEC was designed to form a common market with free movement of goods, capital, labour and services. Phased progression towards a customs union was a major goal. The introduction of a Common Agricultural Policy (CAP) also emerged as an immediate priority. The underlying political purpose to create 'an ever closer union among the peoples of Europe' accommodated different views about integration and avoided any specific reference to the supranational principle contained in the ECSC treaty. The EEC's first tariff reductions were made in January 1959 and later that year (November) the Six agreed to accelerate their tariff cutting programme. Meanwhile, seven member states of the OEEC including Britain signed the Stockholm Convention (July 1959) establishing the European Free Trade Association (EFTA). By the end of 1959, therefore, Western Europe was divided into two trade blocs, a Europe at Sixes and Sevens in the newspaper headlines of the day.[5]

Second, the fate of the common market project hung in the balance for much of this period. French membership of the EEC, for example, was not assured until late in the process of treaty making, as France wrung concessions out of the rest of the Six on such matters as agriculture and the association of colonies with the EEC. At the same time, the collapse of the Fourth French Republic and the emergence of the Fifth Republic under Charles de Gaulle in 1958 gave rise to further doubts. The sheer rapidity of events and the uncertainty of outcomes often meant Whitehall assessments were either incorrect or quickly overtaken by events. Such assessments were in any case coloured by a strong tendency to underestimate the Six's seriousness of purpose and to overestimate British influence on the continent.

Third, any generalizations about underlying patterns across this period require critical scrutiny. They may fail to take account of the increasingly equivocal attitudes of British political leaders and officials against the background of a fast-changing European political landscape. In these circumstances, the parameters of the earlier approach to European integration eroded away to leave both government departments and individuals with changing motivations and divided opinions. British aims and motives, therefore, could be so unclear, mixed and varied across time and across personnel as to defy any single or blanket explanation.

Finally, Britain's relations with the Six throughout this period did not amount to a priority item on the international agenda of Britain's interests and concerns. At the beginning of the period this issue was overshadowed by the course, outcome and significance of the Suez crisis. By the end of the period it was judged less important than, for example, the intensification of the Cold War following Soviet moves (November 1958) on the Berlin question or the second major phase of decolonization in the period 1958–62. Predictably, therefore, when Spaak, the Belgian foreign minister, claimed in September 1959 that the main problem facing Britain was the future organization of Europe and especially Britain's relations with the EEC his comment met with a mixture of incomprehension and ridicule in the Foreign Office.[6]

The character of British policy and attitudes towards the Six during much of this period is best gauged by examining the origins, course and outcome of a British proposal for a Free Trade Area (FTA) originally known as Plan G.

Plan G proposed to turn the OEEC into a tariff-free trading bloc for manufactured but not agricultural goods. There was to be no common external tariff against non-members of the FTA, nor any of the other deeper forms of economic integration evident in the common market project. The Board of Trade and the Treasury were the principal authors of this proposal. They were to remain the dominant government departments in shaping British policy towards the Six over the next few years. In these circles, the EEC was stripped of any political connotations, was classified as commercial policy in Cabinet discussions and was usually called the Common Market over the next twenty years. Both departments insisted that Plan G offered safeguards for British manufacturing exports to the Six, while preserving the free entry of Commonwealth agricultural goods into Britain. Furthermore, Plan G maintained national freedom to determine tariffs on imports from non-members of the FTA, and it generally upheld the principle of British association with the Six. In short, the scheme seemed to offer Britain the best of all possible worlds. It preserved the Commowealth preference system, maintained the 'one world' or GATT approach to freer trade, and held out the prospect of reasserting British commercial leadership of Europe. In the event, the scheme, which was announced by Macmillan (November 1956), was formally approved by the OEEC as a basis for negotiations (February 1957). These negotiations began in October 1957 but eventually collapsed in November 1958 when France vetoed any further negotiations.

The meaning and significance of Plan G for Britain's relations with the emerging EEC has attracted various assessments. It was portrayed at the time and by some since as a deliberate spoiling tactic by the British government to frustrate the Six's plans for a common market: a malicious sabotage effort by 'perfidious Albion'. This charge was initially levelled by some of the foremost supporters of European integration at the time.[7] There were clearly some self-serving, polemical functions in casting the British in the worst possible light as an untrustworthy spectator of the Six's efforts. For example, the alleged existence of an external opponent like Britain helped to unify the Six and gave momentum to their process of integration. The sabotage charge was also skilfully used by French policymakers, for whom arousing deep-seated mainland European suspicions of British policy and motivations throughout this period was both a useful negotiating tool when dealing with the rest of the Six and a means of highlighting France's leadership credentials.

It is fair to say, however, that the charge is not without some substance, at least prior to and during preparatory work on Plan G when British tactics contributed to the poisoning of relations with the Six and intensified suspicions among the Six about British motives. Immediately after the British withdrawal from the Spaak committee, for example, there was a blatant attempt to undermine the Six's efforts. The Foreign Office mounted a diplomatic offensive that unsuccessfully sought to persuade the Germans and the Americans of the disadvantages of the common market idea. It also issued a warning about the damaging effects of the Six's plans on the political cohesion of Europe and on progress towards freer trade. Shortly afterwards, Macmillan, Chancellor of the Exchequer since the Cabinet reshuffle of December 1955 and the prime mover in the origins of Plan G, left several observers, including Spaak, in no doubt that the government would fight against the common market scheme (Spaak 1971: 232; Charlton 1983: 200).[8] Treasury papers for early 1956 also suggest clear opposition to the Six's plans. Negative impulses towards the Six, however, increasingly formed part of a confused mixture of doubts about the wisdom of waiting on events and about whether 'to undertake a rearguard action or an advance' (Macmillan). There was also some acknowledgement of the case for a counter-initiative. Such a measure was clearly intended, initially at least, as a substitute for the Six's common market plan or as a way of demonstrating British willingness to associate with Europe while at the same time hoping to sideline or smother the Messina proposals. In its early formulation, moreover, Plan G ignored the proposed common market of the Six as a special, distinctive group within the proposed FTA. Furthermore, British politicians only welcomed the Treaty of Rome on the assumption that there would have to be a FTA including the Six.[9]

An altogether different, and more sympathetic, understanding of the British position in this context views Plan G as a well-meaning and necessary defensive measure. According to this view, Plan G was basically designed to effect changes to British trading policy in the light of the emerging EEC and also to bridge the gap between the Six and other European states; bridging the gap was to become the overworked expression of British politicians in seeking to come to terms with the EEC over the next few years.[10] Plan G was most especially conceived to protect Britain's trading relations with the rest of the Commonwealth. Macmillan explained to Eden at an early stage in the exercise that the first question to be tackled was whether Britain could make a closer tariff association with Europe without weakening links with the Commonwealth.[11] A preoccupation with protecting Britain's trade with the rest of the Commonwealth was partly a reflection of the still substantial size of that trade and of the continuing, if waning, importance of imperial preferences. It was also an indication of divisions within the Conservative government and party between the strongly imperial and protectionist wing of the party led by ministers like Butler, Kilmuir and Salisbury and the more free trading, modernizing European wing represented by Macmillan, Sandys and Thorneycroft, for whom Plan G represented a reversal of the protectionist policy adopted in the early 1930s.[12] The substance of Plan G was largely a successful attempt by Macmillan to satisfy both wings of the party. Doing nothing was no longer an option so far as Macmillan and Thorneycroft were concerned, in Macmillan's case because of his long-standing fear that this would lead to a German-dominated Western Europe while Thorneycroft was concerned that Britain would thereby forfeit the leadership of Europe and would be left with only the remnants of the imperial preference system.[13]

Some studies of Plan G suggest more plausibly a mixture of motives. In short, the origins and pursuit of Plan G reflect a transition from initial attempts to sabotage the common market idea through the use of Plan G as a counter-initiative to the subsequent presentation of Plan G as a way of coming to terms with the Six through an FTA including the common market as a single entity. According to this view, assessing the rights and wrongs of the charge of perfidy against Britain simply obscures rather than reveals the policy formation process underlying the Plan G proposal.[14] If most trace elements of British hostility to the Six's plans gradually disappeared, it was certainly the case that Britain's benevolent neutrality towards the Six's form of integration since 1950 was now exchanged for the appearance of neutrality as one Treasury paper described the matter.[15]

The collapse of the intergovernmental negotiations on the FTA proposal with the French veto of November 1958 indicated the limitations of this proposal. It was unclear from the outset how a scheme that was so obviously tailored to suit British trading interests, that was presented on an almost take-it-or-leave it basis, and that had little or no regard for the different interests of the Six was likely to appeal to the Six, except to certain largely politically uninfluential industrial interests especially in Germany. It was equally unclear why the Six should endorse an arrangement whereby Britain derived maximum benefit without submitting itself to the disciplines of a common market. The exclusion of agricultural trade from the proposed FTA was a major obstacle to its acceptance. France, in particular, insisted on the inclusion of a common agricultural policy in the common market and was ill-disposed to grant favourable access of British manufactured goods to the common market without comparable access of French agricultural goods to the British market. Besides, the French constantly insisted that Britain could not belong to two discriminatory trade clubs, i.e. the common market and the Commonwealth. The FTA negotiations became increasingly bogged down in technical questions about how to run a customs union within a free trade area at a time when the political will for success had greatly diminished by late 1958.

There is much substance to the view that British politicians and officials generally overestimated the strength of their bargaining position and also the attractions of the Plan to the Six. True, some ministers like Butler, who remained a thorn in Macmillan's side on the question of relations with the Six, was always sceptical of the likelihood that the Six would be 'all eager to receive us on our terms'.[16] Reginald Maudling, the Paymaster-General who was made responsible for conducting the FTA negotiations, came to share Butler's scepticism, notably on the likely French opposition to the FTA proposal. A post-mortem on the FTA negotiations by Whitehall officials, however, pinpointed what were undoubtedly major weaknesses on the British side. Among other things, it concluded that the government had embarked on the project without being prepared to pay an adequate price and had initially antagonized the Six by failing to recognize the common market project.

Furthermore, there was a lack of political weight behind the negotiations, while Britain's negotiating position suffered from 'woodenness'. Perhaps most importantly, the introverted nature of the Whitehall policymaking exercise meant that much time and energy went into the management of interdepartmental and departmental differences and 'the effort and achievement of having formulated a plan breeds some arrogance and lack of willingness to understand the Europeans' ideas'. Bretherton, the British observer at the post-Messina talks, noted at this time that any Whitehall document passed by ministers left little room for 'flexibility or frills' and that while this approach worked all right for 'Lutheran Scandinavians' it did not awake any response in 'Catholic Latins'.[17]

A further feature of the FTA negotiations, evident also in the unsuccessful British applications for EEC membership in the 1960s, was that British policymakers before, during and since the Second World War were accustomed to dealing with a succession of weak French governments. Following de Gaulle's accession to power, however, they faced a strongly nationalist and self-assertive French government. On a number of occasions, British officials felt outsmarted by their French counterparts. They often believed that the French were in a weak position, were invariably in the wrong and were acting unreasonably, and yet they had to acknowledge that the French always got their way and that support for the British position among the Six (often dubbed the 'friendly Five') always seemed to melt away when it came to the crunch (Bloemen 1995). A key element in this situation was that shortly after coming to power in 1958 de Gaulle cultivated a good relationship with Adenauer, the West German Chancellor, which assisted his veto of further FTA negotiations and also of the first British application for EEC membership. Macmillan's relations with Adenauer, however, were at best lukewarm and often downright poisonous. Macmillan's attitude reflected the intense Germanophobia among the British population at large through this period and beyond that loomed large in the opposition to a close relationship with Western Europe. Macmillan treated Adenauer as a junior international player on probation who was vain, suspicious and grasping, while Adenauer regarded Macmillan as comparable to Neville Chamberlain in his willingness to ease Cold War tensions by appeasing or making concessions to the Soviets at the expense of the Germans.[18]

The formulation of and negotiations surrounding the FTA proposal in 1956–58 figured to a very limited extent in the minds of ministers, if only because of the Suez crisis of November 1956 and the 'lessons' drawn from this episode by the principal beneficiary of the crisis, Harold Macmillan, who succeeded the demoralized Eden as Prime Minister in January 1957. The Eden government was plunged into the most serious crisis confronting a post-war British government, first when President Nasser of Egypt nationalized the Suez Canal (July 1956), which had hitherto been funded by the British- and French-dominated Suez Canal Company, and then by the outcome of British, French and Israeli military action against Egypt (31 October–6 November

1956). This action was opposed by the US, whose economic pressure and particular threat to withhold support for sterling was instrumental in achieving a ceasefire and a withdrawal of British and French forces from Egypt. When a chastened Eden phoned Guy Mollet, the French Prime Minister, to inform him that he was bowing to US pressure, Mollet was with the West German Chancellor Adenauer who immediately consoled him: 'Europe will be your revenge'. The reactions of Britain and France to the aftermath of the Suez crisis were totally different. France was determined never to trust the US again and this paved the way for France's withdrawal from the US-led NATO ten years later. Britain, however, emerged from this episode fully determined to repair the damage to relations between London and Washington. Suez as military failure and political disaster was a humiliating outcome of the first order. Eden was the last British Prime Minister, as *The Times* commented, to believe Britain was a great power, and the first to confront a crisis which proved she was not. Suez (or 'Suezide') thereafter became a byword for British weakness. The episode finally exposed the country's decline in the international system that had been masked by the victory of 1945, and thus ended the twilight zone of great power status. It also highlighted Britain's inability thereafter to attempt any global military action without first securing the acquiescence of the US. 'No solo flying' by post-imperial Britain also signified that Suez was to mark a turning-point in Britain's retreat from empire. In the longer term, too, Suez was to prompt a review of Britain's European policy. Shortly before the end of his premiership, Eden offered a reappraisal of the post-Suez position in which he trailed the possibility of working more closely with Europe, but he warned 'Europe will not welcome us simply because at the moment it may appear to suit us to look to them'.[19]

Macmillan paid no heed to such advice, though there was a fruitless attempt by the Foreign Office to tilt British policy towards Western Europe at this point.[20] Now, as later, Macmillan was anxious to appease the Americans, thus perpetuating a policy that can be traced back to Churchill's wartime relations with the Roosevelt administration. Macmillan's reaction to Suez was to give far higher priority to restoring relations with the US than to developing closer relations with Western Europe. If Macmillan so often blew hot and cold about Europe, as some of his critics maintained, then this was one such occasion. Only two months before he became Prime Minister, his announcement of the FTA proposal suggested a new, more positive relationship between Britain and mainland Europe. In the early years of his premiership, however, this was far less evident. The centrepiece of his foreign policy, as under the Labour government of 1945–51, was to harness US power to upholding British interests. Such assistance was judged vital, partly to overcome the problems of overstretch and the mismatch between Britain's resources and its global commitments and partly to shore up Britain's, and thus Macmillan's, standing on the international stage. What this meant, in particular, was that Macmillan assumed the role of a reliable and trusted

confidant of the US, with a keen attention to fostering notions of partnership and interdependence which were the new labels for the 'special relationship' by the late 1950s.

It was largely in retrospect that the significance of the French veto on further FTA negotiations became apparent as France effectively strengthened its leadership of the Six while Britain was shut out of the EEC for the next fifteen years with a consequential loss of prestige and influence in Europe. At the time, there was irritation and anger on the British side at the French veto, with some recognition that the Franco-German accord represented a great 'landslip' in history (B.J. Jones 2003). In addition and in the months before the veto, Macmillan gave vent to one of his periodic outbursts of isolationist, 'Fortress Britain' sentiment. He suggested the possible withdrawal of British military forces from mainland Europe and of Britain from NATO if the common market came into being without a wider free trade area.[21] Such views were widely ridiculed by Foreign Office officials, some of whom brutally dismissed the Macmillan notion that Britain had a choice in the matter.

In the wake of the veto, Britain moved swiftly with six other countries to establish the EFTA which aimed to create by 1970 a free market in industrial goods only. This essentially defensive measure arose out of the wreckage of the FTA negotiations and out of a palpable need to do *something* to protect British interests following the failure of the negotiations; 'if we do nothing we are a sitting rabbit' Butler warned Macmillan.[22] It was also undertaken in the largely ill-considered expectation that a close form of association could be established between the EEC and EFTA. It was out of the evident failure to establish any such form of relationship – 'close', 'closest', 'near identification' in the language of the time – that there emerged the earliest signs of a sea-change in Whitehall opinion and a move towards the possibility of applying for full membership of the EEC. Meanwhile, the Conservatives fought the ('You've never had it so good') general election of October 1959, returning to power with an increased and substantial majority that had seemed highly unlikely in the immediate aftermath of the Suez debacle and that owed much to Macmillan's leadership. There was no reference to the EEC nor to the possibility of British membership in the Conservatives' election manifesto. Meanwhile, efforts to instruct the British public in the mysteries of the EEC were pitched at and remained on an elementary level; a Conservative Party publication of 1957 included the reassuring advice that the Treaty of Rome had nothing to do with the Vatican, the Pope or religion. After the election Macmillan merely noted that the question was how to live with the Common Market and turn its political effects into harmless channels. Why, then, less than two years later did Macmillan make the first British application for membership of the EEC?

The question has attracted many answers. Press comment at the time of Macmillan's announcement in July 1961 was often at a loss to either explain the decision or determine the advantages and disadvantages of EEC membership; *The Economist* in July 1961, for example, noted that the reasons that had impelled the British government to consider EEC membership in recent months had become obscure, while *The Times* maintained that the question of EEC membership involved a complex account of advantages and disadvantages.[23] In the extensive historiography of the first application, the emphasis on a particular factor or dimension – strategic, political, economic, diplomatic and others – often reflects the expertise of the individual historian.[24]

What can be said with some degree of certainty is that the application did not arise out of a single imperative or driving force but rather demonstrated the interaction of often unquantifiable influences whether at the individual or collective level. What is also evident is that in so far as a single individual was responsible for mounting this application it was Macmillan whose serpentine mind and manoeuvres were evident throughout this episode. Any study of the first application also involves taking account of the distinction between the private discourse of the policymakers and their public rhetoric in support of a policy.

At the time of EFTA's formation in 1959, the obstacles to British membership of the EEC still seemed to obtain. The Commonwealth dimension still loomed large, particularly in the form of trade ties. The Commonwealth still accounted for approximately 30 per cent of British trade, largely comprising the low or duty free import of food and raw materials into Britain and the export of manufactured goods to the rest of the Commonwealth, again with variable, preferential rates of duty. Then, too, Britain's self-styled role at the centre of the three interlocking circles of Europe, the Commonwealth and North America was still intact. Where this left British policy towards the EEC by late-1959/early-1960 was in limbo. EFTA had emerged on the assumption that there would be bridge-building between the EEC and EFTA, though nobody in the Foreign Office seemed to know what bridge-building meant in this context.[25] The Six had no interest in such an exercise, and easily represented the EFTA as just another example of the British at their old game of organizing counter-coalitions.[26]

It was at this point that a heightened sense of panic, drift and indecision reigned in government circles. The crisis of confidence, albeit hidden from public view by Macmillan's appearance of self assurance, was reflected at the time and later in his handling of the issue. The immediate cause of alarm was the EEC decision in November 1959, which took effect in July 1960, to accelerate its programme of internal tariff cutting and the creation of the common external tariff, thereby increasing the degree of discrimination between the EFTA and itself. This move further magnified what Macmillan perceived as a major external threat. This threat was framed and conditioned by some of his large stock of historical analogies, all of which represented the EEC not as an opportunity or as a risk worth taking but as a menace. In talks with US officials in March 1960, for example, Macmillan expatiated on the political dangers of the EEC. In particular, he expressed his fears about a Nazi revival in Germany after Adenauer. He also lashed out at the French by claiming that the EEC was comparable to the Napoleonic continental system and that the EEC/EFTA division was reminiscent of the Napoleonic period when Britain had allied with Russia to break French ambitions. When news of this outburst was leaked to the press by the Americans, it was widely regarded by the press across the EEC states as yet further confirmation of British opposition to the EEC and of another British operation to disrupt the organization.[27]

It was, however, indicative of the utter confusion and mood of desperation at the heart of government that a month later Macmillan agreed to a re-consideration of the case for British membership of the ECSC and of the EAEC. This Foreign Office-led operation was actually masterminded by Macmillan and resulted in an announcement (June 1960) that the government was prepared to consider the possibility of joining these two communities.[28] Charges of sabotage yet again rang through the EEC states, not least because the long-term plan of the Six was to merge the executives of the three Communities. Any consideration of joining two of the three Communities seemed a particularly crude piece of divide and rule strategy on the part of the Macmillan government. Unsurprisingly, the British ambassador in Bonn reported that the German press portrayed the British government as following an unsteady and unplanned course. To some mainland European observers it seemed that the British ship of state was zig-zagging from one destination to another, occasionally appearing to dock at mainland Europe only to reverse direction and make its way back across the Channel. Its course appeared even more directionless when two months later Macmillan fleetingly associated himself with the idea of the EEC joining the EFTA. At this same time, however, Walter Hallstein, the first President of the European Commission, claimed that the British were pursuing a clear strategy which meant that any initiative by the Six for tighter co-ordination was met by a British response which appeared to dilute the Six's unity with something wider and weaker, a commonplace observation that had more validity in later years than at the time.[29]

Macmillan's cackhanded moves in this period suggested perplexity in his own mind which sometimes resulted in a threadbare strategy born of wishful thinking and a lack of decisive leadership. This was particularly evident in July 1960 when the Cabinet discussed a report recommending EEC membership. Macmillan failed to provide any leadership from the front in favour of membership. The Cabinet concluded that there were insuperable difficulties in the way of accepting EEC membership under the existing provisions of the Treaty of Rome. According to one source at the time, it seemed that Macmillan's views on Europe simply reflected those of the average civil service and ministerial and establishment man.[30] It can be argued that Macmillan was skilfully playing a complex, convoluted game in building Cabinet support for a major change of policy. A Cabinet discussion of the principle of EEC membership, however, was not the way to do it according to Freddie Bishop, one of Macmillan's most trusted advisers. It is in any case easy to under-estimate the uncertainties in Macmillan's mind about the issue of EEC membership right through to July 1961. In particular, he harboured doubts about whether to apply, how to apply, when to apply, on what terms to apply and with whom to apply, all of which seemed to confirm that on Europe, as one observer commented, Macmillan was 'Forever amber' and in other quarters was repeatedly criticized for dithering.[31] In later years, Philip de Zulueta, Macmillan's Private Secretary during his premiership (1957–63) who had special responsibility for foreign affairs, commented that there was no single day on which Macmillan decided to apply. On 22 July 1961, the Cabinet unanimously decided in principle to apply formally to enter the EEC, though on the understanding that the application simply asked for negotiations to enquire if Britain could get terms on which it could then decide to join. Beyond that formal decision, however, Macmillan's handling of the matter puts to the test any fine-meshed discourse analysis or decoding of hidden meanings and ambiguous language. This was particularly the case as his representation of the possible relationships between Britain and the EEC melded into each other from association, close association and closest association to near identification and full membership. Thus, for example, Macmillan's 'Grand Design' paper, which was typical of a man who prided himself on seeing the 'big picture' and on responding to problems with grandiose strategies, has been regarded in some studies as confirmation of his determination to join the EEC. The paper does not say as much, however, but refers only to the possibility of an accommodation between the EEC and the EFTA.[32]

As compared with Macmillan's indecision, certain elements in the Foreign Office were very much to the fore in contributing to a major review of British policy, in pressing the case for EEC membership and in taking a distinctive line on matters concerning the timing, substance and character of the application. True, Selwyn Lloyd, Foreign Secretary, was no driving force and was at best ambivalent towards the possibility of EEC membership. However, there developed among senior officials by mid-1960 a solid body of support for an application. Several influences were at work including a determination to reassert the Office's voice on Europe in Whitehall together with a recognition of the absence of viable alternatives to membership and a deep sense of despair at the drift and lack of purpose among ministers. Following the formation of the EFTA the Office was determined to wrest control of policy towards the EEC away from the Treasury and the Board of Trade. The latter had taken the lead since 1956, as noted above, in the unsuccessful attempt to establish a FTA including the Six and then in forging the EFTA (Ludlow 2003). By late 1959, both ministries were, with certain exceptions, so satisfied with having ushered the EFTA into being that they were optimistic about the future. In the Foreign Office, however, the prevailing view was that the FTA negotiations had not been well-handled by the economics ministries and that the formation of the EFTA contributed to the division of Western Europe. Furthermore, it was believed that since the collapse of the FTA negotiations Britain's negotiating position and prospects vis-à-vis the EEC had on balance deteriorated. The formation of the EFTA was regarded as a net loss in terms of British bargaining power in any negotiations with the EEC.

A more serious concern among senior Foreign Office officials was the increasing absence of a credible British policy towards the EEC and the limited prospects for a major change. In July 1960 and ahead of the Cabinet meeting on European policy that month, for example, Gore Booth, head of the Office's Economic Relations Department who later became Permanent Under Secretary, noted the element of groupthink at work in the reluctance of policymakers to challenge the existing consensus on Europe. It was unlikely, he maintained, that anyone in British political circles would acknowledge the mistake of failing to join the EEC at the outset and say 'OK we're wrong and will do it your way'. To emphasize the 'never apologize, never explain' mantra of his peers he broke into German 'Das gibts nicht' ('It's impossible'), a characteristically melodramatic touch from someone who, as President of the Sherlock Holmes Society, enjoyed dressing up as Moriarty in his spare time.[33]

In the first year of the new Macmillan government several major reports reflected, and in turn influenced, Whitehall thinking. These collectively demonstrated the often finely balanced arguments about policy towards the EEC. One of them, *Future Policy Study 1960–70*, emerged from a Foreign Office-supervised interdepartmental study in February 1960.[34] Macmillan found its conclusions so depressing that, contrary to his original intention, he decided that it was not fit reading for the full Cabinet. Butler, one of the few senior ministers to see the report, judged it too defeatist and he thus prefigured the charge of appeasement made by later right-wing historians against Macmillan and his successors who sought EEC membership and in doing so symbolized national decline.[35] Butler was particularly critical of the insufficient stress that the report placed on the development of the Commonwealth and the colonial system. The report conveyed what was now the dominant view in the Foreign Office: that the Commonwealth could be more of a liability than an asset and that as a source of power it was not comparable with the USA or possibly Western Europe. By this time, too, it was calculated that the margin of trade discrimination against Britain in the markets of the Six if Britain remained outside the EEC would be much higher than the margins of preference currently enjoyed by Britain within the Commonwealth. Furthermore, British exports to the EEC were on a rising curve, while British exports to the rest of the Commonwealth were on a declining curve by the late 1950s.[36] Meanwhile, as Empire Day was increasingly disregarded and finally went out of fashion in the second wave of decolonization in the period 1958–62, the attempt to hold a Commonwealth Week in 1959 failed to capture the public imagination and was abandoned a few years later. Negative views of the political and economic value of the Commonwealth in the Foreign Office and elsewhere carried over into the 1960s.[37] The Foreign Office was thereafter increasingly prominent in pressing the case for making concessions on the Commonwealth front to ease Britain's passage into the EEC while Downing Street refused to contemplate such a possibility. In a commentary on the report to Macmillan, Patrick Dean, a weighty figure in the Foreign Office who was principally responsible for writing the report, echoed a view shared by others in British policymaking circles, including Macmillan, that while Britain's relative power in the world declined, its non-material goods of good sense, first class brains and ideas could more than compensate for the lack of real power in the world.[38]

A more substantial and influential report was supervised by Frank Lee, the Permanent Secretary at the Treasury, who had the sense and brains to recognize that to rely on non-material goods for trading in international relations was a precarious basis on which to conduct foreign policy. As chairman of the official Economic Steering (Europe) Committee, Lee was asked by Macmillan to undertake a review of British policy towards the EEC. The main conclusion of the Lee committee was that the most advantageous solution, with the possible exception of an Atlantic free trade area, was EEC membership.[39] In its conclusion, the report hit a note that continued to ring throughout policymaking circles, this being the difficulties involved in measuring or quantifying the impact of EEC membership on British trade and especially on British industry. How British industry was likely to react remained a mystery throughout this debate, even among some of the advocates of economic modernization. At a meeting chaired by Macmillan, it was noted that EEC membership was one of the few ways in which the government in a largely non-interventionist economic culture could bring pressure to bear on industry to make it more competitive. This argument seemed all the more persuasive in view of what were perceived as the limitations of government attempts to rejuvenate industry and improve productivity by a mixture of exhortation, patriotic appeals to the 'Dunkirk spirit', cajolement and incentives.[40] But the rhetoric of EEC membership as a necessary cold shower in Macmillan's view and as the astringent of competition according to one of his ministers did not receive unqualified support. Bishop advised Macmillan that making industry more competitive by exposing it to greater foreign competition might well be a case in which theory would not be borne out by practice.[41] A Treasury paper (May 1961) merely noted that opinion was divided between those who thought industry was fully capable of exploiting new opportunities for growth and those who believed that it was so sluggish and backward that it needed the shock produced by the removal of tariff barriers to wake it up. The report dryly observed 'This is an act of faith'.[42] In other quarters, meanwhile, there was considerable doubt about the view that Britain's economic problems could be automatically solved by EEC membership.[43] The Lee report is commonly cited in the literature as having had a considerable influence on Macmillan's thinking, though Lee receives only half a sentence in Macmillan's multi-volume autobiography. Lee's impact on Macmillan was probably less in the detailed economic arguments for and against EEC membership than in the sharply-cut word pictures and the trail of status and value statements that were likely to catch Macmillan's eye. Thus, he described the EFTA as a body brought together by ties of 'common funk' while immediately noting of the EEC that 'nothing succeeds like success'.[44] Nevertheless, economic uncertainties still remained in Macmillan's mind, especially as to whether the EEC would be a dynamic, modernizing force. There was too perhaps the lingering hope that the EEC would eventually disintegrate or, as he confided to his diary as late as December 1958: 'It will be the EDC story all over again'.[45]

The eventual decision to apply for EEC membership was taken not in a fit of euro-enthusiasm, but out of a reluctant, if not desperate, recognition that it represented the lesser of two evils. Britain's economic problems were undoubtedly a contributory factor and were highlighted in July 1961 when, only a week before the announcement of the EEC application, the Chancellor of the Exchequer introduced emergency measures to deal with a mounting balance of payments crisis. This situation presented the worst possible conditions in which to make an application, because not only did it convey the impression of entering the negotiations with the EEC from a position of economic weakness but it also allowed the Labour Opposition to portray the application as a form of economic escapism. Macmillan's announcement was cautious and unenthusiastic. The dimness of the presentation, according to one account, masked the boldness of the decision. In another, he was presented as attempting to slide sideways into the Common Market without any fanfare or excitement according to another account and with much emphasis on conditions that had to be satisfied, notably the Commonwealth, domestic agriculture and EFTA; 'The plunge is to be made' commented the *Manchester Guardian* 'but, on yesterday's evidence, by a shivering Government'.[46] Meanwhile, Jean Monnet, one of the EC's founding fathers, repeatedly advised the British government that it should sign the Treaties of Paris and Rome immediately (Monnet 1978).[47] During the course of the negotiations the EEC Commission strongly defended the *acquis communautaire* (the existing body of EEC legislation) and insisted that the principal onus of adaptation lay on the side of the applicant state and not the EEC (Ludlow 2005).

Macmillan's presentation emphasized the importance of the EEC membership application as an economic move dictated by commercial imperatives, with arguments largely couched in tradesmen's terms. There was, moreover, only limited substance to some of the political arguments publicly paraded to justify the decision, most notably that British membership of the EEC would help to overcome the division of Western Europe into two trade blocs and thereby strengthen the West's position in the Cold War.[48] Such an approach, however, scarcely inspired popular interest in the prospect of EEC membership. Nor did it allay or confront fears about particular issues such as the loss of sovereignty. The loss would be substantial according to Lord Kilmuir, the Lord Chancellor, who warned Edward Heath, the Foreign Office minister with special responsibility for European affairs and leader of the British negotiating team in Brussels.

Macmillan's handling of the announcement had the desired effect of concealing the more political considerations that underlay the decision and that figured prominently in private calculations. Much of the economic decline of Britain debate that accompanied this and subsequent applications for EEC membership had not figured in Whitehall's collective understanding of what had changed since 1956 to account for the decision to apply for EEC membership. The principal changes, according to the Whitehall version of events, were that in 1956 it seemed doubtful that the Common Market would come into being and that if it did Britain could make its own terms. In addition, France was no longer as weak as it had been in 1956, while earlier fears that EEC membership would weaken the 'special relationship' with the US were far less evident. Finally, whereas in 1956 Britain gave as much prominence to relations with the Commonwealth as to relations with the US and Europe, it now seemed likely that remaining outside the EEC would seriously affect Britain's position in the world and would damage the relationship with the rest of the Commonwealth.[49] Nevertheless, Macmillan had no sooner made the application than the British press was full of doom and gloom stories, often echoing Macmillan's private moan at the time of a sterling crisis in 1960: 'Everyone believes in Britain, except the British' (Sandbrook 2005: 352). A rash of books, articles and headlines appeared on the theme of 'What's wrong with Britain?', with detailed commentary on particular aspects of the decline of national prestige and competitiveness. One devastating critique appeared in the form of a collection of essays in July 1963 entitled *Suicide of a Nation?* in which Macmillan, exuding a flavour of mothballs in the view of one commentator, was portrayed as emblematic of a general sense of national decline.

What tipped the scales in favour of an application were political factors that often involved matters of status and prestige.[50] These considerations weighed heavily with British policymakers like Macmillan. This was particularly the case in view of the diminishing number of symbols of Britain's world power rank and an increasingly acute consciousness of relative decline and of the complex problems involved in the management of this decline. In their response to a rapidly changing and unexpected course of events in the successful launching of the EEC, policymakers reflected a longer-standing set of attitudes about Britain's role in the world and about its standing in relation to the mainland European powers. At a time of changing power relations, as in Europe with the emergence of the Six, British policymakers were all the more sensitive about status in the international system and about the need to ensure that Britain's allies 'understand and appreciate us and that our claim to rank as leader does not lapse by default'.[51] Macmillan led the way in this respect. In November 1959, for example, he insisted that Britain must try to preserve its position as a great nation with world-wide responsibilities and implicitly his own standing as an international statesman. The Foreign Office in response was primarily anxious to restore Britain's status in Europe in the wake of what it regarded as the devastating blow of the collapse of the FTA talks; Selwyn Lloyd, Foreign Secretary, argued that what was required was a political settlement that would stop the split in Europe and 'save our face'.[52]

Other ministers were no less status conscious: David Eccles, President of the Board of Trade, spoke disparagingly of the EFTA as a second class club and of British membership as 'a climbdown – the engineer's daughter when the general manager's had said no'.[53] International affairs invariably brought out the snob in Macmillan who had a punctilious regard for standing and for top table imagery of international relations, noting at one conference of western leaders, for example, that Adenauer was not invited to the main course.

Britain's status symbols and prestige considerations in the international system appeared most under threat during the first six months of 1960 which was a critical period in terms of strengthening the case for an EEC membership application. Arguably no other six-month period in the country's history since 1945 witnessed so many status symbols under threat or disappearing at an alarming rate. Historians have particularly highlighted the abortive Four-Power summit of May 1960, occasioned by the shooting down of a US spy plane by the Soviet Union. This event was certainly a public relations disaster for Macmillan who was far more committed to a positive outcome than any of the other participants. According to de Zulueta, it was as a result of this experience that Macmillan realized Britain counted for nothing in terms of great power status (Charlton 1983: 237).[54] During this same period, other long-standing symbols of Britain's international standing were under threat or being removed. At the time of the summit meeting, for example, the issue of apartheid in South Africa was exacerbated by the Sharpeville massacre (March 1960) and threatened to tear apart the Commonwealth during a Commonwealth Prime Ministers' conference; Macmillan confided in his diary (7 May 1960) 'Quite a pleasant Sunday – the Commonwealth in pieces and the Summit doomed!' (Horne 1989: 226). Macmillan increasingly came to view the diplomatic management of Commonwealth Prime Ministers' conferences as the latest version of the white man's burden.[55] Other developments conveyed a similar meaning in terms of the haemorrhaging of status symbols. British leadership of the OEEC ended at this time as this body was turned into the Organization for Economic Cooperation and Development (OECD) at the behest of the Americans and under American leadership. In this same period (February 1960 but announced in April), the Cabinet cancelled Britain's Blue Streak missile project and consequently an updated delivery system for Britain's nuclear weapons could be obtained only from the Americans. Macmillan's concept of interdependence to describe Britain's relations with the US began to resemble even more a culture of dependency. Finally, in June 1960 de Gaulle launched a plan for political union of the Six which further emphasized the heightened prestige of France in Western Europe and the diminished standing of Britain.

This loss of the trappings of Britain's world power status in the first half of 1960 often went largely unacknowledged even in the private confines of policymaking circles. There were coded references to the unspoken fears and psychological dimensions of relations with the EEC, but a marked reluctance to delve too deeply. For example, in May 1960 Anthony Rumbold, head of the Western Department in the Foreign Office who was one of the first senior officials in the Office to advocate EEC membership without special terms or conditions, suggested that the Office should embark on a detailed study of what he called the consequences of status consciousness. The reaction to this particular suggestion was uniformly negative. It seemed that Rumbold had touched a raw nerve among his peers and that they had no intention of inquiring into the degree to which their attitudes towards the Common Market were conditioned by a reluctance to recognize the decline in Britain's relative wealth and importance in the world. At the same time, the US ambassador in London advised the State Department that 'Decline of influence [here] is either unnoticed and unacknowledged, or, if publicly manifest, can embitter a proud people against those to whom the torch has passed'.[56]

The reverse side of the loss of status coin was that EEC membership could enhance Britain's status and particularly its leadership aspirations. In these circumstances, policymakers stressed their credentials for leading the EEC on the flimsy assumption that the Six needed, required, requested or even pleaded for British leadership. Harold Watkinson, Minister of Defence, envisaged that Britain would emerge as the leader of the EEC, while Macmillan advocated membership on the grounds that Britain could lead better from within the EEC than outside.[57] Meanwhile, a Foreign Office paper at the time of the application announcement suggested that sterling might become the EEC's common currency in the longer term. At a cabinet committee attended by Macmillan in May 1961, it was noted that Britain might be the most powerful member of the EEC, and there was no doubting that leadership status in Europe on British terms was an ingrained feature if not obsession of British policymakers. At the same time, it was agreed that perhaps the strongest argument for joining the EEC was based on the potential dangers of staying outside, but that this was 'a difficult argument to present publicly'.[58] One of the unspoken difficulties was how to explain the Conservative government's complete reversal of attitude on the question of EEC membership after six years of opposition to such a prospect. A particular problem was how to change direction without recourse to arguments that smacked of national decline and without admitting that the existing policy had been a disastrous failure. In the event, Macmillan, who had demonstrated his skills as actor manager at the time of Suez, was to ensure that a humiliating U-turn was smoothed over without sounding too desperate in public. Another area of concern lay in public attitudes towards the idea of EEC membership. In July 1960 officials warned ministers that if the government changed its policy towards the EEC it would have to contend with the ordinary Englishman's almost 'innate dislike and suspicion of "Europeans"' and that would require careful handling and intensive re-education.[59] In September 1962 the results of the government's own findings, based on national opinion polls and soundings taken by Conservative Party agents, revealed that only 40 per cent favoured EEC membership, while the same soundings reported increasing distrust of foreign political connections and especially of being forced 'to

surrender our independence to "Frogs" and "Wogs"'.[60] While EEC membership offered the possibility of projecting the Conservative Party as a rejuve-
nated, progressive, modernizing force and became the central feature of the
Macmillan government's forward thinking, there was little evidence here to
suggest that the party was likely to reap electoral dividends in advocating
EEC membership.[61]

The toxic mixture of declining status, inflated leadership aspirations, reversal of policy and public hostility typified in many respects the beginnings of a
longstanding unwillingness or inability by the political class to educate the
public about EEC membership. It was rather the case that there was a strong
preference for resorting to propaganda that often highlighted the gulf between
pro-EEC membership politicians and large sections of public opinion (Mullen
and Birkitt 2005). At the official level the combination of grandiose claims
and the growing perception of Britain's relative decline in the international
system affected all and sundry, even those who might have been expected to
take a more clear-eyed view of matters. For example, in a preliminary draft of
his report, Lee stressed that there was no evidence that British membership of
the EEC was desperately needed by the Six. Nevertheless, he concluded this
draft with a flourish in the words of William Pitt: 'We will save England by
our exertions and Europe by our example'.[62] This conclusion was scarcely
consistent with the burden of his message, but it was nonetheless indicative of
the doublethink characteristics of British politicians and officials born when
British imperial and maritime supremacy was at its zenith or on the turn.
Herbert Andrew, a senior Board of Trade official, drew an altogether different
conclusion from Lee's paper, insisting that 'Europe will change us, not we
them', and he added for good measure that EEC membership would have
profound effects: 'It is as if another planet were crashing into us. The kingdom and the power and the glory will pass from us and leave us naked, face
to face with our real selves at last'[63] – unusually apocalyptic language for a
Board of Trade official. The marked disconnection between the intellectual
and the emotional appreciation of Britain's changing position in the world
was perhaps best expressed by Hoyer-Millar, the most senior official at the
Foreign Office. He supported EEC membership, thinking that it was the correct policy but feeling otherwise. Against the background of such ambivalence,
the construction of a coherent and convincing case for EEC membership
remained problematical.

Some invincible wishful thinking on Macmillan's part also entered into the
diplomacy surrounding the origins and outcome of this application. He was
clearly aware that de Gaulle represented the most formidable obstacle to a
successful application. He was repeatedly warned by some of his Cabinet
colleagues and by diplomats, like the UK ambassador to France, of the seemingly insuperable problem of persuading de Gaulle of the merits of the
British case for EEC membership. Despite this, Macmillan believed that an
agreement was more likely with de Gaulle than with any of his successors
who would probably be strong supporters of European integration. He did

not fully realize at the time, as he later noted, that de Gaulle wanted the kind of EEC that Britain would feel able to join, but without the British in: *L'Europe à l'anglais sans les Anglais* [*sic*] (Macmillan 1973: 118). He later claimed that, while de Gaulle did not want Britain to join the EEC, once the negotiations had started he could not reject the application, especially as he would be left with no excuse to exclude Britain.[64] De Gaulle made no secret of his serious reservations about the possibility of British membership of the EEC, often recycling arguments that had been used on the British side to explain Britain's aloofness from the origins of the EEC. He especially capitalized on the difficulties of reconciling Britain's Commonwealth trade arrangements with EEC membership. Commonwealth trade issues took up a considerable amount of time in the negotiations between Britain and the Six that formally opened in October 1961 and lasted until the French veto in January 1963. The negotiations covered all manner of Commonwealth imports from the major, problematical issue of Temperate Zone foodstuffs to the treatment of relatively minor items such as kangaroo meat and cricket balls.

Status and prestige considerations in the international system, most especially in the triangular relationship between Britain, France and the USA, entered into and ultimately determined the fate of the Macmillan government's application for EEC membership. British, and in particular Macmillan's, perceptions of the value and future of the 'special relationship' with the US were important in accounting for both the origins and the failure of EEC membership application.[65] US support for British membership of the EEC was evident in the later years of the Eisenhower administration and became even more pronounced under the incoming Kennedy administration of January 1961. This support was expressed by Kennedy at his first major meeting with Macmillan in April 1961, following which the Communist *Daily Worker* ran the headline 'Mac given his orders'. In view of the importance that Macmillan had attached to US/UK relations since the beginning of his premiership,[66] there was good reason to pursue EEC membership if it meant protecting Britain's standing in Washington. The case was all the more compelling in view of the fact that Macmillan was not best placed to resist US pressure after his agreement with President Eisenhower (March 1960) that US-built Skybolt missiles should be provided for British nuclear weapons. A Foreign Office paper in January 1960 typified British assessments at the time, and also over the longer term, in its treatment of the advantages of EC membership that might accrue to Britain in Washington.[67] The paper took the view that Britain's standing in American eyes would be enhanced. The US could rely on Britain as an EEC member to consider policy questions from the standpoint of the Atlantic Alliance as a whole and thus be more alert to American views and also help to combat neutralist elements among the Six. Such views largely coincided with de Gaulle's opinion that Britain within the EEC would act like an American Trojan horse and that Macmillan rather than choosing Europe was seeking to shore up Britain's international position by adding a new European dimension.[68]

This period in UK/US relations culminated dramatically in two events that had a direct bearing on the fate of the EEC membership application. First, as a result of negotiations between Macmillan and Kennedy at Nassau (19–21 December 1962) Britain was offered US-built Polaris missiles for its nuclear weapons instead of the recently cancelled Skybolt. In pressing the case for Polaris with Kennedy, the status-conscious Macmillan explained that possession of nuclear weapons was partly 'a question of keeping up with the Joneses' and that a country like Britain that had played a great role in history had to retain its dignity.[69] In the view of some commentators, the acquisition of Polaris had less to do with protecting the country than with protecting the standing of Macmillan and of the Conservative government. Second, a month after the Nassau meeting, de Gaulle vetoed the British application for EEC membership. Status considerations also entered into account in Macmillan's dealings with de Gaulle. Before and during the UK–EEC negotiations of 1961–63, Macmillan toyed with the idea of assisting the French nuclear weapons programme in return for obtaining de Gaulle's agreement to British membership of the EEC.[70] Britain was ahead of France in its nuclear weapons programme, possessing the hydrogen bomb and a fully operational V-bomber force. France, however, did not test its first atomic bomb until February 1960. Furthermore, the limited range of its bomber force, as the Foreign Office noted with some satisfaction, meant that it could deliver the bomb to Moscow but could not make the return trip. Macmillan's handling of the issue occasionally smacked of social engineering at the international level. In a memorandum to the Foreign Secretary, for example, in January 1961, he considered the respective merits of levelling up or down; the choice was between stepping down to the same level as France by bringing Britain's independent nuclear strength entirely under NATO control or trying to help France to rise up to the special position of Britain. In Macmillan's view the first alternative ran the risk of Britain becoming a European power on terms of equality and surrendering too much of its 'special relationship' with the US and its special position as leader of the Commonwealth which were the main marks of Britain's standing as a world power. The second alternative was likely to be more palatable to France and also to British public opinion as it would mean 'we regarded ourselves as retaining a special status as something more than a "European" country'.[71] A major obstacle to the use of a nuclear bribe to win French acquiescence in British membership of the EEC, however, was the restriction on bilateral cooperation with third countries under the contractual obligations of the British–US nuclear partnership established in 1957–58. The Foreign Office under Home as Foreign Secretary generally exercised an important, restraining influence on Macmillan, and in this case was very uneasy about any prospect of nuclear cooperation with France, to the point where Macmillan tried to hide his intentions from the Office (Holt 2005).[72] In the end it was power rather than status that took the matter out of Macmillan's hands and determined the outcome. The decisive blow against any nuclear deal with France was administered by President Kennedy when he informed Macmillan that it would be undesirable to assist France's efforts to create a nuclear weapons capability.

While his consideration of a nuclear deal with de Gaulle was never put to the test, Macmillan continued to believe that once the negotiations got underway de Gaulle could not reject British membership. Yet in view of Macmillan's indecision about the application, the emphasis on its conditionality, and the preoccupation with status symbols and leadership claims, there was substance to de Gaulle's argument that Britain was not yet ready for EEC membership. It was equally evident that no conceivable French national interest would be served by permitting Britain to join the EEC at this stage, least of all in de Gaulle's view when Britain wanted to have the best of the Atlantic and European worlds and the advantage of 'winning at both tables'. The veto poleaxed Macmillan, who 'could not remember going through a worse time since Suez', while a popular British retort at the time to de Gaulle's action attempted to disguise the hurt of humiliation: 'Take your dreams of independent power, and stick them up your Eiffel Tower' (Horne 1989: 449; Wall 2008: 1). De Gaulle's veto shattered what had increasingly become the centrepiece of the Conservatives' modernization programme. Furthermore, it demolished Macmillan's 'Supermac' image and made him the first of a long line of British leaders seriously damaged by the politics of European integration.

De Gaulle's veto was to be repeated four years later when the Wilson Labour government made the second attempt to join the EEC. On this occasion, the veto was less surprising than the fact that a Labour government and Harold Wilson in particular were following in Macmillan's footsteps. The Labour Party conference in September 1962 under the leadership of Hugh Gaitskell had strongly opposed the Macmillan application by setting out five conditions for entry which amounted to rejection of the application. As Shadow Chancellor of the Exchequer Wilson had figured prominently in parliamentary debates on the application and was particularly critical of what he regarded as the government's failure to safeguard Commonwealth interests. On coming to power in October 1964, there was no indication that Wilson was about to abandon either this negative stance or the domestic and international priorities with which he came to office as Prime Minister. His list of priorities included economic planning, the regeneration of Britain's links with the rest of the Commonwealth and the modernization of the British economy via science and technology. Neither the EEC nor the EFTA figured on this agenda. This omission was most evident when, immediately after coming to power, the government imposed a 15 per cent surcharge on all Britain's imports regardless of source in response to a colossal balance of payments deficit inherited from the Conservative government. In any case the first Wilson government (October 1964–March 1966) had a wafer-thin majority of five and survival was the top priority until the next election produced a larger majority and the second Wilson government (March 1966– June 1970). Furthermore, Wilson possessed none of the European interests and connections of Macmillan and none of the pro-EEC convictions of Edward Heath who became leader of the Conservative Party in 1965. In his early period of office, he maintained a position on the issue that was very similar to Gaitskell's, stipulating conditions which in fact stood no real chance of acceptance by the Six.

What exactly induced Wilson to change his mind on the EEC membership issue was a matter of dispute among his political colleagues at the time and it has also attracted different explanations ever since, as has the question of whether his conversion to EEC membership was sudden or gradual. Explanations run the gamut from the high politics of global strategy and retreat to the low politics of party and personal advantage. Some accounts view Wilson's handling of the issue as a largely tactical manoeuvre that was rooted in the exigencies of Cabinet, party and inter-party politics and reflected his talents as a master tactician and political manipulator. According to this version of events, the application was a short-term gimmick typical of the man who coined the expression: 'a week is a long time in politics'. In short, the application was a misconceived, diplomatically inept venture predictably ending in another veto by de Gaulle. This type of assessment was often based on the observations of some of Wilson's ministerial colleagues who believed he was devoid of a clear and coherent strategy, lacked firm principles and was thus unable to provide visionary leadership; Richard Crossman, one of Wilson's ministers, commented: 'Does he really want to go into Europe, or doesn't he? I don't think he knows himself' (Dorey 2006: 376–78). One or two such explanations have more validity than others. For example, there is little or no substance to the view that in making the application, Wilson was engaged in a Machiavellian exercise, knowing that there was no chance of securing membership and using the application to demonstrate that this was so. Had that been the case, he would not have become so personally involved as to risk exposure to humiliation (Pimlott 1992: 438). A more convincing explanation in terms of party advantage is that Wilson wanted to deprive the Conservative Party of electoral ammunition, as its new leader, Edward Heath, strongly supported EEC membership.

Other and often more recent assessments, however, have viewed the application as a serious, strategic and positive response to changing domestic and international conditions that confronted and, at times, almost overwhelmed Wilson's government. According to this view, the Wilson application was a 'successful failure' in its achievement of a number of immediate and longer term objectives such as managing divisions of opinion in the Labour Cabinet and Party, fending off the criticisms of the pro-EEC Conservative Party, and assisting Britain's eventually successful passage into the EEC. Interpretations of the application have also attached varying degrees of importance to strategic, political and economic factors as well as to the domestic and international dimensions of policymaking.[73] At the very least, therefore, Wilson cuts an enigmatic figure in the history of Britain and European integration. No single explanation, except at the highest level of generality such as the impact of the experience of government, satisfactorily captures a wide variety of influences, some of which carried over from the Macmillan bid for EEC membership but were now more pronounced.

Few accounts doubt that economic considerations contributed to the application decision, as the Labour government's economic and monetary policies failed to overcome Britain's laggardly economic growth rate and fed into the 'decline of Britain' debate of the 1960s and 1970s. Wilson had come to power promising to solve the persistent problem of slow economic growth. The centrepiece of his economic strategy was the coordination of resources and investment by means of the National Plan that was announced in September 1965. The Plan set an ambitious economic growth target averaging almost 4 per cent per annum over the next five years, as against the trend growth rate of the British economy of 2.5 per cent over the past sixty years. The expansionist emphasis of this plan, however, was completely at odds with the steadfast refusal of the Wilson government to contemplate devaluation of the pound in the fixed exchange rate system of the time, at least until forced to do so (November 1967). Wilson did not want his government to be branded a devaluing one like the Labour government of 1949 in which he had served. This determination to maintain the parity of the pound, with US financial support, required retrenchment, as became all too evident in July 1966 when a heavy run on sterling compelled the government to introduce a severe deflationary package, including a freeze on prices and wages. These measures sounded the death knell of the National Plan and so stripped the government of the central plank of its economic policy that the entire affair was immediately dubbed Labour's 'Suez'. In these circumstances, an application for EEC membership could at the very least serve as a diversion from the catastrophic failure of the government's domestic policy. It also offered an alternative route to economic salvation for what one government minister described as a 'defeated cabinet' that was persuaded to see EEC membership as an external solution to Britain's economic problems (Benn 1988: 490).

Furthermore, following the general election (March 1966) that gave Labour an overall majority of 97, the government was in a stronger position to advocate EEC membership if it so wished. Wilson proceeded cautiously, however, in view of deep divisions within the Cabinet and in the Labour movement at large on the question. Besides, he was by no means convinced of the case for membership or at least the process for achieving membership; in discussions with US officials in July 1966, for example, he opposed the prospect of joining an inward-looking Europe, expressed his Atlanticist leanings and resisted the view that Britain should enter the EEC and subsequently negotiate concessions.[74] Now, as later, there was a correlation between enthusiasm for EEC membership and pessimism about the domestic economy. A further complicating factor in this situation was the relationship between EEC membership and devaluation. There was general agreement among policymakers at home and abroad that before Britain could join the EEC it would need to improve its economic competitiveness by devaluing its overvalued currency. Strong supporters of EEC membership in the ministerial ranks like George Brown and Roy Jenkins had no qualms about such a course of action, while others like Wilson clung to the determination to maintain parity and still viewed sterling as a virility symbol or a sign of Britain's greatness.

In the aftermath of the July sterling crisis, the beginnings of a drive towards reviewing the question of EEC membership became discernible. Key developments here were the appointment of Brown as Foreign Secretary (August 1966) and the Cabinet decision (October 1966) that Wilson and Brown should undertake an exploratory probe by visiting each of the capitals of the Six to sound out opinion and convince EC leaders of the seriousness of British intentions. The political fall-out from the July sterling crisis and other, arguably more significant factors than immediate economic problems, however, prompted the Wilson government to seek EEC membership. One of the most important was the growing awareness that a future outside the EEC had diminishing attractions. The possibility of EEC membership was pushed into the foreground for want of a better alternative in what was perceived as the increasingly bleak and changing international landscape facing Britain by 1966–67. This was especially the case in view of growing concerns that the Commonwealth was a busted flush, that Britain's east of Suez, and therefore global, role could not be sustained, and that a 'special relationship' with the US relations was less and less in evidence.

The Wilson government came to power with a keen determination to reinvigorate political and economic ties with the rest of the Commonwealth. Wilson was a strong upholder of the idea of the Commonwealth as an interracial community with an important part to play in world affairs. He had a particularly fond regard for the old Dominions, later boasting that he had some 44 relatives in New Zealand alone. In the election campaign of 1964 he promised a substantial expansion of British trade with the rest of the Commonwealth, thereby reversing the rest of the Commonwealth's declining share of trade with Britain that had fallen from 44 per cent to 30 per cent under the Conservatives. In the event, there was no reversal of this trend, and Britain's trade with the rest of the Commonwealth continued to grow at a much more modest rate than its trade with the EEC (Holt 2005).[75]

The Wilson government also had its authority battered by its response to events in Rhodesia where a white minority led by Ian Smith, the Rhodesian Prime Minister, was determined to preserve its privileged position and announced a unilateral declaration of independence (UDI) in November 1965. Wilson ruled out the use of force and relied on the imposition of economic sanctions. The failure of sanctions and the serious impact of the protracted Rhodesian affair on Commonwealth unity dealt a major blow to British prestige and contributed to Wilson's growing disenchantment with the Commonwealth. It was as a result of a rancorous Commonwealth Prime Ministers' Meeting in September 1966 – the worst ever held up to that time according to Wilson – that he became convinced of the need to apply for

EEC membership. It was in the immediate aftermath of this meeting that the Cabinet agreed to the joint Wilson/Brown probe to the capitals of the Six. This same Cabinet meeting also noted in a paper by Brown and his predecessor as Foreign Secretary, Michael Stewart, that Commonwealth developments might make it more difficult for Britain to exercise world-wide influence as the central nation in the Commonwealth (Alexander 2000: 201–2). It was scarcely surprising that a Whitehall assessment of the value of the Commonwealth to Britain expressed government disillusionment with the enterprise.

There was also an important, if slightly less clear-cut, relationship between the EEC application and the ending of the British role east of Suez. By 1966 and above all in the aftermath of the July sterling crisis of that year, it was evident that Britain's east of Suez role was beyond its financial and military resources. The Defence White Paper of February 1966 heralded the beginning of the end, with heavy cuts in naval expenditure, including the decision not to build a new aircraft carrier. Two years later and following the devaluation of sterling, the process of withdrawal from east of Suez was accelerated as a result of further public expenditure cuts made by Roy Jenkins, the newly-appointed Chancellor of the Exchequer. Jenkins himself was convinced that Britain's global commitments and outdated imperial pretensions were an unwelcome distraction from the key priority of achieving EEC membership (Roy 2000; Pickering 2002).[76] The process of withdrawal from east of Suez was influential in persuading some Cabinet ministers that another EEC membership bid should at best receive their support or at worst their grudging acquiescence, safe in the knowledge that de Gaulle was likely to exercise yet another veto.

The case for another EEC membership bid was further strengthened by the need to compensate for the growing trend of drift and disillusion in US/UK relations. There was a gradual distancing in relations that reflected the priorities of the Johnson administration in Washington, the growing economic and financial weaknesses of Britain and the at best lukewarm relations between Johnson and Wilson. Widespread opposition within the Labour movement to the escalation of the Vietnam war meant that while Wilson did not dissociate himself from US policy he refused Johnson's request to send a contingent of British troops to Vietnam; Wilson also argued that if Britain remained outside the EEC it might be forced into closer association with the US in Vietnam.[77] The Johnson administration continued to support British membership of the EEC. It had little interest in the issue of European unity, however, and increasingly viewed Britain as at best a medium-sized European power with residual extra-European responsibilities and a continuing, if diminished, status as a favoured partner of the US. Johnson himself took the view that it was no longer worth spending two days with the British Prime Minister because Britain was not that important anymore. The US ambassador in London at this time commented that the so-called Anglo-American special relationship was now little more than sentimental terminology (Colman

2004). According to most accounts, Johnson had little regard for Wilson, while the mock heroics in Wilson's personality often meant that he thought that his relationship with Johnson was warmer than it was in reality. This distancing in relations helped Wilson to persuade de Gaulle that Britain had made progress in detaching itself from the 'special relationship' with the US, as de Gaulle himself moved towards the climax of his stormy relations with the Johnson Administration by announcing the French withdrawal from military participation in NATO (March 1966).[78]

The Wilson application was also influenced by the views of significant bodies of opinion within and beyond Whitehall. The Foreign Office, for example, was by now convinced that there was no alternative to membership and exerted strong pressure on Wilson to undertake a bid. The substance of the Foreign Office argument was that EEC membership was essential to bolster British power in the world and that in the absence of membership Britain would be forced into political neutrality and would become 'a greater Sweden' (Parr 2005: 450). In short, Britain could only maintain the semblance, if not the reality, of world power status through joining the EEC. Wilson was receptive to such arguments, not least because he was convinced that Britain's great power status was supported largely by the twin pillars of the east of Suez role and sterling's position as a major reserve currency, both of which were in a state of terminal collapse. The Treasury, however, counselled against any immediate application. It feared that a move towards the EEC could precipitate the devaluation of sterling. Such warnings often meant that ministers viewed the economic pros and cons of EEC membership as at best finely balanced and that political considerations ultimately figured more prominently. At the Chequers Cabinet meeting (23 October 1966), for example, at which it was agreed that Wilson and Brown should conduct an exploratory probe, Brown and Stewart (now Secretary of State for Economic Affairs) insisted that EEC membership was essential not for economic reasons, but rather to keep up Britain's international status and its place at the 'top table'.[79] According to this view, Britain would not only be giving the Six the benefit of its long experience as a parliamentary democracy, but would also be providing the type of British leadership eagerly awaited by the Six. Brown was so supremely confident in this respect that he informed Willy Brandt, the West German foreign minister: 'Willy, you must get us in [the EEC] so we can take the lead' (Brandt, 1978: 161).

Unlike the Macmillan negotiations with the Six between 1961–63, the Wilson government's application reached closure even before the negotiations stage. Wilson skilfully and often stealthily secured the approval of a divided Cabinet for an application. In November 1966 he announced to Parliament that the government intended to enter the EEC, provided essential British and Commonwealth interests could be safeguarded. Following their exploratory probe in the period January–March 1967, Wilson and Brown reported to Cabinet (21 March) that de Gaulle did not favour EC enlargement and that the other members of the EC (the 'friendly Five') were not prepared to challenge France. During April 1967, the question of whether or not to apply was the subject of regular discussions by the Cabinet. The opponents of entry in the Cabinet formed a disparate group. There were principled opponents of entry like Barbara Castle on the left and Douglas Jay on the right who were joined by more centrist and more pragmatic opponents like Denis Healey and Richard Crossman, the latter of whom took the view that there appeared little reason to put up a fight to the finish or to threaten resignation, since de Gaulle was likely to exercise a veto.[80] In the end, Wilson, Brown and the pro-entry group secured a majority of 13 votes to eight in Cabinet to apply to join. This decision was announced to Parliament (2 May). A fortnight later, however, de Gaulle made a dramatic intervention in the course of a press conference at which he applied the so-called 'velvet veto', insisting that Britain was not yet ready to join the EC. He also placed great emphasis upon the weakness of sterling and on the more fundamental difficulty of incorporating it into any form of European monetary system. Despite this major setback, Wilson remained determined to persevere, having a further meeting with de Gaulle (18 June). British hopes were finally dashed when de Gaulle formally vetoed the application in November 1967.

In some respects it is puzzling that the Wilson government pressed ahead with the application in the face of French opposition and at a time when the British negotiating position was at its weakest in the period culminating in the devaluation of sterling in November 1967. To a large extent, the case for an application gathered momentum to the point where it was almost too late to draw back without suffering a humiliating loss of face. Wilson exhibited many of his Walter Mitty characteristics throughout the episode whether in extravagant claims about his abilities as a top-flight diplomat or in assessments suggesting that he had charmed de Gaulle. He misjudged de Gaulle, evidently believing that while the French president was opposed to British membership he might lack the strength to exercise a veto if the British government continued to beat at the door and did not falter in its purpose.[81]

Both Wilson and Brown believed that the 'friendly Five' could successfully bring pressure to bear on de Gaulle. This was despite all evidence to the contrary, including the failure of the Five to reverse de Gaulle's veto in 1963. Brown was arguably even more wilfully determined than Wilson to rely on the Five, unsuccessfully imploring the Americans after the veto to stiffen the Five's opposition to de Gaulle.[82] Brown also downplayed any reports indicating the likelihood of a French veto, largely for fear that Cabinet opponents of an application might capitalize on such assessments. Thus, for example, he insisted that the Foreign Office should report as positively as possible on the prospects for a successful application, and he ordered Patrick Reilly, the UK ambassador in Paris, not to send negative signals about de Gaulle's intentions. Reilly, however, continued to warn that de Gaulle was extremely sceptical about British entry and intimated that the only way to avert a French veto was to offer de Gaulle joint Franco-British development of thermonuclear weapons. Now, as in the early 1960s, this suggestion was anathema to the Foreign Office on the grounds that it threatened Britain's 'special relationship' with the US. Such messages ultimately led to a complete breakdown of trust between Brown and Reilly, so much so that Brown prematurely relieved Reilly of his ambassadorship in 1968 and forced him to take early retirement. On the whole, there is no reason to doubt the general conclusion that Wilson and Brown, like Macmillan before them, failed to make sufficient use of the best tools the Foreign Office provided them with – a UK embassy only a few hundred yards from the French presidential palace (Boehm 2004). Once again, securing a domestic basis, and in this case Cabinet approval, for a European initiative took precedence over preparing the ground abroad for a successful initiative and for exploring the consequences of the possibility of a French veto.

Following de Gaulle's veto, several aspects of British policy assisted the third and successful application by the Heath government. First, Wilson left the application on the table so that whenever an opportune moment arose, by which it was now generally understood to be de Gaulle's retirement from office, negotiations could proceed without delay, as in fact they did only 12 days after the defeat of the Wilson government in the general election of 1970. Second, the Wilson government had crossed an important bridge in deciding to apply for membership unconditionally, thereby avoiding a repetition of the seemingly interminable negotiations that had followed Macmillan's application. Third, the government did not deviate from its declared policy in support of membership. In the wake of the veto, Wilson informed the US President Johnson that there was no 'Little England' spirit in the country but rather a determination to hew out a new role for Britain in the world.[83] At the same time, Wilson was advised by one Foreign Office minister to aim at a position of 'dignified resolution' which meant, among other things, that when de Gaulle tried to draw the Wilson government into bilateral discussions about the future of Europe, through the so-called Soames affair, the government refused to deviate from its declared policy of seeking EEC membership.[84] Finally, there was now a widespread consensus in government circles that there was no viable alternative to EC membership. It was this mind-set together with the departure of de Gaulle from office in April 1969, and the emergence of a Conservative government under Edward Heath a year later, which shaped the third and successful application for membership.

In the 1980s the acronym Tina (There is no alternative) was commonly used as a dogmatic assertion or an article of blind faith by the Thatcher governments that there was no alternative to free market capitalism. To a large extent, similar status was given to the importance of EEC membership by the political establishment of the late 1960s and early 1970s. A classic exposition of this view found expression in a Foreign and Commonwealth Office study of the options for British external policy if the third application for EEC membership ended in failure.[85] Douglas Home, the Foreign Secretary, and Geoffrey Rippon, Chancellor of the Duchy of Lancaster who headed the British team in the negotiations on the third application, broadly agreed with the conclusions of this study.

This paper maintained that the arguments for EC membership were 'overwhelming' while acknowledging that the prospect of EC membership and potentially of a unified Europe did not enjoy substantial support among the British public. The four alternatives to EC membership were 'Go-it-Alone policies', co-operation with European countries outside the EC, new forms of association with non-European countries, and policies involving co-operation with the EC states. As compared with EC membership, even the best of these options was judged to be not 'merely second but fourth or fifth best'. A key argument against 'Go-it-Alone policies' was that these would do lasting damage to Britain's relations with the EC and with the US without deflecting the EC from its course. Nothing would be more likely to unite the Six than disruptive tactics on Britain's part; 'We have tried disruption before, in the 1958/59 free trade negotiations, and failed', this being an acknowledgement of British subversion tactics denied at the time and also of Britain's weaker position ten years on. The second option was rejected on the grounds that there was no realistic prospect of the EFTA becoming either a stronger, more cohesive body or a unit in international relations. Close ties with Eastern Europe offered only limited commercial gains and ran the risk of adversely affecting relations with the US, as any British move to draw nearer to Eastern Europe and the Soviet Union would be regarded as a defection from the Western camp. The third option of new forms of association with non-European countries was ruled out on several counts. The Commonwealth and especially the old white self-governing Commonwealth states were adjusting to new centres of power in the world, and Britain lacked the leverage to arrest or reverse this trend. The other set of ties under this option concerned trans-Atlantic relations and in particular the idea of a North Atlantic Free Trade Area (comprising the US, Canada, Britain and possibly other EFTA states), an evergreen favourite of opponents of British membership of the EC in later years. The NAFTA idea was here dismissed on the grounds that the US showed no interest in such a scheme and that British industry would be brought face to face with US competition. Besides, it would offer Britain no political base in the world but would rather mean that the country would be increasingly overshadowed by the US. The final option of co-operation with the EC held out some advantages but these were far outweighed by disadvantages. Most notably, such cooperation might meet public opposition following a third failure to secure EC membership and that some form of association with the EC was not available for a developed European country like Britain. Furthermore, any possibility of a trading arrangement between the EEC and the EFTA would fall foul of the same obstacles encountered by the Macmillan government in 1959–60.

To some commentators at the time and since, this sort of analysis smacked of weakness and defeatism. Pro-marketeers were routinely criticized for losing faith in Britain's ability to solve its problems outside the EEC and the assumed economic stimulus that EEC membership would bring. In October 1970, for example, *The Spectator*, the leading pro-Conservative weekly, claimed that the British public was being taken into the EEC under false pretences. It was being misled by a formidable establishment masterminded by a group of British politicians and intellectuals unable to think of any acceptable diversion with which to conceal the country's political and economic weakness. At the same time, George Gale, its editor, claimed that the paper stood fast on the principle of national identity in opposing membership, insisting that to join the EC would be an unnatural and unhistorical and therefore ignorant folly. Some later right-wing historians further expanded on this theme, accusing the Heath government of acting as an abusive parent towards the Commonwealth and of entering the EEC under the 'moral cowardice' of Heath in 'the dour, drab defeatist Seventies'.[86] The course and outcome of the third set of negotiations for EC membership bore out some of the charges levelled against the Heath government by such opponents of membership.[87]

Heath came to power with a strong commitment to modernize and regenerate the British economy through a radical reform of industrial relations and exposure of domestic industry to fierce competition within the EEC. By this time, the far higher standard of living of the Six was fast becoming a matter of common knowledge (J.W. Young 1996: 260–61). EEC membership, however, was never merely a question of economics for Heath but rather amounted to a political crusade (Campbell 1993: xv–xviii). He pursued this goal in such a single-minded, uncompromising manner that possibly Thatcher and himself were the only two post-war British Prime Ministers to have personally changed the course of British history by sheer force of character and conviction. Some observers have noted the contrast between the persistence, drive and energy devoted to obtaining EEC membership under Heath's leadership and the overall sense of drift and abandonment of other policies when the going got rough (Day 1989: 229; Tebbitt 1989:135, 149). He was undoubtedly the most European-centred of any British Prime Minister since 1945. Unlike all his postwar predecessors and successors as well as the British public at large, he took the view that the EEC was a dynamic and unfinished creation that might in the course of time evolve into a federation. Furthermore, and again unlike his predecessors and successors, he had no interest in the maintenance of a special relationship with the US, but recognized that shedding the special relationship for a natural relationship, as he put it, would be more difficult psychologically than the withdrawal from Empire.[88] Certain elements in the Foreign Office were already challenging the view that Britain still benefited substantially from bilateral relationships with the US in the field of nuclear technology, defence and intelligence co-operation.[89] Heath steadfastly resisted attempts by the Nixon administration in Washington to establish more cordial relations, and he was particularly critical of the administration's handling of international trade and monetary policy.[90] Nor did he feel any sentimental attachment to the Commonwealth, and he was invariably unimpressed by rhetoric about the future role and value of the Commonwealth. At a particularly fractious Commonwealth Prime Ministers' conference in Singapore in 1971, he expressed such irritation with some of the other Commonwealth representatives for their criticism of certain aspects of British policy that one commentator concluded that the imperial menopause was over.

Heath's passionate commitment to EC membership was both an asset and a disadvantage in the negotiations between Britain and the Six. It provided a fund of goodwill among the Six that smoothed the path towards entry. However, it left him open to the accusation that he was willing to pay any price or to sign a blank cheque to fulfil a cherished political ambition. It also exposed him to the charge that his European convictions were, like his interest in classical music, far removed from the common culture of most Britons and indicative of the High-Brow/Low-Brow gulf between the pro- and anti-marketers that W. H. Auden, the poet, had detected at the time of the first application.[91] Certainly, Heath's basic approach to the 1970–72 negotiations was to concentrate on securing EEC membership and to defer any attempt to modify its institutions and practices until after that goal had been achieved. His firsthand experience of the 1961–63 negotiations had convinced him that there was no point in trying to obtain fundamental changes to existing EC arrangements; 'Swallow the lot, and swallow it now' commented Con O'Neill, Britain's most senior official in the course of the negotiations, when emphasizing the importance of accepting all of the EC's existing legislation (*acquis communautaire*) (O'Neill 2000: 3). Meanwhile, Crowther, in the House of Lords, stressed one of the important reasons for doing so among advocates of EEC membership: 'You do not haggle over the subscription when you are invited to climb aboard a lifeboat' (H. Young 1998: 239). Heath was equally determined to avoid any attempt to mobilize the 'friendly Five' against France on Britain's behalf, as the Macmillan and Wilson governments had unsuccessfully tried to do. British membership of the EEC would only become possible when the French government was prepared to sanction it.[92]

At an important stage in the negotiations between Britain and the Six, when the talks were in danger of stalling, Heath made a decisive personal intervention by arranging a meeting (21–22 May 1971) with Georges Pompidou, the French President.[93] The course and outcome of this meeting virtually signalled the success of the negotiations, while the entire episode of access negotiations demonstrated that Heath possessed the temperament, experience and mindset to achieve his principal objective. The successful negotiation of EEC membership, however, was not without drawbacks, since it meant a reluctant acceptance by the British of terms about which they had serious reservations. These terms ultimately reflected the fact that Britain negotiated from a relatively weak bargaining position because of its long delay in seeking admission and the rejection of its earlier applications. By the early 1970s it was left with little room for manoeuvre and no real alternative but to accept what was on offer, subject to some fairly minor concessions in certain key areas such as imports of New Zealand meat and dairy products and of Caribbean sugar. Not unnaturally, the organization that Britain had joined belatedly was fashioned to suit the interests of existing members. Great care had been taken, especially by the French, to ensure that arrangements on such crucial matters as the CAP and the financial mechanism for providing the EEC with its 'own resources' were in place before negotiations on Britain's entry got under way.

Several aspects of the terms and concessions left a legacy of problems and conflict. A key problem concerned the British contribution to the EEC budget and the financing of the CAP. Following an agreement by the Six (December 1969), the EEC's 'own resources' were to come from levies and tariffs on all external imports, plus up to 1 per cent of receipts from Value Added Tax (VAT). These arrangements placed Britain at a double disadvantage. In the first place, Britain imported more from outside the EC than any of the EC states, and consequently its contribution to the EC's coffers would be disproportionately great. Second, the bulk of the money (almost 90 per cent) raised for use by the EC was devoted to the CAP. Britain's agricultural base was relatively small, and thus it stood to gain less than other member states from the CAP. As a result, Britain would be making a contribution to EC expenditure which was wholly disproportionate to the benefits it received and also to the size of its GDP. In some respects, this financial penalty was the price that had to be paid for Britain's tardiness in seeking and securing EC membership. In these circumstances, the Heath government sought to cushion the shock of adjustment to the EC budgetary regime by negotiating a five-year transitional period. It also managed to extract what proved to be a largely worthless assurance that the EC would be impelled to find equitable solutions in the event of an unacceptably high British contribution to the EC budget. Almost inevitably, the question of the British contribution to the EC budget became the focal point of a more or less continuous process of renegotiation long after Britain joined the EC. Heath also pinned his hopes on clawing back some of the money that Britain paid to the EC through the EC's European Regional Development Fund (ERDF). In the event, the introduction of this EC policy was delayed and received only limited funding. Another EC policy, the Common Fisheries Policy (CFP), was developed by the Six at this time and presented to Britain and the other candidates for EC membership (Denmark, Ireland and Norway) on a 'take it or leave it basis'. When presented with this prospect in the course of the entry negotiations, Geoffrey Rippon, the government minister at the head of the UK delegation, immediately consulted a large map of the UK, tracing the coast of the UK from Conservative seat to Conservative seat in order to work out how many Conservative MPs might be at risk if Britain adopted this policy. This exercise, indicative of the interplay of domestic politics and the government's negotiating stance, produced a satisfactory answer, at least according to Rippon's calculations (Menon 2004: 8). In the longer term, however, the CFP was often at the centre of controversy in particular parts of the UK, chiefly Scotland (see Chapter 5).

Another aspect of the entry negotiations and debate that had lasting consequences concerned the government's handling of the question of the loss of national sovereignty. This issue attracted less public attention than it had done ten years earlier, partly and ironically because throughout the 1960s de Gaulle had firmly defended the concept of national sovereignty and had frustrated efforts to promote political integration of the EEC, and partly because public opinion tended to focus on economic issues such as rising food prices and unemployment.[94] Nevertheless, fears on this score were expressed by the maverick Conservative former minister Enoch Powell; a loss of parliamentary sovereignty was the theme of his speech to the 1971 Conservative Party conference.[95] Heath's response was to insist that EC membership did not entail a loss of national identity or an erosion of essential national sovereignty. Furthermore, he always defended his position by drawing a distinction between 'pooling' sovereignty and 'surrendering' it.[96] Heath's critics, however, have frequently complained that he was guilty at best of being economical with the truth, at worst of deception (Castle 1993: 444).

A further element in this episode that remained in play long after Britain signed the Treaty of Accession (22 January 1972) and became a full member of the EC (1 January 1973) was the question of membership itself. It was widely believed that Heath failed to honour his much-quoted undertaking that entry would only take place with the full-hearted consent of parliament and the people. Public opinion polls and the muted celebration of Britain's accession to the EC indicated all too clearly the limited popular support for membership. In the period 1967–71 support for EEC membership fell from 65 per cent to 22 per cent. There was a revival of interest and support in the period leading to membership; in January 1973 Gallup found that 38 per cent supported EC membership and 36 per cent were against (Mullen and Burkitt 2005). At the same time, the Fanfare for Europe to mark Britain's entry into the EC completely failed to capture the public imagination as three out of four Britons opposed the venture (Weight 2002: 497). It seemed that most people accepted EC membership with resignation, if not enthusiasm, according to *The Times* which claimed that the issues were too complicated for mass enthusiasm and might also have added that large sections of the public were content to remain half-hearted and ignorant.[97]

Whether or not the British public was ill-informed about the key issues at stake is debatable. Particular attention has focused on whether the government deliberately embarked upon an exercise in the management of public ignorance that duped the public about the advantages and disadvantages of EC membership. In some respects the public heard what it wanted to hear so that the issue of food prices completely overshadowed the sovereignty question. For its part, the government was acutely aware of the need to overcome public opposition by a variety of means, including such suggestions as mounting a campaign to discredit the opinion polls and also inviting the French ambassador in London to make a rousing speech in favour of British membership of the EC.[98] More generally, in a paper that Heath himself regarded as a good basic document, the government was advised that the full weight of its campaigning should be directed at the prices issue and that it should err on the optimistic side in its estimates of economic growth and wages.[99] On balance, it is fair to say that both government and public were to blame for what has been portrayed as a compact between a disingenuous governing class and a people too preoccupied by the economic problems of the day to bother overmuch about constitutional issues (Weight 2002: 438). The Heath government did not shy away from the sovereignty and primacy of EEC law issues, but was loath to dwell on the precise implications for fear of strengthening the anti-marketeer case. In this context, there is substance to the view of Richard Wilson, a former Cabinet Secretary, that British entry into the EEC was indicative of the British habit of undergoing big changes 'under anaesthetic' (Trewin 2008: 670).

One of the most significant and enduring aspects of the Heath government's negotiation of EC membership lay in the internal convulsions and divisions between and within the political parties. These were first paraded on 28 October 1971, when the House of Commons voted in principle for EC membership, and they have rarely disappeared from view ever since. Labour Party unity was the major casualty in the first instance. Immediately after its electoral defeat in June 1970, Labour Party opinion, greatly influenced by the growing strength of the Left, turned against EC membership. Wilson faced major problems in view of his 1967 EC membership application and also in holding together a party bitterly divided over the issue. In the event, he took the line that he was not opposed to entry in principle but he made the unlikely claim that he would not have accepted the terms negotiated by the Heath government, an inglorious if politically convenient compromise. This stance placed the staunchly pro-European Labour MPs led by Roy Jenkins, deputy leader of the party, in a quandary; they viewed EC membership as a matter of principle which they were not prepared to sacrifice for party advantage. In the event, 69 Labour MPs defied a three-line whip and voted with the government on 28 October while a further 20 abstained, thus helping to ensure a government majority of 112. This whole episode left a legacy of deep bitterness within the Labour Party and set the scene for the vicious internecine conflict of the early 1980s. Meanwhile, as early as March 1970, John Biffen, a Conservative government minister in the 1980s, warned that a struggle was just beginning for the soul of the Conservative Party which would be focused on the Common Market and would continue for years after British entry into the EC (Trewin 2008: 11). Indeed, the fact that 33 Tory MPs voted against EC membership in principle was indicative of a strand of opinion within the party that in different circumstances was to command greater support. It eventually ensured that as the pro-Europe party of the 1970s the Conservatives underwent a deeply damaging metamorphosis over Europe in later years.

3 Adjustment to membership, 1973–84

The process of British adjustment to being a member of the EC in the decade after entry proved to be a long, complicated and troublesome one. In other member states the UK quickly acquired a reputation for being awkward and uncooperative, while in Britain itself substantial sections of opinion remained either opposed to membership or at best doubtful as to whether the benefits which it brought outweighed the costs. It was the persistence of such widespread hostility and scepticism that led to a continuing and highly divisive debate on the issue and to the holding of a referendum in the summer of 1975.

The suggestion has been made by one inside observer that the early strains which arose between the UK and its European partners were caused to some extent at least by a tendency on the part of British policymakers to adopt an aloof and superior attitude.[1] This was allegedly accompanied by a failure to adapt to the country's new role within the EC (Denman 1996). According to this interpretation, successive political leaders remained locked in a mind-set which accorded priority to links with the Commonwealth and the United States rather than Europe. Heath, with his deep conviction that Britain's future was bound up above all with that of the other major European states, was a solitary exception to this trend. He was, in any case, soon to be out of office, brought down in February 1974 by a combination of domestic and international crises. His successors – Wilson (1974–76), Callaghan (1976–79), Thatcher (1979–90) and Major (1990–97) – 'chose to pursue a policy of quarrelsome obstructionism' in their dealings with EC colleagues and thereby squandered valuable opportunities to consolidate Britain's position as a leading player (Denman 1996: 243). What they lacked was a real understanding of the drive to unity engendered on the other side of the Channel by the experience of defeat and occupation during the Second World War. They 'knew nothing of Europe's history or its culture ... Towards the Continent their incomprehension led to indifference and at times a chauvinist hostility' (Denman 1996: 277).

While there is considerable substance in this analysis, to accept it in its entirety, including the degree of deliberate intention which it implies, would be to underestimate the extent to which all British leaders during this period were trammelled in their conduct of European policy by serious internal and external constraints that were largely beyond their control. Even so, it seems clear that the undoubted continuation of pre-entry habits of thought within the UK's political elite added to the difficulties of adjustment.[2] Nor was such thinking confined to policymaking circles. Rather, it reflected the general public mood. Heath's stated hope was that membership of the EC would bring an end to the distinction that many of his countrymen routinely drew between 'them' and 'us' when discussing Europe. This did not happen, however, and long after entry had been achieved, it was (as it still is) common-place for the term 'Europe' to be used as if it applied to a separate and distinct entity to which Britain did not fully belong.

At the root of the protracted struggle to come to terms with life in the EC, then, was a problem of cultural and psychological adjustment. This was compounded by the need to resolve many practical and political difficulties in the immediate aftermath of entry. An example of these was the sharp disagreement that soon arose between Britain and its partners over energy policy. The quadrupling of international oil prices during 1973–74 raised the question of whether the EC should adopt a common energy strategy. There was a limit to how far Heath was prepared to go along those lines. While he was strongly in favour of forming a united front for dealing with the oil producing countries, he refused to accept a proposal from the French and Germans that all EC energy resources should be pooled in times of crisis. His attitude was strongly influenced by the fact that North Sea oil was about to come into production. This was also a prime consideration for Heath's successor. Wilson was adamant that the UK's reserves should be kept outside the scope of EC legislation. He also demanded (unsuccessfully) that Britain's new status as an oil-producing country should be recognized by the granting of separate representation at the international conference on energy that was held in Paris in December 1975.[3]

Another significant question that had to be addressed shortly after the UK's accession to the EC was that of fishing rights, an area in which substantial British interests were at stake. The starting point for what developed into the CFP was an agreement reached in 1970 which granted free access to EC waters for the fishermen of all member states. When Britain subsequently joined the EC, it was allowed to retain its existing national 12-mile limit until 1982. Concerns were raised in 1976, however, when the EC adopted an exclusive fishing zone of 200 miles. It was now unclear how far British fishing interests would be protected after the special transition period came to an end, and the uncertainty created by this state of affairs provided critics of EC membership, including Enoch Powell, with powerful ammunition for their attacks. As a result of the CFP, Powell complained, the fate of Britain's fishing industry would henceforward be in the hands of 'the landlubbers of Brussels'.[4]

The evolution of the CFP was only one aspect of a general movement towards closer integration in the 1970s. During these years the EC experienced one of the recurrent phases of dynamism and radical change that have characterized the way it has developed since its inception. For British governments in general, such phases have invariably presented a particularly difficult challenge, requiring them to perform a complex balancing act in the face of conflicting domestic and international pressures. While attempting to block or at least delay unwelcome reforms, they have simultaneously sought to prevent Britain from being left behind or becoming completely isolated. At the same time, they have needed to formulate a policy in response to proposed changes which was acceptable to both pro- and anti-EC opinion in the UK. This was the formidable task that confronted Heath, Wilson, Callaghan and Thatcher.

Some of the changes that took place within the EC after British entry involved detailed implementation of decisions taken at The Hague summit of December 1969, the most important example of this being the attempt to promote Economic and Monetary Union (EMU). The first practical step towards this goal had been the creation of the 'snake in the tunnel' whereby the exchange rates of each of the national currencies were tied together within a narrow band of fluctuations. Although the UK was not at the time a formal member of the EC, Heath had agreed that sterling should take part. By the time the pound had joined in May 1972, however, the whole system was already coming under severe strain because of turbulence on the international money markets and in July it was forced out as a result of intense speculative pressure.[5] The disastrous experience of this short-lived involvement with the 'snake' was one of the reasons for Callaghan's cool and suspicious reaction to the European Monetary System (EMS) in 1978, a posture which only served to reinforce Britain's reputation as an uncooperative partner.[6]

That Britain joined the EC when the latter was going through one of its periodic bouts of radical change scarcely facilitated a smooth entry. The timing of the British accession was in fact doubly unfortunate, since it also coincided with the onset of a global recession which ended the long period of prosperity that the western world had enjoyed almost without interruption from the early post-war years. The collapse of the Bretton Woods fixed exchange system in 1971, followed by a fourfold increase in international oil prices during 1973–74, triggered off a new phase of monetary instability and sluggish economic activity. So far as Britain was concerned, the situation was aggravated by the impact of the 1974 miners' strike and the major sterling crisis that blew up in 1976. From the mid-1970s the UK economy was in the grip of 'stagflation' – a pernicious combination of low growth and high inflation – and there occurred a marked deterioration in all the key economic indicators, with investment and production falling sharply, unemployment more than doubling between 1973 and 1979, the balance of payments moving into massive deficit and inflation soaring to an annual rate of more than 25 per cent in 1975. All the available evidence conclusively showed that Britain's economic performance was significantly worse than it had been in the years immediately before entry to the EC. It also remained inferior to that of most of the other member states, with output growing at little more than half the EC average between 1973 and 1979.[7]

In the years after accession to the EC, therefore, the UK experienced depressed economic conditions which bore no relation to the optimistic predictions made by pro-market enthusiasts in general and the Heath government in particular.[8] It was impossible to determine with certainty, however, to what extent, if at all, the dismal state of the economy could be attributed to joining the EC.[9]As might be expected, pro- and anti-marketeers offered completely different analyses on the subject. According to the former, the country's economic downturn was a consequence of other factors, notably the current international crisis and long-standing structural weaknesses in British industry.[10] The latter, by contrast, focused attention on the part played by membership of the EC. They identified this as a major direct cause of rising unemployment and balance of payment difficulties, pointing to the UK's disproportionately large trade deficit with the original member states to support their case.[11] Strictly accurate or not, such a claim was at least plausible and, together with the actual state of the economy, helped to foster from the outset a negative image of the EC and an atmosphere of disappointed expectations. In this respect, Britain's early formative experience within the EC formed a marked contrast with that of the Six, for whom it had been synonymous with progressively improving economic conditions and prosperity.

Another factor that complicated British adjustment to membership of the EC was the unsatisfactory nature of the terms of entry. In a sense, these terms reflected the fact that the UK had been negotiating from a relatively weak bargaining position because of its long delay in seeking admission and the rejection of its earlier applications (see Chapter 2). This meant a reluctant acceptance by the British of terms that they had serious reservations about and which they regarded, in essence, as temporary necessities. The inevitable consequence of this outcome was that entry was followed almost at once by the start of a more or less continuous process of renegotiation, both formal and informal, in which the Wilson, Callaghan and Thatcher governments were successively involved. This was a recipe for friction between the UK and its new partners. On the one hand, it served to fuel the smouldering sense of grievance felt by many in Britain over what seemed to them the unfair conditions that had been forced upon them as the price of admission. On the other, Britain's partners resented being subjected to an endless stream of complaints about matters which they believed to have already been satisfactorily dealt with.

In its election manifesto of February 1974, Labour committed itself to a 'fundamental renegotiation' of the terms of entry, with the results being submitted to the electorate for approval.[12] The avowed reason for this proposed course of action was that Britain had been taken into the EC on the basis of unduly onerous conditions and without the consent of the people. According to many commentators at the time and since, however, the real motivation behind the policy was to be found in Labour's disarray over Europe and its leader's preoccupation with maintaining party unity.

The renegotiation exercise began formally in June 1974, several months after the formation of Wilson's third government. At an early stage in the proceedings the Cabinet decided not to seek changes to the existing EC treaties, thereby limiting the scope of British demands. Those which figured most prominently on the agenda were the reform of the CAP, a reduction in the UK's contribution to the Community budget and an extension of guaranteed access to EC markets for Caribbean sugar producers and New Zealand farmers beyond the agreed cut-off date of 1977. Only on the last item did Wilson obtain any tangible results, securing a number of concrete concessions at the Dublin European Council of March 1975. With regard to the others, even the modest achievements that he claimed proved to be illusory.

Wilson himself acknowledged that renegotiation had brought no changes of substance in the CAP. The regime was deeply unpopular in Britain. It was widely regarded as an expensive and wasteful system which produced artificially high food prices. In addition, it was commonly portrayed, especially by the tabloid press, as a racket for subsidising inefficient French and other continental farmers at the expense of the British taxpayer and consumer. The Wilson government was dissatisfied with the arrangement negotiated by Heath, whereby Britain would have a five-year transition period in which to absorb the shock of changing from a completely different agricultural support system. It considered such a provision to be wholly inadequate and was committed, like all its successors, to a fundamental overhaul of the CAP. For various reasons, however, no immediate steps were taken to bring this about. To begin with, the issue was rendered less urgent and emotive by the fact that by 1975 food prices outside the EC had risen to a general level where they were at least as high as those within it.[13] In any case, if only because of the French government's absolute determination to preserve the CAP in its current form, it was recognized that there was not the slightest chance of securing changes in the near future: it was to be another ten years before real progress was made in that direction.

Wilson's efforts to reduce Britain's net contribution to the EC budget were equally unproductive. At the time he assumed office, only estimates were available on what the UK would be required to pay: the actual sums would depend on the future growth of EC spending. It had been agreed that between 1973 and 1977 the amount that it contributed would rise in annual stages from 8.64 per cent to 18.92 per cent of the budget, the latter figure being regarded as broadly comparable to the proportion of its GNP to that of the EC. During the following two years the increase in British contributions would remain subject to limits.[14] What caused concern was the scale of payments that might need to be made from 1980 onwards, the fear being that these would be disproportionately high in relation to the national wealth. The vague assurance given in 1972 that the whole arrangement might be reconsidered in the event of an unfair situation arising provided no firm guarantee against this danger. To make matters worse, British hopes that generous subsidies from the recently created ERDF might help to compensate for the UK's hefty budget contribution were not fulfilled. By the time the new body had been set up (after much delay) in 1975, the prospect of large-scale receipts was receding rapidly, partly because of the continuing growth of expenditure on the agricultural sector, partly because of the impact of the world economic crisis, but also because of West Germany's unwillingness to provide the necessary level of funding.[15]

It was against this unpromising background that Wilson sought to tackle the problem of Britain's net budget contributions by means of a general system of rebates. With assistance from Helmut Schmidt, the West German Chancellor (1974–82), and Valéry Giscard d'Estaing, the French President (1974–81), he was able to conclude an agreement on the matter. In order to clinch this, however, he was obliged to go along with a French proposal for direct elections to the European Parliament (EP), a concession which was to cause his successor, James Callaghan, some embarrassing political difficulties. The fatal weakness of the budgetary agreement itself was that the criteria which it laid down for determining both eligibility for a rebate and the amount to be received were so complicated as to rob it of any practical value. Indeed, the financial mechanism which was meant to trigger a rebate never actually came into play and it was not until 1984 that a workable formula was provided by the Fontainebleau Agreement, which went some way to meeting British requirements (H. Young 1998: 312–25; Wall 2008: 5).

Wilson's renegotiation exercise was formally concluded at the Dublin European Council. Domestic opinion was sharply divided on what it had achieved. Some observers shared Wilson's own view that the new terms represented a significant improvement on the original ones. The verdict of many others, however, was a great deal harsher. The Conservative Opposition predictably dismissed the whole episode as a political stunt whose sole purpose had been to paper over cracks within the Labour Party. This was a judgement echoed by many Labour pro-marketeers, while Labour opponents of EC membership complained bitterly that the changes which had been obtained were only marginal and in some respects, indeed, for the worse.[16] The Labour movement's general lack of enthusiasm for Wilson's handiwork was reflected in a decisive rejection of the new terms at the special party conference called in April 1975. Fewer than half of the PLP voted for them in the Commons and within the Cabinet itself they encountered stiff resistance, with around a third of its members, including Benn, Castle and Foot, voting against their acceptance.

Despite these signs of dissent, Wilson proceeded with plans to submit the renegotiated terms to a popular vote by means of a referendum and to ask the electorate at the same time whether Britain should remain a member of the EC.[17] When the idea of such a referendum had first been mooted by Benn in late 1970, it had aroused little interest among his colleagues.[18] Wilson, for his part, had been lukewarm and it was only gradually, as Labour's internecine quarrels over Europe intensified, that he began to appreciate its potential usefulness as a device for preventing the party, not to say the Cabinet, from tearing itself asunder – a 'life raft', as Callaghan put it, aboard which the warring factions could clamber. In a tacit admission of how badly his government was split, Wilson decided that ministers should be allowed to take part in the forthcoming referendum campaign on either side of the argument.

The referendum of 5 June 1975 was an unequal contest.[19] Those who campaigned for Britain to stay in the EC had access to far greater financial resources than their opponents.[20] In addition, the umbrella organization which co-ordinated their activities, Britain in Europe, was considerably more efficient than its tiny, cash-strapped and somewhat ramshackle opposite number, The National Referendum Campaign. The pro-marketeers enjoyed the backing of practically the whole of the press, as well as the business and commercial world.[21] All of the three main party leaders, Wilson, Thatcher, who had replaced Heath in February 1975, and Jeremy Thorpe, threw their weight – albeit with varying degrees of commitment – behind the 'yes' campaign. So too did the Liberal Party, the overwhelming majority of the Conservative Party and centre-right members of the Labour Party. The pro-European camp, in other words, commanded the support of the political mainstream. As against that, the opposing side consisted of an ill-assorted coalition of political interests, riven by internal feuds and damaged by association with various extremist groups. Its principal spokesmen, Benn, Foot and Powell, were certainly high-profile personalities and effective communicators, but they were also mavericks who aroused strong negative as well as positive feelings among the public.

In the event, the referendum provided a clear endorsement of British membership of the EC. This outcome was ironic, given that the initial impulse for holding one had come from anti-marketeers, who were convinced, on the basis of evidence from opinion polls, that they would win a resounding victory. On a high turnout of almost 65 per cent of the electorate, there was a two to one majority in favour of staying in the Common Market. At the time, the result of the referendum was seen by many commentators, including critics of the tactics he had employed, as a triumph for Wilson, since he had attained his main objectives of keeping Britain in the EC and the Labour Party in one piece.[22] With the benefit of hindsight, however, it can be seen that his success was only partial and short-term. The referendum put an end neither to discord between Labour's pro- and anti-European factions nor to the corrosive national debate over British membership of the EC.

In the period following the referendum, Labour's internal quarrels over the EC reached new levels of bitterness, as the Left gradually established a dominant position within the party and drove it in an increasingly anti-European direction. The anti-marketeers refused to accept the referendum verdict as binding and, with Benn and Foot in the vanguard, set out to reverse Labour policy on Europe. In this they enjoyed a large measure of success. Labour's manifesto for the 1979 European elections listed what it regarded as the adverse consequences of EC policies for Britain, attacking the 'expensive farce' of the CAP and the UK's 'monstrously unfair' contribution to the Community budget. It called for 'tough negotiations and hard bargaining' to secure wholesale changes, including a major revision of the Treaty of Rome, and declared that if this did not happen within a reasonable period of time it might be necessary to consider whether continued EC membership was in Britain's best interests.[23] This implied threat became explicit when the 1981 party conference passed a resolution calling for a negotiated British withdrawal from the EC, a stance which was adopted as official Labour policy for the 1983 general election.[24]

Not surprisingly, Labour pro-Europeans viewed these developments with a mixture of alarm, distaste and despair. They felt increasingly alienated, especially after Foot was chosen to succeed Callaghan as party leader in 1980, and in the following year the so-called 'Gang of Four', Roy Jenkins, David Owen, Bill Rodgers and Shirley Williams, took the dramatic decision to leave Labour and form a new political movement, the Social Democratic Party. While dissatisfaction with Labour's new stance on Europe was by no means the only factor that precipitated their departure, it was undoubtedly the decisive one.[25] Available evidence also suggests that their experience of cross-party collaboration during the referendum campaign in itself played a significant part in loosening ties with left-wing colleagues and paving the way for future collaboration with the Liberals.[26]

For public opinion in general, as for Labour, the outcome of the referendum did not signal an unreserved acceptance of EC membership. As analysts of the voting have pointed out, the substantial 'yes' majority reflected a preference for the status quo rather than enthusiastic approval.[27] Nor had the opportunity given to the electorate to express its opinion on the subject completely dispelled a widespread feeling that the decision to join the Common Market lacked popular legitimacy. In this connection, great play continued to be made with Heath's much-quoted undertaking that he would only take Britain into the EC 'with the full-hearted consent of Parliament and the people'.

In the years after the referendum, the British public's attitude towards EC membership remained less than enthusiastic. This was the unequivocal message that emerged from numerous opinion polls, as well as from the first direct elections to the EP (1979), in which the UK turn-out of less than 33 per cent was far lower than that of any other member state. Such a mood hardly encouraged the adoption of bold and positive policies by whatever government was in power. At times, Wilson, Callaghan and Thatcher all sought to exploit public dissatisfaction with the EC for party or personal political advantage. Wilson notoriously played to the gallery throughout his renegotiation exercise, deliberately exaggerating opposition from other leaders in order to magnify his achievements. He also threw his weight behind tabloid scare stories about 'Euro ale' and 'Euro bread' by publicly pouring scorn on EC Commission harmonization plans. As Foreign Secretary, Callaghan mounted a provocatively strong defence of British oil interests during discussions in 1975 over the establishment of a common EC energy policy. With her defiant rhetoric and 'handbag' diplomacy, Thatcher surpassed them both, and in the early years of her premiership the popularity that she gained from her strident demands for a fair budget rebate proved invaluable at a time when her personal standing was at a low ebb and the government's deflationary policies were under fierce attack. While the public's unsympathetic attitude towards the EC could sometimes serve as a useful tool, however, it was for the most part a constraint on the conduct of policy.

At the same time, the extent to which the prevailing public mood acted as a brake on the desire of successive governments to play a more positive role within the EC must not be exaggerated. It has to be borne in mind, indeed, that much of the caution and scepticism to be found among the public at large was mirrored in governing circles. By no stretch of the imagination could Wilson be regarded as an ardent pro-marketeer in the mould of Heath or Jenkins. His attitude was essentially pragmatic. The same could be said for Callaghan, as well as for Thatcher during the period of her first government. For all three, British membership of the EC had less to do with vision than with a hard-headed calculation of national interests.

This low-key approach helps to explain why Britain played a less important role in EC affairs during its first decade of membership than had been generally expected. In the period before entry, it had always been regarded as axiomatic in British governing circles that the UK would enjoy a status equal to that of France and West Germany, operating alongside them as part of a dominant informal grouping. In the event, however, the Franco-German axis continued to be the main driving force within the Community, with the leaders of the two main continental states exerting noticeably more influence than their British counterparts. Close collaboration between France and West Germany was underpinned by the extensive network of institutional links which had developed between the two countries since the conclusion of the Franco-German Treaty of Friendship and Cooperation in 1963. In addition, Giscard and Schmidt enjoyed an exceptionally cordial personal and working relationship. Under these circumstances, it proved impossible to convert the Franco-German special partnership into a *directoire à trois*. This situation was not entirely unwelcome to Callaghan in particular since he had little wish to be seen as a prominent mover in an organization which was viewed with scant sympathy by the British public in general and with positive hostility by much of the Labour movement.

In the case of Wilson and Callaghan at least, there were two domestic factors that undoubtedly did impose strict limits on their room for manoeuvre: the lack of a solid base in the Commons and the internal politics of the Labour movement. Following his success in the February 1974 general election, Wilson headed a minority government. Although the election held in

October 1974 strengthened his position somewhat, he was still left with an overall majority of only three. For Callaghan, who became Prime Minister after Wilson's surprise resignation in March 1976, the parliamentary arithmetic was even grimmer. Within a matter of months Labour's wafer-thin majority had disappeared completely and the government was only able to survive by concluding a pact with the Liberals in March 1977.[28] The Lib–Lab pact meant that Callaghan's European policies were subject to still more restrictions. This became evident in connection with his government's failure to meet its commitments over direct elections to the EP. It will be recalled that in the course of his renegotiation exercise Wilson had agreed to this innovation in return for French support for a system of rebates on EC budget contributions. Callaghan was called upon to deal with the practical consequences of this pledge after EC leaders agreed in September 1976 to set a deadline for completing all necessary legislative preparations for the first direct elections. By the terms of the Lib–Lab pact, Callaghan was bound to respect Liberal wishes that the UK vote would be on the basis of proportional representation. Thus a Bill was introduced into the Commons to that effect in June 1977. This encountered determined opposition from a majority of Conservative and Labour MPs, however, and was defeated in December. As a result, the UK was unable to meet the agreed timetable for the first direct elections and these were then postponed until June 1979.

It was significant that the government had decided to allow a free vote on the Bill. This was a clear acknowledgement both of continuing Labour divisions over Europe and of the difficulty of managing the party. It has been seen to what extent the decision to hold a referendum on EC membership had been dictated by such considerations. Indeed, the referendum had served Wilson well not only as a means of limiting the damage caused by party quarrels, but also as a weapon in his struggle with the Labour Left in general and with Benn in particular. It has been convincingly argued by a close associate of Wilson, Bernard Donoughue, that he used the EC issue as a means of distracting left-wing attention from more troublesome activities such as implementation of 'Labour's Programme 1973', with its panoply of proposals for increased state control of the economy. Thus, Benn's 'army of the left was diverted from the dangerous fields of British industry onto the deceptively inviting marshes of the EEC. Once committed and trapped there, Mr Benn was blown up by a referendum of the British people'. It is no coincidence that the defeat of the anti-marketeers in the referendum vote was followed almost immediately by a Cabinet reshuffle in which Benn was moved from his post as Industry Secretary to the Department of Energy. Once again this provides a clear illustration of the degree to which Labour politics and the EC were inextricably linked, for Benn's departure from Industry was intended both to put a stop to the campaign of systematic obstruction that he had been waging against the ERDF and to deprive him of a strategic base from which to push for more government intervention in the running of the economy.

In almost every respect, the close interconnection between Labour infighting and government policy towards the EC was carried over into the years of the Callaghan premiership. There was, though, one major difference: in contrast to what had happened with Wilson, Callaghan's manoeuvring in relation to the EC was not influenced by a perceived challenge to his leadership. Wilson had become obsessed by this danger, seeing Jenkins and Callaghan as the two ministers from whom he had most to fear. The latter was rightly regarded as a more serious potential threat because of the wider support that he enjoyed throughout the Labour movement, and there is general agreement amongst historians that Wilson's 'shadowing' of his main rival's tortuous policy shifts over the EC was prompted chiefly by his concern to deny the other any tactical advantage.

By the time Callaghan took over from Wilson, left-wing, anti-European elements had already gained a firm grip on key parts of the Labour movement, and during his three-year premiership their dominance was further strengthened. In his new post as Energy minister, Benn continued his relentless campaign of non-cooperation with EC colleagues, sometimes carrying it to extraordinary lengths, as on the occasion when he delayed an EC Council of Energy Ministers because of his insistence on attending a local Labour Party meeting (George 1990: 96). His behaviour was as irritating for Callaghan as it had been for Wilson, but it represented only one small element of the broader problem that faced him: an unbridgeable gulf between his own views on Britain's role within the EC and those which held sway in the Labour movement at large. There was a clear majority in favour of a negotiated withdrawal on the influential NEC. This line also received powerful backing from local activists and at the annual party conferences. In addition, the trade unions were overwhelmingly hostile to EC membership, the two largest of them, the Transport and General Workers Union (TGWU) and the Amalgamated Union of Engineering Workers (AUEW), being led by inveterate anti-marketeers, Jack Jones and Hugh Scanlon. What this meant was that there existed a deep cleavage between the main body of the party and the government, with Callaghan and ministers who broadly shared his opinions, like Denis Healey, the Chancellor of the Exchequer, coming under constant pressure to pursue and defend policies which they regarded as completely unacceptable. Whatever reservations Callaghan and Healey had about the EC, they did not subscribe to left-wing assertions that it was nothing more than a 'capitalist club' and that British membership had been an unmitigated disaster. Nor did they believe that pulling out was either desirable or feasible.

Although Callaghan disagreed profoundly with the stance adopted by the Left, it inevitably influenced his calculations.[29] An early indication of his sensitivity to left-wing views on the EC was the decision which he took when forming his government not to appoint Jenkins as Foreign Secretary on the grounds that to do so would infuriate anti-marketeers.[30] This set the tone for the approach that he subsequently adopted. In general terms, he sought to avoid an open confrontation between government and party which would be highly damaging to both. This was especially the case since the EC was not the only area where the two were at loggerheads. There were also fundamental differences over economic policy which came to a head during the 1976 sterling crisis and which were aggravated by the manner in which that was resolved.

In his first few months as Prime Minister, Callaghan was faced by a grave deterioration in the country's economic and financial circumstances, one of the most disturbing features of which was a rapid fall in the value of sterling.[31] By September 1976 the pound was coming under such intense speculative pressure that the government felt obliged to negotiate a large-scale credit from the IMF in order to prop it up. In return, it agreed to drastic curbs on public expenditure. Coming on top of the deflationary package already announced in the 1975 and 1976 budgets, these new cuts provoked intense anger among Labour left-wingers who favoured a completely different way of dealing with the current crisis and with the underlying problem of the British economy's lack of competitiveness. The prescription that they proffered was expressed in the 'alternative economic strategy', a programme which strongly reflected Benn's ideas and which proposed (amongst other things) the introduction of import and exchange controls in order to protect British industry and obviate the need for austerity measures. These proposals received short shrift from the Cabinet, not least because they were wholly incompatible with continuing British membership of the EC. For Benn and his left-wing allies, by contrast, this aspect of the matter constituted an additional advantage.

There were two important issues on which the Left's antipathy towards the EC had a discernible influence on government policy. The first of these was the introduction of direct elections to the EP. Given that anti-marketeers had been highly critical of the EC for its supposedly undemocratic nature, it might have been expected that a move which was intended to increase the EP's accountability would be welcomed by them. Yet that was not the case. On the contrary, it encountered strong opposition from the NEC and other quarters as a development which would encourage undesirable federalist tendencies. The depth of hostility that the proposed reform aroused throughout the party was manifested in its rejection by a two to one majority at the 1976 annual conference. It was also apparent in the vote by a majority of Labour backbenchers against the parliamentary Bill providing the necessary legislative framework for direct elections.

The other EC issue on which a negative reaction from within the Labour Party helped to determine the line taken by Callaghan was the EMS. Like its ill-fated predecessor, the 'snake', the EMS was designed to promote greater monetary stability within the EC. It was first proposed at the Copenhagen European Council of April 1978 and the purpose behind it was to provide a viable alternative to the floating exchange rate arrangements which had emerged after the collapse of the Bretton Woods system a few years earlier. The principal architect of the scheme was Schmidt, who had become increasingly concerned at the damaging effect that general monetary instability, and more especially the weakness of the American dollar, was having on the West German economy. Giscard immediately threw his full weight behind the new project, but Callaghan, while initially voicing broad approval, soon made it clear that his government was not prepared to give it unqualified support. The government's most serious reservations centred on the Exchange Rate Mechanism (ERM), the device for controlling fluctuations between the different participating currencies, and in December 1978 it was announced, at the Brussels European Council, that the UK would not be taking part in this crucial feature of the EMS.

There were various reasons for this decision. The Schmidt initiative came at an inopportune time. Callaghan was preoccupied with the next general election and with mounting difficulties over implementation of the government's incomes policy. He was also heavily engaged in launching a scheme for joint European–American collaboration to revive the western economies and anxious that this should not be put at risk by proposals for a new EC monetary bloc. Quite apart from these considerations, Callaghan felt that it would be imprudent to enter the ERM until there was a greater degree of convergence between the different EC economies.[32] The Treasury shared this concern. More specifically, it was worried that tying sterling to the deutschmark might have an adverse deflationary impact on the domestic economy. City and business opinion was at best lukewarm, while the attitude of the Conservative Opposition was decidedly hostile. What needs to be emphasized here, however, is that Callaghan was faced with strong opposition to the EMS at all levels of the Labour movement. The Cabinet was divided, but a majority of ministers took the view that Britain had more to lose than to gain from sterling's entry to the ERM.[33] In addition, the EMS as a whole came under fierce attack at Labour's 1978 annual conference, where it was repeatedly denounced as a threat to national economic sovereignty and a decisive step on the road to a federal Europe. The mood of the conference made a powerful impression on Callaghan and banished any lingering thoughts he may still have harboured about accepting the EMS in its entirety.

Following Labour's defeat in the May 1979 general election, Thatcher formed the first of her three governments (May 1979–June 1983, June 1983–June 1987 and June 1987–November 1990). The initial reaction to her advent to power was that it would almost certainly bring an improvement in Britain's relations with its European partners. This assumption was understandable, given the Conservatives' justified reputation for being more pro-European than Labour (Thatcher 1993: 63). Yet there was little concrete evidence to suggest that the new Prime Minister was herself any more enthusiastic about Britain's role in the EC than her Labour predecessors had been. Certainly she had campaigned for a 'yes' vote during the 1975 referendum. It was a matter of common observation, however, that she had done so with only a fraction of the commitment and vigour displayed by Heath.[34] If one compares her general attitude to the EC with that of Heath, in fact, it is immediately apparent that it was fundamentally different. It might be argued, indeed, that Thatcher's approach was much closer to that adopted by Callaghan. Like him, she was unimpressed by extravagant rhetoric about Europe and instinctively suspicious of ambitious projects for its future development. In sharp contrast to Heath, she also shared Callaghan's view on the cardinal importance of relations with the US. She gave immediate backing in 1979 to President Carter's strong stand against the Russians' invasion of Afghanistan and later went on to develop an extremely close rapport with Ronald Reagan throughout the period 1981–89, one that was grounded in personal friendship and shared political convictions: an unquestioning belief in free market economics and a profound aversion to the Soviet Union.

If Thatcher adopted an approach to the EC which was not dissimilar to that of Callaghan (or for that matter Wilson), she was in a number of respects far less hampered than he had been by domestic political constraints. At no time did she lack a secure parliamentary majority. Nor was she plagued by internal party divisions over Europe – at least during the early years of her premiership. It is true that there were some misgivings within the Cabinet over Thatcher's abrasive approach towards Britain's European partners, two of the most prominent dissenting voices being those of the Foreign Secretary, Peter Carrington, and his deputy, Ian Gilmour, the spokesman on Foreign Affairs in the Commons, both described by one historian as 'wet Europeanists' (H. Young 1998: 317). As against that, Thatcher's unapologetic defence of national interests struck a chord with the broad mass of the party, while opposition from senior colleagues, always limited, became increasingly ineffective, as those who disagreed with her were either cowed into silence or dismissed. Having incurred Thatcher's displeasure because of his critical attitude towards the government's economic as well as its European policies, Gilmour was sacked as part of the 'anti-wet' Cabinet reshuffle of September 1981. Carrington chose to resign the following summer, believing that he had mishandled the crisis preceding the Falklands War. Following her triumph in that conflict and her subsequent success in the 1983 general election, Thatcher's authority over the Cabinet and the party as a whole was assured.

The issue that dominated EC affairs between 1979 and 1984 was the British Budget Question (BBQ), sometimes referred to by Roy Jenkins as the Bloody British Question. This was a running sore in the UK's relations with its partners. Neither Wilson nor Callaghan had managed to produce a satisfactory solution to the problem of Britain's disproportionately large budget payments and Thatcher was determined to succeed where they had failed. Her attempts to do so precipitated what has been described as 'the most long drawn out and bitter battle yet fought in the EU' (Wall 2008: 8).

By the time Thatcher came to power, the need for action had assumed a new urgency. The seven-year transition phase was drawing to a close and there was thus the immediate prospect of a steep rise in British contributions. As it was, even with the temporary protection afforded by the 1972 agreement, there had been a remorseless increase in the sums paid by the UK. In

1979 it was paying twice as much as France, which had a higher GDP, and was one of only two net contributors among the nine member states, the other being West Germany. Its net payment for that year amounted to some £900 million. This was certain to climb higher still when the transition period came to an end the following year. It was reliably forecast, indeed, that Britain would be paying more than West Germany in 1980, despite the fact that its GDP was considerably smaller. In the event, this proved to be the case, the figures being £1.184 billion and £750 million respectively.

To Thatcher the issue was perfectly straightforward. It was undeniable that the existing method of financing the EC budget placed Britain at a fundamental disadvantage. This basic inequity was aggravated, moreover, by a decline in the country's relative prosperity compared to that of most other member states since 1973, as a result of which it now had only the seventh highest per capita GDP. The current situation was therefore 'demonstrably unjust', as well as 'politically indefensible', and Thatcher found it impossible, as she declared in a speech made in October 1979, to 'play Sister Bountiful to the Community while my own electorate are being asked to forego improvements in fields of health, education, welfare and the rest' (Thatcher 1995: 79).

Thatcher's many continental critics accused her of demanding the so-called *juste retour* – the recovery of exactly the amount that Britain paid out. Given her rhetoric, such an accusation was understandable. It was not, though, entirely fair or accurate (Wall 2008: 6, 9, 25–26, 29). In reality Thatcher was always prepared to accept a position where Britain was a net contributor. Her overriding objective was to achieve on a permanent basis a 'broad balance' between British outgoings and receipts. This was to be brought about within the framework of a fundamental restructuring of the EC budget aimed at controlling total expenditure and reducing the proportion of it devoted to agriculture.

So far as tactics were concerned, the available options were limited. Some months before Thatcher came to power, David Owen, the Foreign Secretary in the Callaghan government, who felt no less strongly that Britain had received a bad deal over its budget contributions, attempted to use the threat of blocking the EC's annual farm price increases as a means of exerting pressure for a rebate, but had not succeeded. When Peter Walker, the Minister of Agriculture in Thatcher's first administration, actually tried to put the threat into effect in May 1982, he was equally unsuccessful, with ministers from other member states overriding his efforts to exercise the right of national veto embodied in the Luxembourg Compromise of 1966 (Thatcher 1995: 85; Wall 2008: 10–17; Young 2000: 142).

In the aftermath of this inglorious setback, the Labour Opposition called upon the government to take tougher action, including the withholding of Britain's contribution to the EC budget. This possibility was given serious consideration from the beginning of 1983. It was realized at an early stage, however, that such a course would be fraught with risks. The FCO urged caution, warning of the likelihood of damaging political consequences. A number of other difficulties were identified, not least the danger of retaliatory measures, and in the end the idea was ruled out as being both illegal and impracticable (Wall 2008: 27, 33). At the same time, Thatcher made no attempt to discourage press reports that such a move was in prospect, seeing speculation of that kind as a useful adjunct to her diplomacy (Thatcher 1995: 79–80, 83).

The principal weapon in her armoury, however, was dogged persistence. It seemed inconceivable to Thatcher that such a manifest injustice could continue to be tolerated indefinitely. It followed that if the British case was put with sufficient conviction and determination, it must eventually win general acceptance. Such an approach was well suited to her combative personality and she quickly demonstrated that she was fully prepared to reiterate the same arguments ad nauseam, even at the risk of alienating all the other EC leaders and becoming completely isolated. As Thatcher's self-assurance grew, her negotiating style increasingly came to resemble a form of brinkmanship carried to extreme lengths. As one British diplomat expressed it, she would 'take the wheel of the European car and drive it at full speed to the cliff's edge, confident that the others would lose their nerve before she did'.[35]

As early as the Strasbourg European Council of 21–22 June 1979, the first one that Thatcher attended, there were ominous signs that the path to an agreement on the British rebate might not be a smooth one. Thatcher had been led to believe by Giscard, who was presiding, that the budget question would be the first item on the agenda. Yet the opening session began instead with discussions on energy policy, world economic problems and the EMS. Thatcher therefore felt cheated and reacted angrily, becoming embroiled in a series of fractious exchanges not only with Giscard, but also with several other EC leaders, including Schmidt. She had thus, as Jenkins was later to observe sardonically, 'performed the considerable feat of unnecessarily irritating two big countries, three small ones and the Commission within her opening hour ... at a European Council' (Jenkins 1992: 495; Thatcher 1995: 63–64). Her squabble with Schmidt was especially unfortunate, given that his cooperation was indispensable to any settlement.

The procedural wrangle at Strasbourg was followed by differences of a more substantial nature when negotiations were resumed at the Dublin European Council in November 1979. From the outset Thatcher insisted that she would accept nothing less than the return of 'our money', peremptorily rejecting the offer of an annual rebate of some £350 million, which she later described as being only 'one third of a loaf'. Other leaders were infuriated by the challenge which Thatcher's reference to British money appeared to mount to the concept of the Community's 'own resources'. They were also indignant at being subjected to a lengthy and hectoring monologue, in the course of which Schmidt famously feigned sleep. For the West German Chancellor in particular the experience must have been profoundly disappointing, since he had intimated to Jenkins (President of the European Commission 1977–81) shortly before the Dublin European Council met that he would do all he could to facilitate an agreement, provided Thatcher adopted a less confrontational approach than she had so far done (Gilmour 1992: 235; Jenkins 1992: 496–99; Thatcher 1995: 80–82).

What both the Dublin and Strasbourg European Councils had clearly demonstrated was that the prospects of settling the budget question were adversely affected by a serious personality clash between the British Prime Minister and a substantial majority of her EC counterparts. Thatcher liked and admired Schmidt. Most of the others, however, made a highly unfavourable early impression upon her, as is revealed in the scathing comments she made about them to Jenkins in October 1979: 'They are a rotten lot', she complained. 'Schmidt and the Americans are the only ones who would do any standing up and fighting if necessary' (Jenkins 1992: 495). Relations between Thatcher and Giscard were particularly strained. Despite her self-confessed 'soft spot for French charm', she found his personality unappealing and, as she herself later conceded, the feeling seemed to be mutual (Thatcher 1995: 70). Thatcher regarded the French president as cold, aloof and arrogant, while for his part he made little effort to hide his contempt for the person he referred to dismissively as 'the grocer's daughter' (H. Young 1990: 187).

The acrimonious and fruitless discussions in Dublin were the prelude to almost five years of what has been termed 'megaphone haggling' over Britain's budget contribution (Sanders 1990: 159). Although it proved possible to put in place a series of short-term arrangements for the early 1980s, it was not until the summer of 1984 that an agreement was finally reached on a permanent rebate formula. This long delay was partly the result of a general unwillingness to compromise. The stiffest resistance to British demands came from the French. They were by no means alone in their reluctance to make concessions, however, since any reduction in the UK's net payments would inevitably entail financial sacrifices for others and for the Germans in particular (Wall 2008: 6, 9, 25). On the opposite side of the negotiating table, Thatcher was obduracy personified, for a long time insisting on terms which stood no chance of being accepted. Addressing a press conference at the end of the EC summit held in March 1982 to celebrate the twenty-fifth anniversary of the Treaty of Rome, she said: 'I am stubborn and I intend to go on being stubborn. I have much to be stubborn about' (Wall 2008: 10).

In this respect, her attitude stood in sharp contrast to that which prevailed at the Foreign Office, where it was always felt that there must be an element of flexibility in the British negotiating position and that a rebate amounting to two-thirds of the difference between UK outgoings and receipts was the most that could be reasonably or realistically expected. To Thatcher such an approach was pathetically weak, reflecting the department's institutionalized tendency to seek compromise and consensus, as well as its pro-European zealotry. For their part, Foreign Office officials and their political chiefs were frequently reduced to despair by Thatcher's intransigence. These different perspectives on Europe underlay the long-running feud which developed between Thatcher and the Foreign Office and which was to culminate in Howe's removal from his post as Foreign Secretary in the summer of 1989.[36]

In January 1980 Howe, then the Chancellor of the Exchequer, and Gilmour embarked on a round of visits to EC capitals in search of a basis of agreement. Their mission was doomed to failure, however, since they had been given no authority to consider any offer of a rebate which fell short of Britain's total net annual contribution to the EC budget (1.5 billion ecus). Some progress was made at the Luxembourg European Council of 27–28 April, when Schmidt and Giscard proposed what amounted to a rebate of £760 million for each of the two years 1980–81. This clearly represented a significant improvement on what had been offered in Dublin and made a favourable impression on the Foreign Office. Carrington and Michael Palliser, the Permanent Under-Secretary, both urged acceptance, as did Robert Armstrong, the Cabinet Secretary. To their surprise and disappointment, however, Thatcher demurred. She was also initially inclined to reject a deal which Carrington and Gilmour hammered out during an all-night meeting of EC foreign ministers in Brussels on 29 May 1980, reacting with ill-concealed fury when the two negotiators, who were themselves delighted by what they had achieved, reported back to her at Chequers (Wall 2008: 7). After venting her anger, though, Thatcher grudgingly acquiesced.[37]

Conflicting explanations have been given of why she did so. According to Thatcher's own later account, she herself concluded that the package offered the 'great advantage' of providing a three-year solution, while its other elements, including a 5 per cent increase in farm prices, were 'more or less acceptable'. Taken as a whole, she writes, 'the deal marked a refund of two-thirds of our net contribution and … huge progress from the position the Government had inherited. I therefore decided to accept the offer' (Thatcher 1995: 86). A somewhat different version of events is offered in Gilmour's memoirs, where Thatcher is depicted as having her hand forced by strong pressure from within the Cabinet, a resignation threat from Carrington and a skilfully judged press leak by Gilmour himself suggesting that she had won a resounding diplomatic triumph (Gilmour 1992: 237–41).

In June 1982 Francis Pym, who had just replaced Carrington as Foreign Secretary, negotiated another short-term deal, this time for one year. Yet a permanent resolution of the problem seemed no closer. Throughout 1983 the British negotiating position was based on a 'safety net' mechanism, an idea developed within the Treasury and first submitted to Thatcher in February 1982 by the Chancellor of the Exchequer, Howe. The proposal aimed at fixing an upper limit, set in relation to GDP, on the budgetary burden of each member state. While it was intended to be of general application, in practice it was the UK which would be the principal beneficiary, standing to recover some 70 per cent of its current net contribution. Not surprisingly, therefore, the scheme was given a frosty reception by Britain's partners. What made it even more unpalatable to them was the fact that it was so complicated as to be virtually unintelligible to most people (Wall 2008: 19).

In the absence of any significant movement towards a lasting settlement during 1982–83, there was a marked hardening of attitudes all round: in June 1983 Thatcher made it clear at the Stuttgart European Council that she would obstruct progress in all other spheres until a satisfactory agreement was reached on the rebate question; and the Athens European Council of December 1983 ended in complete deadlock, mainly because of the gulf separating the French and British negotiating positions. At Athens, François Mitterand, the leader of the French Socialist Party, who had succeeded Giscard as president in May 1981, argued strongly for another temporary rebate agreement, apparently unaware that his stance ran counter to proposals put by his own finance minister, Jacques Delors. Thatcher, on the other hand, demanded a lasting settlement which contained two essential elements: a mechanism for ensuring that the contribution of each member state was related to its ability to pay, and a reduction in the share of EC spending allocated to the CAP.[38] Her suggestion that Britain's net contribution should be broadly similar to that of France did nothing to improve the atmosphere. A headline in *Le Monde* aptly captured the intransigence displayed by both leaders when it characterized their confrontation as 'Iron Lady versus Man of Marble'.

Within months of the failed Athens European Council, which Thatcher was later to describe as a 'fiasco', a comprehensive agreement was at last reached on the British budget contribution. By early 1984 a number of factors were at work which contributed to this outcome. On the British side, Thatcher was both keener to settle the issue and at the same time in a stronger position to obtain most of what she wanted than had previously been the case. Notwithstanding her natural relish for dramatic clashes, even Thatcher was beginning to recognize the futility of perpetual wrangling over the budget. This was especially the case since she was increasingly impatient to push on towards completion of the single market, an item which figured prominently in *The Future Development of the Community*, a paper published by the government in September 1983 (Wall 2008). It is possible that she was disturbed by Mitterand's recent references to a 'two-speed Europe', with their implied threat that Britain might be relegated to the periphery of EC affairs. Of more immediate concern, however, was the absence of any rebate arrangements for the current financial year or thereafter. This difficulty was compounded by the fact that the £400 million refund which Britain was scheduled to receive for 1983 had been blocked by the foreign ministers of France and Italy immediately after the Brussels European Council of March 1984 and was still not being paid (Thatcher 1993: 539–41; Wall 2008: 33). Another important consideration was the advisability of settling during the French presidency – due to finish at the end of June 1984 – in order to take full advantage of the moderating influence that this must necessarily exercise upon Mitterand's pursuit of narrow national interests.

A combination of circumstances provided Thatcher with the opportunity to obtain the permanent agreement that she was now seeking with a greater sense of urgency on terms which she judged to be acceptable. A victorious conclusion to the Falklands War in June 1982, followed by a Conservative landslide in the general election of May 1983 and some early signs of economic recovery, had all served to strengthen her domestic political position by the beginning of 1984. At the same time, recent changes of French and West German political leadership also worked in her favour. In 1979 it had been Thatcher who was the newcomer to EC politics, while Giscard and Schmidt had been experienced practitioners. Now the roles were reversed and it was the new leaders of France and West Germany who were the apprentices. When it came to hard bargaining, neither Mitterand nor Helmut Kohl, the leader of the Christian Democrats who had replaced Schmidt as Chancellor in October 1982, was as much of a match for Thatcher as their predecessors had been: it was noticeable, for instance, that they were often poorly briefed in comparison with their British counterpart, whose conference preparations were always meticulous (Thatcher 1995: 337). Nor was their collaboration as close or effective as that of Giscard and Schmidt had been. In any case, both men were prepared to make some concessions at least in order to dispose of an issue which had already absorbed an undue share of time and energy and which was continuing to divert attention from other matters that they considered to be of far greater importance.

By the mid-1980s a powerful momentum was building up for another 'relaunch' of Europe, akin to that of the late 1960s and early 1970s, with Kohl and Mitterand each playing a leading role in the growing campaign for deeper integration. In the case of the latter, his preoccupation with reform of the EC was closely linked to the twists and turns of French domestic politics. Following his advent to power at the head of a left-wing coalition in May 1981, Mitterand had initially attempted to tackle the problems of low growth and high unemployment which he had inherited by a programme of nationalization, increased state spending and a boost to wages. By the spring of 1983, this 'Socialist experiment', as it was called, had clearly failed and Mitterand began to pursue an alternative strategy, one which was based on a policy of austerity at home and the forging of closer ties with France's EC partners and with West Germany in particular. Mitterand had now become an enthusiastic advocate of a far-reaching reform of the EC. His priorities included liberalization of the internal market, an increase in Community funding and a streamlining of decision-making procedures through an extension of majority voting on the Council of Ministers and the granting of greater powers to the Commission. He was also eager to press ahead with the early admission of Spain and Portugal. The continuing saga of the BBQ was a major obstacle to the achievement of these objectives and Mitterand was determined that the issue should be settled as soon as possible.

This in itself strengthened Thatcher's bargaining position. What gave her additional leverage was her ability to block any increase in EC funding, without which all the ambitious plans for change currently under consideration would be impossible. By 1983 EC finances were in a parlous state:

expenditure on the CAP continued to rise unchecked and the accession of Greece in 1981 had added to the burden of regional subsidies. The impending entry of two other relatively poor states, Spain and Portugal, together with the heavy costs involved in projected administrative and political reforms, could only intensify the existing financial strains. Thatcher was acutely conscious of the strong position in which this scenario placed her, noting with considerable satisfaction at the time of the Stuttgart European Council in June 1983 that the EC was on the edge of bankruptcy and could only retrieve the situation by raising the 1 per cent ceiling on VAT receipts from which it derived a large part of its 'own resources'. That could only be done by means of a unanimous vote and Thatcher left no room for doubt that the price of her consent would be a satisfactory outcome to negotiations on the British rebate (Thatcher 1995: 312–14).

In January 1984 France assumed the EC presidency. Both for reasons of national prestige and in order to enhance his own political standing, Mitterand attached great importance to ensuring that the problem of Britain's budget contribution was resolved during this six-month period. He immediately began an intensive bout of diplomatic activity, involving visits to all of the EC capitals, with the announced intention of having the issue settled by the time of the forthcoming Brussels European Council of 19–20 March. Although this self-imposed deadline was not met, the discussions in Brussels nevertheless brought significant progress on a number of key points. It was agreed that there should be an increase in the share of VAT receipts allotted to the EC. There was also a major concession by Thatcher on the contentious issue of how to calculate net budget contributions and hence the size of the rebate to which Britain might be entitled. The British government had so far always maintained that the proceeds from the tariffs and import levies that it paid to Brussels should be counted as part of its gross budget contribution. This argument, however, had never been accepted by the other EC governments: they insisted that such revenues should be treated not as national contributions, but as part of the EC's 'own resources'. In an effort to bridge the gap between these conflicting standpoints, the French now produced a compromise formula on VAT contributions that was to apply only to those member states which in the previous year had paid more in VAT contributions than they had received from the budget by an agreed amount – a figure which was to be settled at a later date. Thatcher accepted this formula as a basis for negotiation. Proceedings were brought to an abrupt end, however, by a clumsy intervention from Kohl, whose proposal of a flat-rate annual rebate of 1 billion ecus between 1984 and 1986 was rejected out of hand by the British.

What Kohl did not know when he intervened was that some useful behind-the-scenes discussions were currently taking place between French and British officials. The important breakthrough over calculation of the rebate referred to above was the result in part of these talks, and in the period following the Brussels European Council a small group – comprising Roland Dumas, a close friend of Mitterand and Minister for Europe since December 1983, Howe, the Foreign Secretary, and two senior officials, Guy Legras and David Hannay of the FCO (later replaced by Robin Renwick) – continued to hold regular private meetings. The main value of these sessions was that they provided an opportunity to explore and whittle away areas of disagreement without exposure to the public gaze or to the pressure of national expectations.[39] This was all the more important in that Mitterand's diplomatic activity was hampered at this time by his concern to avoid being seen to make too many concessions to Britain in the run-up to the European elections of June 1984.

By the time proceedings began at the Fontainebleau European Council of 25–26 June 1984, the gap between the British and French positions had been considerably narrowed. There remained few outstanding points of substance to be resolved, and the settlement that was negotiated there followed closely the lines laid down in Brussels three months earlier, with some subsequent fine-tuning. It was quickly agreed that Britain should receive a rebate of 1 billion ecus for 1984. Making arrangements for later years inevitably proved more complicated.

In essence, the final stages of negotiation on this point centred on the question of what percentage of the net British budget contribution should be refunded. There were some unhelpful interventions. Thus the French Foreign Minister, Claude Cheysson, who had never shown any sympathy for Britain's demands, made what has been described as a 'last-minute, and potentially derailing, attempt' to fix the figure at between 50 and 60 per cent, an offer that was unrealistically low (Wall 2008: 36). On the British side, Treasury officials likewise played a less than constructive role, advising Thatcher not to settle. The Treasury remained wedded to the 'safety net' scheme that it had devised two years before and was extremely reluctant to see negotiations focus purely on percentages. It was also insistent that if an agreement was reached on the basis of a percentage and if, in addition, account was taken solely of Britain's VAT contributions, without regard to the sums contributed from import taxes and levies, there would need to be a rebate of 75 per cent of the deficit. Only thus, the Treasury argued, would Britain recoup two-thirds of the total difference between its outlays and receipts (Wall 2008: 35).

Such special pleading, whether by the Treasury or by Cheysson, counted for little when set against the political imperative that there now existed to reach agreement. What guaranteed a successful outcome to the negotiations was the fact that the three key participants were all determined to produce a settlement and prepared to make concessions in order to do so. Thatcher believed that the time had now arrived to clinch a deal, as she told Foreign Office advisers with whom she held talks to discuss progress to date during the Fontainebleau negotiations (Wall: 2008 36). With Mitterand and Kohl inclining to a similar view, there was no real danger of failure.

The final bargaining over percentage points was essentially a form of shadow boxing, in which the amounts of money involved were arguably less important than the need to impress domestic opinion, especially in France and Britain, with a display of firmness in protecting national interests. Kohl and Mitterand initially proposed an annual rebate which was equivalent to 60 per cent of the difference between Britain's VAT contributions and its receipts from 1985 onwards. Thatcher countered with 70 per cent and sought to enlist Kohl's support for her demand. When her efforts were rebuffed, a meeting was arranged between Thatcher and Mitterand, at which the latter made an improved offer first of 65 per cent and then of 66 per cent. In terms of political presentation, this extra 1 per cent was crucial to Thatcher, since it enabled her to speak of a rebate of two-thirds, a figure which she could 'sell' to the British public with at least some plausibility as the target she had been aiming for all along. Thatcher accepted Mitterand's second offer. In addition, she conceded an increase in the EC's 'own resources': it was agreed that the contribution from VAT revenues would definitely rise the following year from 1 per cent to 1.4 per cent of the national total, with the possibility of a further increase (to 1.6 per cent) in 1986.[40]

It took five years of bruising diplomatic activity to resolve the notorious BBQ. It is not surprising, therefore, that the question prompted a great deal of debate at the time, much of it of a highly political nature. It is equally unsurprising that it has also been the subject of a great deal of detailed study by historians. From the beginning, attention has tended to focus on the role played by Thatcher and, more especially, on three specific issues relating to her policies: the extent to which she was responsible for delaying a settlement; the effectiveness of her tactics; and the degree of success that she achieved.

It has sometimes been claimed that Thatcher deliberately prolonged the crisis over Britain's budgetary contribution for domestic political reasons and, in particular, to boost both her own popularity and that of the Conservative Party. One of the most prominent exponents of this view is Ian Gilmour, who in his memoirs explains Thatcher's extreme reluctance to accept the deal that he and Carrington brought back from Brussels in May 1980 by her desire to keep the 'grievance' alive as a means of diverting public attention from the disastrous state of the British economy. 'However badly things were going for Britain', Gilmour writes, 'Mrs Thatcher could at least win some kudos and popularity as the defender of the British people against the foreigner. Hence a running row with our European partners was the next best thing to a war … ' (Gilmour 1992: 240). Given that Gilmour was a long-time critic of Thatcher and had been sacked by her, his views must be treated with a considerable degree of caution. At the same time, more impartial commentators, including Stephen George and Hugo Young, have offered a similar interpretation, noting that it served Thatcher well to mount a robust defence of national interests at a time when her government's popularity was at a low point and the economy was in deep recession (H. Young 1990: 189–90; George 1990: 162–63).

Whether or not Thatcher was motivated by such political calculations, it is undoubtedly the case that her obduracy and intransigence increased the difficulty of reaching a settlement. She was not alone, however, in her unwillingness to compromise. The French, in particular, were equally capable of digging in their heels when important national interests were felt to be at stake, and the blanket refusal of both Giscard and Mitterand to contemplate a reduction in the share of the EC budget spent on agriculture was a major obstacle to an agreement on the British rebate.

Nor was Thatcher's truculent and aggressive style of diplomacy unrelated to her treatment by other EC leaders. Certainly it reflected her personality and her natural taste for a confrontational approach. It was also, however, a reaction to the behaviour of Giscard and Schmidt during the early stages of negotiation. Both of them had been in power since 1974 and by the time Thatcher became Prime Minister they already formed an assured and dominant partnership within the EC. Evidence from a number of first-hand observers – Carrington, Michael Butler, the British ambassador to the EC between 1979 and 1985, and Roy Jenkins, the President of the EC Commission from 1977 to 1981 – strongly suggests that the newcomer was treated in a condescending manner and made to feel like an intruder. Christopher Tugendhat, a former Conservative minister and a European Commissioner during the early part of the first Thatcher government, draws a similar picture in his memoirs, adding that the problem was probably compounded by the fact that the British Prime Minister was a woman (Tugendhat 1986: 122). According to Tugendhat, the French and West German leaders were guilty not only of a lack of courtesy, but also of a serious failure of statesmanship in making what he calls a 'derisory' offer at the Dublin European Council. By doing so, he argues, they provoked Thatcher into taking a harder line than she might otherwise have done (Tugendhat 1986: 120–22).

As regards the tactics employed by Thatcher, opinions differ widely on the question of how effective they were. Her approach to negotiations owed little to subtlety. It consisted in essence of setting out the British position and then refusing to budge, no matter how intense the pressure that was exerted or how great the risk of total isolation. Critics of Thatcher's reliance on sheer bloody-mindedness have argued that it was more often than not counter-productive, its main effect being to stiffen the attitude of other leaders and thus lessen the chances of coming to a sensible agreement. Others, including Robin Renwick, have reached precisely the opposite conclusion. A senior official in the Foreign Office, Renwick was closely involved in the final stages of the negotiations leading up to the Fontainebleau Agreement and, in his opinion, a successful outcome there was only possible because of Thatcher's stubbornness and extraordinary tenacity (Wall 2008: 39).

This leads on to the question of how successful Thatcher was in her attempt to secure a fair deal over Britain's contribution to the EC budget. From a narrowly financial point of view, she clearly achieved her goal. Certainly that was the judgement of Michael Butler, who regarded the Fontainebleau Agreement as a 'major victory for the UK' (Wall 2008: 37). Hugo Young comes to the same conclusion, writing: 'The Thatcher technique was brilliantly successful in a certain task. It got the money back' (H. Young 1998: 325). The agreement provided a guaranteed rebate of at least £1 billion annually – a massive advance on the £350 million offered in 1979. What was more, the mechanism that had been set in place meant that the amount which Britain received would rise automatically in line with the growth of the EC budget. If the UK continued to be one of the few member states which were net contributors, its financial position had been greatly improved. It is worth noting, indeed, that during the 1990s and the following decade the deal obtained by Britain became an object of envy to most of its EC partners. The demand for a 'Thatcher rebate' of their own was voiced with ever greater insistence by the Dutch and, above all, by successive German leaders, starting with Kohl. In addition, there was a growing determination to scale down the sums refunded to Britain. Such a change could only be brought about by a unanimous vote, however, and because of that the Major government was able to resist all the pressure to which it was subjected on the matter. For most of his premiership Blair insisted that the subject was not open to discussion and that he would veto any attempt to cut the rebate: it was not until the Brussels European Council of December 2005 that he was finally obliged to give ground.

On the debit side of the balance sheet, the financial gains outlined above had been secured at a very heavy political cost. Relations between Britain and the rest of the EC had been badly strained and the experience of five years of acrimonious disputes had left a legacy of deep bitterness and mistrust on both sides. At the personal level, Thatcher emerged from the episode with an even lower opinion of her European colleagues than before, more firmly convinced than ever that they were almost without exception unprincipled, hypocritical and not to be trusted. She, for her part, had forfeited whatever goodwill that had existed towards her when she first came to power and was left almost completely friendless within the EC. This was to be a grave handicap over the next few years, as she struggled to come to terms with a sustained drive for deeper integration.

4 Trench warfare, 1985–97

This chapter deals with a turbulent phase in the history of Britain's relationship with the EC/EU and it also covers a period of transformation in the character of the EC/EU. Much of the chapter focuses on the interrelationship between these two developments, as the emergence of new forms of European integration in this period was accompanied by deepening divisions over Europe within the Conservative governing party under the leadership of Thatcher until 1990 and thereafter of John Major until 1997. During this period, there was a decisive shift towards a degree of dynamism and integration in the EC that was comparable in scale and intensity to the formative years of the EC in the 1950s. Furthermore, in this period, as in the 1950s, the landscape of European integration often changed faster than the perceptions of British policymakers and in ways that confounded their expectations; significantly the word 'ambush' was used on several occasions in the second half of Thatcher's premiership to describe her experience of dealing with an unexpected turn of events in the management of EC affairs in the domestic and wider EC context.

The quickening pace of European integration in this period was most evident in the Single European Act (SEA) of 1986 and in the Treaty on European Union of 1992. During the same period, the seemingly immutable division of Europe and of Germany dramatically dissolved in 1989–91 with the end of the Cold War, the unification of Germany, the disintegration of Soviet dominance in Eastern Europe, and the collapse of the Soviet Union. This chapter briefly outlines these principal landmarks in the history of the EC/EU during the period 1985–97. It also offers some comparative assessment of the Thatcher and Major governments in their handling of these EC developments, and finally it provides detailed treatment of particular features of EC policy under each premier.

The SEA originated in a decision by the EC heads of government at the Milan European Council (June 1985) to convene an intergovernmental conference (IGC) on the EC's future. The SEA, which was signed by all EC states in January 1986, aimed to create a single market by the end of 1992. This goal involved the elimination of all impediments to the free movement of capital, goods, services and persons, thereby creating the largest frontier-free market in the advanced industrial world. The institutional provisions of the SEA established an important new principle in the decision-making procedure of the EC. The Council of Ministers was now empowered to take decisions by qualified majority voting (QMV). This innovation overcame the use of the national veto and immediately expedited the passage of the large amount of legislation required to give effect to the SEA. The significance of the SEA for the future development of the EC gave rise to a fierce debate that left its mark on the EC/EU in the 1990s. Some states, most notably the core or founding member states of the EC led by France and West Germany, saw the SEA as a means of advancing the cause of political, economic and monetary integration. They particularly emphasized general commitments in the SEA to the further development of European unity and of the EMS in particular. This view was strongly championed by Jacques Delors, whose presidency of the Commission (1985–94) restored its role as a dynamic force in promoting new schemes, most notably a three-stage plan for full economic and monetary union (April 1989) and also for a social charter of workers' and citizens' rights (May 1989). The debate over the EC's future after the completion of the single market project intensified when the EC (April 1989) agreed to convene an IGC on economic and monetary union and subsequently decided (June 1990) to establish an IGC on political union. These IGCs opened in December 1990 and culminated in the signing of the Treaty on European Union in Maastricht (commonly referred to thereafter as the Maastricht Treaty). This treaty coined a new name for the EC – the more federal-sounding 'European Union'. The centrepiece of the treaty, however, was the commitment to forge an economic and monetary union (EMU) by means of three stages with the final stage to be completed by 1999 at the latest. The treaty also included provisions for a Social Chapter (previously known as the Social Charter) and for a common foreign and security policy (CFSP) which envisaged a more influential role for the EU in the international system.

Between the making of the SEA and the signing of the Treaty on European Union, two concepts increasingly crept into EC parlance, at least one of which had a bearing on the evolution of British policy through these years, while the other came to express a British preference in terms of the overall organization of the EC. At the time of the Fontainebleau European Council (June 1984), there was considerable talk, especially from President Mitterand of France, about the possibility of a 'two-speed' Europe and of pressing on with desirable changes to the EC: an implicit reference to Britain as a likely laggard. The idea of a two-speed or multi-speed Europe meant that some of the EC states, which were able and willing to integrate in a particular way should be free to do so in the expectation that the other member states would follow them in due course. What this meant in practice became evident in the negotiations on the Maastricht Treaty when the Major government secured two opt-outs, one of which allowed Britain to defer a decision on participation in the third and final stage of EMU while the second opt-out concerned the Social Chapter of the Maastricht Treaty. The other concept was variable-geometry Europe. This expression was used to describe an EC/EU within which a group of member states able and willing to integrate in a particular way did so but was fully aware that other member states had no intention of following them, thereby making for a permanent difference in the degree of integration. This concept had a particular appeal to the British government in that it relieved the government of the necessity of participating in an EC/EU-wide uniform approach to integrative projects (Wall 2008: 64), though at the same time such an arrangement held out the unwanted prospect of a two-tier EC/EU with Britain in the second division.

Thatcher and Major shared a number of common features and conditions in the course of their management of EC/EU policy at home and abroad. Both Prime Ministers had to respond to a substantial advance in European integration: Thatcher in relation to the SEA and Major in the form of the Maastricht Treaty. In both cases they faced a formidable coalition for major change in the EC that was spearheaded by France under the leadership of President Mitterand, (West) Germany under Chancellor Kohl, and the EC Commission under the leadership of Delors. In these circumstances, Thatcher and Major often found themselves on the defensive in their relations with their EC/EU partners and also with elements in their own party. Certainly, at one point each of them imagined an enhanced role for Britain in the EC. Thatcher, for example, seemed to open a new chapter in Britain's relations with the rest of the EC in the mid-1980s, insisting that Britain was 'ahead of the pack' in its support for the single market project. Major came to power with the intention of putting Britain 'at the very heart of Europe'. By the end of their period of office, however, each Prime Minister was increasingly isolated in domestic politics and largely ignored in EC/EU circles. In negotiations with their EC/EU partners each had entered into agreements that stored up trouble at home, and each recognized that the SEA and the Maastricht Treaty went somewhat further in a supranational direction than either had wished. In some respects the SEA was a fatal attraction for Thatcher. She strongly supported the idea of a single market, yet she disliked the introduction of a greater element of majority voting in the Council of Ministers and she failed to appreciate at the outset the significance of the SEA as a launching pad for further integration. For his own part, Major viewed the Maastricht Treaty as an unqualified triumph for his diplomacy, a case of 'game, set and match',[1] but the opt-outs were a measure of how far the full treaty fell short of an ideal outcome for Britain. The ensuing parliamentary struggle to ratify the treaty, moreover, later described by Major as 'the longest white-knuckle ride in recent British politics' (Major 1999: 384), further exposed the increasingly deep divisions over Europe within his government and in the Conservative Party at large.

Thatcher and Major also shared common ground in their approach to EC/EU matters in so far as there were few, if any, substantial differences between them over policy. Major shared both Thatcher's support for the creation of a genuine single market and her hostility to any further ceding of national sovereignty. His views on the future development of the EU, as expounded in an article which he wrote in September 1993, were in line with Thatcher's in that he entered a strong plea against 'ever tighter political and economic integration'.[2] Both opposed the substance of the plan for EMU in the form of a single currency, fixed exchange rates and a European Central Bank. Both wished to stay in the EC/EU game but with qualifications or opt-outs. Certainly, there were differences of emphasis between the two Prime Ministers, whether over their contrasting degrees of enthusiasm for the prospect of putting sterling in the ERM in 1990 or in their responses to German unification. That said, Thatcher and Major were of one mind both on entry to the ERM[3] and in terms of the meaning of German unification for Britain's EC/EU policy. Unlike the French government, neither was prepared to participate without qualification in further European integration in the form of EMU as a necessary price for controlling Germany.

There were considerable differences of style between the two leaders that entered into and influenced their conduct of policy. Thatcher was variously abrasive, obstinate or confrontational in her dealings with EC matters or with other member states. Major, however, was far more emollient and more intent on negotiating or finding a way through the new process of integration. Differences of style, for example, were evident in their handling of the question of German unification. Thatcher barely concealed her dislike and suspicion of the Germans, and her opposition to the unification of Germany was a matter of common knowledge. Major, who had no memories of the Second World War, did not share Thatcher's stance. One of his first objectives on coming to power was to mend fences with the other EC states and especially to establish a close personal rapport with Chancellor Kohl of Germany.

A very important difference between Thatcher and Major that had a direct bearing on their EC/EU policy concerned domestic political conditions and Major's relatively weak political position from the beginning of his premiership. Throughout her premiership Thatcher commanded substantial parliamentary majorities: 43, 144 and 119 respectively as a result of the general elections of 1979, 1983 and 1987. By contrast, Major not only suffered from comparison with his successor and was haunted by the spectre of Thatcher (Seldon 1997: 252–55) but also had a small and dwindling parliamentary majority of 21 as a result of the general election of 1992. This majority was gradually whittled away to an overall majority of only one by 1996, partly as a result of defections but mainly because of an unbroken run of by-election defeats. The question of EC membership in the closing years of Thatcher's premiership sowed divisions in the upper echelons of the party especially within the Cabinet itself and also among MPs fearful of losing their parliamentary seats. It was ultimately the tide of opinion against her at this level that made Thatcher the victim of a palace coup. Major, however, faced a 'peasants' revolt' in that the issue of EU membership now generated deep and widespread concern throughout all sections of the Conservative Party. Eurosceptic opinion was increasingly in the ascendant, so much so that under his leadership the European issue was sometimes referred to as the party's 'San Andreas Fault'. At the same time, Major unlike Thatcher had to deal with a revitalized Labour Party which had gradually repositioned itself on the question of EC/EU membership and was not slow to take advantage of a Conservative Party at war with itself over Europe.

The evolution of Thatcher's European policy after the Fontainebleau European Council of June 1984 and throughout the remainder of her premiership admits of no easy explanation. However, the handling of three policy areas in these years – CAP and the EC budget, economic and monetary integration and the emergence of EMU, and British membership of the ERM – shed light on why Britain at this time was embroiled in increasingly acrimonious clashes with most of the other EC states and why at the same time deep divisions over European policy emerged in Thatcher's Cabinet.

The period immediately following the Fontainebleau agreement of 1984 saw a marked reduction in friction between Britain and its EU partners. Even so, differences persisted, not least over British efforts to curb the remorseless growth of the EC budget which on several occasions during the 1980s brought the EC to the verge of insolvency. The root problem was the CAP, which was extremely expensive and absorbed a large proportion of the total EC budget (65 per cent in 1986). The British strategy for getting the budget under tight control was to set strict limits on the growth of spending and to press for a radical reform of the CAP. However, the large farming constituency within the Conservative Party ('The National Farmers' Union was the Conservative Party at prayer' in the words of Geoffrey Howe) meant that even Thatcher was not prepared to be as tough on CAP reform as she sometimes appeared to be (Wall 2008: 81–82). In yet another crisis over the EC budget in 1987, the Thatcher government agreed to an increase in overall resources only on condition that it would be accompanied by binding agreements to restrict the production and price levels of surplus agricultural products such as milk, beef and cereals (G. Howe 1994: 522–23; Thatcher 1993: 728–37). Throughout all the tortuous negotiations over the budget between 1984 and 1988, British tactics conformed to a common pattern. Initially, the government took the line that it could not possibly agree to any increase in spending. Then, at length after a great deal of argument, it finally acquiesced in return for tighter curbs on the amount devoted to agriculture. The procedure was 'messy and negative' (Riddell 1991: 193), and it was also a recipe for discord between Britain and the other EC states.

From the mid-1980s onwards, however, there emerged a far more fundamental divergence between Britain and a majority of other EC members than differences over CAP and budgetary reform. This arose from differing reactions to proposals for a greater degree of economic and political integration. The Thatcher government viewed this drive towards greater unity with distinctly mixed feelings. On the one hand, it strongly disapproved of any changes which might have the effect of weakening British sovereignty. It was therefore adamantly opposed to suggestions that the powers of the Commission should be strengthened and also to the introduction of a greater element of majority voting at meetings of the Council of Ministers. On the other hand, it saw considerable merit in some of the other ideas currently under consideration. Thus it strongly supported the removal of all hindrances to the free movement of goods, capital and labour. Its attitude here was influenced by a combination of political ideology and considerations of national self-interest. The elimination of commercial restrictions was fully in accord with the government's staunch adherence to free market economics. But it was also hoped that Britain's air transport and financial service industries – believed to be the leaders in their field – would derive great benefits from the establishment of unfettered competition (Thatcher 1993: 552–53). Another area in which the Thatcher government welcomed moves towards closer cooperation was foreign policy. European Political Cooperation (EPC) represented an attempt to extend the principle of harmonization to foreign affairs. The Thatcher government consistently took the lead in pressing for its further development, not least because it thereby obtained some protection at least from the charge of being wholly negative towards the development of the EC. In addition, there was no question of any surrender of sovereignty. The basis of EPC was close cooperation between independent governments – a formula that was always likely to appeal to any British government.

The Thatcher government's thinking about moves towards closer economic and political union was set out in a discussion paper which it submitted to the Fontainebleau European Council of June 1984. The document, entitled *Europe – The Future*, advocated the abolition of impediments to trade within the EC. So far as constitutional change was concerned, though, the paper had very little to offer. There was a modest proposal for codification of existing procedures for political cooperation. In addition the paper emphasized the importance of retaining the national veto.[4] The British government liked to portray this particular contribution to the debate about the EC's future as a positive one. It claimed to be offering progress on the basis of sensible and practicable reform, as opposed to the more fanciful ideas emanating from the Commission and other quarters. It is possible, however, to view the British paper in a somewhat different light. Against such a background, the proposals put forward at Fontainebleau can be seen as an essentially defensive tactic – an attempt to avoid complete isolation in EC circles and to divert the general enthusiasm for political integration and institutional reform into channels that were more congenial to Britain.

In the period after Fontainebleau, the Thatcher government continued to fight a rearguard action against the drive for institutional change. But it was in a difficult position. There was powerful pressure from the Commission whose President, Delors, insisted that a single market was out of the question without the necessary political reforms to override national interests. Moreover, Britain was in a clear minority in its refusal to accept a greater degree of political integration. This became clear at the Milan European Council of June 1985 where, as noted above, it was agreed in principle to establish a fully integrated single market by 1992. Thatcher acknowledged that this would mean abandoning the veto in the Council of Ministers in certain areas and was ultimately prepared to accept that. What she was opposed to was the establishment of an intergovernmental conference (IGC) to consider a wide range of institutional reforms and a possible revision of the Treaty of Rome in order to carry them through. She was under the impression that this could only be done on the basis of unanimity. In the event, however, Bettino Craxi, the Italian Prime Minister, who was chairing the session, called a vote – the first time ever in a European Council – and the majority approved the IGC, with only Britain, Denmark and Greece voting against (Thatcher 1993: 548–51; G. Howe 1994: 409; Urwin 1995: 226–28). This was the first of several miscalculations by the British Prime Minister which she regarded as the Milan ambush (Wall 2008: 63).

Despite this setback, the SEA was accepted by the British government. Equally surprisingly, it was approved by the House of Commons with minimal opposition. Among those who voted for its acceptance, indeed, were Conservative backbenchers like William Cash and Peter Tapsell, who were later to be among its bitterest critics on the grounds that it represented an intolerable erosion of national sovereignty (H. Young 1998: 334–35). Their subsequent explanation for their acquiescence – that they trusted Thatcher's judgement – is perhaps understandable.[5]

What is more puzzling is the attitude of Thatcher herself and her motives for going along with the SEA including the commitment in its preamble to look at 'further concrete steps towards the progressive realization of Economic and Monetary Union' and also the adoption of QMV. It is possible that she felt unable to offer further resistance to the growing momentum for political integration (Thatcher 1993: 547–48). Another likely explanation is that she wholly underestimated the seriousness of intent behind yet another in a long line of vague, ambitious commitments to the goal of European unity. That would certainly be consonant with her dismissive attitude towards enthusiasm for political integration. Given her desire to achieve a single market, subscribing to what she regarded as meaningless declarations no doubt seemed a small price to pay. In her memoirs, she claims to have been misled and betrayed by duplicitous EC partners (Thatcher 1993: 555–56; 1995: 473). Some of her closest confidants at the time, including Charles Powell, her foreign policy adviser, have echoed this charge. They have also alleged that Thatcher was badly misinformed by Foreign Office advisers about what precisely was involved in the SEA. This allegation has been denied, however, by one of the officials concerned, Michael Butler, according to whom Thatcher insisted on having every line of the Act explained to her. Another official has said that she boasted of having read it in minute detail.[6] Certainly it seems implausible that a politician who was famed for mastery of a brief should have been unaware of what she was signing up to.

A no less puzzling feature of Thatcher's policy in the aftermath of the SEA and as its implications became clearer in detailed plans for economic and monetary union is why she did not perceive the dangers of such a project at an earlier stage. At their summit in Hanover (June 1988) the EC Heads of Government, including Thatcher, supported a study of European economic and monetary union by a committee chaired by Delors and comprising the central bankers of the EC states. Thatcher's involvement in this decision made her an easy target for criticism from Neil Kinnock, the Labour leader, who accused her of selling the pass on EMU at Hanover (Wall 2008: 83). The report of this committee favoured a three-stage approach to EMU, beginning with all member states joining the ERM in the first stage, a transitional stage two and a stage three in which exchange rates would be fixed and the European Central Bank would be established. This report was submitted to the Madrid European Council (June 1989) and eventually formed the basis of the conclusions of the later IGC on EMU. Thatcher did not take the threat seriously enough, despite warnings from Chancellor of the Exchequer Nigel Lawson about the dangers of EMU and about the fact that it would be an integral part of the EC system unlike the intergovernmental EMS and its ERM framework. She took little interest in the proceedings of the Delors committee and believed that any scheme for a European central bank would be opposed on the committee. In any case, she contemptuously declared that she did not expect to see a European central bank in her lifetime 'nor, if I'm twanging a harp, for quite a long time afterwards'.[7] Besides, she had been assured by Helmut Kohl, the West German chancellor, that he was opposed to EMU and understandably so in view of the fact that the deutschmark and the Bundesbank (the West German federal bank) were held in the highest regard in West Germany. These were after all key emblems of the country's economic success since 1949, or as Delors put it: 'Not all Germans believe in God, but all believe in the Bundesbank'. Furthermore, other matters crowded out the question of EMU in British government circles at this time. There was of course the growing importance of developments in Eastern Europe and Germany as the Soviet grip in the area began to loosen. There was, too, the increasing preoccupation of Thatcher and her senior ministers with the possibility of sterling joining the ERM. Indeed, there is no little significance in the fact that while the currencies of the other EC states had been in the ERM for almost ten years by this stage, and these states were thinking beyond ERM to the creation of EMU, the British government was still debating whether to enter the ERM. According to the British ambassador in Bonn in 1987, this was far removed from the type of European leadership that might have been expected from a British Prime Minister who had been in power for nine years (Wall 2008: 76). Be that as it may, there is little reason to doubt the conclusion of one authoritative study covering this episode that Thatcher misread the seriousness of intent of most of the other EC states over EMU and their determination to turn what she saw as airy declarations into hard policy (Wall 2008: 85). If, as this same study maintains, Thatcher woke up late to the impending reality of EMU, she was inclined to see it as a more cataclysmic event than some of her advisers and ministers, as became apparent in her mounting suspicion of and hostility to Delors, whose presidency of the EC Commission was renewed in 1988.

In fact, there developed between Delors and the British Prime Minister something approaching a personal feud (Grant 1994: 87–90; H. Young 1998: 326–27; Thatcher 1993: 547, 551, 558–59, 742). Delors seemed to bring out the instinctive euroscepticism and English nationalism in Thatcher. He had his own vision of what the SEA entailed. He insisted that it was not simply a question of sweeping away obstacles to a free internal market: the creation of a single market must be accompanied by full economic and monetary union. There must be a greater role for the Commission and the EP, as well as the provision of comprehensive welfare measures throughout the EC. Such notions were anathema to Thatcher who saw them as a blueprint for federalism, a diminution of national sovereignty and the establishment of a centralized European superstate dominated by Brussels. Delors expounded his views in a number of highly publicized speeches. In July 1988 he told the EP that in ten years' time 80 per cent of economic, financial and social legislation affecting members of the EC would emanate from Brussels. Thatcher was infuriated and criticized his remarks as grossly exaggerated and 'over the top' (Grant 1994: 88).[8] Delors' speech to the TUC annual conference at Brighton two months later, in which he spoke of the need to protect workers' interests,[9] produced an even stronger retort. Addressing an audience at the College of Europe in Bruges in September 1988, Thatcher denounced the idea of a 'European susperstate' and poured scorn on many of the policies advocated not only by Delors but also by most EC governments. She condemned Delors' projects, notably the Social Charter, as 'creeping back-door Socialism', she spoke out against centralized direction of the economy, and complained bitterly about the proposed new social dimension. New regulations to safeguard workers' interests would make the European economy less flexible and competitive. Similarly, harmonization of social benefits would impose a cost handicap on European industry. But the centrepiece of the speech was its strident assertion of the crucial importance of the individual nations: Europe would be stronger with 'France as France, Spain as Spain, Britain as Britain, each with its own customs, traditions and incentives. It would be folly to try to fit them into some sort of identikit European personality'.

The views that Thatcher expressed at Bruges and elsewhere caused strained relations with Britain's EC partners, though arguably this was due more to the presentation as to the substance of the speech as in some respects it offered a classic exposition of British views.[10] The speech also occasioned mounting disquiet at home. Although the speech was based on a Foreign Office draft, it had been substantially rewritten by Charles Powell and undoubtedly represented the Prime Minister's authentic feelings. Howe, the Foreign Secretary, was aghast when he first saw the amended version (H. Young 1998: 348–50; G. Howe 1994: 536–38). Thatcher's attitude towards the EC seemed to a growing number of critics to be narrow, blinkered, outdated and contrary to Britain's own long-term interests. Misgivings had already begun to surface even in the ranks of the normally loyal Conservative Party, and these were greatly strengthened by the party's disastrous performance in the EP elections of June 1989 following a campaign fought on a platform of outright hostility to Brussels.

The Conservatives' presentation and performance in the EP elections of 1989 formed a marked contrast to that of the Labour Party whose more constructive attitude to the EC resulted in 45 seats, 13 more than the Conservatives. This result for Labour was the culmination of a fifteen-year period of repositioning the party on the question of British membership of the EC. As noted in Chapter 3, the Labour Party conference in 1981 passed a resolution calling for a negotiated British withdrawal from the EC, a stance which was adopted as official Labour policy for the 1983 general election. Defeat in that election brought a change of leadership, a radical overhaul of party organization and a major reappraisal of all areas of policy. Neil Kinnock succeeded Michael Foot as leader in 1983. The scene was set for yet another reversal of policy on Europe. Kinnock had no regrets about the decision to drop the party's existing stance on the EC. From 1983 onwards he became increasingly enthusiastic about Britain's role in the EEC. According to Barbara Castle, who declared herself 'startled' by Kinnock's change of heart, for him 'European unity had become an emotional crusade' (Castle 1993: 545). Kinnock's 'conversion' was symptomatic of a general trend within the Labour movement as a whole during the second half of the 1980s. The beginning of the change of emphasis was discernible as early as the 1983 party conference which endorsed without a vote a National Executive Committee (NEC) statement that there could be no question of leaving the EC during the lifetime of the next Parliament. Over the next few years the Labour Party continued to retreat from its earlier hard-line, anti-EC stance. By the 1987 general election, the policy of withdrawal had been abandoned. In the 1989 EP elections Labour fought on the basis of a solid commitment to closer cooperation with Britain's EC partners, and a year later John Smith, Labour's Shadow Chancellor, argued in favour of entering the pound in the ERM.

Several explanations account for this fundamental change of sentiment. In part, it reflected a gradual and final acceptance by the broad mass of the Labour Party that there was no realistic alternative to remaining in the EC and, further, that EC membership brought benefits as well as advantages. Some of the Labour Party Members of the European Parliament (MEPs) came to believe as a result of their experience that many of the negative stereotypes that had coloured Labour thinking were not entirely justified.

Party-political considerations also helped to nudge Labour in a pro-EC direction. From the mid-1980s the party felt the need to move closer to the stance adopted by its main rival for the anti-Conservative vote, the staunchly pro-EC Liberal-SDP alliance. At the same time, the inherently adversarial nature of British politics meant that it adopted almost as a reflex action the opposite policy on the EC to that of the Conservatives. This tendency was accentuated by Thatcher's own combative style and the visceral dislike that she provoked in many of her political opponents. It was reinforced by Labour's belief that the electorate was losing patience with the kind of abrasive approach to Britain's EC partners that it had broadly approved during the struggle to secure a budget rebate in the early 1980s. For her own part, Thatcher taunted the Labour Party for its change of policy on EC, portraying Kinnock as a tool of Brussels. This set the pattern for the 1990s when Major routinely used the same tactic against Kinnock and his successors, John Smith and Tony Blair. By the later 1980s, however, there were good reasons for thinking that Europe was becoming a political liability for the Conservative government and for Thatcher in particular. From the time of the signing of the SEA in January 1986, Thatcher found herself increasingly at odds with her EC colleagues and almost totally isolated in her dogged rearguard action against the Social Charter, EMU and deeper integration. This produced a widespread feeling that she was overplaying her hand and that her continuing truculence was having a detrimental effect on the national interest. Equally damaging to the government's cause was mounting evidence that Thatcher's views on Europe were not shared by some of her most senior colleagues. Her determined resistance to British entry into the ERM led to barely disguised disagreements with successive chancellors and foreign secretaries and, eventually, to the resignations of Nigel Lawson and Geoffrey Howe in October 1989 and November 1990 (see p. 115). Predictably, the Labour Opposition sought to capitalize on this dissension and, in order to exploit dissatisfaction with Thatcher's tactics to the full, tended to play up its own pro-EC credentials with evident success in the EP elections of 1989. Its manifesto for these elections claimed that Thatcher's confrontational style had left Britain friendless and isolated within the EC.

Apart from electoral calculations, however, Labour was becoming increasingly attracted to many aspects of the economic and social policies associated with the EC Commission and the majority of EC governments, particularly the 'social market' philosophy embraced by the EC Commission and most of the EC governments. Certainly, such policies appeared far preferable to the economic policies of the Thatcher government. By the second half of the 1980s, little was to be heard in Labour circles of the former staple complaint that the EC was a capitalist club. On the contrary, the legal protection, working conditions and welfare provisions enjoyed by workers in France, Germany, Italy and other EC member states were an object of envy. This was especially true as far as the trade unions were concerned. Demoralized and weakened by persistently high unemployment, a declining membership, recently enacted legal curbs on their activities and their exclusion from the corridors of power, they looked to the Social Charter of May 1989, with its programme of minimum rights for workers and citizens, as a shield against the harshness of market forces. Equally, they had come to regard Delors, the main inspiration behind the Charter, almost as a surrogate champion for the British worker at a time when the trade union movement and the Labour Opposition in Parliament seemed unequal to the task (Butt 1992: 161–62).

The fact that Delors was detested by Thatcher, who denounced the rather modest provisions of the Social Charter as 'Marxist', only enhanced his popularity in the eyes of British trade unionists and no doubt contributed to the friendly reception he was given when setting out his vision of the future for European workers in his celebrated speech to the Trades Union Congress (TUC) annual conference in September 1988.

Dissatisfaction with Thatcher's European policies – not least among Cabinet colleagues – was to play a significant part in her fall from power. It is, of course, difficult to separate out the EC issue from many other strands of discontent at that time. The poll tax was proving to be a political nightmare. There were also justified fears that the economy was becoming dangerously overheated after the euphoria generated by Nigel Lawson's 1988 tax-cutting budget. Above all, there was growing criticism of the Prime Minister's personal style, which was widely viewed as autocratic and uncaring. In the early part of the decade, her strident defence of British financial interests had clearly struck a chord with domestic opinion, but this was far less the case by the late 1980s when she appeared 'tired, closed and cut-off from outside advice' (Wall 2008: 85). What ultimately sealed Thatcher's political fate was the sense that she had become an electoral liability rather than an asset. Her stance towards the EC was nevertheless a major reason for her loss of support within the Conservative Party and more generally. Moreover, it was an EC issue – membership of the ERM – that was the immediate cause of her terminal difficulties.

Like her predecessor, Callaghan, and as noted in Chapter 3, Thatcher was against placing the pound in the ERM, though she had described the other's decision in December 1978 as 'a sad day for Britain'.[11] In accordance with her free-market principles, she favoured a floating exchange, believing that fixed rates were inherently unworkable. As she put it: 'There is no way in which one can buck the market' (Thatcher 1993: 703). By the mid-1980s, however, several of her Cabinet colleagues had come to the conclusion that going into the ERM would enhance economic stability and provide a more effective weapon against inflation than control of the money supply. This was certainly the view taken by Nigel Lawson, the then Chancellor of the Exchequer, and at a meeting of senior ministers in November 1985 there was an overall majority in favour of entry. Thatcher, however, opposed this view and declared that if the government decided to go in, it would have to do so without her (G. Howe 1994: 449–50; Lawson 1992: 497–500; Stephens 1996: 48–51; Thatcher 1993: 697). There the matter remained until on the eve of the Madrid European Council (June 1989) when Howe, Foreign Secretary, and Lawson obliged Thatcher to soften her opposition to British membership of the ERM. At what Thatcher later called 'an ambush' and 'a nasty little meeting', they threatened to resign unless she agreed to change her current stance. The loss of two such senior figures would have been politically disastrous and Thatcher therefore reluctantly capitulated. Prior to Madrid, she had stuck to the formula that the pound would enter the ERM 'when the time was right'. At Madrid, more precise conditions were laid down. Although a Downing Street spokesman later claimed that there had been no change of policy, the truth was that it was now a question of when, rather than whether, entry into the ERM took place (Thatcher 1993: 710–13; G. Howe 1994: 576–84; Lawson 1992: 928–34; B. Anderson 1992: 150–51).

This episode marked the beginning of a protracted bout of ministerial wrangling, with the Prime Minister effectively exercising a veto until 1990.[12] Unable to take sterling into the ERM, for a number of years Lawson did the next best thing, pursuing a policy of 'shadowing the deutschmark' – that is, acting as though the pound was actually inside by keeping it at a fixed rate against the West German currency. In the spring of 1988 Thatcher openly blamed this policy for stoking up inflation, and from that time onwards differences between Thatcher and Lawson became increasingly public. The quarrel was inflamed by the embarrassing intervention of Alan Walters, Thatcher's personal economic adviser, who was described by an anonymous mandarin as the man who 'provided her with the algebraic equations for her flat-earth economics' (Stephens 1996: 129). Walters not only ridiculed the ERM as a 'half-baked idea', but also claimed that the Prime Minister agreed with him.[13] Meanwhile, Kinnock, the Labour Party leader, taunted Thatcher in parliamentary exchanges about having two Chancellors. Not surprisingly, Lawson found the situation intolerable and he resigned on 26 October 1989.

Despite her enforced climbdown, Thatcher remained unhappy about the prospect of ERM membership. She rightly saw it as a preliminary step towards full EMU, complete with a single currency and a European central bank, with a consequential loss of sovereignty. In October 1990, however, she was persuaded of the need to go in by the joint efforts of John Major, who had replaced Lawson as Chancellor in October of the previous year after a three-month spell at the Foreign Office, and Douglas Hurd, who had become Foreign Secretary as part of the same Cabinet reshuffle. By the beginning of 1990, Major was firmly committed to securing British entry to the ERM at the earliest opportunity, after he had undergone a bewildering series of changes in his attitude towards the issue during the 1980s (B. Anderson 1992: 120–32). In alliance with Hurd, he set about persuading Thatcher, whose continuing resistance was now the last remaining obstacle. For various reasons the two held a strong hand. They were both on better terms with Thatcher than Howe and Lawson had been. Moreover, their leverage was increased by the fact that she could not afford to risk any further resignations after the ministerial musical chairs of 1989. Besides, Thatcher's opposition was weakening. She was by this stage almost totally isolated on the question, so much so that Michael Heseltine, who was not the most disinterested commentator on Thatcher in general or on the EU in particular, was probably correct in his reported observation about how few people Thatcher spoke to by this stage and how she was simply not exposed enough to people with 'a proper Euro point of view' (Trewin 2008: 291). Furthermore, the resignation of Nicholas

Ridley, the Secretary for Trade and Industry, in July 1990 removed an important anti-ERM voice from the Cabinet. Ridley was forced to resign following publication in *The Spectator* of an indiscreet interview in which he referred to monetary union as 'a German racket designed to take over the whole of Europe', to the French as 'poodles' of the Germans and to the EC commissioners as 'unelected, reject politicians'.[14] The fact that he was widely – and probably correctly – assumed to be uttering Thatcher's own thoughts was symptomatic of the depth of unease that had grown up about her attitude towards Europe.[15] Finally, the economic and financial situation seemed to demand a change of policy. By the Spring of 1990 the government's anti-inflation policy was in tatters, destroyed by the boom of the late 1980s. Interest rates were at a higher level than at any time since 1981 and the pound was dangerously vulnerable to speculative pressure (B. Anderson 1992: 137–46; Stephens 1996: 148ff.).

At a key meeting with Major on 13 June, Thatcher agreed that Britain would join the ERM subject to certain safeguards, and over the next few months they held a series of highly secret meetings to discuss arrangements for going in. Thatcher finally gave her consent at a meeting on 4 October with Major and officials from the Treasury and the Bank of England. According to one account (Stephens 1996: 171–73), this meeting had two extraordinary features. First, Thatcher appeared to be principally concerned with how the news should be released to the press – thus giving substance perhaps to the jibe of Ian Gilmour, a member of Thatcher's first government, that she was the 'mistress of irrelevant detail'. Second, she insisted that the right to determine interest rates must remain with the British government, not seeming to realize that this would not be possible. The decision to join was announced after the markets had closed on Friday 5 October and membership took effect from the following Monday. This decision and its timing were dictated almost entirely by domestic political considerations. As a substantial section of informed opinion noted at the time, sterling went in at too high a rate – DM2.95 – and at a time when inflation was well above the ERM average. What the government was interested in was securing a cut in interest rates – and mortgage rates in particular – before the Conservative Party conference, and it was felt that this could only be done without endangering the value of the pound if it was in the ERM and backed by the resources of the West German Bundesbank. The announcement of entry was accompanied by a cut in bank rate from 15 per cent to 14 per cent.

Even after entry, Thatcher remained deeply sceptical. This was reflected in highly critical comments about monetary union during and after the Rome European Council of October 1990 and in her defiant rejection of Delors' plans to bring it about – 'No, no, no',[16] she exclaimed in the course of parliamentary exchanges on the Rome meeting. Shortly before this outburst, she had told a press conference that the EC was 'on the way to cloud cuckoo land' (G. Howe 1994: 643). These remarks, in turn, prompted the resignation of the long-suffering Howe from his position of Deputy Prime Minister at the beginning of November. In his resignation speech – later described by Thatcher as 'a mixture of bile and treachery' (Thatcher 1993: 840) – Howe attacked Thatcher's whole attitude to Europe, dismissing her vision of a continent that was 'positively teeming with ill-intentioned people, scheming, in her words, to "dissolve our national identities", to lead us "through the backdoor into a federal Europe"'.[17] It was a devastating critique from a politician not noted for his biting invective. Howe's resignation and speech played a major part in precipitating a challenge to her leadership of the Conservative Party and her subsequent resignation on 22 November 1990. Only two years earlier, however, Howe had strongly asserted that the EC owed Britain and Thatcher a huge debt for helping to launch the single market, for settling the British budget question, and for starting the reform of the CAP (Trewin 2008: 275). This was but indicative of Thatcher's mixed and divisive legacy in her handling of Britain's relationship with the EC during her premiership. There was a paradox at the very heart of her EC record. It was perhaps best expressed by William Hague, one of her successors as leader of the Conservative Party, who later observed that Thatcher was the prime exponent 'of taking us further in [the EC] and taking us further out [of the EC]' (Trewin 2008: 586). In effect, Thatcher had taken Britain further into the EC than any premier since Heath by signing the SEA and by placing the pound in the ERM. But she also cut an increasingly isolated figure in EC circles and her angry rhetoric against EC institutions and personnel left to her successor a Conservative government and party increasingly divided over Europe and affected by a rising tide of euroscepticism.

On November 22 Thatcher resigned and she was succeeded by John Major, after he won a contest to become leader. In some respects the situation was not dissimilar to Tony Blair and Gordon Brown in 2007. The incumbent Prime Minister had become an electoral liability and although their successor did not require a mandate from the people (i.e. an endorsement via a general election), there was the expectation that there would be a change of mood and tempo at Downing Street. Whilst Thatcher had the reputation for operating outside Cabinet Government (something that contributed to her political demise), Major set out to be a consensus builder – however he lacked a distinct 'group of followers' within the party (J.W. Young 2000: 150). Whilst Thatcher had become increasingly out of step with public sentiment over issues such as the Poll Tax (which culminated in riots), Major hoped to engender a calmer political environment in Britain. Thatcher had served to inflame sections of opinion on the Celtic Periphery – most notably amongst the Catholic community in Northern Ireland and amongst those Scots who sought greater autonomy from London. Major aimed to secure a peaceful resolution to the conflict in Ulster and to forge a new partnership between the Government in London and Scotland. Last, but not least, there was the issue of European integration – something which had proved so inflammatory during Thatcher's period in office. Here too John Major aspired to reconfiguring the political landscape.

'Europe' was one of the largest challenges in John Major's in-tray. He wanted to heal the rifts with other member states, particularly with Germany, where relations had deteriorated markedly during the latter part of Thatcher's period in office (Gowland and Turner 2000b: 276). He also wanted Britain to play a more constructive role in Europe – as mentioned above – and in essence he hoped it would be 'at the very heart of Europe'.[18] As suggested in previous chapters, the issue of European integration had long been a poisoned chalice for whoever was resident at Number 10 and Major would be no exception. Central to this was the issue of which strategic position would best suit the UK. Thatcher had signed up to the SEA on the basis that this would liberalize markets and diminish barriers to trade. That suited the Conservative's neo-liberal ideology. She had objected to the Social Charter in 1989 on the grounds that it could re-empower the unions in the UK. The issue of EMU was more complex, however. On the one hand it marked a natural end-point for the Single European Market. Equally, when John Major was Chancellor at the Treasury in October 1990, she was persuaded by his arguments that Britain should enter the ERM – something that he had come to favour – despite the fact that he had been opposed to this in 1987. In so doing, this was indicative of Major's position on the EU. He could and did change his position on major strategic issues. Was his approach to European integration therefore essentially pragmatic? If so, was it purely dependent on a mix of domestic politics and Britain's economic situation, which was in a state of decline at the time he became Prime Minister?[19]

As far as domestic politics were concerned Major led a deeply divided party, which still had to come to terms with the putsch which led to Thatcher's downfall. However the party was split not just over its leadership but more particularly over Europe. On the one hand there were those like Kenneth Clarke who favoured the EU and on the other were those like John Redwood and Michael Portillo who were much more sceptical. Transcending that was Thatcher herself. Although she was no longer leader, she still commanded support from within the parliamentary party and amongst the rank and file membership of the party. Whilst some of this could be attributed to a sense of nostalgia which harked back to the party's golden age when it was a formidable electoral machine during the 1980s, there was also the perception amongst those opposed to European integration that she had stood up for Britain. As her chosen successor, Major was to some degree a marked man. Although he wanted to change tack and work more closely with his European partners and European institutions, if he appeared overly supportive of the European project then he would face the wrath of Thatcher and her acolytes within the party. With the party divided, Major set out to restore a degree of harmony not least because disunited parties lack electoral appeal. He therefore adopted a more inclusive style of leadership and he hoped that there would be a return to cabinet government. But events in Europe ensured that this was not to be.

Major became leader just at the moment that European integration was set to gather pace once more and he was therefore faced with a dilemma. Whilst he wanted Britain to be 'at the very heart of Europe', he was confronted with Thatcher's legacy and the eurosceptics within his own party – including members of his cabinet, who expected him to take a robust line in the run up to the Maastricht summit.

The origins of EMU went back many years (e.g. the Werner Plan of the 1970s) but these earlier attempts had foundered due to a lack of political co-ordination. Consequently, it was believed, especially in German circles, that if there was to be a realistic attempt at EMU, there also had to be a greater degree of political union in order to avoid earlier setbacks. That said, the EC found itself in a similar position to the situation in 1985 before the SEA. A majority of the member states wanted closer integration, as was the case with the Single Market, but before they could realize their aims, the EC needed to acquire new powers if it was to achieve the second and third stages of EMU. The provisional agreement on EMU in turn led to calls for Political Union. It was therefore decided that two IGCs should be held in 1990 – one on EMU and the other on Political Union. This resulted in the Treaty on European Union (TEU) in 1992.

The TEU was another milestone on the road to a potential European federation. Once again some of the EC's institutions acquired new powers and a further range of policies fell within its ambit, with the consequence that there were few areas where it had no involvement at all. There were two entirely new areas of cooperation between the member states – the Common Foreign and Security Policy (Title V) and Cooperation in Justice and Home Affairs (Title VI). On this occasion the organizational changes were to be more far reaching because the structure of the Community itself was transformed. The EC formed the first pillar, where there was a relatively high level of integration encompassing the Single Market, Community Policies and eventually EMU. The Provisions on a Common Foreign and Security Policy (CFSP) formed the second pillar and the Provisions for Cooperation in the Fields of Justice and Home Affairs (JHA) the third. However, the UK Government had a number of concerns. Whilst Britain had signed up to the ERM, there remained strong opposition to EMU.[20] This was true not just of the party, it also applied to UK society more widely (still the case at the time of writing)[21] and to sections of the media.[22] As Geddes observed, 'the UK has powerful eurosceptic voices in the press and much EU coverage tends to be negative' (Geddes 2004: 224). Any party in government faces the same challenge, as Blair discovered when he succeeded Major. Second, the Conservatives remained steadfastly opposed to signing up to a European social policy (now known as the Social Chapter), the origins of which could be traced to the Social Charter, which Thatcher had rejected in 1989. Third, the UK position was that decision-making in the last two pillars should be intergovernmental. Last, but by no means least, the Government was especially concerned about any inclusion of the word federal in the TEU because of the perception that it would call into question the UK's sovereignty.

Whilst the outcome at Maastricht from Major's perspective was a success in relative terms, there were some setbacks. The Social Chapter was relegated to a protocol in the TEU, thereby excluding the UK from its provisions. In a similar vein, the UK secured the right to opt out of the third stage of EMU. Decision-making for the second and third pillars was intergovernmental, albeit that there remained the concern that 'joint action' over security policy was the thin edge of the wedge as regards the framing of a Common Defence Policy. On the minus-side, the power of the European Parliament was strengthened as a result of it securing the right of co-decision with the Council of Ministers where the TEU so allowed. Although the Council retained its primacy as decision-maker over legislative proposals, in as much as only it could adopt the latter, the EP had acquired the power of veto. Consequently by default in an institutional sense, the EU itself had gained potentially more authority, thereby adding to its supranationalism. As mentioned above, the potential federal characteristics of European integration increasingly vexed the Conservatives, and the UK Government worked hard behind the scenes to ensure that the phrase 'a federal goal' was not included in the first article of the treaty.[23]

However, that concern had ramifications for the interpretation of the references to subsidiarity (potentially a surrogate for 'federal') in the treaty. From one perspective this could be viewed as a federal concept because nominally it related to the division of competence with some areas of decision-making being assigned to the European/supranational level and others at the state/sub-state level (depending on a member state's internal constitutional arrangements). As such it represented a significant challenge to those in the UK who were concerned about Maastricht acting as a one-way street to a federal EU. In the immediate aftermath of the Maastricht Summit there were three possible interpretations of subsidiarity. First, that where appropriate some functions should be transferred upwards to the European level, second that it delineated competence between the member states and the EU but in so doing it protected the sovereignty of the former, and third, that where appropriate, authority should be devolved to the sub-state tier.[24] This last interpretation posed its own problem for the UK Government, because the Conservatives were opposed to devolving power to Scotland and Wales.

The Government therefore worked behind the scenes to ensure that the second interpretation prevailed and its goal was realized at the Edinburgh Summit in 1992. Despite the reiteration of Article A ('decisions are taken as closely as possible to the citizen'), in essence the conclusions of the Presidency confirmed that subsidiarity 'safeguarded' the powers of the member states.[25] In November 1993, when the Commission made its report to the Council on the adaptation of Community legislation to the principle, it maintained that subsidiarity was to be applied on a case-by-case basis:

> Subsidiarity is first and foremost a political principle, a sort of rule of reason. Its function is not to distribute powers. That is for the constituent authorities – the authors of the Treaty. The aim of the subsidiarity principle is, rather, to regulate the exercise of powers and to justify their use in a particular case.

The 'authors of the treaty' were the member states and in the first instance it was up to them to decide where the ECU should act (viz. they might or might not decide to adopt on EU-wide income tax policy).[26] From this perspective subsidiarity effectively related to the separation of authority between the EU and its member states; by default it was up to the member states themselves to decide individually as to whether the principle also applied to the sub-national level. As such it could be regarded as a recognition of Britain's position. However, the outcome at Maastricht was not an unqualified success, despite Major's claims.

Following the meeting of the Council the previous December, the treaty was signed at Maastricht on February 7 1992. But it now had to be ratified by the member states if it was to take effect. As Major was to discover, this was by no means straightforward despite the fact that concluding a treaty is a prerogative power and as such it rested with the Prime Minister and was essentially extra-parliamentary. Nonetheless the existing legislation concerning the UK's membership of the EU had to be amended and that led to *The European Communities (Amendments) Bill*. The Bill took a considerable time to pass through parliament and it attracted controversy, not least from within Major's party.[27] Initially, there was little sign of the rows that would follow when a debate was held in the Commons on December 18–19 1991 on the outcome of the Maastricht summit.[28] However, the timing of the debate was significant because an election was in the air and that had the effect of uniting the party in public at least.

Although Major's election victory in May 1992 surprised some political pundits and it did help legitimise his premiership, from this moment on his period in office became considerably more turbulent. To no small extent this was a reflection of his strategy towards the EU and widening divisions within his party over Europe. Although the election victory was welcome, the result was also something of a poisoned chalice for Major. That can be attributed to two dynamics. Some of the new intake of Conservative MPs proved to be highly eurosceptic; Iain Duncan-Smith and John Townsend were two such examples. Second, the Government's majority in the Commons had been slashed from 88 to just 21 (and subsequently 18, dropping to just 1 by April 1996), which further added to the influence of the Tory cabal which opposed Maastricht.[29] Within the month 22 Conservative MPs voted against the European Communities (Amendment) Bill, when it underwent its second reading in the Commons. Shortly thereafter, Danish citizens rejected the TEU in a referendum and in so doing fuelled the zeal of those across the political spectrum who called for a referendum in the UK as well.[30] On June 3, 70

MPs, a good number of whom belonged to the Conservative Party, signed an Early Day Motion demanding that the Government embark on a 'fresh start' over its approach to Europe. Even within the Cabinet, ministers such as Michael Howard, Peter Lilley and Michael Portillo flirted with the notion of the UK withdrawing from the treaty.[31] Unsurprisingly, however, Major supported what had been agreed at Maastricht, not least because he had claimed the outcome a success. To adopt a different tack now would have called into question his political judgement, as it would have represented a complete reversal of course. However, Major's troubles had only just begun, thanks to the debacle over the ERM.

The ERM was not only a central element of Major's strategy towards Europe, it also underpinned the UK's macro-economic policy. Whilst Major had become one of its most ardent supporters in the UK, it proved to be deeply damaging to him politically. The motives for the UK joining ERM were wide-ranging. Thatcher had been persuaded to join as a result of a 'combination of Cabinet pressure, business influence and economic and political necessity' (Blair 2002: 162). But as Blair observed, the ERM was becoming less stable by the time the UK joined and when the country did enter it, the rate against the deutschmark at 2.95 to the pound would prove unsustainable. The situation was exacerbated further by the UK's economic decline. Whilst GDP had fallen in Germany, France and Italy between 1989 and 1991, the UK was the only member state that recorded negative growth during this period.[32]

The UK economy was therefore particularly vulnerable at this time and like other countries in Europe its interest rate shadowed that set by the German Bundesbank. As a result of unification, there was greater inflationary pressure on the German economy and in order to reduce this threat the Bundesbank retained a high interest rate. That had the effect of lowering the value of currencies of other member states, with the result that they were driven ever closer to the lower limit of the ERM. One possible solution would have been a devaluation of their currencies against the deutschmark but France resisted this. In the meantime, on three occasions Major appealed to the German Chancellor, Helmut Kohl, to act over the deutschmark. Theformer Prime Minister observed ruefully in a subsequent interview for *BBC TV*:

> The German Government were talking about European Union and the spirit of European unity and the Bundesbank were following policies that were absolutely damaging in almost every respect to the economies of Germany's partners across the European Union. The two things didn't match up. They were inconsistent and that point needed to be made to the German Government.[33]

When the EU's finance ministers and central bankers met in Bath during the first part of September for an emergency meeting, the UK Chancellor Norman Lamont called on the Germans on four occasions to cut their interest rate but to no avail.[34]

The UK had no option but to quit the ERM on Wednesday September 16 after the pound came under overwhelming pressure from currency speculators on the financial markets and it fell beneath its (ERM) 'floor' of DM 2.778 to the pound. Lamont increased the base rate twice during that day (11 per cent initially, then 15 per cent). As events unfolded in the currency markets the day was one of high political drama. Kenneth Clarke and Douglas Hurd remained by Major's side. Hurd, as Foreign Secretary was concerned that if the UK quit the ERM abruptly that could have adverse repercussions for the UK's future relations with its European partners.[35] For his part Lamont was 'flabbergasted' that other ministers were being consulted by Major, not least because in his view 'they had nothing to do with the Treasury and frankly they did not understand the issues at all'.[36] Clearly the highest echelons of the Government were deeply divided over the matter, with Major apparently clinging onto the notion that the UK could remain within the ERM. But as the afternoon drew to a close that was no longer tenable.

Major subsequently conceded that the UK's exit from the ERM had been 'a political disaster' and he did consider resigning.[37] Hurd described the mood as follows:

> We, certainly John Major, and I think all of us were aware that what we were seeing was not something that could be shrugged aside. We were seeing the destruction of our economic policy and of our European policy, both. And for weeks after that the Prime Minister was deeply depressed. Not panicky but depressed.[38]

The reason that the pound had been forced out was that it was costing too much to support it. At the end of so-called 'Black Wednesday' the Government could not resist pressure from the currency markets any longer. By then government intervention had cost the Exchequer billions of pounds, which the country could ill-afford.[39] After quitting the ERM the pound was allowed to 'float' on the markets with the result that devaluation followed (Blair 2002: 171).

Just a few days later on September 20 France held its referendum on the TEU. There was a small majority in favour, but given that it was one of the founding member states the result called into question the future trajectory of European integration. It also helped galvanize those in the Conservative Party who opposed Maastricht. Just a short while later the Conservatives held their party conference. Instead of it being a celebration of the election victory earlier that year, Major complained that Europe dominated the agenda:

> It was unlike any party conference I had been to before or since. It was the first within a few months of winning a general election. Yet from the attitude, we might never have won it, we might even have lost it. There was no post-election feeling of euphoria, though everyone had thought we would lose. The issue was Europe, Europe, Europe.[40]

Norman Tebbitt was deeply critical of Major's approach to the ERM in a speech at the conference, which further served to undermine the Prime Minister's credibility. Thatcher, who had been elevated to the House of Lords, also opposed the Government's policy on Europe, so much so, according to Major, that divisions within the party directly contributed to the scale of the election defeat in 1997.[41] September 1992 was therefore something of a critical juncture for Major and his Government. The exit from the ERM had undermined his economic policy and his policy on Europe never recovered its sense of direction.

As the Bill on Maastricht underwent its legislative stages, it only served to highlight how split the Conservatives were.[42] Kenneth Clarke recounts how it became something of an open sore for the party:

> For weeks upon weeks upon weeks, the thing lingered on the floor of the House of Commons, with animated debates going on all sides but including Conservatives debating against Conservatives on the floor of the House at enormous and ridiculous length.[43]

Major complained subsequently that Norman Tebbit 'encouraged MPs to vote against the Government', whilst Thatcher called 'new and often impressionable backbenchers' to her office to do the same.[44] On November 4 1992, the Government won a so-called paving motion by the slimmest of majorities (319 in favour with 316 against). But the matter was not laid to rest.

The UK's exit from the ERM also made Lamont's position as Chancellor increasingly untenable (plus the depressed state of the economy and a loss of confidence amongst both the party and the business sector) with the result that he was replaced by Kenneth Clarke in May 1993. Although Lamont was offered the post of Environment Secretary, he quit the Government and the relationship between him and Major never recovered (Blair 2002: 187). Whilst Clarke proved to be a valuable ally at the Treasury not least because he was a political heavyweight and a good communicator, he was also a europhile. That was problematic at a time when sections of his party believed the EU had been both damaging to the electoral future of the Conservatives and to the country more generally. Matters came to a head on July 22 1993, when the Government lost the vote on an amendment to the Maastricht Social Chapter (316 against 324). By now it appeared that the parliamentary party was not just divided over Europe but over Major's leadership too. Consequently some Conservative MPs voted on the amendment because they 'would do anything to stop the treaty' whilst others were simply 'anti-Majorites'.[45] However, the following day, Major won a vote of confidence and the treaty was ratified on August 2 1993. Although the storm over Europe abated slightly, the issue of EU membership remained a thorn in the side of the Conservative Party for years to come. In addition, for the first time since 1975 eurosceptics in parliament had substantive allies well beyond Westminster. Maastricht had helped them forge a common identity and seek links with like-minded groups elsewhere in the EU (Forster 2002: 103). In the meantime the EU remained an easy target for those inclined to pursue the struggle.

Despite the UK's exit from the ERM, the issue of EMU remained contentious. That was because the adoption of the single currency remained on track for those EU states which were committed to it. Under stage I, they aimed to align their currencies with each other under the ERM. In 1994, stage II commenced with the establishment of a European Monetary Institute. Stage III ran from between 1997 and 1999, during which time the single currency would commence and it would be overseen by a European Central Bank. As far as the single currency was concerned, Major was initially content to sit on the fence. No action was required by the UK regarding its opt-out until December 1997. It therefore seemed pointless to adopt a position before then, as it would further divide the party. Major also believed that there was a possibility that EMU might not even come to fruition due to political and economic pressures. However, attempts to avoid the issue eventually proved impossible due to pressure from eurosceptics within the parliamentary party. They believed that there should be a rejection of membership of the euro in the party's manifesto at the next election. But Major faced a dilemma. Kenneth Clarke favoured EMU and might have resigned from the Treasury if rejection was formally adopted by the government. The formation of the Referendum Party by James Goldsmith (who threatened to fund candidates in those constituencies where the MP did not support a referendum) complicated matters further. Major came under intense pressure to relent over the manifesto and Clarke compromised on April 3 1996. It was agreed that there would be a referendum commitment in the manifesto but it would only take effect if and when the Cabinet of the day decided that the UK should sign up to EMU and Parliament had also assented to the move.[46] For the time being EMU was laid to rest but European integration remained controversial for Major and his Government. Enlargement of the EU was another issue where the UK potentially diverged from its key partners in the EU.

With Maastricht behind it, the EU was set to enlarge once more with the accession of Austria, Finland and Sweden.[47] But that was overshadowed by the break-up of the former Soviet bloc with the result that a clutch of states from Central and Eastern Europe also hoped to secure membership. The UK had long been keen on 'widening' the EU (i.e. increasing its membership), as that diluted not only its tendency to centralize power but also the potency of the Franco-German axis. In September 1994, during a speech at Leiden University, Major maintained that widening the EU came before 'deepening' it (i.e. enhancing the depth of integration). This was a corollary of his view on Britain and Europe, which had been central to the Conservatives' European election campaign earlier that year, when he called for a 'multi track, multi-speed, multi-layered' Europe in a speech at Ellesmere Port on May 31.[48] Such a notion was a precursor to the forthcoming IGC and was a reflection of a multi-speed approach to European integration, which had originally been formulated by Douglas Hurd.[49] There was further controversy over who should succeed Delors at the European Commission.

In June 1994 Major vetoed the preferred candidate for the President of the Commission, Jean-Luc Dehaene, at the Corfu summit. Although Italy had initially objected to Dehaene, this was lifted at Corfu, potentially leaving the UK isolated (J.W. Young 2000: 168). However, it is worth noting that other countries were concerned about how the Germans had set about promoting Dehaene (George 1998: 262). Major held his ground however, and Jacques Santer became the next President. From that moment on the relationship between Kohl and Major fractured, although the origins of the breakdown can be traced back to Maastricht and the ERM debacle.

Yet despite facing down Germany, Major still endured problems in the UK over Europe. Senior ministers did not disguise their hostility towards the European ideal – examples include Michael Howard, John Redwood and Peter Lilley. Michael Portillo, the Secretary of State for Defence, in an emotive speech at the 1995 party conference, had already rebuffed any idea that there should be a European army with its own administrative infrastructure.[50] He was but one of a group of senior figures in the parliamentary party who were suspicious of Europe. A year earlier Lamont had questioned whether the UK should quit the EU during a fringe meeting at the party's annual conference.[51] More particularly there is reason to suppose that between 1995 and 1996, a majority of the Cabinet were eurosceptics.[52] Determined to call his critics' bluff, Major resigned on June 22 1995 and invited one of his rivals to stand against him for the leadership. John Redwood duly took up the challenge. He resigned as Secretary of State for Wales but Major won with 218 votes against 89 (J.W. Young 2000: 169). Whilst this was intended to lower the political temperature within the party, the fact that Major even thought it was necessary was indicative of how serious the situation had become. However, European matters remained high on the political agenda.

The review of the Maastricht Treaty necessitated an IGC at Turin in 1996. The UK policy had already been formulated in the White Paper – *A Partnership of Nations*.[53] The UK line was essentially in keeping with the Conservatives' earlier approach – namely opposition to greater use of QMV in the final two pillars of the treaty (Common Foreign and Security Policy and Justice and Home Affairs), a refusal to end the opt-out of the Social Chapter and the cessation of national vetoes. The Government also objected to greater powers for the President of the European Commission. However, the White Paper supported the notion that the EU should have its own Foreign Affairs spokesman, albeit that the post-holder should be 'fully answerable to the Council of Ministers, representing the views of Member States, not deciding them'.[54] There was also a call for amendments to the Common Fisheries Policy so that 'quota-hopping' would cease (this related to UK quotas for fishing entitlements being purchased by nationals from other countries – notably Spain). In addition, the Government wanted the powers of the European Court of Justice (ECJ) to be reformed (it had recently lost a case over quota-hopping). In sum, the White Paper was indicative of the difficulties facing Major over Europe. He wanted to have a better relationship with his European partners than was the case when Thatcher was Prime Minister, but the UK was out of step with most other EU countries over a whole range of important issues and the UK lacked allies if a crisis arose.

The 'Beef Crisis' added to Major's woes with Europe during the spring and summer of 1996. The potential threat posed by eating UK beef had been latent for some while. But it exploded onto the political stage when Stephen Dorrell, the Secretary of State for Health, warned that there might be a link between Bovine Spongiform Encephalopathy (BSE) in cattle and Creutzfeld-Jacob disease (CJD) in humans. The UK Government was wrong-footed from the start. First, it had long denied that there was such a link between the two. When Dorrell performed a U-turn, little thought had been given as to how the news might go down with the EU and its member states. Although EU agriculture ministers had met two days before Dorrell's announcement, Douglas Hogg, the UK minister, had not been present and no advance warning had been given to Franz Fischler, the Agricultural Commissioner.[55] Given the gravity of the situation, on April 25 Fischler decided to instigate a global ban on the export of UK beef and allied products. His decision followed a meeting by veterinary experts and was endorsed by the Commission within 48 hours.[56]

Over the coming months there followed a series of disagreements between the UK and the EU over how best the crisis should be resolved. The UK government was concerned at the cost of wholesale slaughter, with the result that it proposed that only a selective slaughter should be conducted for cattle over 30 months old in those areas with a record of the disease. It was also hoped that the EU would bear 80 per cent of the cost but the ban remained and the issue of financial compensation proved contentious. Transcending that was the growing view in the UK that the ban was illegal and that a case should be brought before the ECJ, despite the fact that the Government's own White Paper on the 1996 IGC called for a curb in the ECJ's powers (as mentioned on p. 125). After the standing veterinary committee of the EU decided to retain the ban at its meeting of May 20, the UK Government responded by announcing on the following day that it would commence disrupting EU business, which in effect became a policy of systematic disruption.[57]

Whilst disruption played well to the gallery at Westminster, placating Conservative eurosceptics especially and their friends in the UK media, it antagonized other EU member states. The UK's relations with Germany, already low after the exit from the ERM and the dispute over the Commission Presidency, now plummeted still further. One of Major's goals when becoming Prime Minister had been to restore relations with Germany but that objective had come to nought. In contrast, Tony Blair, Labour's leader, called for a more productive approach based on co-operation in a speech in Germany on June 18.[58] Meanwhile, the Commission, which hitherto had been seeking to remove the ban behind the scenes, stood its ground in the face of the UK's intransigence,[59] and the chance for compromise ebbed away. By this time, the UK, already relatively isolated in the EU, was left to plough its own furrow. It was at this juncture that Conservative europhiles decided to take on the eurosceptics. The party was now in a state of virtual civil war and there was the attendant threat that it could split in two after its anticipated defeat in the next general election. Faced with a stalemate at the EU, Major decided on a climb down and an end to disruption. But the deal that was agreed was little different from that which the UK could have secured through negotiation and compromise.

In sum, a combination of factors had served to undermine Major's policy on Europe. The UK joined the ERM at the wrong rate, its economy was in recession, and the Germans were unwilling to assist by cutting their interest rate when they were suffering from rising inflation. 'Black Wednesday', as Major conceded, was a political disaster and he never fully recovered from it (though supporters of retention of the pound referred to it as 'White Wednesday'). He led a minority government, which was increasingly divided over Europe, and his consensual style of leadership only fuelled the Conservatives' fratricide. In addition, during his final year in office he was at the mercy of events such as the BSE scare. However, it would be unreasonable to suggest that there was a lack of direction over Europe and that Major's administration was completely rudderless. Stephen George observes that, the Government did have a clear, coherent and positive vision of Europe at Maastricht and the 1996 IGC, but it differed from that of France and Germany. More particularly Major felt 'let down' by his colleagues in the EU as time went by (George 1998: 273). Yet other elements were unplanned – such as the compromise on EMU in the manifesto and the policy of disruption in 1996. All in all, far from the UK being at the heart of Europe, the country remained isolated and on the sidelines during Major's period in office.

5 Northern Ireland, Scotland and Wales in the European Community/Union 1973–98

Despite its supranational characteristics, the EU remains to no small extent an intergovernmental entity. By default, therefore, its key players are the governments of its member states. Consequently the EU has posed something of a challenge for its regions and stateless nations. Until recently, to no small degree, they were relegated to mere bystanders as the European 'experiment' progressed. Indeed, for the EC's first three decades, formally, they were for the most part excluded from a direct involvement in EC policy formulation. More particularly, as the EC acquired more and more competence it encroached increasingly on those areas of policy which, hitherto, fell within the exclusive competence of the regions, or which they shared with their central governments. The net result was that, over time, authority to make decisions in a swathe of policy fields resided increasingly in Brussels. However, in the aftermath of the SEA, it became increasingly untenable for governments, in federal polities especially, to monopolise the conduct of European affairs. It was less feasible for them to defend the premise that relations with the EC in a classic sense could be regarded as 'foreign policy' and thus should remain purely within the ambit of the central government. Rather, domestic policy had been 'Europeanized'. In effect the dividing line between domestic and European policy matters had become 'blurred' as a result of European integration (Jeffery 1997a). Accordingly, territorial administrations in the regions and stateless nations began to undergo 'Europeanization'.

Europeanization is a multifaceted term, and there is no consensus on its exact meaning. Olsen suggested that there was a number of possible interpretations, including 'the emergence of European level institutions' and the 'domestic impact of European-level institutions'. Essentially, these two forms of Europeanization were inter-connected. Institutionally, the extent to which Europeanization evolved at the European tier of government had a resonance domestically (J.P. Olsen c2002). Thus it could be supposed that Europeanization has been an incremental process at the territorial level.[1] Primarily, this can be attributed to the manner by which the EU has evolved as a result of successive treaties starting with the EEC (1957), followed by the SEA (1986), the Treaty on European Union (1992), the Treaty of Amsterdam (1997), the Treaty of Nice (2001) and (if it is ratified) the Treaty of Lisbon (2007). As the

EC and its policies began to affect the regions directly, the latter had little option but to respond. In addition, the reform of the structural funds in 1988 helped to fuel regional mobilization. Not only was EC regional aid more substantive than hitherto, from this point on, in theory at least, the regions were supposed to be 'partners' with regard to the implementation of the funds (Marks 1993). Yet territorial Europeanization was not merely concerned with acquiring EC aid, it was more pro-active. For example, it involved collaboration and networking, an underlying aim of which was to influence EU policy making. It therefore included the direct lobbying of the EU's institutions and attempts to influence the EC's wider agenda (John 1997: 133). In sum, sub-state actors re-structured their organizations over time and they re-orientated their strategies, as bit by bit the EC began to affect their activities (see for example, Keating and Jones 1985; Jones and Keating 1995; Jeffery 1997b).

Whilst few, if any, regions could ignore European integration, some were better able to mobilize than others by virtue of the political authority which they had at their disposal. This appeared especially to be the case in federal polities, where authority was 'shared' between the state and sub-state tiers of government. Transcending that was the ideal that both tiers of government aimed to work well together by dint of their commitment to 'federal loyalty'. Consequently, the German Länder attained greater influence over European affairs during the latter part of the 1980s and continued into the 1990s (Gerstenlauer 1985, 1995, Jeffery 1997b). Initially they adopted a twin-track approach in their bid to secure more influence over the EC during the late 1980s. They played a leading role in the mobilization of the 'third level' (i.e. the territorial tier of government in the EC), and they also endeavoured to secure certain rights over the formulation of European policy in Germany (Börzel 2002, Jeffery 1997b). Third level mobilization did yield some tangible results at Maastricht, thanks to pressure from the Länder and the Belgian Sub-national Entities (SNE). Under the Treaty on European Union, where their state's constitutions so allowed, ministers from sub-state administrations could vote in the Council (initially as representatives of their state). The formation of the Committee of the Regions (CoR) formally incorporated the regions into the EU's policy processes in those areas which fell within its competence. Last, the principle of subsidiarity promised much. It was in part intended that where possible, as a matter of principle, decisions would be taken at the closest level to the citizen (see Chapter 4 for further material on subsidiarity).

By the early 1990s, the Länder had also secured a number of mechanisms within the German polity which ensured that they enjoyed, collectively, greater influence over those EU matters which fell within their competence, as well as a potential veto over further transfers of competence to Brussels. The same applied to Belgium's SNEs (Kerremans and Beyers 1997). The situation was less clear-cut for Spain's Autonomous Communities, however, with the Basques, in particular, appearing to lose a degree of autonomy as a result of

European integration (Bourne 2000, 2002). Consequently, it could be supposed that a region's constitutional status could have a distinct bearing on its
potential influence vis-à-vis the EU, both internally in relation to its central
government's formulation of EU policy, and externally with regard to the EU
itself (Bourne 2003). Given the relative success of the Länder and the Belgian
SNEs, it could therefore be inferred that regions in federal polities were best
equipped to reap the benefits of Europeanization, thereby calling into question the influence of territories in more centralized states, such as the UK.

As far as the UK is concerned, it is a union state, comprising a number of
distinct territories, where formally sovereignty resides with the Westminster
parliament. In theory, this is where supreme political authority is situated.
This arrangement does not lend itself to a federal system of government,
whereby sovereignty is 'shared' between the different tiers of government,
because that would subvert the Westminster model (Keating and Jones 1995)
and so threaten the current constitution in its entirety. However, sovereignty
itself is something of a chimera, thanks in part to European integration. It
could be claimed that by virtue of their membership of the EU, the member
states are no longer wholly sovereign, whilst the EU itself is not yet sovereign
either. Thus the term 'post-sovereign' could be a more apt description of the
current situation for the EU and its member states (MacCormick 1999,
Keating 2001). Even so, a primary concern of successive UK governments
since the UK's accession to the EC in 1973 has been, where possible, to
defend the country's (perceived) 'sovereignty'.

Prior to constitutional change in 1999, the UK's situation was complicated
further by the system of government in the UK, or more precisely by the
distribution of authority between the 'centre' and the 'periphery'. So far as
Northern Ireland, Scotland and Wales were concerned, each had its own territorial
branches of government, albeit that its autonomy differed. In the decades
following the establishment of a Scottish Office in 1885, Scotland enjoyed
what can be termed 'administrative devolution', whereby it possessed a degree
of autonomy in relation to the implementation of domestic policies that were
purely Scottish (Mitchell: 2003). Under the Government of Ireland Act
(1920), the North of Ireland secured a form of executive devolution, which
lasted until the imposition of 'direct rule' by Westminster in 1972 as a result
of 'the Troubles'. Wales did not secure its own territorial branch of government until 1965 and to begin with at least the Welsh Office had a much
smaller remit than its counterpart in Scotland. That began to change in 1975
when it secured 'significant economic powers'. During the Thatcher and
Major governments it was assigned a tranche of additional responsibilities
including agriculture, health, and education (B.J. Jones 1997: 61).

Despite the initial absence of Welsh self-government, there was the view
that the periphery enjoyed a fair degree of autonomy from the centre – especially between 1926 and 1961. According to Bulpitt, there existed within the
UK a 'dual polity'. In effect the centre had its own polity which concentrated
on matters of 'high politics', such as defence and foreign policy, whilst the

periphery also had a distinctive polity, which focused on domestic or 'low politics'. According to this perspective, the periphery tended to be governed by acquiescent Conservative elites. Bulpitt's thesis partially rested on the premise that the efficacy of this arrangement was dependent on the existence of an amenable external environment (e.g. empire, victory in war and the Commonwealth). Conversely, therefore, a hostile environment could undermine the dual polity. Hence, membership of the EC posed its own threat to the dual polity, not least because potentially it could undermine elite consensus (Bulpitt 1983).

Bulpitt believed that from the 1960s onwards, the dual polity was increasingly under threat. First, the Conservative elites in the periphery were losing electoral support. Second, in the face of the UK's economic decline, the centre intervened directly in the periphery as part of its attempts at economic modernization, which called into question the worth of the local elites. In addition, the dual polity was weakened further by the deteriorating security situation in Northern Ireland and the growing support for nationalist parties in Scotland and in Wales in the years immediately pre-dating the UK's accession to the EC in 1973. Thus, just as the UK was set to join the EC, it was faced not just with a loss of political authority to Brussels but also pressure from the periphery for greater autonomy. Cumulatively, these various forces threatened to strain a system of government which, though superficially pragmatic and informal, was also inherently hierarchical. Ultimately, as far as EC affairs were concerned, the peripheral administrations were subordinate[2] to the centre, where nominally (in the aftermath of accession) supreme political authority continued to reside at Westminster.

From the perspective of the Welsh and Scottish administrations especially, accession to the EC was something of a step into the unknown. Potentially, they stood to lose autonomy, as decision-making looked set to become both physically and politically even more remote. Instead of decisions being taken in London, all that would occur in the aftermath of accession was that, where the EC's treaties so allowed, policies would be determined in Brussels. Hence, it could be claimed that their political dependency[3] would be exacerbated further by European integration. Hitherto, they had enjoyed direct access to decision-makers in London. For instance, each territory had its own Secretary of State, who was a member of the UK cabinet, thereby ensuring that their interests could be promoted and defended at the highest levels of government. But now their access to decision-making would be indirect, in those areas of policy which fell within Brussels' ambit. As far as intergovernmental channels were concerned, their interests would be represented by UK ministers from the 'lead departments'[4] in the Council of Ministers (since re-named the Council of the EU). Thus, right from the moment the UK joined the EC, this threatened the relative autonomy Scotland and Wales enjoyed (Northern Ireland possessing little, if any, substantive autonomy following 'direct rule').

However, the UK's accession coincided with growing demands for constitutional change. This was most pronounced in Northern Ireland where secessionists had been engaged in armed conflict, the aim of which was the re-unification of Ireland. Whilst the situation in Northern Ireland was somewhat exceptional, compared to that of Scotland or Wales, as far as the latter were concerned there had been mounting pressure for greater autonomy during the late 1960s as the nationalist parties looked set to make headway at the polls. That contributed to the establishment of a Royal Commission on the Constitution in 1969, the aim of which was to assess whether there was a favourable climate for legislative devolution.[5] Clearly this stood to be affected by the UK's membership of the EC and the issue led to deep divisions within the Commission when it published its final report in 1973. Whilst the report maintained that the case for devolution would not be weakened as a result of the EC, two of its members, Crowther Hunt and Peacock, published a Memorandum of Dissent.[6] The latter believed that devolution would be a recipe for confusion, as there would be ambiguity over the divisions of competence and there was no formal access point for regional governments in the EC, at that moment in time. They therefore argued that there was little scope for legislative devolution as a result.

Despite the concerns of the 'dissenters', the UK Government published a White Paper in 1975 proposing legislative devolution for Scotland and Wales.[7] The Government viewed devolution as a priority after the Scottish National Party (SNP) made significant gains at Westminster during 1974. However, the issue of how the (proposed) devolved administrations could best be represented in Brussels still had to be resolved. The paper therefore explained that European affairs rested with the UK government and that the representation of territorial interests would be based primarily on 'pragmatic arrangements'.[8] As it happened, legislative devolution came to nought on this occasion, following referendums in Scotland and Wales in 1979. Even so, it had been apparent for some time that the EC would have far reaching consequences for the UK's territories, regardless of the constitutional architecture within the UK.

One such example was Scotland where well before the UK's accession to the EC, its political and economic elite was divided over the pros and cons of EC membership. In 1961 the leadership of the SNP wrote to Harold Macmillan, demanding the 're-convention' of the English and Scottish parliaments on the basis that Westminster lacked the authority to cede sovereignty to the EC. In 1967 the Scottish Trades Union Congress was strongly opposed to membership on the grounds that it would weaken trade with the Commonwealth. However, the Scottish branch of the Confederation of British Industry was broadly in favour. By this time, civil servants in Edinburgh viewed the impending accession with a combination of trepidation and excitement. On the one hand they were concerned that it might result in extra work. On the other they wondered if the Scottish Office would take the lead in relation to those areas of policy which affected Scotland most, otherwise they risked being related to little more than 'an English appendage'. By 1971, however, it was apparent that this was not to be, but senior figures were intent at the very least on ensuring that key individuals were seconded to Brussels, so that they could 'work away on the inside' (Wright 2005).

In the aftermath of accession it soon became clear that EC membership was less popular in Scotland and Northern Ireland than in Wales or England. As far as Northern Ireland was concerned, the Protestant majority's doubts stemmed from the perception that membership eroded UK sovereignty, and in so doing, it posed, potentially, a threat to the Union. Equally, sections of the Catholic community regarded membership more positively for much the same reasons (Keating and Jones 1995: 94–95). With regard to Scotland, there was the concern that the EC was too remote and that the terms of entry did not suit the country. Thus in the run-up to the 1975 referendum on membership of the EC, some in the SNP called for a 'no vote' on the basis that Scotland should secede from the rest of the UK and re-apply for membership on its own terms. In addition elements within the Scottish Labour Party were opposed on the grounds that the EC was concerned primarily with promoting the interests of big business (Wright 2005). Plaid Cymru, Wales' nationalist party, shared similar misgivings to those of the SNP. But Welsh support for the EC during the early years of UK membership differed markedly from that of Scotland and Northern Ireland. Whilst 66.5 per cent voted in favour in Wales during the 1975 referendum, the figures for Scotland and Northern Ireland, were 58.4 per cent and 52.1 per cent respectively. That compared with 68.7 per cent for England and an average of 67.2 per cent for the UK as a whole.[9] Yet even though it was early days, as far as the UK's membership of the EC was concerned, it was already apparent that the latter was having an impact at the territorial level.

The Scottish Office, for example, could not avoid becoming entangled in European affairs. It took a close interest in EC funding and the CAP.[10] It had also been concerned with the evolving CFP, the legitimacy of which was open to question. That was because the original six member states had established a policy on fisheries just prior to the UK's accession with the result that the UK Government was presented with a *fait accompli*, whilst Heath and his government did not view fisheries as a 'red line' issue. The CFP was especially contentious north of the Border because the bulk of UK catches was landed in Scotland and the industry was a significant employer in the north and east of the country. Consequently, during the first ten years of membership, the Scottish Office sought, with some success, to defend the interests of Scottish fishermen as the CFP developed more fully. The eventual agreement on quotas in 1983, the preservation of the six- to twelve-mile coastal bands (around the UK) and the creation of a Shetland Box could each be regarded as positive outcomes (Wright: 1996). However, as time went by, the CFP became increasingly unpopular both in Scotland and in parts of England (e.g. the South West).

During the 1980s, the Europeanization of the Scottish Office gathered pace, with the SEA being of particular significance. As more and more decisions were taken in Brussels, responsibility for European matters was gradually decentralized from London to Edinburgh. This did not relate so much to strategic matters, which remained the preserve of the lead departments in Whitehall. Rather it was concerned with more technical areas of policy such as water purity or conservation. This was because the departments in London were becoming overloaded. So, it made sense for the Scottish Office to take on additional European work. In addition, it was apparent that the Scottish Office needed to influence the EC more directly, as it could not wholly rely on the lead departments to promote Scottish interests (Wright 1995). Thus, towards the end of the decade the Scottish Office increasingly opened up informal channels with the European Commission, albeit that it was intent on ensuring that its activities would not conflict with the UK line on any given policy.

The Welsh Office also underwent a degree of Europeanization. In particular, its Economic Regional Policy and European Affairs Divisions became key players (B.J. Jones 1997: 66). As far as the former was concerned, that was unsurprising given the prominence of EC structural funds. In addition, at the instigation of Peter Walker, its former Secretary of State, it established relations with four other regions in the EC.[11] Links such as these were significant, because they affirmed that the Welsh Office was not wholly dependent on the conduits provided by departments in London when it wished to engage in the European political arena as a player in its own right. However, as was the case with the Scottish Office, in essence much of this was inherently informal.

Whilst a number of Northern Ireland departments was involved in EC affairs (e.g. the departments of agriculture and education), the Department of Finance and Personnel had the 'central co-ordinating role, in so far as it existed'. That was primarily by virtue of its involvement in the implementation of EC structural funds in the province (McGowan and Murphy 2000:11). However, that meant that most of its effort was devoted to the management of the funding schemes *per se*.[12] Arguably, therefore, Europeanization in Northern Ireland was relatively limited prior to 1999. Moreover, what Europeanization there had been, was to no small degree driven by its civil service. More particularly, there was an absence of political leadership. Given the circumstances, deficiencies such as these were understandable. UK ministers would have been more concerned about resolving the conflict than defending the province's European interests. Despite the deficiencies which they faced, the territorial offices of government were by no means alone in developing links with the EC, however.

Local authorities also took an interest in European matters.[13] Although their European activities dated back to the 1970s, when Strathclyde Regional Council succeeded in securing EC funding, the SEA was something of a turning point. From that moment on, local councils were faced with a plethora of European regulations. The SEA also presaged the reform of the structural funds in 1988, a result of which was that local authorities participated in the funding partnerships which bid for and, if they were successful, implemented EC aid programmes. Consequently, a number of Scottish councils established specialist EC units in order to co-ordinate their EC work, and some employed consultants or seconded staff in Brussels. For their part, the eight Welsh county councils established the Assembly of Welsh Counties, part of whose remit was to promote Wales' interests in the EC (Keating and Jones 1995). However, the capacity of the Welsh local authorities to forge links with other regional bodies in the EC was potentially circumscribed by legal and economic factors. Nonetheless, the Assembly of Welsh Counties did eventually develop relations with pan-European networks such as the Conference of Maritime Regions and the Assembly of European Regions (B.J. Jones 1997:67). Although the Convention of Scottish Local Authorities (COSLA) acted as the umbrella body for Scottish local government, individual councils, or more especially the former Regional Councils, tended to deal with the EC on a bilateral basis. That came to a halt, when they were abolished in 1996. For a short while thereafter, COSLA took a more leading role but that was somewhat curtailed when it lacked sufficient finance and its EC specialists left.

Governmental bodies were by no means the sole actors from the UK's territories to take a close interest in European affairs The same applied increasingly to territorial pressure groups. Some, such as the fishermen and the farmers, had been involved in lobbying Brussels right from the moment the UK joined the EC. The same applied to the Scotch Whisky Association. Others became involved in lobbying Brussels after it became apparent that they could no longer ignore the EC. One such example was Scottish Financial Enterprise (SFE). This organization had been established in part because of the 'big bang'[14] and also because of the inception of a single market in the EC. As far as the latter was concerned, the underlying concern was that regional financial centres such as the one in Edinburgh could find themselves marginalized. Consequently, SFE helped to establish the Association of European Regional Financial Centres, thereby enabling its members to mount a joint lobby in the EC. The situation for Wales differed inasmuch as until 1964 a distinctive Welsh lobby was less evident. That changed with the creation of the Welsh Office and the manifestation of a Welsh interest became more evident during the years of Thatcher's government (Keating and Jones 1995: 103). Over time Welsh pressure groups did lobby Brussels direct in part because they did not perceive that they would get much sympathy from Thatcher.[15] In sum, from a territorial perspective, activities such as these indicated that authority across a swathe of policy areas no longer necessarily resided in London. Rather, increasingly it was situated in Brussels – something which was to attract the attention of nationalist parties in Wales and also in Scotland.

Despite their initial scepticism, the SNP and Plaid Cymru became rather more amenable to the EC, as time went by. Plaid Cymru's enthusiasm stemmed from the EC's assistance for small farms and minority languages in rural Welsh-speaking areas in the west of the country (Keating and Jones, 1995: 97). The SNP's change of tack can be attributed, in part, to Jim Sillars. Originally a member of the Scottish Labour Party, he had once been opposed to EC membership. He eventually quit Labour to form his own splinter party, after which he joined the SNP. By the mid-1980s he warmed to the idea of Scotland seceding from the UK and becoming a member state in the EC in its own right (see, for example, Sillars 1986). Within the SNP he was by no means a lone figure with regard to this, however, and the SNP's key objective became 'independence in Europe' as the 1980s drew to a close. All in all, therefore, the adequacy of territorial representation in the EC became ever more politicized during the late 1980s and on into the 1990s. The net effect was that, increasingly, the onus rested with the UK government to demonstrate that territorial interests were safe in its hands, during a period when the impact of the EC was becoming ever more extensive. That was especially so for Scotland.

In the run-up to the Maastricht Treaty, the Scottish Office undertook a review of its EC work. Such a review was by no means restricted to the Scottish Office, however, as other departments in the government did much the same (Smith 2003). However, the findings of the review were notable by virtue of the extent to which the EU had impacted on its activities. The review noted that some 1,200 officials (amounting to 20 per cent of its staff) were engaged in EC-related work and that few of its departments were unaffected. The ensuing recommendations called for EC training to be up-graded, more staff secondments to the EC's institutions and a further enhancement of informal links with the EC (Scottish Office 1991a, 1991b). As far as the latter was concerned, it was suggested that officials should remain in Brussels for an extra day or so when they visited so that they could network with European officials. However, by this time each of the three territories was set to have its own bureau in Brussels.

The establishment of Scotland Europa, the Northern Ireland Centre in Europe (NICE) and the Wales European Centre in Brussels was indicative of the need for a more permanent presence in the EC's capital. Even so, their conception was potentially contentious. The attendant risk was that they might be misconstrued as quasi-embassies. That particularly applied to Scotland Europa, as both the Scottish Trades Union Congress and local authorities viewed it with concern as a vehicle to promote a distinctively Scottish agenda in the EC (Mazey and Mitchell 1993: 115). In time however, neither the Scottish Office nor UKRep objected. As far as UKRep was concerned, it would 'siphon off' some of its workload and the Scottish Office had no objection as first and foremost, Scotland Europa's role focused primarily on economic rather than overtly political matters. The latter therefore took a close interest in EC aid, and it provided its clients with regular briefings on EC policies. Despite the concern that they must not have a political remit, however, it was hoped that these bureaux would enhance their territory's influence within the EC. That particularly applied to NICE. As one of its founder members later observed, the *rationale* behind its inception was that it would help offset the weakness of the province's representation in the EC. On the one hand he believed that 'it played a very important role'.[16] Yet it was also evident that NICE faced a number of hurdles, including a lack of resources and a somewhat strained relationship with the direct rule administration. He claimed that not only did ministers fail to appreciate the 'need to act quickly and to build on the work of NICE', but also the direct rule administration had a 'cumbersome and old fashioned approach to policy making and doing business'.[17] For its part, whilst the Wales European Centre could be viewed as something of a 'success' because it 'raised Wales' profile in Brussels', it too was burdened by increased costs and strains with the Welsh Office over its role (B.J. Jones 1997: 68). Hence, although each of these bureaux endeavoured to cultivate informal links with the EC's institutions and with other regional bureaux, their capacity to influence the EC's policy agenda appeared to be somewhat limited during the 1990s. That rather stood in contrast with their German counterparts, which enjoyed better resources and which were more pro-active (Jeffery 1997c).

Although it is tempting to believe that there was something of a Westminster by-pass, in the sense that territorial pressure groups in Scotland, Wales and Northern Ireland tended to circumvent London when they wished to influence the EU, the reverse was more apt. To no small extent the UK government acted as a gatekeeper between the territories and Brussels by virtue of the primacy of the Council of the EU. In addition, the government was ultimately responsible for overseeing the implementation of EU policy in the UK. Moreover, the Scottish, Welsh and Northern Irish Offices were all territorial branches of the UK government. The net result was that few interest groups chose to ignore or circumvent the territorial administrations when they sought to influence EU policy making. That particularly applied to the farming lobby for example, despite the fact that the sector had its own trans-European umbrella group.

During the 1990s the farming community faced a number of challenges, a good number of which was connected to the EU. That is unsurprising, given that competence for agriculture rested with the EU as a result of the CAP. Two issues which particularly occupied the minds of the farming lobby were the proposals to reform the CAP and the (then) forthcoming accession of states from Central and Eastern Europe. Rather than deal direct with the (former) Ministry of Agriculture, Fisheries and Food (MAFF) in London, the National Farmers Union Scotland focused its efforts on the agriculture department at the Scottish Office. In so doing, it typified the decentralized approach adopted by agricultural pressure groups in Scotland, Wales, Northern Ireland and England (albeit in the latter's case it did not have its own territorial department as such and it therefore lobbied MAFF direct). The underlying intention was that by mounting joint lobbies of their respective territorial administrations, in relation to a given issue such as the reform of the CAP or the terms of accession, they could bring greater pressure to bear on the government. That, however, rested on the twin assumptions that their territorial departments enjoyed sufficient influence within MAFF, and that the UK government itself was able to influence decision-making in Brussels. That, though, was not always the case.

The BSE scare was particularly illuminating (see also Chapter 4) because it demonstrated just how little influence the UK farming community possessed at times over EU affairs. The crisis came to a head in 1996 following global concern that BSE, which had affected livestock, could be transmitted to humans. The UK government hoped that UK exports of beef products would be maintained but the EU decided that there should be a global ban. Although this eventually did not apply to farmers in Northern Ireland, their colleagues elsewhere in the UK fared less well. Despite the objections of the UK government, effectively there was nothing it could do (apart from mount a challenge in the ECJ and disrupt EU business) and the ban remained in force, much to the dismay of the farming community. The BSE crisis was particularly salient as far as the promotion of territorial interests was concerned. First, it was indicative of the extent to which 'authority' now resided in Brussels. It served to affirm that the EU could impose its will on parts of the UK, regardless of whether the UK government agreed or not. Second, it served to highlight the UK's relative lack of allies within the EU at that moment in time. That is understandable, given the increasingly, eurosceptic attitude adopted by the Thatcher and Major governments (see Chapter 4). The BSE crisis, however, was by no means the only issue that called into question the extent to which territorial actors in the UK could influence European matters.

Whilst the UK fishing sector secured a reasonable outcome with regard to the CFP in 1983 (see p. 133), by the end of the decade and on into the 1990s the industry was in crisis as fish stocks began to decline markedly. The root cause was technology creep whereby the fishermen were more successful due to new aids such as sonar. In effect their potential to catch fish increased three to four per cent year-on-year. Faced with the slump in fish stocks, one option would have been to decommission a proportion of the fleet. In return the EC would have made aid available for modernization under its Multi-Annual Guidance Programme. But the then-Conservative government decided to abandon decommissioning temporarily in 1989, with the result that the Scottish fleet, for example, did not markedly decline in terms of the number of fishing vessels and stocks came under even more pressure during the 1990s (Wright 1996, 2000c). The situation was apparently exacerbated further, according to *The Royal Society of Edinburgh*, when scientists recommended over-generous catch limits for North Sea cod during the 1990s.[18] That said, if an effective decommissioning scheme had been *in situ* at the start of the decade then the crisis might not have evolved in the way that it did.

The implementation of the structural funds also served to expose the extent to which the UK's territories could be affected adversely by decisions taken in London. In theory, EC aid was supposed to be additional to UK regional expenditure. In the event, the decision was taken by successive UK governments that this was not to be, as EC structural funds were to be used to offset the UK's contributions to the EC's budget (Rhodes 1974; Keating and Waters 1985; Mitchell 1997, Wright 2005). That was primarily because the UK was a net contributor to the EC. The net result was that EC monies were not genuinely additional until the Kerr/Millan agreement of 1991 at the earliest. Even then the issue of additionality helped bring down Alun Michael, Wales' First Minister, as late as February 2000, indicating that problems persisted beyond the constitutional reform of 1999. Consequently, Scotland and Wales received less regional aid than they were entitled to. This was especially significant in the aftermath of the funds' reform in 1988 when the amount of money allocated by the EC to the funding schemes increased markedly. In sum, these deficiencies served to exemplify the potential inadequacy of the largely pragmatic inter-governmental mechanisms within the UK.

Essentially the pragmatic arrangements, which governed territorial influence over the formulation of European policy within the UK, were a mix of the formal and the ad hoc. The pre-1999 arrangements have been well documented by Bulmer *et al.* in *British Devolution and European Policy-Making*. These were an amalgam of committees in Whitehall, a forum which convened on Fridays, together with a plethora of less formal meetings.[19] Although the Cabinet Office European Secretariat was 'the key co-ordinating agency (Bulmer *et al.* 2002: 20), individual departments in London acted as the lead with regard to sectoral policies. When EU legislative proposals were despatched to the lead ministry, it was up to the latter to decide if there was a territorial dimension to a particular proposal. If that were so, then the proposal would be despatched to the relevant territorial departments (e.g. the Welsh Office). This arrangement was not always satisfactory. For example, there were times when the Scottish Office was forgotten completely or consulted too late in the day (Wright 2005). However, attempts were made to remedy this in 1995 (Bulmer *et al.* 2002: 111).

Where necessary, the lead department would convene an inter-departmental committee which would be attended by officials from a variety of government ministries including, if necessary, those from territorial departments. But this was not without its deficiencies; some Scottish interest groups maintained that the officials from the territorial departments were too junior and risked being out-gunned (Wright 2000a, 2000b, 2005). When officials were unable to influence the outcome to their satisfaction, and where the issue was sufficiently important to warrant it, the matter could be referred to their ministers. In the main, however, ministers from the territorial departments rarely attended the Council of the EU, although of the three departments, ministers from the Scottish Office tended to be more prominent in Brussels (Bulmer *et al.* 2002: 19). Consequently, ministers at the territorial ministries were in some respects 'bargain hunters' within the UK polity, so far as European affairs were concerned. They could act as a fallback if their officials lacked the necessary influence in London. If they wished to influence a colleague in the lead department with regard to a legislative proposal emanating from the EU, they could write to the individual concerned or have a quiet word 'behind the speaker's chair' in the House of Commons. If necessary, they could refer the matter to their Secretary of State. The territorial Secretaries of State sat on Cabinet committees, one of which dealt with European matters.[20] So, they already had an involvement in EC affairs, albeit that this related primarily to matters of high politics such as enlargement or the single currency, rather than technical/routine policy matters, such as a regulation on water purity.

In sum the efficacy of these arrangements was dependent first, on the extent to which the relevant territorial minister could promote and defend the issue at hand, within the UK polity. Second, it was also dependent on the willingness of the relevant UK department to accommodate a particular territorial interest when it was formulating its position with regard to EC policy. Third, it was also dependent on the *capacity* of the department and by default the UK government to promote and defend that interest within the EC. This became more problematic as the 1980s drew to a close and it was further exacerbated during Major's administration, not least because he led an administration which was deeply divided over the EU. More particularly, there was little evidence of strategic political leadership at the territorial level with regard to Scotland (Wright 2005) and arguably the same applied to Wales, which shared a similar form of territorial administration, albeit with less autonomy than the Scots enjoyed. Moreover, there was no sign that subsidiarity would apply to the territories of the UK in the aftermath of the TEU.[21]

As far as Northern Ireland was concerned, the imposition of direct rule brought its own problems (see the earlier section on NICE). Whilst Westminster was responsible for the government of Northern Ireland, the latter's civil servants played a key role with regard to determining the province's European 'priorities'. But according to Kennedy *et al.* (1998) there was 'a minimum of input from any political or democratic master at either regional or national level'. Consequently, there was little, if any, accountability. In addition, the imposition of direct rule meant that Northern Ireland was governed by ministers from parties which lacked a 'constituency base' in the province.[22] Hence, unlike Scotland, for example, the Secretary of State was not elected from a constituency in the province and the situation was complicated further by the absence of mainland UK political parties in Northern Ireland. This remained problematic right up to 1998, and it contributed to the difficulties in assessing whether the province exercised any substantive influence over the formulation of EU policy within the UK.[23]

Wales too suffered from a relative lack of influence over EU affairs.[24] For example, Jones observed:

> The Welsh Office was inhibited from pushing the Welsh case because it had to balance a specific Welsh interest against a more general British interest, and the European Commission, although eager to establish contacts with British regions, was under no illusion as to where

political power resided and in its negotiations dealt exclusively with the UK government.

(B.J. Jones 1997: 67)

All in all, therefore, Welsh influence in the EU was questionable prior to devolution – something that clearly came to the fore in 1995 when the Welsh Affairs Select Committee at the Commons published a critical report on the Welsh Office's handling of EC matters.

Thus, by the time Tony Blair became Prime Minister in 1997, the influence of territorial administrations over the formulation of EU policy in the UK was open to question. From a civil service perspective, the current arrangements were something of a success, as far as day-to-day issues were concerned (see Bulmer *et al.* 2002, for example). That though was not the whole picture. An underlying deficiency was that there had been a lack of political leadership at the territorial level regarding EU integration. In addition there had been too little democratic oversight on the part of MPs from Wales, Scotland and Northern Ireland and little transparency over inter-governmental mechanisms within the UK. By 1997, however, the issue of European representation was but one facet of a state which needed to modernize if the Union was to remain *in situ*.

Consequently, when 'New Labour' won its election victory, devolution was one of the lynchpins of its modernization agenda. As such, it was expected there would be greater democratic accountability, whilst the decentralization of authority would ensure that the country would be better governed, on the basis that territorial politicians would be more sensitive to local needs. Even so, European affairs in particular, and international relations more generally would remain something of a challenge for the new constitutional arrangements. On the one hand, devolution portended that the territories would secure more autonomy. But on the other, as was the case prior to 1999, many of the areas of domestic policy which fell within the remit of the newly created institutions also fell within the competence of the EU, whilst the UK government retained its role as gatekeeper to the Council.

6 The Blair governments and European integration 1997–2007

Major's increasingly desperate efforts to maintain a semblance of party unity over Europe proved unavailing: Conservative infighting carried on undiminished into 1997. Even the approach of a general election, announced in mid-March and scheduled to take place on May 1, failed to end the internecine warfare, and throughout the unusually lengthy electoral campaign the Conservatives' internal differences, especially on the issue of the single currency, were repeatedly exposed. So deep were the divisions, indeed, that a large number of candidates issued individual constituency manifestos setting out personal positions on the euro which were mutually contradictory and often at odds with official party policy. Not surprisingly, the outcome was a crushing defeat at the hands of New Labour, as the Labour Party now called itself. It would be simplistic to attribute the Conservatives' abysmal performance, involving a loss of 177 seats, solely to their public quarrels about Europe. Other factors were at work, including Major's perceived lack of authority, competition for votes from the Referendum Party, the lasting damage inflicted by the disastrous events of 'Black Wednesday', the outgoing government's reputation for 'sleaze'[1] and a widespread feeling that it was time for change after eighteen years of being governed by the same party. Even so, there can be little doubt that the Conservatives paid a high price at the polls for their disarray over Europe.

In comparison with the Conservative Party, Labour displayed a united front on the EU in the run-up to the election. Its leading figures assiduously projected a pro-European image, while those within the party who were of a more eurosceptic disposition refrained from attempting to embarrass them. It was a thoroughly disciplined performance which threw into relief, as it was fully intended to, the turmoil in their opponents' ranks.

The contrast with the bitter feuding of the late-1970s and early-1980s could scarcely have been greater. In the intervening period Labour's stance towards the EU had undergone a process of radical change (as part of a comprehensive policy review) under the leadership of Neil Kinnock and John Smith,[2] and by the time Tony Blair succeeded the latter in July 1994 the party was committed to establishing a harmonious working relationship with Britain's European partners. This general evolution of Labour thinking had been paralleled by a shift in Blair's own views. At the time of his first election to parliament in 1983 Blair had strongly supported the party's current policy of withdrawal from the EC, writing in his address to the voters of Sedgefield that British membership had 'drained our natural resources and destroyed jobs'.[3] According to Stephen Wall, his senior adviser on the EU between 2000 and 2004, Blair did not really agree with the official line.[4] Others, however, take a different view, with one first-hand observer commenting that 'there is no evidence that he [Blair] was ill at ease with the stance taken by the Labour Party led by Michael Foot'.[5] Whatever the truth of the matter, what is certain is that in the course of the next few years Blair's public attitude towards Europe had become increasingly favourable and from the mid-1990s, as Leader of the Opposition, he launched regular attacks on the government for what he saw as its negative approach to the EU. If he were in power, Blair insisted, Britain would never be isolated and marginalized as it had been in the Thatcher and Major years.

Throughout the 1997 election campaign the Labour leadership was anxious to enhance its pro-European credentials. It nevertheless took a cautious line, not least because of concerns about how the eurosceptic press might react. Thus the party manifesto contained little on the subject of Britain's relations with the EU to distinguish it from that of the Conservatives. The only real difference of substance was on the issue of the Social Chapter, with Labour pledging to end the opt-out negotiated at Maastricht and the Conservatives giving a commitment to maintain it. Both manifestos expressed opposition to a federal Europe and a strong preference for the EU as a partnership of nations. In both of them, moreover, it was urged that British policy should be focused on such items as enlargement, reform of the CAP and completion of the single market. On the question of EMU, there was equally a marked similarity between the two party positions. While keeping open the possibility of joining the single currency, the Conservatives stressed the importance of the opt-out and a referendum. Labour, for its part, spoke of 'formidable obstacles' to Britain joining as part of the first wave in 1999, adding that entry would only ever take place if it had been approved by the Cabinet and Parliament and in a referendum.

As the election campaign progressed, Labour caution increased in response to evidence from opinion polls suggesting a growth of eurosceptic sentiment among voters.[6] Blair reacted to Conservative taunts that his determination not to be isolated in the EU would lead him to play a subservient role by writing jingoistic articles in the *Sun* in which he proclaimed, amongst other things, his 'love for the pound' and his determination to slay the 'dragon' of a European superstate.[7] He set out his position in more measured fashion in a speech which he made in Manchester on April 21. In this speech, Blair struck a carefully calculated balance between his desire to establish better relations with Britain's EU partners and his determination to defend vital national interests, even if that meant having to stand alone. A Labour government, he said, would be prepared to consider a limited extension of QMV, but would insist on retaining a right of veto where it was felt to be necessary. As regards EMU, which he described as the 'hardest question', Blair ruled out any 'fudge' over British entry to the single currency: that would only take place, he asserted, if there was a genuine and sustainable convergence between the UK's economic cycle and those of the other countries concerned. One of the most interesting aspects of the whole speech was Blair's admission that in many areas, including EMU, the 'formal' positions adopted by the Conservatives and Labour were virtually the same. Where there was a difference, he argued, was in his party's ability to deliver what was promised:

> We agree on the maintenance of the veto in vital areas like tax and treaty change. We agree on the single market. We agree on our attitude to the single currency and the referendum. The real dividing line is between success and failure. The fundamental difference is in Party management, attitude and leadership.

Blair's advent to power at the beginning of May was received with undisguised satisfaction by most EU officials and statesmen, many of whom had by this stage become completely disillusioned with Major.[8] The new man was seen as providing a chance to make a fresh start in relations between Britain and other EU states and to repair the damage done by his predecessor. Certainly that was the prospect held out by Blair himself, as well as by his Foreign Secretary, Robin Cook, and the Europe Minister, Douglas Henderson. The message from all three and from other senior ministers was relentlessly positive: Britain's membership of the EU was presented as an opportunity rather than a threat, and it was stressed that the government would pursue a policy of 'constructive engagement', working closely with France and Germany and playing a central role in the direction of EU affairs instead of sulking on the sidelines.[9] Major had engaged in the same kind of well-meaning rhetoric at the start of his premiership, but had been unable to put his good intentions into practice. It remained to be seen whether this pattern of disappointed hopes and expectations would be repeated during Blair's tenure of power.

Initial indications were that the new government was in earnest about adopting a more cooperative approach to its EU partners. As early as May 4 it was announced that Britain would soon be ending its opt-out from the Social Chapter. The appointment to a key post in the Department of Trade and Industry of the prominent industrialist David Simon, who was known to be an enthusiastic supporter of the single currency, was generally interpreted as a sign that the government favoured British participation.[10] This impression was powerfully reinforced when Gordon Brown, the Chancellor of the Exchequer, disclosed his intention to hand over control of interest rate policy to the Bank of England. Brown himself claimed that the decision had nothing to do with preparations for the euro and was solely for the purposes of domestic monetary management. His protestations were taken with a large pinch of salt, however, and most expert observers viewed the move as an important preliminary step towards meeting the Maastricht convergence criteria.[11] It appears, indeed, that this was the prevalent assumption even at the Bank of England and the Treasury.[12]

Despite these auspicious beginnings, the Blair government soon ran into difficulties with the majority of its EU counterparts as well as Brussels. Its decision to reduce the rate of VAT on domestic fuel provoked a row with the Commission, being regarded as a contravention of directives on tax harmonization.[13] A disagreement arose concerning the procedural technicalities involved in reversing the British opt-out from the Social Chapter.[14] In addition, the long-running dispute over the ban on UK beef exports flared up again. Hopes of an early lifting of the embargo were quickly dashed with the rejection in June 1997 of proposals previously submitted by the Major administration to provide the basis for a partial resumption of the trade.[15] The French in particular continued to take a hard line and it was not until March 2006 that the EU standing veterinary committee finally sanctioned an end to all restrictions.[16] In the meantime, the issue remained a cause of ill-feeling between Britain and its EU partners. The problem of 'quota-hopping', the practice whereby fishermen from other EU countries operated in British-registered vessels, likewise continued to be a source of persistent friction, notwithstanding misleading claims by Blair that he had secured adequate protection of national interests in the matter at the Amsterdam European Council of June 1997.

At a more fundamental level, it soon became apparent that the Blair government's strategic thinking on the EU diverged in a number of important respects from that of most of its partners. Its circumspect approach towards the Social Chapter was symptomatic of the gap that existed. Having agreed to end the British opt-out, the new government quickly set limits on how far it was prepared to go. This was in keeping with prior assurances that had been given to employers both privately and in a special election manifesto prepared for the business community in April 1997.[17] Blair, who wished to keep on good terms with the CBI, was acutely aware of its dislike of the Social Chapter. He himself had mixed feelings about it and lost little time in making it clear that he was against any significant enlargement of its scope of the kind that was currently being prepared by the Social Affairs Commissioner, Padraig Flynn. Speaking at a mini summit held at Noordvijk on May 23 and again at a meeting of European Socialists at Malmö on June 6, he warned that his government would not agree to a raft of new regulations which might damage the competitiveness of British industry. This was a hint of some of the difficulties that were to arise in the lead-up to the Amsterdam European Council of June 16–17.

At both Malmö and Noordvijk Blair set out his vision for the future development of the EU, adumbrating a number of themes which were to run like a continuous thread through his ten-year tenure of power. At the top of his agenda was tackling unemployment. This was to be done by means of a strategy based on job creation rather than job protection, the main features of which would be reducing excessive bureaucracy, especially as it applied to small businesses, completing the single market, promoting labour flexibility and 'keeping a watchful eye on the Social Chapter' to prevent it from becoming too costly and intrusive. The overall aim was to raise the efficiency of the EU economy towards the American level and thereby enable it to compete successfully not only with the US, but also with emerging industrial giants such as China and India. Other priorities for Blair included enlargement of the EU and a radical overhaul of the CAP. He also called for more attention to be paid to meeting the concerns and aspirations of ordinary citizens and less to debating esoteric issues which were of interest only to a narrow political elite. As he said at Malmö: 'We must stop talking about European theology and start doing things from which real people see real benefits'.[18]

With its emphasis on economic reform, market forces and the need to reconnect with 'the people', the programme outlined by Blair represented in many ways a continuation of ideas enunciated by Major, notably in an article which the latter contributed to *The Economist* in September 1993.[19] There was one aspect, however, that was authentic Blair. This was the reference to a 'third way', a concept which he had been developing and seeking to promote, in enthusiastic partnership with President Clinton, for several years. Blair dealt with the idea in more detail in the speech with which he launched the British presidency of the EU during the period January–June 1998. Outlining the main themes of the presidency, he said:

> First, we must build support for what we call the third way in Europe. The focus of economic reform should be a social model based on improving the employability of the European workforce.
>
> This means education not regulation, skills and technology, not costs and burdens, and open competitions and markets, not protectionism. There is a way between the old-style intervention and laissez-faire and we must take it. The crucial tests will be in completing the Single Market and in labour market reforms.

There has been much debate about whether the idea of a 'third way' ever amounted to much more than a political gimmick, with one historian dismissing it as 'vogue-ish and insubstantial'.[20] In so far as it did constitute a coherent political philosophy, it embodied an attempt to adapt social democracy to the realities of the late twentieth and early twenty-first centuries. Paradoxically, most of the EU leaders who showed an initial interest in Blair's 'third way' were not Social Democrats. Gerhard Schröder, the SPD leader who replaced Kohl as German chancellor in September 1998, was something of an exception, producing a joint paper on the subject with Blair, *Europe: The Third Way/Die Neue Mitte*. The publication made little impact in Germany, however, and Schröder's own enthusiasm proved to be short-lived, partly because of a critical reaction from within his own party. In France, the attitude of the left-wing government of Lionel Jospin, which assumed power in June 1997, was from the outset openly sceptical, not least because the doctrine was seen as being essentially Anglo-American (Scott 2004: 22–21; Seldon *et al.* 2005: 132–33).

The 'third way' was meant to make possible the simultaneous pursuit of two potentially conflicting goals: economic efficiency and social justice. The approach was seen to be applicable in both the domestic and the foreign spheres. At home, it found expression in efforts to reform the welfare state and public services in general through the introduction of business methods. In the European context, the 'third way' was presented as a compromise between, on the one hand, the traditional continental emphasis upon state intervention and social protection and, on the other, the British preference for deregulation and economic liberalism.

Blair's preoccupation with a 'third way' epitomized his determination to shake up existing economic and political structures both in Britain and in the EU as a whole. So far as the EU was concerned, his overriding objective was to equip it to meet the new challenges presented by globalization. What this entailed for Blair was an abandonment of shibboleths which had long held sway among most of the member states, including France and Germany. Foremost among these was the automatic assumption that progress could only be achieved through ever closer integration and the extension of harmonization to more and more fields. For Blair such a credo was the product of particular historical circumstances which no longer obtained and reflected the thinking of an older generation of European leaders whose ideas on European integration had been born out of their personal experiences of the Second World War and the immediate post-war years.

As a man who was only in his early forties when he formed his first government, Blair was necessarily untouched by such influences. His attitude was shaped less by a resolve to prevent another European Armageddon than by a mission to modernize and promote greater efficiency. In essence, what he aimed to do was to extend to other EU states the guiding principles of New Labour's domestic programme of economic and social reform and in doing so to update the current European model. His ambition, in other words, was to provide the framework for a thriving enterprise culture, through deregulation, the elimination of remaining obstacles to a single market, especially in energy, telecommunications and financial services, and the promotion of more flexible market conditions.

Blair was not alone among EU leaders in seeking such reforms. His main allies in the early years included the centre-right Spanish and Italian Prime Ministers Jose Maria Aznar and Silvio Berlusconi; and it was they, along with the Portuguese Premier Antonio Gutteres and Blair himself, who helped to secure at the Lisbon European Council of March 2000 the adoption of proposals intended to make the EU 'the most competitive and dynamic knowledge-based economy in the world' within ten years. Focusing as it did on increased investment in education, training and research, the Lisbon Agenda stood as a powerful symbol of the direction in which the Blair government wanted the EU to move. By contrast, the CAP was regarded by the same government as one of the most serious impediments to modernization since it absorbed a massive share of EU expenditure, at least some of which might be channelled more productively into research and technological innovation. Not unexpectedly, this was a viewpoint which commanded little sympathy in France, the principal beneficiary of the CAP, and persistent British attempts to prune agricultural spending provoked fierce opposition from Jacques Chirac, the French President (1995–2007). Given the strength of the French farming lobby, any other course would have meant political suicide. Quite apart from this consideration, Chirac regarded his clash with Blair on this particular issue as being part of a much wider struggle, the outcome of which would determine whether or not the EU would henceforward be dominated by the free market approach favoured by the British. For a man who famously dismissed neo-liberalism as the 'new communism', such a prospect was abhorrent.

For much of his premiership Blair was to be engaged in a prolonged, and sometimes acrimonious, debate with Chirac and other EU leaders about the EU's long-term future. When he first took office, however, his government was immediately faced by a number of specific issues which needed to be addressed without delay. The most urgent of these was the negotiation of a new EU treaty.

By the beginning of May 1997, preparations for this treaty were entering their final stage. The process, initiated in Turin in March of the previous year, was due to be completed at the Amsterdam European Council of June 16–17 and the new government therefore had less than seven weeks to prepare its negotiating position. Henderson, the Europe Minister, gave the first official indication of what that was likely to be when he set out its main features at a meeting with his EU counterparts in Brussels on May 5. From the statement made by Henderson and from London's subsequent reactions to the various draft treaties emerging from the IGC, it was evident that the new government shared many of the basic reservations felt by its predecessor about closer integration and that this was likely to cause difficulties. The French, German and most other EU governments were pressing for more use of majority voting. They also wanted to see a pooling of sovereignty in spheres that were currently in the second and third pillars of the complicated three-pillared structure established by the Maastricht Treaty and therefore on an intergovernmental basis: defence, foreign policy and justice and home affairs. The response from the British government was largely negative. It had no difficulty in accepting an extension of QMV to such areas as anti-fraud measures, regional aid and environmental policy. At the same time, it was not prepared to give up the national veto on a number of key matters, including taxation, defence and security, immigration and treaty changes.

From the outset the Blair government made it clear that it was opposed, as the Conservatives had been, to the idea floated by France and Germany that the WEU should be absorbed into the legal framework of the EU, fearing that this might pave the way to a fully fledged common defence policy which would pose a threat to the primacy of NATO. The most that it was prepared to concede was that some broad principles might be laid down governing EU involvement in peace-keeping and humanitarian missions of the sort assigned to the WEU by the 1992 Petersberg Agreement. The government was equally opposed to proposals for incorporating the Schengen agreements into the new treaty in order to eliminate border restrictions between all of the 15 member states of the EU. What it demanded was that Britain should be given a legally binding guarantee, written into the Amsterdam Treaty, of its right to retain permanent control over its own frontier checks. Other member states were generally sympathetic to this claim, readily acknowledging that Britain, along with Ireland, should be treated as a special case because of its island status.[21] The British government was, in any case, in a strong bargaining position since its consent was needed to permit incorporation of the Schengen agreements into the new EU treaty, a goal to which other governments attached great importance.

There was one further important point on which the Blair government found itself out of step with most of its EU partners in the run-up to the Amsterdam European Council. Ironically, this arose from attempts to avoid deadlocks by introducing a greater element of flexibility into decision-making. As was noted in Chapter 4, during the early part of 1997 a great deal of attention had been focused on the possibility of a 'multi-speed' or 'variable geometry' EU whereby a group of member states might agree to share sovereignty in certain areas without the participation of the rest. The idea was not without appeal for the Major government, which saw it as a way to avoid being dragged along unwillingly in a general drive to deeper integration. Approaching the matter from a different angle, after some initial misgivings, Kohl and Chirac increasingly came to regard selective pooling of sovereignty as a useful tool for overcoming British obstructionism. There was, in any case, a growing recognition all round that the admission of ten or more new states within the next few years made it essential to have greater flexibility if the EU was not to be reduced to deadlock. While accepting the logic of this analysis, the Blair government, like its predecessor, saw a real danger that Britain might be marginalized if an inner core of states, headed by France and Germany, decided to forge ahead with further integration. It therefore insisted that such selective pooling of sovereignty should not be permitted in some spheres, including the single market and defence, and that in all others there must be stringent safeguards to protect the interests of those countries which chose not to take part.

The central purpose of the Amsterdam European Council was to finalize the work of the IGC and produce a treaty which prepared the way for a successful enlargement of the EU to up to 27 members by the early years of the new millennium. In this, it was only partially successful. Indeed, the

Amsterdam Treaty contained a tacit admission of this in its provision for the convening of another IGC to complete unfinished business in the near future.

The reforms which the treaty brought about fell well short in a number of important respects of what was originally envisaged when the IGC began. Some useful changes were made in the workings of the EP. Its size was capped and its functions were rationalized. In addition, it acquired the power to approve or reject nominees for the post of President of the Commission, as well as an enhanced role in co-decision with the Council of Ministers. The scope of the co-decision procedure was extended to several new policy areas. The use of QMV in the Council of Ministers was similarly broadened in scope. It proved impossible, however, to reach agreement over changes to the weighting of votes or to the composition of the EU Commission. As had already been agreed, the Schengen agreements were incorporated into the new treaty, with signatories being required to remove all internal frontier controls within five years. Britain and Ireland were permitted to retain their own border checks, while being granted the right to collaborate with the others at any time and to the extent that they wished. Common procedures and standards were to be introduced for dealing with immigration, asylum, visas and other matters relating to the EU's external frontiers, and policy decisions concerning these questions were to be decided by QMV after a period of five years from the coming into force of the treaty. In addition, the jurisdiction of the European Court of Justice was extended to this sphere.

As regards foreign and defence policy, the formulae agreed in this part of the treaty were extraordinarily convoluted – deliberately so in the opinion of one well informed observer in order to paper over irreconcilable differences.[22] The British and those who shared their views on the importance of doing nothing that might undermine NATO (the Danes, the Austrians, the Irish, the Finns and the Swedes) succeeded in blocking the incorporation of the WEU into the EU. On the other hand, the treaty did call for progress towards a common defence policy and established the principle of EU involvement in humanitarian and peace-keeping tasks. Despite British resistance, moreover, the power of veto in foreign policy decision-making was somewhat weakened.

A major innovation in the Amsterdam Treaty was the inclusion of a special section dealing with flexible decision-making. In this, a mechanism was established to enable some EU states to move towards closer integration in certain areas without needing to wait for others. As the British government had insisted, this procedure was subject to strict conditions to protect the interests of non-participants.

A further innovation in the treaty was that for the first time the promotion of a high level of employment was laid down as one of the EU's main objectives. Most of the measures set out for furthering this goal were permissive and it was emphasized that responsibility for employment policy rested principally with individual governments. Supplementing the chapter on employment was a resolution on economic growth and employment. This was strong on exhortations to share experiences and examine good practices, but weak on financial and institutional support. Arrangements were made for a 'summit on jobs' to be held in the autumn in Luxembourg, the intention being that this would serve as a forum for exchanging ideas and information on how to tackle unemployment. The British government viewed the projected meeting as an ideal opportunity to publicize its 'welfare to work' programme.

Finally, in addition to this side agreement on employment there was another one concerning the problem of quota-hopping. Although Blair claimed that this fulfilled his pledge to protect the interests of the British fishing industry, the reality was much less impressive. All that he had obtained was an inconclusive exchange of letters between himself and Santer, the President of the EU Commission, in which the latter simply pointed out the existence of a long-standing legal remedy against quota-hopping which was available to all EU members and which was already well known to the British government, This was a far cry from a protocol completely outlawing the practice which Blair had originally declared to be his objective.

It might be said that Blair's exaggerated claims on this particular point epitomized his general presentation of what he had achieved at Amsterdam. Disregarding the new treaty's shortcomings and echoing Major's jubilant reaction at the close of the Maastricht negotiations, Blair told the Commons on June 18 that what had been agreed represented a triumph for his government and for Britain. The treaty, he said, protected essential national interests on immigration, defence and foreign policy. It would also encourage the development of job skills and a flexible labour market, and was based squarely on the prescription offered by the British government for dealing with unemployment within the EU. Not surprisingly, the verdict delivered by the Conservative Opposition was less flattering. The main thrust of the onslaught launched by Major, who was soon to be replaced as party leader by William Hague, was that the government had surrendered to pressure for closer integration on defence, asylum and immigration and employment. In a similar vein, Michael Howard, the Shadow Foreign Secretary, complained that the treaty marked 'an unacceptable step towards an integrated federal superstate'. Taking a more moderate line, Kenneth Clarke spoke of it as a 'balanced document' which 'did not involve some fundamental transfer of power to Brussels'.[23]

It is hard to disagree with this last assessment. The institutional changes brought about by the Amsterdam Treaty undoubtedly fell well short of initial expectations. They were also a good deal less substantial than those negotiated at Maastricht five years earlier. Indeed, the obvious lack of appetite for more radical reform on the part of those involved in the negotiations reflected a general reaction against the Maastricht Treaty and its ambitious plans for deeper integration. Over the next few years this tendency was to become increasingly evident, as major problems were encountered over ratification of the Treaty of Nice (2003) and the new EU constitution (2004).

The Amsterdam Treaty left various unresolved issues to be settled. It remained to be seen how the arrangements agreed for reducing unemployment would actually be implemented. A number of major institutional reforms needed to be carried out before enlargement of the EU could take place. In addition, many critical decisions had to be taken regarding the launch of the euro. The period following the Amsterdam European Council saw much hard bargaining on all these matters, with the Blair government seeking to play a leading role, especially after Britain assumed the EU presidency in January 1998.

In the lead-up to the planned Luxembourg job summit, which was scheduled to take place in mid-November, it soon became apparent that there were competing views on how to deal with the problem of unemployment. Broadly speaking there were two main schools of thought on the subject. First, there was the approach favoured by the French in particular, according to which the most effective way to create new jobs was by giving Brussels more power to co-ordinate policy, set targets and provide the necessary funding to meet them. The other approach, which was associated above all with the British government, laid greater emphasis on deregulation, more labour market flexibility and the encouragement of small and medium-sized enterprises. In the event, the employment blueprint unveiled by the EU Commission on October 1 drew upon both of these models. The plan, which aimed at the creation of 12 million new jobs over the next five years, acknowledged the need for greater flexibility and called upon governments to compare each others' performances in tackling unemployment. At the same time, it stressed the importance of job security and set specific targets for increasing the number of those on job creation schemes in the EU as a whole. The package of proposals which emerged from the job summit on November 21 likewise reflected a combination of the two approaches. According to Blair, the outcome demonstrated that there was broad backing for the line advocated by the British government.

In the meantime, preparations for the opening of formal negotiations on enlargement had been proceeding without any serious setbacks. On July 16 1997 the EU Commission announced that six of the total number of 12 applicants had met the necessary criteria for membership established at the Copenhagen European Council of June 1993: Hungary, Poland, the Czech Republic, Estonia, Slovenia and Cyprus. It was confidently expected that these would become full members by 2002. Another five applicants – Bulgaria, Romania, Slovakia, Latvia and Lithuania – received a clear signal that they were next in line. Admission of the final applicant, Turkey, raised some highly sensitive political issues and it was regarded as highly improbable that it would happen in the near future.

It was self-evident that the accession of such a large number of widely differing states would impose enormous strains on the EU. The central problem was how to accommodate the diverse interests of all the new members while at the same time avoiding unacceptable sacrifices for existing ones. The total failure at Amsterdam to grasp the nettle and make necessary changes in the composition of the EU Commission or in the weighting of votes in the Council of Ministers provided an early warning of how difficult this task might be.

Britain was perhaps the most committed supporter of enlargement and was to remain so throughout the next decade. Although the argument was never spelt out explicitly, the Blair government undoubtedly shared the long-standing assumption of previous British policymakers that one of the most effective ways of countering moves towards closer integration was to increase the number of EU states. It was thought desirable to admit the eastern European countries, recently freed from Soviet control, in order to strengthen their democratic institutions. In addition, the Blair government attached great weight to the economic advantages to be gained from trading in a much bigger internal market. While there was general support for enlargement among other EU governments, some of them tended to be less enthusiastic. The French had never been more than lukewarm about it, fearing that it would lead both to institutional paralysis and to a diminution of their own influence within the EU: their instinctive preference was to concentrate instead on deeper integration. Some of the smaller states were worried about a possible reduction in their voting power, while those which were receiving generous EU subsidies, like Greece, Ireland, Italy and Spain, were understandably reluctant to see them being channelled instead to economically backward newcomers. The reservations felt by the German government centred on the financial implications of the enlargement. The costs would undoubtedly be huge and if past experience was any guide Germany was almost certain to pay a disproportionately large share of the bill.[24]

The issue triggered an acrimonious debate which was to rumble on for several years and which was to focus in its latter stages on the British budget rebate and reform of the CAP. What enlargement did was to bring to the surface latent dissatisfaction among some member states, and Germany in particular, about their respective contributions to the EU budget. Germany was by far the largest net contributor, followed by Britain, the Netherlands and Sweden. All the other member states were net gainers. During the summer of 1997, Chancellor Kohl began to express impatience with the current situation, calling for a fairer system linking contributions to national GDP. This marked the beginning of a sustained campaign for reform that was to culminate in his demand at the Cardiff European Council of June 1998 for a cap on Germany's budget contributions and a rebate similar to that enjoyed by Britain since 1984. The Netherlands and Sweden also pressed for a better deal for themselves. Such changes could only be brought about by unanimous vote, however, and would depend on the willingness of others to make concessions. The uncompromising response from Blair was that whatever else might be changed the British rebate was not negotiable.[25]

While this financial wrangling was taking place, various plans were being drawn up in preparation for enlargement. The EU Commission's main contribution to this process was a document entitled *Agenda 2000: For a Stronger and Wider Union*, issued on July 16 1997 and containing proposals for a radical restructuring of the CAP and the system of regional funding. Between them these two items accounted for almost four-fifths of the EU budget. The CAP was a particularly heavy drain on resources, absorbing some 50 per cent of a total annual expenditure of £60 billion. Although some changes had been introduced in 1992, they had failed to achieve the desired cutbacks and the Commission warned in *Agenda 2000* of the need for further action to avert a crisis of overproduction. The prospective accession of Poland and the other central and eastern European states made major reform imperative, not least because any attempt to extend the existing regime to regions where a quarter of the population worked in agriculture would be financially ruinous.[26]

The Blair government had consistently attacked the CAP as indefensibly wasteful. It is therefore not surprising that it welcomed the Commission's proposed reforms – even though some of them were considered to be disadvantageous to British farmers.[27] The reaction from some of the other EU governments, however, was decidedly hostile. This was especially so in the case of the French and the stage was thus set for a long-running and bitter squabble over reform of the CAP between Blair and Chirac.

Of all the issues to be addressed by the British government after the Amsterdam European Council, the launch of the euro was the most challenging by far. It provided the acid test of Blair's claim that Britain was now one of the leading players in the EU. One obvious problem for the government was that it had to work to an extremely tight timetable. The projected starting date was January 1 1999. Under the Maastricht Treaty, however, any country wishing to be in from the beginning was required to give notice of its intentions before the end of 1997. This stipulation left very little time in which to make all the necessary practical and legislative preparations, especially since the government was committed by its election manifesto to hold a referendum on the matter.

Extraordinary though it may seem, Blair appears to have believed that he could persuade Britain's partners to allow some additional time for reaching a decision: at a meeting held soon after the 1997 election and attended by Jonathan Powell, his Chief of Staff, Robin Butler, the Cabinet Secretary, Nigel Wicks, the Second Permanent Secretary at the Treasury, Ed Balls, Gordon Brown's economic adviser and Brown himself, he allegedly indicated that he might telephone his friend, Helmut Kohl, to ask him if the project could be delayed until Britain was ready to take part.[28] Needless to say, there was never the remotest chance of such a postponement at the British leader's behest. Nor was there any realistic prospect, as Blair and Brown seemed to think initially, that the launch might be deferred because of difficulties experienced by a number of states, including France and Germany, in meeting the Maastricht criteria on debt and inflation levels. By the autumn of 1997 the economic and fiscal situation in both of these countries was beginning to look a great deal healthier than it had done only a few months earlier: the improvement in the French position was so dramatic, indeed, that the Jospin government felt able to call for the EMU timetable to be speeded up. On October 14 the European Commission published a report indicating that all EU states, with the sole exception of Greece, were on course to qualify for membership of the euro zone from its inception. This effectively banished any lingering doubts about beginning on time.

Against this background, the government was urged by supporters of British membership of the single currency to sign up as soon as was practically possible. The former Chancellor Kenneth Clarke was a prominent advocate of this course of action, arguing that there would probably never be a better opportunity. The government had just received an overwhelming mandate from the electorate and enjoyed a massive parliamentary majority. It had inherited a strong economy. The popularity of Blair himself, both within his own party and in the country at large, was exceptionally high. According to Clarke, there was thus a compelling case for acting boldly and swiftly in order to take advantage of this highly favourable combination of circumstances. Delay could only make the task harder, Clarke maintained, since the honeymoon period would not last indefinitely and the government was bound to run into difficulties in other areas of policy which would weaken its overall authority.[29]

Even Clarke could not have realised quite how prescient his warnings were to prove. Hostility to the euro hardened during the late 1990s and early 2000s. The government's parliamentary majority was reduced as a result of the 2001 and 2005 general elections. More seriously, Blair suffered a disastrous fall in his personal ratings. A key factor here was the Iraq War, which began in March 2003, and the loss of trust that it cost him. After 2003, and largely because of the war and its aftermath, he increasingly lacked the authority to win support for a policy that was in any case generally unpopular. At the same time there was increasing restiveness and indiscipline within the Labour Party over a wide range of issues, including foreign policy, pensions, university top-up fees and private finance initiatives in the NHS and elsewhere. Matters were made worse by Blair's unwise announcement after the 2005 general election that he did not intend to stay on as Prime Minister for the full five-year term. This marked the beginning of a period of debilitating speculation about the precise date on which he would be stepping down, the effect of which was to reduce his status to that of a 'lame duck' leader. From the tactical point of view, Blair's difficulties over entry to the euro were compounded by the debate over a new constitution for Europe during 2004–5. The proposed constitutional treaty provoked widespread opposition in the UK and the controversy surrounding it made it even harder for Blair to rally enough support for membership of the euro zone. The treaty's rejection by the French and Dutch electors in May/June 2005 put an end not only to the possibility of an early adoption of the new constitution, but also to the chances of a British referendum on the single currency in the near future.

At the time of writing (2009), when Britain is arguably as far away as ever from adopting the euro – notwithstanding recent claims to the contrary by the President of the EU Commission Barroso – there is now broad agreement that the early part of the first Blair government was probably the best time to sign up.[30] It is equally agreed, however, that there was never any real possibility of that happening. According to Terence Burns, then the Permanent Secretary at the Treasury, there was 'not a cat in hell's chance of joining in the first wave'.[31] This was certainly not because of any difficulty in meeting the key economic and financial preconditions established at Maastricht. Unlike many of the other EU states, including France, Germany and Italy, Britain was at this time in a position to satisfy them with ease, as Brown indicated in his first budget statement on July 2 1997, in the process provoking groundless eurosceptic fears that the government was making preparations for entry on the launch date.[32] The hesitation and reluctance shown by Blair and his colleagues proceeded from other factors.

To begin with, the weight of expert opinion that was available to them strongly suggested that entry to the euro in January 1999 would be risky and might well have a damaging impact on the economy. On more than one occasion Eddie George, the Governor of the Bank of England, who was in the habit of describing himself as either a 'Europragmatist' or a 'Eurorealist', expressed misgivings about a fundamental lack of convergence between the UK and other EU business cycles.[33] The Treasury likewise had serious doubts on this score. In addition, it warned that adopting the single currency on the launch date would mean public spending cuts of some £20 billion or an increase in taxation equivalent to 10p in the pound on the standard rate of income tax.[34]

The only senior figure at the Treasury who was in any way favourable towards the euro was Nigel Wicks, the Second Permanent Secretary, who (as chairman of the EU's monetary committee) had played a key role in making the necessary technical preparations for its introduction. The rest, including Terence Burns, the Permanent Secretary, Alan Budd, the Chief Economic Adviser, and Robert Culpin, the Director of Public Spending, were against British entry. As for joining at the beginning of 1999, even Wicks thought that would probably be a mistake.[35]

Such a negative reaction was hardly surprising, given the Treasury's consistent record of scepticism towards the EC/EU in general and towards EMU in particular over several decades. Amongst other things, it had emphasized the heavy costs rather than the potential benefits of joining the EC at the time of the Heath application, raised objections to full participation in the EMS in 1978 and argued against acceptance of the Fontainebleau rebate deal in 1984, wishing to hold out for a better offer. Following Britain's humiliating exit from the ERM in September 1992, the Treasury's underlying scepticism had been greatly reinforced. The experience of 'Black Wednesday' and the events leading up to it had a devastating effect on Treasury morale and an exhaustive internal enquiry was immediately begun into what had gone wrong. From departmental papers released in February 2005 under the Freedom of Information Act, it can be seen that officials were appalled at the extent to which the decision to enter the ERM in 1990 had been affected by political factors, especially by tensions between Thatcher and Lawson. One of the main lessons that they drew from the whole episode was that any future attempt to participate in EMU must be dealt with on a purely financial and economic basis. Another was that it should only proceed if and when a genuinely sustainable convergence had been established between all the economies concerned.[36] These considerations continued to loom large in Treasury thinking from the mid-1990s and help to explain the department's ultra cautious approach to joining the euro in the years that followed.

A second factor contributing to government indecision was the mixed message coming from industry and commerce. While generally favourable to joining the single currency at some point, the business community was nevertheless dubious about doing so in January 1999. This was not only because many companies had so far done little by way of preparation,[37] but also because of uncertainty about the impact such a move would have on domestic interest rates and the international value of sterling. Many industrialists were worried that the strength of the pound and the current high level of British interest rates – more than 3 per cent above the EU average – were having a damaging effect on exports. They therefore lobbied the government to give a firm commitment to an early adoption of the euro as a means of exerting a downward pressure on both.[38] As against that, there were widespread fears of a consequent resurgence of inflation. This underlying ambivalence was reflected in a survey of its members published by the CBI in July 1997, the results of which were described by the organization's director general, Adair Turner, as representing a 'contingent yes' to the question of whether Britain should join the euro. Although only 6 per cent of respondents expressed opposition in principle, a substantial majority were against being part of the first wave, mainly on the grounds that it would have inflationary consequences.[39]

Third, the government was extremely nervous about the public's attitude towards the euro and far from confident about securing approval for its adoption in the event of a referendum. Focus studies organized by Philip Gould revealed the existence of strong opposition to joining and this tendency was confirmed in the findings of numerous opinion polls (Rawnsley 2001: 76). A survey conducted by British Social Attitudes in October 1997 was typical, showing that 61 per cent of UK residents were in favour of keeping the pound, with only 17 per cent wishing to see it replaced by the euro. Similar results emerged from a poll by MORI in the same month, this time about how people would vote in a referendum.[40]

Equally disturbing for the government was the stance taken by large sections of the press.[41] With a few exceptions such as the *Guardian*, the *Independent,* the *Financial Times* and the *Daily Mirror,* the majority of newspapers, both broadsheets and tabloids, were highly sceptical in their approach to the EU in general and to monetary union in particular. The *Daily Mail*,[42] Conrad Black's *Daily Telegraph* and *Sunday Telegraph*, and the four British newspapers in the Rupert Murdoch News International empire – *The Times*, the *Sunday Times*, the *News of the World* and the *Sun* – were all fiercely opposed to signing up for the single currency. They could be guaranteed to launch a fierce onslaught on the government at the slightest indication that it might be planning to do so, accusing it of 'selling out' British interests.

Blair was extremely worried (as was his press secretary, Alastair Campbell) about the impact this would have both on the government's general popularity and on its chances of holding a successful referendum on the euro. He was especially anxious about the likely reaction from the *Sun*, whose backing he had only recently secured and was desperate to retain. Described by one inside observer as 'the tabloid that wields the most clout at No. 10' (Peston 2006: 197), the *Sun* was reputed to have a significant influence over large swathes of the electorate. Understandably, therefore, the newly-installed Prime Minister had little relish for the prospect of holding a referendum in which it was to be found campaigning against the government line. Blair's preoccupation with the damage that could be inflicted by the *Sun* was to be a permanent feature of his period in power, with no effort being spared to keep its eurosceptic proprietor on side. Meetings with Murdoch himself or with one of his trusted aides were frequent and usually conducted in great secrecy. So close were the links, indeed, that it seemed to one of New Labour's 'spin doctors' that Murdoch was 'like the 24th member of the Cabinet. His voice was rarely heard (the same could have been said of many of the other 23) but his presence was always felt'.[43]

A further impediment to early entry to the euro was the disagreement that the issue generated at the very top of the government. Each of the three main figures within the Cabinet – Blair, Brown and Cook – held different views on the matter and this in itself precluded the adoption of a clear and coherent policy. In the summer of 1997 Brown was favourably inclined, although not to the extent that he was generally thought to be and already beginning to change his mind. Cook was perhaps the most sceptical of ministers, having made a speech in the run-up to the general election ruling out entry to the euro for the duration of Labour's first term.[44] As for Blair, his attitude was essentially pragmatic: while appreciating the potential benefits of membership of the single currency to the UK, to the government and to himself, he was also anxious about the economic and political risks that were involved.

Overall, then, there were many reasons for the government's cautious approach to taking Britain into the euro in January 1999. As a matter of fact, both Blair and Brown quickly realised that taking part in the first wave was not a feasible option (D. Scott: 2004: 213). Yet neither was prepared to say so publicly. In the case of Blair, this was principally because he wished to preserve as important a role as possible for Britain in the critical negotiations preceding the launch of the euro. Even at this early stage, however, there were already clear indications that he was using a tactic which was later to become his stock-in-trade when dealing with EU (and other) issues – sending at one and the same time contradictory messages to different audiences. On the one hand, the eurosceptic press and eurosceptic opinion in general were appeased by the strong emphasis placed on the 'formidable obstacles' standing in the way of British entry to the single currency. On the other, the reassuring impression conveyed to fellow EU leaders, Brussels and supporters of the euro at home was that going in was merely a matter of waiting for the right time and circumstances. About a month after taking office, for instance, Blair told the President of the EU Commission Santer that 'although Britain was unable to join [the euro] in 1999, he hoped any delay would be short'.[45] It is small wonder that one of his biographers has concluded that 'the euro saw Blair at his most enigmatic'.[46]

In the case of Brown, there were incipient signs of what was to become an obsessive secrecy over matters that he regarded as being within his competence alone. Not only did he say little about his plans regarding the euro to the general public: even senior Treasury officials, including Burns, in whom he had little confidence, were kept in the dark about his intentions. They were left assuming that he wanted to see Britain in as soon as possible.[47] Blair himself was another victim of Brown's determination to keep his cards as close to his chest as possible, only discovering at the last moment the contents of a major speech that the Chancellor was due to make about the single currency at Chatham House on July 17 1997 (D. Scott 2004: 214). Declaring that the government was 'throwing open the EMU debate', Brown used the speech to announce the appointment of a group of business leaders to advise on practical preparations for adoption of the euro – a forerunner of the more broadly based committee set up in February 1999 to oversee the National Changeover Plan. This apart, no new light was shed on government intentions. The official line set out by Brown remained what it had been since New Labour came to power. A decision on entry to the euro would be taken on the basis of a 'hard-headed assessment' of whether it was in the national interest. In principle, the government was in favour of going in, seeing significant potential benefits for the UK through an elimination of exchange rate risks, lower international transaction costs, a long-term reduction in interest rates and a greater degree of financial stability. At the same time, it was 'highly unlikely' that Britain would be joining in 1999.

Continuing uncertainty on the key question of whether Britain would be taking part in the first wave inevitably gave rise to periodic bouts of market speculation, and it was one of these which eventually obliged the government to clarify its position. On September 26 1997 the *Financial Times* carried an article by Robert Peston under the headline 'Cabinet shifts towards EMU'. Said to be based on information from an unnamed minister, the article was widely interpreted as a signal from the government that it was about to adopt a more proactive approach to EMU. The impact was immediate, with shares and gilts soaring and the pound suffering a dramatic fall. In typically robust fashion, Charlie Whelan, Brown's press adviser and general factotum since

1994, dismissed the story as 'lies and bollocks'. Not surprisingly, Whelan's colourful intervention did little to calm market nerves. More sober denials of any impending change of policy from Brown and Cook proved equally ineffective and there followed what has been aptly described as a 'Whitehall farce' (Routledge 1998: 325).

For nearly a month sensational reports appeared in the *Daily Mail*, the *Independent*, the *Times* and other newspapers, most of them inspired by leaks and briefings from members of the warring Blair and Brown factions: Alastair Campbell operating in the former camp and Balls and Whelan in the latter. It was rumoured that Brown was trying to bounce Blair into an early decision in favour of joining the single currency. An alternative theory had them working together to 'talk up' the likelihood of British membership soon after the launch, their motives being to prepare the City and the public for entry, to strengthen the government's hand in euro negotiations with Britain's EU partners and to help exporters by encouraging a fall in the value of sterling. Confusion reigned and the government came under mounting pressure from the CBI, the Conservative Opposition and other quarters to give a definitive statement of policy. Before the crisis erupted Brown had been planning to make such a statement in mid-November. It was now deemed prudent to do so at an earlier date.[48]

On 27 October 1997 Brown made his much-anticipated statement in the Commons.[49] His own and the Treasury's original instinct had been that it would be best to rule out unconditionally the possibility of entry to the euro not only in January 1999, but for the whole of the current Parliament. In the event, however, he added the proviso 'barring some fundamental and unforeseen change in economic circumstances'. This qualifying phrase was of little practical significance and had only been added in response to pressure from Blair and his closest political associate Peter Mandelson, the most pro-euro member of the Cabinet, both of whom wished to keep open at least some faint chance that Britain might join in the near future (Peston 2006: 213–14).

Brown left no room for doubt about the government's basically favourable attitude. 'We are', he said, 'the first British Government to declare for the principle of monetary union'. It was announced that an intensive campaign was to begin to prepare Britain for membership should a decision be made in favour during the next Parliament. Most important of all, Brown set out five key economic tests by which the government would judge whether it was in the national interest to adopt the euro. These tests were not new, having been devised by Balls – possibly in a New York taxi cab – during a visit to the United States (with Brown) the previous February (Peston 2006: 192–93). They were: Would membership of the single currency help to create jobs? Would it promote investment in the UK? Would it be of assistance to the City and the financial services sector? Was the EU economy strong enough and flexible enough to withstand any shocks that might occur if a single currency came into being? Was the British business cycle in harmony with those of the other member states? A 40-page Treasury document which accompanied

Brown's statement, and which had been five months in the preparation, provided a technical assessment of how far the UK economy met these tests. Its conclusions were strongly negative.

The importance of Brown's statement cannot be overstated. The fact that it was the Chancellor rather than the Prime Minister who gave it was in itself an early pointer to who would in future play the dominant role in determining policy on the euro. After October 26 there was never any real doubt that it was Brown and his Treasury team rather than Blair and the No. 10 Policy Unit who had the ultimate say. Brown had insisted that the decision on when and whether to join the single currency must be decided solely on the basis of the rigorous economic criteria set out in the five tests. By acquiescing, Blair had given him 'a permanent veto over British policy on the euro' (Riddell 2006: 135). There is some evidence that Blair initially believed that the tests might be 'conveniently elastic' (Rawnsley 2001: 86). He was soon disabused. That was never Brown's reading of the situation, and every attempt by Blair or others to include non-economic factors in the equation or to deviate from a strict interpretation of the tests was systematically rebutted. Ironically, Blair himself unwittingly tightened Brown's stranglehold over euro policy by suggesting the inclusion in his Commons statement of a stipulation that the economic benefits of British entry must be 'clear and unambiguous'. His gesture appears to have been meant as a sop to the eurosceptic press. Its unintended outcome, however, was to make it virtually impossible to demonstrate with any degree of credibility that the agreed conditions for entry had been met (Peston 2006: 215–16; D. Scott 2004: 217).

By the end of October 1997 two things at least were absolutely clear: first, that the launch of the euro would definitely go ahead on schedule and second, that the UK would not be taking part. This opened up a real danger of British marginalization. Admittedly the UK would not be completely isolated since three other countries would be absent from the starting line up – Denmark and Sweden from choice and Greece because it was judged not to have satisfied the Maastricht criteria. Even so, the fact remained that the British government faced total exclusion from policy-making not only as it related to managing the euro, but also on a much wider range of economic and financial matters.

Some of the practical disadvantages of being in this position were illustrated at a very early stage by the government's experience with the proposed 'euro council'. This was a French-inspired body, the essential purpose of which was to provide a political counterweight to the ECB. Having at first assumed that the new council would be of little significance, the British were shocked when on November 5 1997 the French and Germans unveiled a joint plan which aimed to give it extensive powers. The council was to be called euro X – the X referring to the number of states in the euro zone. Its membership was to be confined to those states. It was to meet immediately before each session of EU finance ministers (ECOFIN) and was to have a wide-ranging remit, covering such matters as EU budgetary policy, fiscal harmonization and employment.[50] Fearing that ECOFIN might be reduced to the role of a rubber stamp, the British government embarked upon a confused strategy which sought at one and the same time to smother the council at birth, restrict its functions as narrowly as possible and obtain a place on it for Britain.[51] Although they received some backing from the Danes and Swedes, the British were in a weak bargaining position: it was repeatedly pointed out to them in no uncertain terms that they had no right to take part in the activities of a club when they were not members.[52] Blair became increasingly desperate to resolve the dispute before the start of the British EU presidency in January 1998 and on December 12 a deal was finally reached after some ill-tempered discussions. Blair believed that this fully protected the interests of the four 'outs'. Events were to show, however, that his understanding of what had been agreed did not correspond with that of the French.

When Blair and Cook set out the government's agenda for the British presidency in a number of keynote speeches, the themes that they outlined had a familiar ring to them. They spoke of the need to make the EU more understandable and accountable to its citizens by taking stronger action on issues seen to be relevant to the ordinary man in the street, like employment, crime, drug trafficking, pollution and global warming. Emphasis was placed on promoting a more flexible labour market. In addition, Blair and Cook pledged to push ahead with enlargement and to cooperate fully with the launch of the euro, despite the fact that Britain would not be a participant. In the event, no real problems were encountered with regard to enlargement. As agreed at the Luxembourg European Council of December 12 1997, negotiations began with six of the candidates at the end of March 1998, while another five were officially admitted to a 'screening process'.[53] The only cloud on the horizon was the mixed reaction to the Commission's detailed proposals, released in mid-March, on reform of the CAP and regional subsidies in preparation for enlargement. From this it was clear that a great deal of hard bargaining lay ahead.

The launch of the euro presented greater and more immediate difficulties. The period of the British presidency (January to June 1998) coincided with a number of crucial developments in this respect. In May 1998 EU leaders designated the founding members and decided the exchange rates at which currencies would be locked together. They also chose the first head of the ECB, the Dutch banker Wim Duisenberg, thereby bringing to an end a five-month long wrangle between France, Germany and the Netherlands.[54] On June 4 the euro council, by now known as Euro-11, held its inaugural meeting: and on June 30, the last day of the British presidency, the ECB officially came into being.

The position of the British government while all these momentous events were taking place was to say the least a curious one. Between them Blair and Brown chaired nearly all of the meetings at which key decisions relating to the launch of the euro were taken. Because of Britain's self-exclusion from the first wave, however, they were unable to play a full role in the way that most other EU leaders did. This reality of limited influence formed a stark contrast with the lofty expectations held out by Blair and Cook at the start of the presidency.

Despite Brown's Commons statement of October 27, there still remained great uncertainty about the government's intentions regarding the euro. All that was definitely known was that Britain would not be joining for the next three to four years: when it would do so, if at all, was a matter of conjecture. There was some speculation that 2002, the year when national currencies were to be replaced by euro notes and coins, might be the time of choice. The government refused to commit itself to this or any other date, however, despite strong pressure from its EU partners and Brussels.

This equivocation provoked growing impatience on the part of other EU governments and contributed to their adoption of a tougher line on two issues: the euro council and the question of whether Britain, along with the other 'outs', should be required to spend two years in the ERM before entering the euro. Blair believed that the deal agreed at the Luxembourg European Council of December 12 1997 guaranteed Britain an automatic right to be present at Euro-11 whenever topics of importance were to be discussed. It subsequently transpired that this was not the case: the eleven members of the euro zone were adamant that they alone had the power to decide when the four 'outs' were to be invited to attend. British humiliation was completed at the inaugural meeting of Euro-11 in Luxembourg on 4 June 1998. Having insisted on his right to chair the opening proceedings, Brown was then obliged to stand down in favour of the finance minister of Austria, the next country to take over the presidency. His conduct provoked an outraged reaction from other finance ministers, and the whole incident provided a telling illustration of the extent to which Britain had become sidelined on the key issue of EMU.[55]

A dispute over British membership of the ERM provided additional evidence. The Treaty of Maastricht made a two-year probationary period in the ERM an essential precondition of entering the euro. The Blair government refused to accept this stipulation, not least because of the psychological scars left by 'Black Wednesday'. All that was necessary, it argued, was to demonstrate currency stability for two years. Only the Swedes, who were in a similar situation themselves, backed the British case: the rest of the EU members were united in insisting that Britain must comply in full with the Maastricht Treaty requirement.

Largely as a result of problems that arose because of the government's anomalous position in relation to the launch of the euro, the general verdict on the British presidency was at best a mixed one. It was not surprising that the Conservatives dismissed it as a 'flop'.[56] More revealing was that the EP took the most unusual step of voting down the customary resolution congratulating the outgoing presidency.

Between the end of the British presidency and June 2003, when the Treasury finally presented its assessment on whether Britain had met the five tests, the government's official position on the euro was 'prepare and decide', a watchword which 'was to become a formula for inertia and prevarication' (Seldon et al. 2005: 330). In practical terms, there seemed little to distinguish this approach from the 'wait and see' policy of the Major government that Blair had derided when in opposition, and there was growing restiveness among supporters of British entry to the euro at the slow rate of progress towards a referendum. Blair himself was in no hurry to hold one. Nor did he wish the single currency to figure as a major issue in the forthcoming general election in 2001 (Price 2006: 14). The public's attitude remained over-whelmingly negative: a MORI poll held in November 2000 showed only 18 per cent in favour.[57] The eurosceptic press was as virulently opposed as ever. In addition, the success that the Conservatives had enjoyed in the 1999 European elections by 'fighting a very effective single-issue campaign on the euro' served as a warning of the electoral risks involved (Price 2006: 116).

Nervous about committing the government to an early referendum, Blair preferred to pursue a gradualist strategy aimed at creating an irresistible momentum in favour of joining the euro. This consisted of two interrelated elements. At the economic level, it involved cooperation between Whitehall and business in making practical preparations for the time when a decision might be taken to join. Brown fired the starting gun at the CBI conference in Birmingham on 10 November 1997, declaring: 'The euro will radically transform the whole single market. So my message is: "Let's get down together to the serious business of preparation."'[58] The process was given fresh impetus on February 23 1999 with the Commons announcement by Blair of a National Changeover Plan: an accompanying 65-page document revealed the various measures that were to be taken by the government, including changes to the computer systems of key departments in order to make them compatible with the euro.[59] Blair's statement provoked fury from the Conservative Opposition and the eurosceptic press, which accused him of trying to bounce the country into the single currency and pre-empting the promised referendum.[60] To business leaders and pro-euro politicians like Clarke, Heath, Heseltine and Paddy Ashdown, however, it was an encouraging sign that the government really meant business, with the Liberal Democrat leader applauding the fact that the government had at last 'crossed the Rubicon'.[61]

At the political level, the government was engaged in a parallel exercise of building up a cross-party pro-European alliance of the sort that had proved so effective at the time of the 1975 referendum. Gaining the cooperation of the Liberal Democrats presented few problems since the party was whole-heartedly in favour of British membership of the euro and its leader, Ashdown, was already working closely with the government in other areas, notably on constitutional reform. The real challenge was to win over leading Conservative pro-Europeans, and here Blair was aided by recent develop-ments in Conservative policy. Under the leadership of William Hague, who had been chosen to succeed Major soon after the 1997 general election, the Conservative Party had moved strongly in an anti-EU direction, calling for a referendum on the Amsterdam Treaty and ruling out entry to the single currency for the duration of two parliaments.[62] Blair's objective was to capitalize on the resulting alienation of senior Conservative pro-Europeans by persuading them to take part in his broad campaign. Apart from strengthening the informal pro-euro coalition that he was seeking to construct, this would have the added advantage of stoking up civil war within Conservative ranks. Blair had been in contact with Clarke since the summer of 1997 (Peston 2006: 191–92, 196–97). In January 1998 he was given an opportunity to sound out other prominent Conservatives when the *Independent* published a joint letter signed by a number of them, including Heath, Heseltine, Carrington, Howe and Patten, which was critical of their party's current policy and supportive of the government's general approach on EU matters and especially of its active preparation for EMU. Blair immediately seized the opening this presented by making overtures to several of the signatories about joining him in a campaign for entry to the euro.[63]

Blair's efforts ultimately bore fruit with the formation of the all-party Britain in Europe. By the time this organization was launched on October 14 1999, with Blair and Brown being joined on the platform by Clarke, Heseltine and Charles Kennedy, Ashdown's successor as leader of the Liberal Democrats, its original purpose had been transformed. At Blair's insistence, it was no longer to campaign specifically on the euro but 'on an overarching message of Britain engaging constructively in Europe, with the underlying message on the euro that you shouldn't rule out any option' (Price 2006: 122–23). The reason for Blair's change of tack is not hard to seek. Realising that the chances of winning a 'yes' vote on the question of entry to the euro were negligible, his response was to change the nature of the debate and the question to be put to voters in the proposed referendum: they would be asked to decide not whether Britain should join the single currency, but whether it should be in or out of the EU. This was a tactic that he was to repeat several years later, and under similar circumstances, in connection with the draft EU constitution. Blair could be remarkably candid about his motives, telling a group of advisers shortly after the launch of Britain in Europe that the debate 'has to be about Europe itself ... we can only win the debate on the euro by winning the wider debate about Europe' (Price 2006: 152). Not everyone agreed. Indeed, one Cabinet minister, Charlie Falconer, thought that it would be 'absurd' for Blair to go on a Britain in Europe platform and refuse to speak about the euro. 'That would be like going to an anti-abortion meeting and saying "I'm not prepared to talk about abortion, just about childbirth in general"' (Price 2006: 123).

From its inception Britain in Europe was bedevilled by underlying tensions and disagreements about tactics. Some of its leading personalities, like Clarke, Heseltine and Mandelson, wanted to see more active campaigning for entry to the euro (Price: 2006: 122–23). They were also keen to emphasize the political aspect of the matter, something which was anathema to Blair, as well as to Brown. Blair was well aware of the potential for embarrassing differences of opinion within the organization and was determined that it should fall in line with the policy that he laid down.[64] It is difficult to avoid the conclusion, indeed, that he saw Britain in Europe as a useful instrument and no more. Certainly it is not without significance in this respect that a prominent pro-European journalist was later to describe it as 'the pet of ministerial patronage'.[65] Where it was particularly useful to Blair was in providing spokesmen for a pro-European message that he was not prepared to give himself because of the eurosceptic flak to which he would be exposed. Extravagant attacks on him by the *Sun* in particular suggested the advisability of such a tactic.

Blair was rather more successful in controlling Britain in Europe than members of his own ministerial team. The government was frequently accused of failing to present a coherent policy on the euro and one of the main reasons for its undoubted weakness in this area was the existence of serious differences of opinion both between senior ministers and between their assorted aides. To begin with, the views of advisers working at No. 10 were sharply divided. Some of them, such as Stephen Wall, Jonathan Powell and Roger Liddle, strongly favoured British membership of the single currency, while others, including Alastair Campbell and Derek Scott, Blair's economic adviser since 1994, were opposed – in the case of the last-named, passionately so. Blair was thus receiving conflicting advice, with no one being able to tell which he heeded (Rawnsley 2001: 74–75). Relations and communications between the No. 10 team and Brown's economic adviser Ed Balls were notoriously difficult. At the ministerial level, moreover, Brown was often involved in clashes over the euro with two of its staunchest supporters, Cook and Mandelson, in which personal animosities and grudges probably counted at least as much as differences over policy (Bower 2007: 315–17). Brown had not forgiven Mandelson for switching his support to Blair during the 1994 leadership contest, while it was a matter of common observation that Brown and Cook always took pleasure in being on opposing sides in any argument.[66]

Having initially been highly sceptical on the question of entry to the euro, Cook had rapidly changed his mind after becoming Foreign Secretary. He was one of the few ministers to speak out publicly in favour of joining, warning of the damaging consequences of staying outside in terms of loss of inward investment and political influence. Demoted to the post of Leader of the Commons after the 2001 general election, he continued to play the role of ministerial maverick until his resignation over the Iraq war in 2003. Numerous attempts were made to rein him in and tone down his speeches when they were felt by Blair or Brown to be excessively favourable to the euro. He was not an easy man to muzzle, however, and on one occasion at least the intervention backfired spectacularly by drawing even more press attention to splits within the government.[67] Mandelson's frequent speeches on the euro presented similar problems.[68]

Brown was reported on a regular basis to be 'grumpy', 'furious' or 'livid' at the activities of both of his colleagues (Price 2006). As Mandelson complained, he had quickly developed a 'territorial fetish' over the government's policy on the euro (Bower 2007: 317): even Blair was effectively excluded from the decision-making. Brown was undoubtedly allowed an extraordinary degree of independence in the conduct of all aspects of economic and social policy, including that on the single currency. This was partly because of the notorious deal reached in 1994 at the Granita restaurant in Islington, by which Brown agreed not to stand in Labour's leadership contest in return for being given both a free hand in those policy areas and (according to Brown) an assurance that Blair would make way for him in the not too distant future.[69] The situation also reflected the fact that Blair had little knowledge of or interest in economic policy and was content to leave it to his Chancellor, especially since the economy appeared to be thriving under his stewardship. Although the arrangement worked well on the whole, serious tensions developed over policy on the single currency.

When he first became Chancellor, Brown was generally thought to be one of the most europhile members of the government and strongly in favour of British entry to the euro. Nor was there anything at that stage to suggest otherwise. As Shadow Secretary for Trade and Industry and later as Shadow Chancellor, he gave wholehearted backing to British membership of the ERM and often spoke in favour, at least in principle, of joining the single currency. Once in office, moreover, his decision to give monetary independence to the Bank of England was seen as being a strong pointer to early entry. What was not appreciated at the time, however, was that Brown already had doubts about whether it was really in the national interest to go in. A key factor in sowing these doubts was Britain's enforced departure from the ERM in 1992, the experience of which was, in the words of one expert commentator, 'probably the most important moment in his [Brown's] European education' (Peston 2006: 182). The debacle 'shaped for ever his views about the practicalities of embarking on a great economic adventure of that kind. The fear of joining the euro at the wrong rate and the wrong time overwhelmed his innate pro-Europeanism when he became Chancellor' (Peston 2006: 186).

As Chancellor, Brown became more and more convinced that taking Britain into the euro would be an unjustified gamble. His own doubts were reinforced by those of senior Treasury officials and above all by the advice that he received from Ed Balls, his economic adviser and closest confidant since 1994. It would be hard to overstate the role that Balls played in providing an intellectual case for the reservations felt by his political master. An economist by profession and a former journalist with the *Financial Times,* Balls was a longstanding critic of EMU. He took a strong line against joining the euro during Labour's first term, arguing that the British economy was neither strong enough nor flexible enough to withstand any serious shocks that it might suffer in the euro zone (Peston 2006: 202). But his objections to entry were of a more fundamental nature. As early as 1992, he wrote a Fabian Society discussion paper entitled 'Euro-Monetarism: why Britain was ensnared and how it should escape', in which he attacked the Maastricht blueprint for EMU as 'an economically and politically misconceived project' whose inflation and fiscal convergence criteria were likely to lead to low growth and high unemployment (Peston 2006: 186–87).

What happened in the years following the launch of the euro gave him little reason to question his basic analysis, as unemployment in France and Germany hovered obstinately around the 10 per cent mark – slightly less than the euro-zone average – and economic growth in both countries consistently failed to match that in the UK.[70] Critics of the euro had predicted that its 'one size fits all' character would inevitably impose limits on governments' freedom to take appropriate actions to deal with their economic difficulties. This argument now appeared to be vindicated as Chirac and Schröder struggled ineffectually to revive the French and German economies, their efforts hampered by having to comply with the Maastricht criteria on budget deficits. Unwilling to adopt the austerity measures needed to meet these criteria, both France and Germany defied Brussels for a period of several years after 2002 and were eventually adjudged by the ECJ to be in breach of their obligations. Throughout the euro-zone there was a growing recognition of the need to make the Growth and Stability Pact more flexible.

Such practical experience of the workings of the single currency offered little incentive for Brown and his adviser to adopt a more favourable attitude towards British entry, especially since the British economy was performing well and did not appear to be suffering unduly from being outside the euro zone. Both were persuaded that the arrangements they had set in place for management of the economy – notably monetary independence for the Bank of England and a flexible inflation target – served British interests well and were reluctant to abandon them in return for a regime that they regarded as excessively rigid. They were especially critical of the role allotted to the ECB and of the Growth and Stability Pact, seeing both as having inherently deflationary tendencies (Peston 2006: 230–32). When Brown spoke of needing to wait for greater convergence between the British and euro zone economies, he was thinking less of changes on the British side than of modifications to the Growth and Stability Pact and to the remit of the ECB.

Quite apart from such technical considerations, Brown's personal contacts with fellow finance ministers did little to increase his affection for the EU. He was not a popular figure. 'In 1997', writes one of his biographers, 'he had been welcomed by his European counterparts, but by 2000 he was loathed' (Bower 2007: 314). As has been seen, he ruffled a lot of feathers during the British presidency by his conduct over Euro-11, and that particular episode set the pattern for future relations. His attendances at ECOFIN were not a success: he felt ill at ease there and spent as little time as possible in meetings. A notorious tendency to deliver lectures on the supposed inadequacies of the continental European economic model compared to its Anglo-American counterpart did not endear him to other ministers, while Brown for his part was deeply suspicious of repeated attempts at harmonization of policies, especially in the field of taxation. It was his opposition to such tendencies that provoked a protracted wrangle with the Germans over a plan which they proposed for a European 'withholding tax' on interest payments: after years of obstructionist tactics Brown finally managed to block it in 2000 (Bower 2007: 314–15; Peston 2006: 198–99).

In the meantime, while Brown was effecting a surreptitious retreat from his earlier support for membership of the single currency, Blair was travelling in the opposite direction. While it is not possible to pinpoint the time when he began to shift from cautious to enthusiastic support, it has been convincingly suggested that the process began as early as the autumn of 1997, although it did not really become evident until 1999 (Peston 2006: 192). His motives were overwhelmingly political. For Blair the issue had never been a matter of economics, despite the fact that he agreed to accept the five tests as the key or even the sole determinant of whether or not Britain should enter. According to his economic adviser at the time, indeed, he never showed any real inclination to discuss that aspect of the question: 'exposure to the economic arguments … left him uncomfortable'. In so far as he did show any interest, it was limited to having a sufficiently convincing economic case to present to the electorate.[71]

Blair's attitude towards the euro was inextricably linked with his ambition to make Britain a leading player in the EU (Seldon *et al.* 2005: 317, 2007: 205). In the early part of his premiership he was able to make an impact on other leaders by the sheer force of his charm and his formidable networking skills (Wall 2008: 177). Such assets were not by themselves sufficient, however, and he soon became frustrated at his inability to exert the influence that he wished to. Nor was he in any doubt that one of the principal reasons for this failure was the fact that Britain remained outside the euro. In December 1999, feeling particularly discouraged after a French government decision to continue the ban on British beef and a difficult EU summit in Helsinki, he gave vent to his impatience at the limitations imposed on his effectiveness by Britain's non-membership of the euro: 'TB says that Britain's problem outside the single currency is that "It's like trying to tell a club you're not happy with the way they're doing things without being willing to pay the membership fee"' (Price 2006: 177).

Although keenly aware of the political handicap of being outside the euro, Blair was unable to speed up progress towards a referendum since one could only be held after the Treasury had delivered a positive verdict on the five tests. In his policy statement of October 25, Brown had implied that the Treasury's assessment would be revealed 'early in the next parliament'. On February 7 2001, in reply to a parliamentary question from Hague, Blair declared that 'early' meant 'within two years'. To the annoyance of Brown, who had not been consulted, the government was now committed to a deadline – the summer of 2003.[72]

A formidable group of Treasury officials, headed by David Ramsden, the head of the department's economic and monetary union team, was already deeply engaged in a preliminary technical study and Brown, who 'took a very proprietary attitude' towards the five tests, made absolutely sure that there was no interference in its activities from No. 10 (D. Scott 2004: 223). Blair's then economic adviser has described the 'absurd' way in which the Prime Minister's efforts to find out how the study was going were systematically blocked.[73] As always the contest of wills between Blair and Brown was not simply about the euro: it also reflected their long-running power struggle about when the latter would be allowed to take over as Prime Minister in accordance – as Brown believed – with the Granita deal. It has even been suggested that Blair sought to exploit the other's prime ministerial ambitions by proposing, through various intermediaries, a bargain whereby Brown would drop his opposition to joining the euro in return for an undertaking that Blair would step down before the next election.[74]

Throughout the period leading up to the publication of the Treasury's assessment, Brown was scrupulously careful that both he and Balls kept their distance from the experts' work in order to avoid any accusation of a political fix. Not that there was any need to intervene, since it was a foregone conclusion that the evidence would lead to a negative verdict. As for Blair, he was presented with an unpalatable fait accompli. He managed to influence the presentation of the findings by making it appear that there had been at least some progress towards greater convergence; but this was only after a series of rows with Brown, in the course of which the Chancellor's resignation or dismissal was mentioned (Seldon 2007: 210–12; Peston 2005: 234–40).

On June 9 2003 Brown duly made his statement on the five tests in the Commons.[75] It was a carefully crafted effort, the result of intensive consultation between the Treasury and No. 10. The central conclusion of the statement and of the accompanying Treasury assessment was clear enough: only one of the five tests – that relating to the effect on the financial services industry – had been fully met. Yet the whole thing was packaged in such a way as to offer something to both supporters and opponents of entry to the euro within the Labour Party, and also to convince Brussels and Britain's EU partners that Blair was serious about joining. It was a typical case of the government facing both ways at the same time, a posture which inevitably invited Conservative scorn. Thus Michael Howard, the Shadow Chancellor, declared: 'This isn't prepare and decide. It isn't even wait and see. It's hope and pray'.[76]

The message delivered by Brown was a deliberately mixed one: realistic but upbeat. Although the tests had clearly not been met, Brown insisted that they 'could and can be'. The Treasury assessment emphasized the danger of cutting interest rates to euro zone levels, saying that the greater volatility of British house prices and the bigger effect of housing on economic activity meant that joining the euro risked destabilizing the economy. Measures were to be taken to tackle the problem, however, with Brown outlining a package of reforms designed to limit swings in the housing market. As a further sign of progress towards convergence, he also announced that the Bank of England's inflation target was to be aligned with that of the ECB.[77]

To reinforce the message that the government was not ruling out the possibility of an early referendum, Blair announced that there was to be a 'road show' designed to highlight the benefits of the euro. True to form, he also went out of his way to reassure EU colleagues that Brown's statement should be seen as a positive sign, telephoning Schröder, Chirac, Jean-Pierre Raffarin, the French Prime Minister, and others to tell them that the UK was actually taking a big step towards joining the euro.[78] Jonathan Powell was more precise, informing surprised German officials that there might well be a referendum in 2004 (D. Scott 2004: 222–23). All this, however, was little more than window-dressing. The reality was that Brown's statement effectively ended the prospects of entry to the euro for the foreseeable future. As David Blunkett, the Home Secretary, noted at the time: 'I think the issue is dead for some years to come' (Blunkett 2006: 511). The promised road show never materialized and the ministerial committee that Brown had established to monitor progress towards convergence proved to be 'more virtual than real' (Wall 2008: 171).

In the course of the next few years the euro referendum receded ever further into the distance. Both Blair and Brown continued to engage in pro-euro rhetoric, but a reduction in the size of the Treasury assessment team from 100 to 10 officials shortly after the Commons statement of October 9 provided a more accurate gauge of government intentions.[79] From 2003 onwards events and circumstances combined to make the prospect of a euro referendum increasingly remote. On September 14 2003, for example, a referendum held in Sweden saw voters reject entry to the single currency by a clear majority on a very high turn-out (81 per cent). The result dealt a heavy blow to the pro-euro campaign in Britain, all the more demoralizing in that conditions in Sweden were in almost every respect far more favourable to a 'yes' vote than was the case in Britain.[80]

The outcome of the Swedish referendum was the first of several major developments that effectively put paid to British membership of the euro for years ahead. Another was the onset of war in Iraq. The wider implications of the war for Britain's relations with its EU partners will be discussed later. What is to be considered at this point is its impact on the British debate about the euro.

The most obvious consequence was that the conflict brought a radical change in Blair's order of priorities. After the general election of June 2001 he had embarked on a programme of domestic reform as one of the main objectives for his second term, in the process pushing the question of the euro further into the background. From March 2003 it was the Iraq War which became the principal focus of Blair's attention, with the inevitable result that the euro was relegated to an even lower position on his agenda. Second, the war created a serious split between Britain and its two main EU partners, France and Germany, both of whose governments were highly critical of American and British policy. The disagreement created a great deal of bitterness between them and the British, with the French in particular coming under strong attack from Jack Straw, the Foreign Secretary, as well as the tabloid press, for what was seen as their unhelpful conduct at the United Nations. The initial concern of Robin Cook, who resigned from the government because of his opposition to the war, was that:

> this breach with our European neighbours would make it tough to persuade the British public to vote for closer union with these same countries. Certainly the buckets of vituperation emptied over the French would have challenged the greatest of spinmeisters to explain why the next logical step was to share a common currency with them.

On reflection, however, he came to feel that there was another aspect of the war which was even more harmful to the prospects for membership of the euro: the loss of trust that it cost Blair. The failure to find weapons of mass destruction, together with revelations concerning the 'dodgy' intelligence dossier of September 2002, raised questions about whether the country had been taken into the war on the basis of misleading information. In the opinion of Cook, it was this damage to Blair's credibility which was 'the bigger obstacle to a successful referendum' (Cook 2003: 168–69). The shadow cast on Blair's reputation as a result of the Iraq War served to weaken his moral authority for the remainder of his premiership, thereby adding to his difficulties over both the euro and the draft EU constitution.

Proposals for a new EU constitution, which were the subject of intense debate between 2003 and 2005, were yet another factor militating against the chances of a referendum being held on the euro. The failure of the Nice summit (December 2000) and its resulting treaty (2003) to provide a wholly satisfactory institutional framework for the accession of ten new member states at the beginning of May 2004, led to the establishment of a Convention on the Future of Europe to consider more extensive reforms. The convention, chaired by the former French president Valéry Giscard d'Estaing, consisted of 105 representatives of existing member governments, the candidate states, national parliaments, the Commission and the EP. It began work in February 2002 and in the following summer produced a package of proposals. These were then discussed by an IGC which concluded in June 2004. For reasons which will be examined later, the draft constitution that emerged from the IGC proved to be extremely controversial, not least in Britain where it was denounced by the Conservative Opposition and the eurosceptic press as a massive step towards the creation of a federal superstate. In response to mounting pressure, Blair reluctantly agreed to demands for a referendum on the matter and in doing so effectively ruled out a referendum on the euro. To win a 'yes' vote on either of the two issues was challenge enough for the government: to attempt to do so on both would have been outside the realms of practical politics.

As has been seen, Blair always regarded entry to the euro as an essential element in his ambition to make Britain a leading player in the EU. At an early stage of his premiership, however, when British membership of the single currency still appeared to be a realistic possibility, he had already begun to explore alternative ways of achieving this goal, notably in the field of defence. Quite apart from wishing to demonstrate that he was serious about putting Britain at the centre of the EU, Blair was also prompted to work for closer cooperation in this area by a conviction – reinforced by his experience of the Kosovo conflict during 1998–99 – that Europe's defence capacity needed to be significantly strengthened.[81] The Blair–Chirac declaration at St Malo in December 1998 marked the beginning of active British participation in the creation of the European Defence Agency, aimed at improving common procurement, and in an initiative concerning EU battle groups (Riddell 2006: 149). Blair sought to take cooperation over defence much further in 2003 when he became involved in talks with Chirac and Schröder over plans to set up a joint headquarters for running European defence operations.[82] On this particular occasion, he was able to secure US approval for his attempts to reach agreement with the French and Germans. As a general rule, however, Washington was hostile to attempts to promote closer EU collaboration on defence.

This leads on to the contentious question of Anglo-American relations during this period – a key element in Blair's strategic thinking about Britain's relations with the rest of the EU.[83] Like almost all British Prime Ministers since the end of the Second World War, Blair attached huge importance to the 'special relationship', going out of his way to establish close personal and political relations with both Bill Clinton (1997–2001) and George W. Bush (2001–9). Blair did not believe that the maintenance of the 'special relationship' was in any way incompatible with his plans to play a leading role in EU affairs. On the contrary, he was convinced that the two roles were mutually reinforcing and that it was in the best interests of the EU as well as the US that Britain should serve as a bridge between the two. This was an image habitually used by Blair, but it failed to impress the French or Germans: Schröder is supposed to have observed tartly that the traffic always seemed to flow in one direction.[84]

Blair's self-appointed role as transatlantic mediator was tenable as long as there existed a sufficient community of interest between the EU and the US. With the advent to power of Bush in 2001, however, it came under increasing strain and finally became impossible because of French and German opposition to the invasion of Iraq in March 2003: as many commentators observed at the time, Blair's transatlantic bridge collapsed.[85] Blair claimed that the only way he could influence the Bush administration's policies was by staying close and giving loyal backing. To a growing army of critics, however, this approach became synonymous with servility. Blair was increasingly regarded as an American poodle, both abroad and at home, and this viewpoint was voiced publicly in November 2006 by a senior State Department analyst, Kendal Myers, who spoke of a 'totally one-sided relationship' in which there was 'no payback, no sense of reciprocity'.[86] In this context, Bush's greeting at the G8 summit in St. Petersburg on July 17 2006 – 'Yo, Blair' – was widely seen as confirmation of an essentially master–client relationship.

The breach that the Iraq War opened up between the British government, on the one hand, and the French and German governments, on the other, constituted a major setback for Blair's strategic goal of aligning Britain with France and Germany as the dominant partnership within the EU. It must be said, however, that an informal grouping along those lines was not the only option available to Blair.

During Blair's first two terms in government, the EU was going through a process of radical change. The situation was more fluid than it had been for some time and many of the developments taking place were undoubtedly to Britain's advantage. Foremost among these was the accession of ten new member states. As the French had feared, this enlargement diluted their influence. It also reduced the relative importance of the Franco-German axis as the EU's centre of gravity shifted eastwards. By contrast, Britain's position in the internal power structure was generally strengthened. Most of the new entrants, including Poland, Hungary, the Czech Republic and the three Baltic states, Latvia, Lithuania and Estonia, shared the Blair government's Atlanticist outlook and its commitment to free market economics. They were therefore useful potential allies, alongside Italy, Spain and Portugal, all of whose leaders collaborated closely with Blair. This new balance of power first became evident in connection with the Iraq War and the events leading up to it. At the end of January 2003 Britain, Denmark, Italy, Portugal and Spain joined three states who were not yet full EU members, Hungary, Poland and the Czech Republic, in signing an article supporting the US–British interpretation of UN resolution 1441, as opposed to that of the French (and Russians) which stressed the need for a further vote to provide a legitimate basis for war. Chirac was furious, especially since the US Defense Secretary, Donald Rumsfeld, had spoken disparagingly a few days before of France and Germany belonging to what he termed 'old Europe' (Riddell 2006: 141–42).

Chirac's irritable response to the central and eastern European states which backed the US was to tell them that they were not yet full members and that it behoved them to adopt a low profile. The effect of his rebuke was the opposite of what he intended since it caused the Poles and the rest to draw closer to the British and Americans. For some time thereafter there appeared to be a possibility of Britain heading a group of EU states acting as a counterbalance to the Franco-German partnership. In the longer term, however, such a grouping was not sustainable and fell apart in 2005 amidst bitter wrangling between the British, the Poles and other new members about the EU budget, reform of the CAP and the British rebate. Nor were the French slow to exploit and deepen the split.[87]

The prize that Blair was really seeking, in any case, was a place at the top table with the French and Germans. This was a tough nut to crack, as the experience of previous British Prime Ministers had shown. For some months after the Iraq War, relations with the French and Germans were fraught. A thaw began, however, with a meeting at the Elysée between Blair and Chirac and this was followed in September by a further meeting between these two and Schröder in Berlin in an attempt to move on from the bitterness caused by the Iraq War. This marked the beginning of a cooperative phase in which collaboration over defence figured prominently. This was not to last, though, and for the next few years relations between the three were patchy. In the case of relations between Blair and Chirac, they became dire from 2005 onwards. Indeed, there was a period following the French rejection of the new constitutional treaty in May 2005 when the British and French leaders seemed incapable of agreeing on anything, becoming embroiled in rows over the EU budget, the British rebate, reform of the CAP and the future accession of Turkey. Even the rivalry between Paris and London over which of them should host the 2012 Olympics was grist to the mill.

In the end, therefore, Blair's attempts at trilateralism ran into the sand. In part, this was because of a clash of personalities, especially between Blair and Chirac. According to Blair's adviser on Europe, the French president never liked Blair, a feeling (he suggests) in which there was perhaps an element of jealousy; and their dealings were punctuated by a series of angry scenes (Wall 2008: 178). The most spectacular of these occurred in October 2002 when Chirac presented Blair with a fait accompli in the shape of a package of proposals on agricultural reform that he had agreed with Schröder.

The differences went beyond personalities, however. Blair angered both Chirac and Schröder by organizing a successful resistance in 2004 to their preferred candidate to succeed Romano Prodi as President of the Commission, while his surprise decision in April of the same year to hold a referendum on the new constitutional treaty was a further cause of irritation to Chirac who was thus put under pressure to have one in France (Wall 2008: 176). But the most important obstacle by far to Blair's plans to establish an informal triple partnership was the special relationship between France and Germany which had endured for more than forty years. It was built on a basic community of interests, which no transient differences could undermine, as well as a dense bilateral network of institutional cooperation.

So far as the EU was concerned, the final phase of the Blair premiership was dominated by four issues which came to be inseparably linked: the new constitution, the EU budget for the years 2007–13, reform of the CAP and the British rebate.

Between 2003 and 2005 Blair went through a series of about-turns on the proposed EU constitution which would have done credit to Harold Wilson at his wiliest. Having at first argued that a constitution was unnecessary, by September 2003 he was welcoming the draft produced by the Convention on the Future of Europe as 'good news for Britain'.[88] At this point, he rejected demands for a referendum, arguing that the new constitutional treaty would involve nothing more than a 'tidying up' of existing ones. In April 2004 he abruptly announced that there would after all be a referendum. The subsequent rejection of the constitution by the French and Dutch voters in May and June 2005 threw the whole ratification process into the melting pot. After a period of reflection and political manoeuvring, a new slimmed-down treaty emerged, no longer called a constitution, and Blair later let it be known that this would not be put to a referendum.

There was much in the original draft treaty that appealed to the Blair government, which was hardly surprising since large parts of it reflected British input.[89] In general terms, the government approved of what it saw as a much-needed rationalization of the current jumble of treaties, as well as a streamlining of decision-making procedures. It was in favour of the proposed change from a rotating presidency to a 'permanent' one whereby a President of the European Council would serve for a period of two-and-a-half years: the new arrangement, it was believed, would make for more continuity, efficiency and accountability. The government also supported the creation of a new EU foreign minister, combining the roles of the High Representative and the Commissioner for External Affairs. There were certain elements, however, which caused concern, including the fact that the new treaty was to be called a constitution and gave the EU a single legal personality. In addition, it was feared that the proposed Charter of Fundamental Rights would provide a loophole for the introduction of new EU laws and regulations affecting British business. To counter this danger the government had secured an amendment to ensure that new rights were not incorporated into British law.

In defending the draft, the government pointed out that the text emphasized the importance of member states and gave national parliaments an effective role in policing Commission proposals. It also insisted that it would preserve the British veto on such 'red line' issues as taxation, social security, criminal justice, defence, foreign policy and security. The Conservative Opposition and the eurosceptic press refused to accept such assurances from an 'untrustworthy' government, however, denouncing the proposed new treaty as a dangerous threat to national sovereignty and demanding a referendum. Even the Liberal Democrat leader, Charles Kennedy, and his foreign affairs spokesman, Menzies Campbell, both of them strongly pro-European, joined in the demand for a referendum.[90]

On April 20 2004 Blair discovered the reverse gear he had previously said he did not have, telling the Commons that the electorate 'will be asked for their opinion' on the matter. Although he took care not to mention the word 'referendum', everybody understood that was what he meant. Blair explained that he had been obliged to change his mind because Michael Howard, the Conservative Party leader, had given a pledge on March 24 to renegotiate the constitution unless it was approved by a referendum and that would weaken Britain's position in the EU.[91] A suitable response to this explanation came from the *Financial Times*, which described it as 'tripe'.[92] The *Sun*, predictably, ascribed the enforced u-turn largely to pressure from its ten million readers, though it did admit that the Liberal Democrats and a growing number of Labour MPs had also played their part.[93]

There can be little doubt that Blair was in fact influenced by the *Sun*, or more precisely by its proprietor, Rupert Murdoch, who was reported to have told him that he would switch his support to the Conservatives at the next general election unless he agreed to a referendum. Press rumours abounded that the American economist Irwin Stelzer, Murdoch's trusted emissary, had been involved, and these were given some credibility by a confirmation from Downing Street on April 19 that a senior figure from the News International Group had held a meeting with Blair the previous month.[94] Another important factor was advice and pressure from Jack Straw. Despite the fact that he was later to express his regret when the treaty was rejected by the French and Dutch, Straw had little enthusiasm for it. What really caused him to propose a referendum, however, was his concern about the likely electoral consequences of refusing one. This was a key consideration. With the EP elections due in June 2004 and a general election likely to follow in 2005, there was a real danger that the Conservatives would have a vote-winning issue in portraying the government as being afraid to trust the people.

Blair's decision to hold a referendum was generally viewed as a sign of political weakness. Certainly he would have preferred to avoid one if at all possible. This was especially the case since there seemed little prospect of winning the vote: in a *Sun*/YouGov poll published the day before Blair's announcement of his u-turn, only 16 per cent of respondents said they would vote 'yes'.[95]

Blair was already constructing a twofold strategy to deal with this difficult situation. First, as early as April 20, he indicated that he did not intend the debate ahead to be a narrowly focused one. The question would be on the treaty. 'But the implications will go far wider. It is time to resolve once and for all whether this country, Britain, wants to be at the centre and heart of European decision-making or not ... whether our destiny lies as a leading partner and ally of Europe or on its margins'.[96] What Blair was seeking to do, in other words, was to repeat the tactic he had already contemplated in connection with a referendum on the euro: recasting the question into one that offered a greater chance of success. The second element in his strategy was to play for time, to delay holding the referendum for as long as possible. In the meantime, votes would be taking place in a number of other countries and there were already indications that some of them would be extremely tight. Since ratification of the treaty needed to be unanimous, a rejection in any one of these polls would remove the necessity for a British referendum: Blair would be off the hook.

In the event, this is precisely what happened. In a referendum held on May 29 2005 the proposed treaty was decisively rejected in France, and the pattern was repeated on June 1 in the Netherlands. The reaction of British eurosceptics was one of delight.[97] In public, Blair, Straw and other ministers expressed disappointment, but they cannot have been entirely dissatisfied with what had happened. The question that now arose was whether the ratification process should continue, given that unanimous approval was no longer possible. Jose Manuel Barroso, the President of the Commission, along with Chirac and Schröder, urged that other countries should go ahead with their planned votes. The British government, on the other hand, suggested that what was needed was a 'pause for reflection'.[98] In the end, the latter argument won the day and at the Brussels European Council of June 16–18 2005 the issue was effectively shelved: it was decided that the agreed deadline for approval, November 2006, should be extended.

The constitution was meant to be the dominant issue at the Brussels European Council. Instead, the questions that occupied centre stage were the EU budget, reform of the CAP and the British rebate. The three issues were inextricably linked and over the next few months they were to generate a great deal of passionate disagreement, especially between the British and the French.

Britain's rebate had been for some time a cause of underlying resentment among its EU partners, and this feeling rose to the surface in the period following the rejection of the constitutional treaty by France and the Netherlands. The British suspected, indeed, that Chirac had chosen to focus attention on the subject as a distraction from his humiliating setback over the French referendum. Chirac had long wanted to get rid of the hated 'chèque brittanique', regarding it as no longer justified because of the growth in Britain's relative prosperity since 1984, the year in which it was negotiated. By 2005 he was far from being alone in this respect. The Germans and Dutch were calling for a rebate of their own if the British continued to receive theirs, and the rest of the EU members were wholly unsympathetic to Britain's case: some of the poorer newcomers were especially resentful at having to contribute to the rebate.

The issue had already begun to take on a much higher profile the previous year in the context of proposals by the Commission for a 35 per cent increase in the EU budget for the years 2007–13 to take account of enlargement. The British response was to reject categorically any idea of abolishing the rebate. Brown defended its retention in characteristically robust fashion at an ECOFIN meeting in November 2004, pointing out that even with the benefit of the rebate Britain had been the second largest net contributor to the EU budget since 1984, paying twice as much as France. Going on to the offensive, he attacked the proposed increase in the EU budget as 'unrealistic and unacceptable', even more so since the Commission was currently criticizing member states for exceeding a 3 per cent deficit in their own budgets. In addition, he demanded that other countries open their public procurement markets to British and other foreign firms – a thinly disguised dig at French 'economic patriotism'.[99] In January 2005 Blair managed to persuade EU colleagues to postpone further consideration of the issue until after the approaching British general election was out of the way, but the respite was brief.

On 5 May Blair won a third term, with a much reduced overall majority (down to 66). A few weeks later he was attending the Brussels European Council fighting to preserve the rebate, reform the CAP and trim and restructure the EU budget. The stage was set for a tough battle. The Treasury had spent a year preparing to defend the rebate and Brown was reported to have appointed some of the department's 'brightest stars' to negotiate the 2007–13 budget.[100] All the indications were that the government was not in the mood to compromise, with Straw threatening to use the veto to protect the rebate shortly before the summit began.

At the Brussels summit Chirac maintained that the British rebate was outdated and had lost whatever justification it ever had since Britain was now much wealthier than in 1984. Currently worth £3.2 billion a year, the rebate was set to rise even higher in line with the growth in the EU budget, and what made it especially indefensible was that the ten new member states, predominantly poor, would be contributing to it.

Blair's immediate response was that the rebate was not negotiable. Even at this stage, however, he was beginning to see that some sort of compromise might be necessary given that not a single one of the other 24 states supported the British viewpoint. The trouble was that any hint of concession would cause enormous political difficulties at home. Blair therefore faced an unenviable choice between total isolation in Brussels or a fierce reaction from domestic critics. Deciding that the latter was the lesser evil, he indicated that there might be some room for negotiation on the rebate – but only as part of a general agreement involving a reduction in the proposed EU budget and a fundamental reform in the CAP. Although the latter's share of overall EU expenditure had fallen from the level of 70 per cent that it had been in 1984, it still accounted for almost 45 per cent of the budget. According to Blair, this was a waste of resources which might otherwise be employed more usefully by investing in education and technology so as to equip the EU to meet the challenges posed by globalization. Blair pointed out that over 23 per cent of agricultural subsidies went to France, compared with only 9 per cent to Britain. He also argued that the protectionist nature of the CAP was extremely damaging to the export prospects of Third World countries.

Chirac was unimpressed, arguing that decisions regarding the CAP budget up to 2013 had been taken unanimously at the European Council of December 2002 and were not open to discussion. His refusal to budge from this position and Blair's continuing insistence that any agreement must include major changes to the CAP meant that the Brussels European Council ended in complete deadlock.

This outcome was profoundly disappointing for Blair. The British presidency was due to begin on July 1 and he had hoped to use the opportunity to promote a programme of far-reaching changes to the EU. Instead, it was now highly likely that he would be embroiled in a protracted and bitter wrangle about finances. The outcome of the recent referendums in France and the Netherlands had sent shock waves throughout the EU, provoking calls for some serious rethinking about whether it was heading in the right direction. Blair was not slow to capitalize on the mood. The day after the French referendum he said that it had left Europe with 'a profound question' to answer about the future of the EU. While the rejected constitution was a sensible attempt to provide effective rules and institutions for an enlarged EU, it reflected the preoccupation of political leaders, not the concerns of ordinary citizens. Nor did it address the need for reforms which were essential for dealing with the challenges of globalization. Straw likewise spoke about the French vote raising serious issues concerning the future direction of the EU.[101]

The political turmoil created by events in France and the Netherlands presented Blair with an ideal opportunity to win backing for the British vision of how the EU should develop. The chief upholders of the traditional 'social model', Schröder and Chirac, were both in bad political shape, weakened by years of failure to deal with mass unemployment. Schröder's position was so tenuous, indeed, that he was soon forced to call a general election (which he lost to Angela Merkel), one year ahead of the scheduled date. As for Chirac, he was faced by a mass of deep-seated problems that he seemed incapable of solving, presiding over a government afflicted by political paralysis. He had suffered serious setbacks in the French regional and European elections of 2003 and 2004 respectively, as well as in the recent referendum on the constitutional treaty. It was now the conventional wisdom that his chances of standing for a third term had completely disappeared and that he would serve out the remainder of his five-year mandate as a lame-duck president. He was engaged in a ferocious struggle with his minister of the interior and nemesis, Nicolas Sarkozy. He was completely out of touch with the public mood, and his poll ratings had sunk to a disastrously low level.[102]

By comparison with the aged and ailing French president, Blair cut an attractive figure: young, dynamic and charismatic. To all appearances, moreover, his government's economic record was superior to that of its French and German counterparts. At a time when doubts were being raised about the traditional nostrums emanating from Paris and Berlin, the prescriptions offered by Blair had an undeniable resonance. The fact that Barroso was president of the EU Commission also strengthened Blair's hand. The former Portuguese Prime Minister, who had been appointed to the post in November 2004, shared much of the other's impatience with the old EU model, as well as his commitment to reform along the lines set out in the Lisbon Agenda.

On July 1 2005 Blair held a joint press conference with Barroso at which he placed an overhaul of the traditional European 'social model' at the centre of his programme for the British presidency. He called for a special informal summit to be held, which would consider the sustainability of this model in the light of the growing challenges presented by globalization and examine a paper on the subject drawn up by the Commission. It was emphasized that the intention was not to abandon the 'social model', but to update and modernize it.[103]

In the event, much of Blair's time during the presidency was spent not in promoting long-term reform of this sort, but rather in seeking to reach agreement on the various financial issues left unresolved by the Brussels European Council. The basic obstacle to a deal remained Chirac's refusal to accept a reduction in the scale of agricultural subsidies and Blair's insistence that this was an essential precondition of a British concession over its rebate.

On November 7 a meeting held in Brussels to settle the issue ended in stalemate, and it was not until December 16, virtually at the end of the British presidency, that an agreement was finally hammered out. Britain agreed to a reduction in the growth of its rebate between 2007 and 2013 by the amount that the ten new member states would have had to contribute. There was to be an increase in the EU budget, although not by as much as the Commission had wanted. In addition, as a sop to the British government, it was decided that there would be a mid-term review of the CAP in 2008. This last concession by the French was of no practical importance, since the 2002 agricultural settlement already made provision for a review on that date. For the Blair government what counted was being able to show that it had managed to wrest some French counter-concession over the CAP to justify the proposed cuts to the British rebate.

The agreement was far from ideal from the British viewpoint and securing it had involved political as well as financial costs. Not the least of these was the deterioration caused in relations between Britain and the new member states, who had reacted with outrage to British proposals for a reduction in structural funds which they saw as detrimental to their interests.[104] The Poles threatened a veto and the Polish and French foreign minister sent a joint letter to the *Financial Times* on December 14 saying that the British proposals were completely unacceptable. This last development was a clear indication of a big improvement in relations between France and Poland since the days of the Iraq War when they had reached a low point.

There was general agreement that Blair had needed the settlement in order to prevent the achievements of the British presidency from seeming meagre. That was precisely the reaction of most commentators, however, with one critical journalist awarding a miserly 'nul points'.[105] Not for the first time a British presidency under the Blair government had failed to justify the extravagant promises that had attended its launch.

Blair made as much as he could from the fact that for the first time the British net contribution to EU budget would in future be about the same as the French. This, however, failed to placate the eurosceptic press which lambasted the settlement as an abject surrender and a blow to the British taxpayer. During the summit, reports had been appearing in the *Financial Times* about a likely reduction of 20 per cent in the rebate and critics were already champing at the bit by the time the accuracy of this figure was confirmed.[106]

With the budget settlement for the next few years in place, attention began to switch to the question of the EU's constitutional future. During the second half of 2005 and much of 2006, the debate over this marked time, although the constitution that had been rejected by the French and Dutch was subsequently approved in 15 other countries. Towards the end of 2006 Sarkozy, the French Interior Minister and a certain candidate for the next presidential elections, began to speculate publicly about the possibility of devising a simpler institutional framework. At the same time the German Chancellor, Angela Merkel, who had replaced Schröder in September 2005, was taking a very different line, indicating that she wanted to retain as much as possible of the existing constitutional treaty. Germany was to take over the EU presidency in January 2007 and she was planning to use the opportunity to push on with preparations for an IGC, to be held during the second half of the year under the Portuguese presidency. Her aim was that the process should be completed before the 2009 European elections.

These developments opened up the prospect of extremely tricky political problems for the Blair government since any new treaty would inevitably raise again the thorny question of whether there should be a referendum. Its manifesto for the May 2005 general election had contained a pledge to hold one. But would that be binding in the case of a new treaty? Much would depend on its contents. In the meantime, Blair refused to be drawn on his intentions.[107]

On April 19, however, he announced that he saw no need for a referendum on the scaled-down treaty that was currently being considered. 'If it is not a constitutional treaty that alters the relationship between Europe and the member states', he said, 'then there isn't a case for a referendum'. As might be expected, this assertion provoked the fury of the Conservative Opposition and large sections of the press, especially since a letter by Merkel had been leaked suggesting that her intention was to reintroduce the essential substance of the old treaty, while trimming away some of its more unpalatable trappings.[108]

The furore came to a head during June. The German presidency was to end soon and Merkel was desperate to secure a deal on the new treaty at the European Council in Brussels on June 21–23. Although difficulties arose because of reservations expressed by the British and the Poles' insistence on keeping the voting arrangements contained in the Treaty of Nice, an agreement was finally reached after a difficult all-night session. The new treaty, which was to be ratified at an IGC later in the year, was not called a constitution. It nevertheless inherited many features from the old one. There was to be a 'permanent' president of the council, for example, as well as a new foreign affairs chief, to be known as the High Representative, an extension of QMV, a smaller Commission (after 2014) and more powers for the EP. Despite this, Blair, who had just attended his last European Council as Prime Minister, insisted that there was no need for a referendum, arguing that the new treaty was not a constitution and was therefore fundamentally different from the one on which a pledge had been given. In any case, he had obtained safeguards to ensure that essential British interests were protected. The Charter on Fundamental Rights would not be justiciable in British courts. In addition, he had negotiated various protocols or opt-outs guaranteeing Britain's continuing right to a veto in foreign policy, justice and home affairs.

The pressure for a referendum was stepped up. Nor was Blair helped by frank admissions from various EU statesmen that there was not really any great difference between the two treaties. Thus the Irish Prime Minister, Bertie Ahern said: 'Thankfully, they haven't changed the substance – 90 per cent of it is still there'. To compound the damage, he promised to hold a referendum.

This gave an obvious weapon to the Conservatives: William Hague, the Shadow Foreign Secretary, said that it was now 'getting clearer and clearer that this is basically the Constitution by another name' and people would not understand why they should not have the same right to vote on it as their Irish neighbours.[109] David Cameron, the party leader since December 2005, raised another point which was highly embarrassing for Blair. Blair would cease to be the Prime Minister within a matter of weeks and was therefore transferring vast new powers to Brussels as one of his final acts.[110]

Blair's final European Council was not his finest hour. He was on the back foot when he returned home to defend the new treaty, facing accusations that he was thoroughly untrustworthy. He had changed his position on the referendum several times and, according to his critics at least, had now reneged on his election pledge. The central charge was that he was not a person to be trusted – one that struck home because of the Iraq War. The chickens had well and truly come home to roost.

The last phase of Blair's premiership formed a stark contrast with the early days. He had come to power promising a new age of harmonious cooperation with Britain's EU partners and an end to the friction and isolation of the Thatcher and Major years. He had been welcomed by other EU leaders as a breath of fresh air – it could hardly have been otherwise given the appalling state in which Major had left British–EU relations – and the honeymoon period was a lengthy one. By the end of his ten years in power, however, much of this capital of goodwill had been dissipated, and he spent the final British presidency of his premiership engaged in a bitter row with Chirac, the Poles and others about money: the British rebate, the size of the EU budget and French agricultural subsidies. It was not an exact parallel with Thatcher's set-piece battles over the British rebate during her first years in power: as has been pointed out, Blair's negotiating style was worlds apart from hers, employing a technique based on ducking and weaving rather than seeking the knock-out blow (Wall 2008: 177). Nevertheless, the comparison is not entirely fanciful.

From as early as the 1997 general election Blair showed a tendency to blend professions of pro-European sentiment with an appeal to national self-interest, the articles which he contributed to the *Sun* in which he proclaimed his love for the pound and his determination to slay the dragon of a European superstate being cases in point. What he was attempting to do was to address two very different audiences at once: other EU leaders, who were delighted to learn of his desire for friendly cooperation; and British voters, many of whom were wary about too close a relationship between Britain and its continental partners and needing to be reassured that national interests would not be put at risk. Any political leader who wishes to stay in power has to be able to perform this exercise to some degree. In the case of Blair, it was carried to extreme lengths. It has frequently been pointed out that he almost always chose to make his most pro-European speeches when he was abroad: his speeches for domestic consumption tended to be far more cautious.

In the longer term, the effect of this dual approach was to create a strong sense of ambiguity about Blair's European policies. His policy on the euro provides perhaps the best illustration of this. There appears to be almost unanimity amongst commentators that Blair regarded entry to the euro as one of his prime objectives: a *sine qua non* of his ambitions to make Britain a leading player in Europe. Yet one historian has written of him being at his most enigmatic over the euro, and it is certainly difficult to reconcile his equivocal approach with the importance which he supposedly attached to the issue. Once again, it was a case of speaking to two (or more) audiences, sending reassuring messages to his EU colleagues that entry would be happening soon, while for the purposes of home consumption stressing the formidable obstacles in the way. With skill and charm, which Blair has in abundance, it was possible to maintain this game for some time – but not indefinitely. The end result was to cause confusion about his real intentions, as well as disappointment on all sides. EU leaders eventually came to feel that he was not serious about taking Britain into the single currency. Eurosceptics at home suspected him of harbouring plans to do it by stealth, while europhiles were puzzled and discouraged by his failure to give a strong lead.

There were certainly good reasons why Blair could not be more straightforward about his aims. One of the main problems throughout was that of reconciling conflicting external and domestic pressures. He wanted to avoid isolation in the EU, but often that could only be done by means of compromises which were extremely difficult to 'sell' at home. This was a genuine dilemma, but some commentators have suggested that Blair should have done more to explain the realities of the situation, that he 'never confronted voters with the necessary compromises demanded by engagement, and influence, in Europe'.[111]

Many europhiles complained about Blair's failure to make the case for Europe. What is noticeable in this connection is that Blair was often reluctant to do this personally, preferring to use confidants, like Mandelson, or aides like Jonathan Powell. On occasion he would make a stirring speech. He was also involved in some eye-catching initiatives like the projected 'road show' that was meant to highlight the benefits of being in the euro. All too often, however, there was little follow-up, as in the case of the 'road show' which never got off the ground. 'It has always been a case of tomorrow' (Riddell 2006: 151).

The effect of Blair's failure to give a lead was to leave the field clear for the eurosceptic press. The latter was certainly a persistent thorn in his flesh and presented him with difficulties that no other EU leader ever faced. It is possible to argue, however, that he was unduly influenced by this factor and especially by the need to retain the support of the *Sun*. In effect, he allowed the European agenda to be dictated by this section of the press.

But there were other constraints apart from the press. The most important of these was the opposition offered by Gordon Brown to British entry to the euro zone. Much has been written about the combustible relationship between

Chancellor and Prime Minister and the extraordinary influence that the former was allowed to have over economic and social policy in general and over the question of joining the euro in particular. It is no exaggeration to say that he exercised a veto on an issue that Blair regarded as being of cardinal importance. The situation was frustrating, almost intolerable, but there was little that Blair could do about it: dismissing the second most senior figure in the government was never a serious option.

It is undeniable that Blair took the initiative in a number of major developments in the EU. He played an important part in promoting cooperation in defence, was an enthusiastic and effective proponent of enlargement, pressed for economic reforms and modernization in order to enable the EU to meet the challenges of globalization, and focused greater attention on such issues as energy and climate change. On the other side of the balance sheet, however, there were some conspicuous failures. His sporadic efforts to establish a triple leadership with the French and Germans were abortive, partly because of his difficulties in working with Chirac, but more basically because of the strength and solidity of the Franco-German partnership. In assuming the role of mediator between the US and Europe, he was simply following the path trodden by almost all of his post-war predecessors, but he underestimated the growing divergence of interests during the Bush years between the US and Europe. The result was disastrous. His transatlantic bridge collapsed under the strains of the Iraq War, causing deep divisions within the EU and undermining his own attempts to make the case for joining the euro. The other outstanding failure in Blair's European policies was, indeed, over the euro. As Blair himself sometimes regretfully recognized, the fact that Britain remained outside the single currency was an almost insuperable obstacle to his ambition of putting Britain at the heart of the EU.

Whether he managed to 'normalize' Britain's relations with the rest of the EU, as is sometimes claimed, is a moot point. He cannot be criticised for lack of effort. He established a network of close personal and working relationships with a wide-cross section of the EU leadership, though he was perhaps not always wise in his choice of friends. In addition, as his adviser on Europe until 2004 has pointed out, he was responsible for the introduction of what is known as 'step change', a policy whereby all Whitehall departments and British embassies throughout the EU are encouraged to come up with projects for new fields of cooperation with other member states (Wall 2008: 178–79). This is doubtless a worthy endeavour, although no real substitute for effective cooperation at leadership level, something which was not always evident. It is debatable, however, whether there has really been a fundamental and permanent change in British attitudes, either among the public in general or at governmental level. Towards the end of Blair's premiership, Eurobarometer polls revealed a continuing high level of dissatisfaction with British membership of the EU. Several months later Blair's successor, Gordon Brown, was to stir memories of a venerable British tradition when he signed the Treaty of Lisbon on his own.

7   The European Union and Constitutional Change in the UK since 1999

Potentially, New Labour's election victory in 1997 marked a critical juncture for politics in the UK. Tony Blair and his colleagues hoped that the incoming administration would herald an era of 'New Politics' whereby sleaze and incompetence, which had hitherto dogged the latter part of John Major's premiership, would be consigned to history. In addition, just as the Labour Party had done, the state itself should undergo 'modernization'. Modernization, it was expected, would act as the antidote to the malaise that had come to afflict politics in the UK. From the Modernists' perspective, government not only required greater transparency and accountability, its efficiency and efficacy also needed to be enhanced (see for example Hassan and Warhurst 1999). More particularly, the relationship between the state and its citizens needed to be put on a sounder footing. As far as the latter was concerned Labour's reforms ensured that from henceforth the European Convention on Human Rights would be enshrined in domestic legislation in the UK. There was also new Freedom of Information legislation. As far as the territories on the UK's 'mainland' were concerned, however, the above were somewhat eclipsed by New Labour's plan to decentralize a measure of authority from the 'Centre' to devolved institutions of government. In so doing, 'power' would be brought closer to the people in Scotland and Wales and, initially, it was hoped also the English regions. As far as Northern Ireland was concerned, however, the situation was more complex due to the 'Troubles'.

The actual implementation of New Labour's programme of asymmetric devolution (i.e. territorial government varied across the UK) was initially not without success. But it was by no means a simple format. Its asymmetric characteristics were a by-product of the underlying drivers for constitutional change in the respective territories. In practice, territorial empowerment in England failed to take root on either a coherent basis (e.g. the creation of one assembly for the whole of England) or incoherently (i.e. the creation of assemblies in those regions which supported such a development). The issue appears to be laid to rest after November 4 2004 when the electorate in North East England rejected proposals for a regional assembly in a referendum. On a turn-out of 47.7 per cent, just 22.1 per cent were in favour and 77.9 per cent were against.[1] As the North East appeared to be the region most amenable to devolution, the result of the referendum effectively curtailed the possibility of it being introduced elsewhere in England. However, London now has its own elected assembly and directly elected mayor but this arrangement is somewhat distinct from the devolved bodies elsewhere in the UK. Primarily that is because the assembly's influence over the mayor is limited at best, thereby calling into question the issue of democratic oversight and accountability.

In Scotland, where the consensus for autonomy was more extensive, the UK government proposed that there should be a Scottish Parliament, with limited tax-varying powers, which could enact primary legislation.[2] That came to pass. But the National Assembly for Wales would have neither a tax varying power, nor (initially) would it possess the authority to enact primary legislation; in part this was because in 1999 the demand for autonomy appeared to be rather less clear-cut (however, see p. 191). In some respects, therefore, to begin with at least, the Assembly's powers could be conceived as being rather akin to that of a local authority, albeit that it possessed the democratic authority to articulate the concerns of the Welsh principality in its entirety.

With regard to Northern Ireland, the new arrangement was first and foremost designed to bring the long-running conflict between the two communities to a conclusion; effectively, therefore, it was primarily a peace settlement. That said, *The Agreement* (1998) ensured that Northern Ireland would once again have its own Legislative Assembly at Stormont. Although the latter did not possess tax-varying power, it did have the authority to pass primary legislation. Northern Ireland's governmental arrangements were complicated further by two cross-border Councils. The North/South Council linked the Northern Ireland's administration with that of the Irish government in the South; this body's European dimension was relatively modest. The British–Irish Council, running east to west, was designed to appease the Unionists. Its constituent members included the Irish government, the devolved administrations in Northern Ireland, Scotland and Wales, as well as representatives from the Isle of Man and the Channel Islands. Both entities appeared to lack any substantive European dimension.[3]

Although there had been a decentralization of political authority to some of the UK's territories, the question arises as to whether the new constitutional arrangements would be of little consequence to the promotion and defence of their interests in the EU. On the one hand the answer is no. Despite the high hopes surrounding constitutional reform, from a territorial perspective, it could be supposed that there would be little substantive difference, as far as European matters were concerned. Primarily that was because European affairs and international relations more generally were 'reserved' to Westminster. Formally, therefore, the UK government retained its primacy over the formulation of foreign policy. Likewise, for the most part, ministers from the departments in London continued to represent the UK in the Council of the EU.[4] Central to this was the belief amongst UK officials that the arrangements prior to 1999, which determined how the European interests of its territories were aggregated and promoted by the UK, 'worked well'. Thus, where possible they should remain undisturbed in the aftermath of constitutional change (Bulmer *et al.* 2002).

Even so, there have been some new developments concerning inter-governmental mechanisms. Effectively, these consisted of three elements (initially, there also was a free-standing Ministerial European Co-ordination Committee – MINECOR – which dealt with 'presentational aspects' of EU policy but from December 2003 this body was incorporated within JMC(E)) (see p. 190).[5]

The first of these elements, the Memorandum of Understanding, affirmed amongst other things, that the relationship between the two tiers of administration (i.e. the Centre and each of the territorial administrations) would be one of collaboration; conflict should be avoided if at all possible. The second element, the Joint Ministerial Committees (JMC), it was expected, would provide a formal setting for dialogue between the UK government and the devolved administrations, including if necessary the potential for conflict resolution (there would also be a JMC (E) which was concerned specifically with the EU). The third element, the Concordats (including one on the Co-ordination of European Union Policy Issues) codified what had been until then informal practice relating to inter-departmental relations within the civil service itself. In part, that was necessary because there would now be different political administrations at the UK and territorial levels. However, none of these arrangements possessed a legal base as such, although they have been referred to as 'soft law'.[6] Furthermore, these arrangements were bound by confidentiality. As such, their efficacy is difficult to discern and should a devolved administration decide to breach confidentiality, then it could find itself 'unplugged' to no small degree by the Centre. More particularly, the JMCs did not convene that often and instead intergovernmental relations between the Centre and devolved institutions was relatively *ad hoc* during the first few years of devolution, albeit that they were underpinned by goodwill on all sides.

The current situation has not been without its detractors, however. One such example was the House of Lords Select Committee on the Constitution which, whilst acknowledging the need for 'goodwill', warned that there had been rather too much informality.[7] Other critics include John Gray, a former Chair of the Wales European Centre and a former ambassador to Brussels. He observed:

> At the level of officials, the concordats have been applied patchily, partly because of resistance from some Whitehall departments, and partly because of a lack of enthusiasm or resources at the Cardiff end. There are even some who believe that there is now less contact between Cardiff and Whitehall civil servants than existed before devolution and what there is, is less structured. At ministerial level things are only marginally better. Assembly Ministers regularly attend meetings of a Cabinet Committee

known as MINECOR, chaired by the UK minister for European affairs, Keith Vaz. However, this is devoted to 'theme' issues rather than addressing individual dossiers on European business. These are the primary responsibility of the Whitehall departments concerned and although machinery exists for problem solving at ministerial level, its efficacy remains very much in the hands of Whitehall Ministers.[8]

It should be noted, however, that these lines were written when Welsh devolution was in its infancy, and that the situation could well have changed radically since then. Even so, there are grounds for supposing that 'in the round', the current arrangements remain overly *ad hoc* (Trench 2003: 164–65). Indeed, as Jones surmised:

> ... The real problem is concerned with developing effective relations between the Assembly and UK government departments to ensure that Welsh interests are fully taken into account at the earliest possible stage of EU legislation.
>
> (B.J. Jones 2003: 132)

Arguably, the current arrangement can be conceived as tantamount to a 'new pragmatism'. While some facets of the previous arrangements have been codified, (see p. 189), the relative informality of intergovernmental relations within the UK, which predated devolution, has been retained under the new constitutional set-up. It could therefore be claimed that this is somewhat akin to a restoration of Bulpitt's dual polity[9] (Wright 2005). It could thus be argued that the deficiencies, which pre-dated the current arrangement, remain *in situ*. For instance, the UK government retains its 'gatekeeping' role as regards the Council of the EU. Furthermore, 'London' continues to exercise considerable political authority over the extent to which the devolved administrations can develop their own quasi-autonomous foreign affairs' agendas. Yet, Jones, whilst acknowledging that Welsh expectations had been 'unrealistic', believed that there were 'opportunities' also.

> In retrospect the great expectations vested in the European connection were probably unrealistic. The fundamentals of the United Kingdom relationship with the EU remain unchanged and the nature of executive devolution left few opportunities for initiatives by the National Assembly. Yet, even within these limitations there were opportunities for the Assembly to develop a closer and beneficial relationship with the European Union.
>
> (B.J. Jones 2002: 57)

For its part, the Scottish Executive has involved itself in European matters to no small degree in the aftermath of constitutional reform (Wright: 2005). In a similar vein, the Scottish parliament (sometimes referred to herein as

Holyrood) has managed to carve out a distinctive role for itself. It succeeded in securing a measure of accountability over the Scottish Executive's (renamed Scottish Government in the aftermath of the 2007 election) handling of European matters (Jeffery 2005: 189; Raunio and Wright 2006; Heggie 2006). In so doing, it rather stood out from its territorial counterparts elsewhere in the EU (Jeffery 2005: 190). Furthermore, as Keating observed, the smaller nations in the EU should have more clout in the aftermath of the recent enlargement, whether or not they are member states in their own right. From this perspective there was a multiplicity of spaces for sub-state actors to exercise a measure of influence over the EU (Keating 2001: 137 and 154). So, potentially, there are grounds for optimism, as far as the UK's devolved territories are concerned. But is that the whole picture?

In practice, the evolution of the European agendas of the territorial administrations has differed markedly, not least because of the diversity of the constitutional settlement in the constituent parts of the UK. With regard to Wales and Scotland, devolution took time to 'bed in'. In Scotland's case there were three First Ministers during the Parliament's first four-year term. Each adopted a rather different approach to foreign affairs. That aside, however, the existing constitutional arrangement enjoyed a measure of stability during its first two four-year terms, albeit that the cost of the new building at Holyrood (circa £400 million) called into question the competence of the new administration. For its part, Wales had two First Ministers during the Assembly's first four years. But the situation was complicated further by two factors. First there was concern that the Assembly possessed insufficient power; that led to the inception of the Richards Commission (it called for more competence to be assigned to the Assembly – see p. 202).[10] Second, until May 2007, legally there was little if any delineation between the ministers on the Executive and Assembly Members; in effect they formed the same corporate body. Thus to no small extent the early years of the Assembly were tantamount to 'a constitutional convention by other means' (Osmond 2000).

Despite the difficulties which they faced during their early years, both the Scottish and Welsh devolved administrations have not shrunk from involving themselves in European matters. In part, it could be claimed that this was little more than a continuum of the scenario which pre-dated devolution. In effect both the former Scottish and Welsh Offices had each taken an increasingly close interest in the EC/EU during the 1980s and 1990s (see Chapter 5) and it followed the same would apply to their respective successors post-1999. Yet in the aftermath of devolution,[11] there had been something of a step change. One explanation is that the EU itself stood on the cusp of further reform – something which was of consequence both to Scotland and Wales and which their political elites could not afford to ignore. An allied reason was the European Commission's paper on Governance, which acknowledged that the EU was increasingly disconnected from its citizens – something that its territorial administrations could potentially ameliorate.[12] More particularly, the newly established administrations in Cardiff and Edinburgh created their own dynamic; namely, that devolution engendered a greater degree of political strategic leadership than had been the case hitherto (e.g. there were more ministers *in situ* and they could lose office if they failed to meet public expectations).

Equally, although European matters and international affairs, more generally, were reserved to Westminster, the authors of the devolved arrangements acknowledged that the administrations in Wales and Scotland would have a 'role' to play.[13] The same applied to the Scottish Parliament and to the National Assembly for Wales. So far as the former was concerned, Scottish and Welsh ministers could not avoid taking a close interest in European issues because of their impact on devolved matters. The net result has been that each administration has formulated its own distinctive foreign affairs' agenda, though this should not be misconstrued as being akin to a form of 'alternative' foreign policy to that of the UK.[14] Moreover, both administrations established their own bureaux in Brussels, thereby supplanting the relatively de-politicized arrangements (The Wales European Centre and Scotland Europa), which pre-dated devolution (see Chapter 5). In the main, this enabled them to garner valuable intelligence about future developments in the EU. Additionally, by having a permanent presence there, they could develop a working relationship with key actors in each of the EU's institutions, (though any such links would be complementary to the role undertaken by UKRep). As such, they lobbied on behalf of their respective territories.[15] Over time, one clear distinction emerged, however. Scotland Europa, which pre-dated devolution, was retained and civil servants from the Scottish Government's EU Office were situated in the same building in Brussels. The Wales European Centre was less fortunate. During the latter part of 2004 it was announced that it would close and that the Assembly Government would set up its own bureau alongside that of the Welsh Local Government centre.[16]

The Parliament and the Assembly have also followed a not dissimilar trajectory, albeit that the status of the two institutions differs markedly. Each has its own European Committee (their remit eventually included 'external relations'). The underlying intention was that European affairs should be subject to democratic scrutiny both in relation to those EU policies which stood to affect devolved matters and also vis-à-vis the implementation of those policies at the territorial level. In practice, however, pre-legislative scrutiny of EU proposals proved elusive for Members of the Scottish Parliament (MSPs) at Holyrood. There was insufficient time for the committee to arrive at a position and transmit its view to the European Affairs committee at the Commons before the proposal had been adopted by the Council of the EU. For its part, the Welsh committee did not attempt this form of scrutiny.

Nonetheless the committees have acted as 'drivers for change' inasmuch as each has conducted inquiries, which in turn has encouraged the relevant devolved administration to formulate its response (see Arter 2004; Raunio and Wright 2006). For example, the Scottish committee's inquiries have ranged from structural funding to how effectively Scotland is promoted world-wide. The net result is that considerably more information about how Scotland and Wales conduct their European relations is available in the public arena[17] than was the case prior to 1999. More particularly, there has been something of a synergy between ministers and the committees. This was especially so in Wales where Rhodri Morgan, the First Minister, chaired the European committee during part of the Assembly's first term.[18] Conversely, the status of MSPs was more akin to their colleagues at Westminster; ministers did not sit on or chair the committee. Instead, where necessary they provided written and oral testimony to the committee. In addition, a convention evolved whereby the relevant Scottish Minister would appear before the committee prior to his or her attendance at the Council of the EU. Ministers also provided an overview of the Executive's priorities concerning the forthcoming presidencies of the EU. Thus, there has been some progress as far as Scotland and Wales[19] are concerned – something which rather contrasted with Northern Ireland's situation.

Initially devolution had been no panacea for Northern Ireland. Although there was much optimism in the immediate aftermath of *The Agreement*, it was soon apparent that the province remained deeply divided, politically. Central to this was the issue of trust, underlying which there was a process of negotiation and re-negotiation over what should stay and what should go (Wilford and Wilson 2000).[20] Whilst initially there appeared to be some progress over the decommissioning of the Provisional IRA's weapons, that eventually stalled, with the result that David Trimble, the First Minister, had no option but to pull out of the coalition with the Republicans. Peter Mandelson, the Secretary of State, then suspended devolution on February 11 2000 (Murray 2000: 126) – the Legislative Assembly having only assumed power months earlier on December 2 1999. On May 29 2000 the devolved powers were restored to the Legislative Assembly (LA). The following year, devolution was temporarily suspended again in August and September 2001. Devolution was eventually restored in May 2007 but problems persisted into 2008 (see p. 201).

It therefore comes as little surprise that between 1999 and 2008 progress on European affairs has been quite modest, as far as Northern Ireland is concerned. As the province was governed by a coalition (when a devolved administration was *in situ*) which itself was a product of *The Agreement* (i.e. the allocation of ministerial portfolios rested on the d'Hondt system), there was an absence of political consensus at the highest levels of the administration over how the province could best be governed. There was also an absence of collective responsibility (Wilford and Wilson: 2000). Presumably that would have had a knock-on effect on the evolution of a more strategic approach to EU affairs. In a similar vein the LA itself made little headway to begin with. Although it had been agreed on December 8 1999 that the LA would have its own European Committee, that was not to be. Instead, European affairs fell within the remit of the newly created Committee of the

Centre. To begin with the committee made little progress due to antipathy between the Sinn Fein members and the chair and sub-chair, each of whom were Unionists. That changed during 2001 when there was a new chair and matters improved into the next year when the committee took a close interest in the EU and its impact on Northern Ireland (Wright 2004). Nonetheless, what progress there was, was overshadowed by the (on-off) suspension of devolution until 2007. Had that not occurred, Northern Ireland's administration could well have found itself pursuing a similar European strategy to that of Scotland and Wales.

Save for Northern Ireland, where devolution was suspended, from time to time, the new constitutional arrangements do appear to have had a marked effect on how the territories have conducted their European affairs' agenda. Though it should also be noted that as far as devolution is concerned, it is early days. There has been a greater degree of strategic leadership[21] than hitherto and the creation of democratically elected bodies has resulted in greater transparency. However, it remains to be seen whether there has been a fundamental step-change, not least because political authority over the formulation of the UK line on EU policy remains in London. Thus whilst the new constitutional arrangements might cultivate new opportunities for Scotland and Wales in the EU, in terms of political authority at least the *status quo* prevails within the UK.[22]

So far as influencing the formulation of UK policy is concerned, historically both Scotland and Wales have had their successes with regard to day-to-day policy making (see for example Bulmer *et al.* 2002). However, as suggested in Chapter 5, there has been a number of occasions where the strategic interests of Scotland have not been well served. One such example was the issue of additionality as regards the EU's structural funds. Until 1991 at the earliest, EU aid should have been additional to UK monies. This was not so and doubts persisted on into the 1990s (Wright 2005). The issue of additionality contributed to the resignation of Alun Michael, Welsh First Minister, when the National Assembly for Wales was in its infancy, although thereafter the issue appears to have been resolved satisfactorily. In terms of power dependency, the devolved bodies are subordinate to Westminster. As constitutional matters are currently a reserved power, formally there is little that the devolved administrations could do to enhance the current inter-governmental mechanisms which exist within the UK – ultimately, that rests with the UK Government. However, that was not the whole picture.

The territorial administrations were also confronted with the fact that responsibility for decision-making in a swathe of areas of policy, which falls within their devolved competencies (e.g. the environment), resides in Brussels. Moreover, there is nothing to prevent a future UK government from transferring even more competencies to the EU in areas that are devolved to the territorial governments. Yet they remain one step removed from decision-making in the EU (i.e. the UK Government is represented in the Council of the EU).[23] Consequently, despite the progress that the devolved institutions have made vis-à-vis European affairs, it remains to be seen if Scotland and Wales have managed to secure substantively more influence over EU policy making than was the case prior to 1999. Devolution in Northern Ireland has only recently been restored at the time of writing and it remains to be seen how the situation evolves.

Indeed, the issue of Scottish representation in Brussels became something of a *cause célèbre* in January 2007, when *The Herald* published details of a confidential report by one of the Executive's top officials in Brussels.[24] The document, it was claimed, warned that the 'Scottish administration was sometimes deliberately excluded' by Whitehall when EU policy was being formulated at the UK level. On occasion, the Executive's views might be ignored altogether or officials might be advised too late in the day about a meeting in London concerning EU affairs with the result that they could not attend. On other occasions Scottish Ministers were part of the UK delegation at the Council of the EU but instead of being able to sit alongside their colleagues from the UK, they had to 'sit in another room'.[25] Jack McConnell, the First Minister, responded by claiming that the document was purely a draft.[26] Nonetheless, allegations such as these are cause for concern, in part because it would appear that the original report was based on a series of questionnaires within the Executive and as such it is difficult to ignore their potential seriousness. In addition concerns such as these are by no means new (see for example Wright 2005; Bulmer *et al.* 2002).

In the meantime, however, the EU had become an increasingly influential political actor in its own right. The exercise of its authority therefore taxed the attention of the new administrations in Edinburgh and Cardiff from the moment of their inception; the EU needed to be 'reined in' just as it was on the cusp of potentially securing more competence.[27]

The Convention on the future of the EU, chaired by Giscard d'Estaing, had a particular resonance for the administrations in Edinburgh and Cardiff. This was because it became a 'marketplace for ideas, where in theory at least, Member States had to compete with others to get their ideas on board' (Clifford 2004: 48). The Welsh and Scottish administrations each had their own agenda, part of which was intended to enhance the status of the regions in the EU. In essence they argued that the delineation of competences did not apply solely to the member state/EU nexus, but also applied potentially to the EU's territories as well. Consequently, in their view, the EU should not involve itself in areas of policy where there is no meaningful justification for it to do so. Allied to which, there was the perception that further seepages of power to the EU risked undermining devolution itself. Jack McConnell was well aware of such a danger, when he called for a Subsidiarity Council on June 6 2002.[28]

The issue of subsidiarity had become increasingly contentious for the Scottish Executive, not least by virtue of how best it could be policed. From one perspective, potentially this rested with the ECJ, but there was no provision in the existing treaties for the regions to bring such cases before the

Court. The Flanders Declaration (May 2001), of which Scotland was a signatory, asked that 'consideration be given' that the Committee of the Regions could bring infringements of subsidiarity before the ECJ. Even though usage of the term 'consideration' ostensibly watered down the demand, the issue raised hackles in London, and Henry McLeish, McConnell's predecessor, faced criticism from sections of the Labour Party and also the Foreign Office (Wright 2005). For his part, McConnell did not think that the Court was of much relevance, even though Scotland was one of the signatories demanding direct access to the ECJ in November 2004 (see p. 197).[29] Instead he called for a 'Subsidiarity Council'. This proposal fell on fallow ground and was not adopted by the EU but the CoR potentially gained (see p. 197).

Nonetheless, the Welsh and Scottish administrations wanted the EU to acknowledge in the constitution that its regions had their own distinctive role within the Union. There was a variety of aspects to this. In part this related to the protection of cultural and national minorities at the sub-state level. In addition, there needed to be a more explicit recognition on the part of the EU that its regional administrations should be 'accommodated in the constitutional treaty'.[30] In effect, whilst the creation of the CoR was not without significance, because it marked the moment when the EU's regions were formally incorporated into the EU policy processes where the treaties so allowed, it was held that the regions' status remained too subordinate within the EU.

In 2002 officials from the devolved administrations worked with the Cabinet Office and the relevant departments in London to agree a paper setting out the position of the Welsh and Scottish governments. This document became official UK policy in January 2003 when it was approved by JMC (Europe). Somewhat fortuitously, perhaps, Peter Hain, the UK's minister for Europe, was also the Secretary of State for Wales. He submitted the paper at the Convention's session on regional affairs during February. The paper contained a number of demands. These included the following. The CoR should have the right of appeal to the ECJ over infringements of subsidiarity. The principle of subsidiarity needed to be delineated more cogently in the (then) forthcoming treaty on the Constitution. There should be greater consultation by the Commission at the pre-legislative stage of the policy process – in effect ideally this should occur well 'upstream' of the publication of a legislative proposal (Clifford 2004: 48).

The Treaty Establishing a Constitution for Europe (signed in Rome on October 2004 but not ratified)[31] was of some succour to the EU's regions and stateless nations. It also took on board some of the demands set out in the paper submitted by Peter Hain on behalf of the devolved administrations in Scotland and Wales. For example, Article 1–3 ('The Union's Objectives') stated that the Union would 'respect its rich cultural and linguistic diversity, and shall ensure that Europe's cultural heritage is safeguarded and enhanced'. More significantly, the regions themselves were directly referred to in Article

1–5 (Relations between the Union and the Member States). It included the following under paragraph 1:

> The Union shall respect the equality of Member States before the constitution as well as national identities, inherent in their fundamental structures, political and constitutional, including regional and local self-government. It shall respect their essential state functions, including the territorial integrity of the State, maintaining law and order and safeguarding national security.

Article 1–11 paragraph 3, relating to subsidiarity also referred to the regions. It stated:

> Under the principle of subsidiarity, in areas which do not fall within its exclusive competence, the Union shall act only if and insofar as the objectives of the proposed action cannot be sufficiently achieved by the Member States, either at central level or at regional and local level, but can rather by reason of the scale or effects of the proposed action, be better achieved at Union level.

Such references to the 'regions' (and stateless nations such as Scotland) in the new Constitution contrasts rather with the TEU in 1991 when they were not directly mentioned in relation to subsidiarity and the division of competences.

When it convened at Edinburgh in November 2004, RegLeg (the umbrella organization representing the regions with legislative power – of which McConnell then held the presidency) welcomed the new treaty, 'as a further step towards full involvement of the regions with legislative power'. Amongst the provisions they approved of were: 'the improved clarification of the competencies of the EU, the provisions that it contains to ensure that the principle of subsidiarity is respected' and the enhanced role that it gives to the CoR. Whilst RegLeg applauded the 'improved provision for pre-legislative consultation, it called for the Commission to consult the regions with legislative power directly as a matter of course'. RegLeg did have a number of reservations however. It suggested that a provision should have been included which allowed a Member State to assign 'Partners of the Union' status to certain regions. In so doing, these regions would 'enjoy specific rights at the European level, where they have exclusive competence or shared competence with their member state'. RegLeg also demanded that regions with legislative powers should have the right of direct appeal to the ECJ (RegLeg 2004).

Although the new constitution did not confer institutional status on the CoR as RegLeg had hoped, nor for that matter did it assign decision-making powers to that body (i.e. it retains its consultative status), it did secure the entitlement to bring cases before the ECJ. However, such cases could only be brought on the grounds that the CoR had not been consulted in those areas of competence where it was so entitled under the treaty.[32] This was indicative of the ambiguity as to how subsidiarity and proportionality[33] would be 'policed' under the protocol in the draft treaty. That, in turn, would have repercussions, potentially for 'national'[34] parliaments, in general across the EU, and for sub-state bodies such as the Scottish Parliament and the National Assembly for Wales.

The protocol sought to ameliorate the democratic deficit by involving the national parliaments more fully in the EU's policy making. But whether this would have provided the national parliaments with more clout in the EU than hitherto is a moot point. The same holds true but more so for the territorial parliaments. Article 6 stated:

> Any national Parliament or any chamber of a national Parliament may, within six weeks from the date of transmission of a draft European legislative act, send to the Presidents of the European Parliament, the Council and the Commission a reasoned opinion stating why it considers that the draft in question does not comply with the principle of subsidiarity. It will be for each national Parliament or each chamber of a national Parliament to consult, where appropriate, regional parliaments with legislative powers.

In effect, whether or not the territorial parliaments were actually consulted by their national parliaments would be dependent on either the current constitutional arrangement (e.g. the German Länder have their own Chamber) or on agreement between the relevant bodies at the state and sub-state tiers. More particularly, there was the possibility that if a sufficient number of national parliaments objected to an EU proposal, then the latter could conceivably be withdrawn, although this was by no means set in stone.

Each Member State would be assigned two votes. Hence in a bicameral parliamentary system such as exists in the UK, the Commons would have one of the votes and the Lords the other. If a sufficient number of parliamentary chambers objected, then this would have implications for the legislative proposal. Article 7 included the following:

> Where reasoned opinions on a draft European legislative act's non-compliance with the principle of subsidiarity represent at least one third of all the votes allocated to the national Parliaments in accordance with the second paragraph [the paragraph above], the draft must be reviewed. This threshold shall be a quarter in the case of a draft European legislative act submitted on the basis of Article III-264 of the Constitution on the area of freedom, security and justice.

Whilst this is worthy in principle, there are a number of practicalities, which may serve to undermine the efficacy of the arrangement. First, the time frame of six weeks left the national parliament with very little time to formulate a position on subsidiarity in relation to a given proposal. Second, there was the issue of co-ordination between national parliaments. Third, legally, the Commission or the relevant EU institution[35] needs only to conduct a review. The proposal could therefore still enter into force, thereby calling into question the point of the protocol. Fourth, Article 7 (referred to above) did not really address the issue of proportionality. Proportionality stems in part from the premise that proposals emanating from the EU should not be disproportional in terms of their cost or their administrative burden vis-à-vis the intended outcome. In practice this is intrinsically related to subsidiarity and that risked creating confusion for the national parliaments, as the House of Lords discovered.

The House of Lords' European Union Committee conducted an inquiry into the provisions for strengthening subsidiarity during 2004. Its report entitled *Strengthening National Parliamentary Scrutiny of the EU – the Constitution's Subsidiarity Early Warning Mechanism* was published in April 2005. Whilst welcoming the new early warning mechanism set out under Article 6, the committee maintained that the short time frame of six weeks was 'regrettable'. The committee also 'regretted' the fact that the early warning system did not apply to proportionality.[36] It also recognized that if the system was to work effectively it should not be abused by the national parliaments. That is to say that they should not engage in 'tactical manoeuvring in order to reach the one third voting threshold or the system would be devalued'. But Peers (i.e. members of the Lords) also observed that even if the threshold figure was not reached it would add to the political pressure for the proposal to be dropped.[37] Effectively, therefore, if a number of national parliaments expressed doubts about a proposal on the grounds of subsidiarity, it would call into question the latter's legitimacy. If the relevant EU body declined to withdraw or amend the proposal to the satisfaction of those parliaments, which had questioned it, then that in turn would serve to undermine further the EU's position.

The inquiry also considered the implications of the new procedure for the devolved bodies. The report advised that there would be 'two phases of involvement' as regards the territorial assemblies. They should be 'consulted at the pre-legislative phase of lawmaking and when potential breaches of subsidiarity are noted'.[38] It also recommended that 'the views of regional assemblies could best be presented to Parliament through a sustained dialogue between the two authorities. Effective communication would help to ensure the smooth operation of the early warning mechanism'.[39] However, the committee raised a number of potential problems. For example what would happen if the national parliament intended to raise an objection to a particular proposal but this was contrary to the wishes of a territorial assembly?[40] The report therefore suggested that a 'system' needed to be devised to 'deal with such differences of opinion fairly and efficiently'.[41]

In response to the Lords' inquiry, the Government submitted a Memorandum, part of which related to the 'role of regional assemblies'. It stated that 'the UK Government intended to involve the devolved administrations as fully as possible' and that the latter would be 'entitled to produce assessments of subsidiarity compliance in their own right'. Accordingly, the 'devolved legislatures could subject these statements to scrutiny but they would not be able to hold the UK Government to account through such an assessment'.[42] In effect this was indicative of how far EU matters were reserved to Westminster. As far as procedural formalities were concerned, the Memorandum, whilst acknowledging that this was a matter for the UK parliament and the devolved assemblies, hoped that the views of the latter would be taken into account by the Commons and the Lords.

The House of Commons European Scrutiny Committee was rather sanguine regarding the involvement of the devolved assemblies. A Memorandum to the House's Modernisation Committee, which was published in the minutes of evidence, observed that the devolved assemblies would have 'an input in the process' but that 'it would not be possible to wait for representations from them'. Instead it proposed that if staff at the Commons perceived that a proposal might be in breach of subsidiarity then the devolved assemblies should be 'alerted' so that they could 'have as much opportunity as possible to make their views known'. It also acknowledged that if the devolved assemblies identified a subsidiarity problem, which the Commons had 'missed', then clearance could be rescinded and an objection would then be raised.[43]

Given the six-week time frame it is unsurprising that there was little confidence that the devolved bodies could have an input (see for example, Heggie 2006:42). But given the considerable goodwill which has existed for some time between the Commons committee and its devolved counterparts, clearly the former would in principle support the latter if they had misgivings over subsidiarity. Even so, doubts remained over whether there is sufficient time. As the Lords' report noted, what would happen if a proposal emanated from the EU which potentially breached subsidiarity when the UK Parliament was in recess? The same could be said of the devolved assemblies. Thus despite the good intentions underpinning the protocol, actually implementing it satisfactorily would be no small challenge, as a pilot project under the stewardship of COSAC (the pan-EU inter-parliamentary body) was to demonstrate. This too revealed how problematic the new warning scheme would be for the devolved bodies.

COSAC's pilot project ran between March 1 and April 12 2005. The object was to assess 'how the subsidiarity early warning system might work in practice'. Thirty-one of the 37 national parliamentary chambers participated. The European and External Relations Committee (EERC) of the Scottish Parliament also took part (albeit that formally it was not one of the chambers cited above). Fourteen of the chambers reported that 'one or more of the legislative proposals in the 3rd Railway package breached the principle of subsidiarity, of which eleven produced a reasoned opinion' (COSAC 2005: section 2). The report identified a number of problems. 20 chambers complained that 'the Commission's justifications regarding subsidiarity were less than satisfactory for one or more proposals' (COSAC 2005: section 3). Some of the chambers claimed that it was difficult to distinguish between subsidiarity and proportionality. A number maintained that the six-week period was far too brief. It was suggested that this would have potentially a number of ramifications. First, as the Lords' report had forewarned, there was the concern that a proposal might be issued when chambers were in recess. Second, there was the view that some chambers might opt to formulate their opinion as late as possible within the time frame in order to assess the positions of other parliaments. It was therefore suggested that some form of informal network had to be established. For its part, 'the House of Commons noted that the timetable was particularly tight if national parliaments were to consult regional parliaments with legislative powers'.

From a Scottish perspective, the pilot project was extremely illuminating. The EERC was allowed just five days to formulate an opinion and that proved to be impractical. Although the proposal could have been passed to Holyrood's Transport Committee, the latter already had a heavy workload and was thus unable to participate in the project. The five-day timetable meant that the EERC had too little time to formulate a view, and thus the trial run served to demonstrate that the subsidiarity early warning system might not be of much use to the devolved bodies.[44] In the fullness of time, that may prove to be overly negative, however, as an official from Holyrood will be permanently based in Brussels. Presumably it will fall to that individual to determine which proposals might risk being in breach of subsidiarity well upstream in the policy process. However, the matter was laid to rest following the rejection of the Constitutional treaty.

Whilst the EU underwent a period of 'reflection' during 2006 (after the treaty's rejection), events were unfolding in Northern Ireland. On October 13 the St Andrews' Agreement paved the way for the restoration of devolved government in the province. That came to pass in May 2007, with Ian Paisley of the Democratic Unionist Party as First Minister, and Martin McGuinness of Sinn Fein as Deputy First Minister. It remains to be seen if devolution can attain greater permanence this time around. Certainly there appeared to have been more goodwill than hitherto with both Paisley and McGuinness apparently getting on well with each other. However, some commentators suggested that the 'honeymoon' may have come to an end in the autumn of 2007 and the relationship between the two parties (Sinn Fein and the Democratic Unionist Party) was not dissimilar to that of a 'shotgun marriage' (Wilford and Wilson 2008: 5). However, it appeared that the two leaders got on rather too well, despite the stance of their parties. Paisley stood down in the Spring of 2008 and it remains to be seen how Peter Robinson, his successor as First Minister, will handle relations with McGuiness.

This era was not just potentially significant for Northern Ireland but also for Scotland. In the first instance May 2007 marked the 300th anniversary of the Union between England and Scotland – which in turn ran close to the

50th anniversary of the EU. That prompted Geoff Hoon, the UK Europe minister, to observe a few weeks earlier:

> There are some interesting parallels to be drawn between the 50th anniversary of the European Union and the 300th anniversary of the Union between England and Scotland. When the Treaty of Union was signed in 1707, the Union represented the largest free trade area in Europe. Similarly today the European Union is the largest single market in the world. Three hundred years ago, a customs and monetary union was also created between England and Scotland. Again the parallels with the EU's origins and its recent history are obvious. Just as this government is of the firm belief that the UK's place is in Europe, equally it is in the interests of both Scotland and the rest of the UK that Scotland remains an integral part of the UK.[45]

In the run up to the 2007 Holyrood election, the SNP had been making headway in successive polls[46] and Hoon's remarks were somewhat overshadowed by the Holyrood election result on May 3. The SNP gained 20 seats and in so doing beat Labour to become the party with the most seats (47 against 46, respectively). However, neither party enjoyed an overall majority (65 seats in a parliament of 129 MSPs). For their part neither the Conservatives (17 seats) nor the Liberal Democrats (16 seats) were willing to enter into a coalition with either the SNP or Labour. Even the Greens (two seats) were unwilling to join a formal coalition with the SNP, but they have formed an alliance of sorts thereby enabling Alex Salmond to become Scotland's first 'nationalist' First Minister.[47] During 2008, the profile of relations with the EU was lower than hitherto, no doubt in part because the new government wanted to focus on domestic issues (an exception being the partial repatriation of fisheries conservation to Scotland – p. 205). Even so, one of the SNP's objectives is to secure direct representation in the EU's fisheries council, but this is likely to be a step too far for the UK Government.

For their part, the Welsh elections, after some discussion amongst the parties, led to Rhodri Morgan becoming First Minister once more but this time in coalition with Plaid Cymru.[48] Wales' situation was also transformed as a result of the Government of Wales Act (2006). Under the Act, Wales could one day acquire primary legislative powers akin to the Northern Irish Legislative Assembly and the Scottish Parliament. But that could only occur after a referendum as well as a two-thirds majority in the Welsh Assembly and approval from Westminster.[49] In the aftermath of the 2007 election, the newly formed governing coalition agreed to press ahead with preparations for securing primary powers for the Assembly. By now the European project looked set to be revitalized once more.

After the EU's Constitutional treaty was rejected it seemed that any further moves to 'ever closer union' had reached an impasse. But that soon proved illusory; in December 2007 the member states signed the Lisbon Treaty.

Whilst the extent to which it retains the key elements of its predecessor is the subject of debate at the time of writing, many of the sections which relate to the EU's regions and stateless nations remain *in situ*. The reference to 'respecting cultural and linguistic diversity' has been retained.[50] So too has 'the respect for national identities, inherent in their fundamental structures, political and constitutional, inclusive of regional and local self-government'.[51] The protocols on the role of national parliaments in the European Union, and on the application of the principles of subsidiarity and proportionality were also retained. However there were some changes to the text, including an extension of the time national parliaments have to despatch a 'reasoned opinion to the relevant institution'.[52] This would be extended to eight weeks, instead of six, which had been originally proposed in the Constitutional treaty. Whether that is sufficient for the Scottish parliament remains to be seen. However, the EU has made one attempt at decentralization of authority which will have implications for Scottish fisheries.

The EU agreed to devolve some fisheries conservation measures to the Scottish Government at the end of 2007, which may defuse SNP calls for repatriation of fisheries to Scotland. In future the latter will decide how many days Scottish fishermen can spend at sea under the new rules. In addition a 'conservation credit scheme' has been introduced which has the potential to allocate more days at sea to those fishermen who undertake new conservation measures such as ceasing fishing in those grounds which have high levels of juvenile fish.[53] Whilst this cannot be regarded as devolution of the CFP *per se* (as the leaders of the industry had once hoped), it is indicative of the EU taking a more regionalist approach to the sector. Some years before, it had agreed to establish Regional Advisory Councils such as the one for the North Sea. These bodies do not have decision-making powers as such but their inception indicates that the EU has recognized that a homogenous approach to fisheries conservation was no longer tenable. In so doing the regionalization of fisheries has offered territorial administrations such as the Scottish Government a chance to involve itself in EU policy making more directly than was the case before. Whether such an approach will apply to other sectors remains to be seen.

In sum, both the Scottish Executive/Government and the Welsh Assembly Government took a close interest in the formulation of the constitutional treaty. Inherently this focused on the need to rein in the EU. When the convention was in session, both First Ministers worked alongside the UK Government to agree a common agenda, which reflected the interests of the devolved bodies. McConnell took this a stage further as a result of Scotland's membership of RegLeg. Wales' status with regard to RegLeg is complicated by the fact that the Assembly did not then possess legislative powers – but it was an observer at a conference of regions with constitutional powers in September 2000.

Whilst the constitutional treaty eventually came to nought, it did contain a number of provisions which could have enhanced the influence of the devolved institutions in the UK vis-à-vis the EU and its policies. The Lisbon Treaty will carry this forward if it is eventually ratified by all the member states including Ireland. But as the COSAC pilot project so aptly demonstrated, it remains to be seen if Northern Ireland, Wales and Scotland will really be any better off with regard to subsidiarity and proportionality than is currently the case. However, anecdotal evidence suggests that, the EU Commission was keen to involve itself more fully with the regions, especially those with legislative powers.[54] Devolution of arrangements on days at sea, which entered into force in February 2008, suggests that the EU does accept that some decentralization in functional areas of policy such as the CFP is desirable (however as suggested on p. 202, fisheries is a sensitive subject for the SNP). How far this applies to other sectors remains to be seen.

All-in-all, despite their relative political dependency (i.e. the UK Government retains its gate keeper status as regards the Council), the actions of the devolved administrations (save Northern Ireland) in EU matters since 1999 very much contrasts with those of their predecessors in the run-up to Maastricht. Where possible, they have involved themselves in the European political arena as players in their own right, albeit with the tacit support of the UK Government. Indeed, it remains impossible for them to avoid an involvement in European affairs, given the extent to which the EU's policies fall within their competence.

Last but not least, there is the issue of the SNP's policy of 'independence in Europe'. This can be traced back to the 1980s. As Jim Sillars, then SNP MP for Glasgow Govan put it succinctly back in 1989:

> In essence the whole issue boils down to whether Scotland will have a full and equal say in the European policies which will shape our future, or be a province which, at best, will enhance our lobbying ability and, as is likely to be the case, remain as we are, powerless, lacking in real influence.
> (Sillars 1989: 196–203)

The SNP's policy of independence in Europe coincided with the inception of the Single Market following the SEA. It represented a challenge to the former Conservative government in London, which was increasingly eurosceptic. It also offered Scotland the chance to join a new union in Europe. Several academic studies have questioned whether Scotland would actually be any better off as an 'independent' state in the EU or even whether it might even be permitted to join the EU. Independence in Europe: Scotland's Choice? (Schieren 2000) and *Scotland's place in Europe* (Murkens 2001) are two such examples. Both authors have produced interesting papers, which examine Scotland's possible secession from the UK and its application for EU membership and each touches on the legalities surrounding such a course of action if it were to come to fruition. Although international conventions and the EU's treaties do provide us with an insight into the complexities which Scotland might face if it were to quit one union and join the EU, only when

Scotland secedes from the UK will this be truly tested. In some respects Scotland's membership of the EU has its attractions, namely, the single market would ensure that the rest of the UK could not impose levies on Scottish imports and potentially the single currency would mean that Scotland would not have to shadow the pound.

The SNP also had concerns about the Lisbon Treaty, most notably the section dealing with fisheries; a policy which the party would like to see assigned to the Scottish Parliament. In the meantime, the Scottish Government conducts its 'National Conversation' concerning more powers for the Parliament, including independence.

In conclusion, the issue of 'Europe' looks set to remain a bone of contention, economically, politically and constitutionally for sub-state institutions. In part that is because from the moment the UK joined in 1973, the EC/EU increasingly impacted on Northern Ireland, Wales and Scotland with the result that the administrations in those territories could not afford to ignore a newly emerging polity at the European level.

8 Continuity and change since 1945

This chapter focuses on British policy and attitudes towards European integration since the end of the Second World War. It ranges across a wide variety of historical, strategic, political, economic and other forces that have shaped policy and attitudes. The chapter also considers some of the immediate, intermediate and distant causes that account for Britain's behaviour as an EU member state. The focus is on identifying major changes as well as elements of continuity in the form of recurring issues, tensions and conflicts. The coverage does not pretend to be comprehensive in scope or explanation. Rather it highlights and reviews some of the key features covered in this book. It also attempts to distil from a welter of evidence a number of the main problems, trends, assumptions, circumstances and factors that accompany and influence policy and attitudes.

The chapter is divided into two sections, one of which deals with the external or international environment, while the other concentrates on internal or domestic conditions. The external environment in this case primarily involves global, European and transatlantic developments that have affected British perceptions of and responses to the EC/EU. Internal conditions include the role of economic, commercial and financial factors, the influence of party and electoral politics, and the impact of divisions over national sovereignty, independence and identity. Neither the internal nor the external context, however, can be examined in isolation from each other and in any case are not easily disentangled. Policy and attitudes have reflected the interplay between internal and external pressures. This process has in turn given rise to a combustible compound of conflicting perspectives, principles and interests concerning the motives and objectives of British policymakers, the value of European integration, and the identity and long-term goals of the EC/EU.

The precise meaning of continuity and change depends on timescale and context. A particular event or episode, for example, may contain trace elements of both continuity and change, while a difference of timescale may affect the degree of continuity and change. For example, the incoming Blair Labour government of 1997 intimated change when it launched what it projected as a new phase of constructive engagement with the EU. It thereby distinguished itself from the rhetoric of previous Labour governments and also of the immediately preceding Conservative government by the end of its period of office. It soon became apparent, however, that the Blair government reflected a high degree of continuity with its predecessor in its defence of British interests within the EU on such matters as membership of the euro zone and national control of borders and immigration policy.[1]

The foremost external feature in this context concerns the EC/EU itself. It is appropriate, therefore, to highlight some of the main elements of continuity and change in its evolution in the first instance that particularly touch on Britain's EU membership, before considering how these have impacted on the British policy and attitudes. The history of the EC/EU, in fact, illustrates the overlap between the internal and external spheres and the changing boundary lines between internal and external policy in the conduct of Britain's relations with mainland Europe. Sixty years ago, mainland Europe was widely perceived in British circles as belonging to the foreign policy sphere. Europe had long figured as the object of British policies of intervention and non-intervention. It was not regarded as a source of institutions and measures penetrating domestic affairs. On the contrary, Europe was invariably viewed as the home of alien and disreputable political systems and customs.

EC/EU membership, however, has profoundly transformed this relationship, at least in terms of formal governmental activities. What were previously classed as 'domestic' or 'internal' affairs wholly determined by national bodies have become Europeanized. EU legislation or forms of cooperation between member states have gradually impinged upon many areas of British national life including foreign, defence and security policy, fiscal and economic policy, judicial and home affairs, border control and asylum, environmental policy, international crime, terrorism and human rights issues. EU business was previously handled primarily by the Foreign Office, the Treasury, the Department of Trade and Industry and the Ministry of Agriculture. Now, however, it engages the interest of all government departments, as there is an EU dimension to a diverse range of issues (Wall 2008: 192). According to one informed estimate in 2002, most of the vital departments in Whitehall spent up to a quarter of their time on EU matters whether coping with the consequences of initiatives taken in the EU or trying to influence projects passing through the EU decision-making system.[2] This seemingly irreversible process is one of the marked elements of continuity. It was evident from the beginnings of British membership of the EC when Master of the Rolls Denning, in his judgment on the first case in the British courts concerning the application of EC law, commented on the immediate and longer-term significance of the EEC Treaty of Rome: 'the Treaty is like an incoming tide. It flows into the estuaries and up the rivers. It cannot be held back'.[3]

Local government, too, has increasingly been drawn into the orbit of EC/EU activities. In the early years of British membership of the EC, European integration appeared to be of little consequence to local government. Even so, a number of Scottish councils, for example, participated in inter-regional associations such as the Conference of Peripheral and Maritime Regions which was formed in 1973 at Brittany's instigation (Wright 2005: 28). Membership of bodies such as these enabled councils to mount joint lobbies with their counterparts on mainland Europe. However, the Single European Act transformed how local authorities viewed the EC. Increasingly, EC/EU legislation would have a greater impact on their activities, ranging from greater competition for council contracts to enhanced environmental standards. The reform of the structural funds in 1988 prompted local government to engage more directly with Brussels, even though problems over whether such funds were genuinely 'additional' to UK expenditure continued to blight local government usage of EC funds. As a consequence councils either opened up their own offices in Brussels – Birmingham City Council being the first in 1984 – or they seconded staff to umbrella bodies such as Scotland Europe (Jeffrey 1997c: 183).

The enlargement of the EC/EU represents one of the major changes in its history over the past thirty years and has often featured as one of the most dynamic elements of the EC/EU. The process of enlargement has often posed key questions about the territorial coverage of the EC/EU, about the purpose of European integration, and about the nature of EC/EU interests in the wider world. For example, the EU has never defined the limits of its possible territorial coverage or what constitutes a European state. Yet the process of enlargement has often raised questions about the European credentials of an applicant state, whether evident when de Gaulle vetoed British applications for EEC membership in the 1960s or currently demonstrated by doubts in some EU member states about Turkey's qualifications for membership.

Among the elements of continuity in the history of the EC/EU, the mainland European parentage of the European 'idea' has had a marked impact on the British debate about Europe. Franco-German relations, in particular, have long played a vital role in acting as the motor of European integration throughout much of this period. The Schuman Plan of 1950, for example, was essentially a French initiative aimed at Germany. The negotiations resulting in the Treaties of Rome hinged on relations between Bonn and Paris, while the launching of the single currency in 1999 was very much the product of close relations between the French President Mitterand and the German Chancellor Kohl and of their responses to the unification of Germany in 1990. More recently, there were strenuous Franco-German efforts, under the leadership of Chancellor Merkel and President Sarkozy, to secure the ratification of the Treaty of Lisbon. These two leaders have also resisted US pressure for the eastern expansion of NATO, and they publicly questioned US policy on this matter by insisting that Georgia and Ukraine were not yet ready to join NATO. Sarkozy and Merkel were also prominent in securing a mediating role for the EU in the Georgian war (August 2008) and in seeking to persuade the Irish government to hold a second referendum on the Lisbon Treaty.

Certainly, personal relations between French and German political leaders have waxed and waned, rarely in recent years approaching the relationship between de Gaulle and Adenauer in the late 1950s and early 1960s or between Mitterand and Kohl in the 1990s. Yet it remains the case that no pair of EU member states has such close institutional ties as France and Germany. The Franco-German Treaty of Paris (January 1963) established the framework for regular meetings between the French President and the German Chancellor and also between ministers to discuss foreign and defence policy among other matters. The treaty also provides for consultation between the two governments before either reaches any important foreign policy decision, so that their actions should correspond as far as possible.[4] The workings of this special relationship were fairly described by the British ambassador to Bonn in 1987 as involving a routine whereby the two Heads of Government 'plant flags far ahead of their respective front line, towards which the troops gallantly struggle. Meanwhile, in the ground already occupied, fraternization continues apace and gaps in Franco-German activity are steadily filled in ... ' (Wall 2008: 76). No comparable arrangement has developed between British ministers and their counterparts in Berlin or Paris.

One long-standing aspect of the Franco-German relationship has concerned security considerations and especially the rationale for European integration as a means of containing Germany, normally expressed in the form of preserving peace on the continent. It is easy to underestimate or dismiss the significance of this development, as British governments have tended to do, whether as a result of the passage of time or as a matter of inconsequential rhetorical posturing in the wider context of Cold War or post-Cold War politics. Yet security concerns and a determination to escape from the flaws and fault lines of Europe's war-torn recent past informed and influenced the vision and activities of the founding fathers of the EEC. The security dimension, however, together with much of the political rhetoric supporting European integration, has entered less and less into public discourse in recent years The reduced force of these influences is partly due to generational change as Kohl and Mitterand were the last of a long line of French and German leaders with personal experience of the Second World War and of the 'never again' mentality. It is also partly a result of a consumerist society within which the EU is primarily judged by its material gains. The recent process of enlargement, for example, highlighted the newcomers' perceptions of the primarily economic benefits of integration.

The Common Agricultural Policy (CAP) is another aspect of Franco-German relations that also points to an element of continuity in the history of the EC/EU. While it may be misleading to suggest that this policy originated in a basic deal between French agriculture and German industry, it was nevertheless the case that France and, to a lesser extent, West Germany were the principal authors of this policy. The main features of this policy have remained intact since they emerged in the 1960s and they have withstood both expenditure and production cuts in the past twenty years. In short, the CAP remains a heavily and notoriously protectionist system. It currently consumes 45 per cent of the EU's budget and provides a subsidy to farmers of

£557 per EU taxpayer. Its cost dwarfs, for example, the much-trumpeted amount of aid that the EU gives to sub-Saharan Africa: at the beginning of this century the EU provided in agricultural subsidies more than 100 times as much money for each EU cow as for each sub-Saharan African human being.[5]

Another enduring feature of the EC/EU is its public image as an elitist, technocratic, top-down, remote and unaccountable organization. It is often portrayed as a source of easy financial benefit and attracts adverse publicity for its unaudited accounts and a shoal of myths surrounding its activities, all of which find ample coverage in the eurosceptic British press.[6] It is a commonplace that the evolution of the EC/EU has resulted in a wide gulf between EU leaders and European public opinion with such a 'democratic deficit' that the institutional structure of the EU is portrayed as failing to meet the democratic requirements that are expected of any applicant state for EU membership. A related major criticism of the EU is that it runs the risk of creating a profound moral and institutional crisis in view of its obsession with market economics and technocratic language combined with little regard for the dispersal of power and strong democratic accountability.[7] The EC/EU has never taken the form of a popular movement with deep, widespread roots underpinning its existence and legitimacy, and it would probably not have emerged if its existence had depended on the outcome of referendums in the 1950s. In its Schuman Plan origins, for example, it was not a grass roots movement, and initially the plan made no provision for any form of popularly elected representative body. A Common Assembly, the forerunner of the European Parliament, subsequently emerged as a result of intergovernmental negotiations on the plan. It was a purely token, consultative body, however, lacking substantive powers, apart from that of dismissing the Commission. The introduction of direct elections to the European Parliament did not occur until 1979. The Parliament remained very much a talking-shop until the past twenty years when, as a result of the SEA, the TEU, and the Treaty of Amsterdam (1997), it has increasingly shared the decision-making role (co-decision-making) with the Council of Ministers. Yet it remains disconnected from the public at large as a virtual parliament divorced from national politics with a limited voting public. In this last respect, at least, it differs little from the election of a Labour government in Britain (2005) in which non-voters easily outnumbered Labour voters; Labour returned to power with only 36.2 per cent of the votes – the smallest percentage vote of any governing party in the democratic states of Europe. Alienation between government and governed is as much a feature of national as of EU political systems.

Finally, the treatment of the EC/EU's history has undergone considerable change as compared with some of the first accounts of the dynamics of European integration. Early histories of the EEC, for example, often gave pride of place to individuals and groups whose pan-European vision and idealism suggested that they were the prime movers in fashioning the EEC. Such grand, heroic narratives frequently belittled the role and importance of the individual states and of national interests and rarely gave detailed attention to hard inter-governmental bargaining and power politics. Some of these studies predicted the withering away of the nation-state and its replacement by a European superstate or federal system. In the past twenty years or so, however, a large body of work on the history of European integration has challenged these earlier accounts, whether by portraying national interests as the motor of European integration or by identifying economic interdependence as the driving force.[8] Other studies have tended to offer multi-causal explanations that stress the changing blend and influence of a number of factors across time and space or deal with a particular episode in the history of the EU.[9]

Much of the debate about the making of the EC/EU in these accounts has centred on such matters as the relative importance of political and economic factors, the influence of sub-national, national, supranational and transna-tional pressures, the relationship between structural conditions and individual agents, and the impact of European and non-European conditions. The debate has taken a variety of forms, from fantasies demonizing or defend-ing the EC/EU to the use of particular representations of the EC/EU's past for current polemical purposes. Meanwhile, political science theories about the process of European integration reflect both change and continuity. The changing character of the EC/EU, for example, has generated a host of theories over time to make sense of the subject, ranging from some of the early or classical theories of European integration like neo-functionalism and intergovernmentalism to more recent developments in EU theory like constructivism, Europeanization and normative theories. The competing character of such theories suggested to one analyst that the origins of theories of European integration were comparable to the fate of a blind person dis-covering an elephant: each blind person touched a different part of the animal, and each concluded that the elephant had the appearance of the part that he or she touched. While nobody arrived at a very accurate description of the elephant, a lively debate ensued about the nature of the beast because each person disbelieved the others.[10] One persistent feature of this academic debate is that the 'practitioners' of EU politics such as politi-cians, diplomats and officials sometimes dispute the extent to which their activities and the daily workings of the organization are in fact captured or illuminated by these theoretical studies (Menon 2004: 43; Wall 2008: 185, 201).

As compared with the early years of British membership, there is a strong case for maintaining that the EC/EU has developed in ways coinciding with British interests during the past twenty years. Consequently, the previously unconvincing claim of British leaders about winning the argument in Europe has had more substance to it in recent years. This view is held, for example, by British diplomats (Permanent Representatives to the EC/EU) who were closely involved in the daily business of representing Britain at the highest level within the EU machinery in the past thirty years (Menon 2004: 44). Several features of the recent evolution of the EU may be viewed as beneficial to Britain: the adoption of economic neo-liberalism (as represented by the so-called Lisbon strategy of 2000) and the erosion of social democratic values and policies (as especially associated with the Commission under the presidency of Delors in the 1980s); the reduction in the amount of EU legislative activity; the collapse of the Constitutional Treaty and the further clouding of any federal vision at the heart of the EU; the increasing doubts about and disenchantment with the 'European project' in many member states suggesting that the EU may have reached the limits of integration; the reform of the CAP; the shifting balance away from institutional preoccupations towards substantive policy issues like climate change and energy; the increasing predominance of English as the working language of the major EU institutions; the greater acceptance of the need for diversity in an EU of 27 member states; and the advantages of enlargement whether in reinforcing British policy on such matters as support for the Atlantic Alliance and relations with the USA or in so paralysing the EU's decision-making system as to make any further steps towards closer integration unlikely. According to Peter Mandelson, the former trade commissioner in the European Commission and currently business secretary in the Brown government, the EU of 27 member states is a place where Britain can feel at home in a way that it has not for much of the past thirty years. Besides evidence of a UK-friendly bias in EU activities, the case for British membership of the EU received greater publicity from Blair during his premiership (1997–2007) than from any of his predecessors with the exception of Heath. In the absence of stiff competition for the title, Blair was arguably the most 'European' Prime Minister since Heath and certainly in terms of his rhetoric.[11]

During this recent period, however, British suspicion of or opposition to the EU, as reflected in press and parliamentary comment, has become more pronounced in the face of the evolution of the EU since the formation of the euro zone. In this respect, it can be argued that while Blair was able to make the case for Britain in Europe he was unable to make the case for Europe in Britain (Geddes 2004: 228). Such developments as the abortive Constitutional Treaty and, at the time of writing, the uncertain future of the Treaty of Lisbon suggest that there is a more widespread perception of what the EU can and cannot do. Few observers doubt that euroscepticism has now supplanted europhile opinion as the dominant position in the British debate about Europe. Apart from Peter Mandelson on the Labour side and Kenneth Clarke, the former Conservative Chancellor of the Exchequer, there are now few heavyweight political figures or national organizations vigorously supporting British membership of the EU. Public opinion polls about attitudes towards the EU often obscure a gallimaufry of motives, some of which have little or nothing to do with the activities of the EU. Nevertheless, a large number of polls conducted in the past ten years has invariably demonstrated a growing and greater degree of lukewarm support for and outright opposition to EU membership in Britain than in other EU states. Eurobarometer polling on British attitudes to the EU for the period 1997–2004, for example, reported a fall from 35 per cent to 29 per cent in the number of people considering EU membership to be 'a good thing' and a rise in the number considering it 'a bad thing' from 26 per cent to 29 per cent. The most recent polling results from the same source for 2007 indicated limited British support for EU membership. They also highlighted considerable differences between Britain and the rest of the EU member states (figures in parentheses refer to the EU-wide average): 34 per cent of those polled saw EU membership as 'a good thing' (58 per cent), 28 per cent viewed EU membership as 'a bad thing' (13 per cent), 31 per cent took a neutral view (25 per cent), and 7 per cent don't know (more than twice the EU average). In response to the question 'Has your country benefited or not from EU membership?' 43 per cent said yes (58 per cent), 44 per cent said no (29 per cent), and 13 per cent said don't know (13 per cent). Furthermore, scepticism and ignorance are often two sides of the same coin so far as British attitudes towards the EU are concerned. In March 2008, for example, an EU-wide survey about attitudes towards the European Parliament found that the British were not only the most sceptical on many EU issues but also the most ignorant. The population of no other member state knew less and trusted less about the EU than the British.[12]

The concepts of continuity and change can be applied to all aspects of British policy and attitudes towards the EC/EU over the past sixty years. British perceptions of the external environment require treatment in the first instance. Some basic parameters of history, geography and culture have had a profound, if not precisely measurable, impact on policy and attitudes. Each has contributed to the uncertainty as to whether Britain is part of Europe and reflects very different readings of the 'island story': insular, European, imperial, Atlantic, global. There are clearly difficulties in determining the precise relationship between British policy and attitudes towards the EC/EU as such and British attitudes towards Europe beyond the exclusive confines of the EC/EU. Europe in the latter sense is a problematical, highly contested concept that attracts a wide variety of definitions, images, representations and explanations. There are, in effect, many Europes, extending, for example, from the 'Europe' of the EU and of the Large Hadron Collider at Cern to the 'Europe' of the Eurovision song contest and European Champions League football. The common expression 'Britain and Europe' and the different connotations attached to the concept of 'Europe' in British political discourse reflect the extent to which a large section of British public opinion seems undecided about Britain's European credentials, standing and identity.[13] Furthermore, the uncertainty surrounding the precise nature and extent of British interest in the EC/EU has long figured as one of the elements of continuity in the British approach to European integration. On the first day of Britain's membership of the EC, an editorial on the event in the *Guardian* feared that 'If the trumpet gave an uncertain sound, who shall prepare himself for the battle?' and it further warned about the need to avoid a new, semi-permanent rift in British society between pro- and anti-Europeans.[14] In the event and less than three years after joining the EC, the battle between pro- and anti-Europeans broke out in the referendum of 1975. The conflict has remained a more or less permanent feature of British politics ever since, though much of the drive and intense campaigning on both sides of the fence has been less evident in recent years.

The idea of 'Europe' as a parallel universe or as a separate entity from Britain is evident in the view that Britain is alongside Europe only as a result of geographical accident and not by virtue of any deep-seated affinity with mainland Europe. Such a position often conveys both a stunning ignorance of the country's place in Europe prior to the rise of the modern nation-state as well as a sweeping tendency to see Europe as an undifferentiated 'abroad'.[15] While the expressions 'joining Europe' or 'going to Europe' are commonplace in Britain, it would be considered illogical to use such expressions in France or Germany. Projections of 'Europe' as the hostile 'other' are often accompanied by definitions of Britishness that contrast what are projected as some of the main features of British identity with what are represented as the principal and deeply rooted unattractive characteristics of mainland Europe. Fairness, tolerance and parliamentary democracy loom large in the case of the former. By contrast, British perceptions of mainland Europe often include centralized government, political instability, undemocratic politics and military weakness in recent times, and militarism, absolutism and Catholicism on a longer time-scale. In short, Britain is viewed as not only different from but superior to Europe.

'Europe' as the hostile 'other' has invariably been underpinned by a deep-seated xenophobia extending to all 'Damn foreigners'. Mainland Europeans, however, have been a particular target. Sometimes, this has taken the form of the crude stereotyping of the EU and of its individual member states in the 'only a bit of fun' presentations of the British tabloid press. In other cases it has found expression in the jokey preferences of political leaders like Attlee, who could not trust the Europeans because they did not play cricket, and John Major who preferred Commonwealth meetings because all participants spoke English. In a characteristically less good-humoured manner, Margaret Thatcher simply complained in her memoirs that her EC colleagues were 'unBritish', and in the case of France and Germany, in particular, were given to plotting against Britain. In addition, there are certain long-standing fears about individual European countries, most obviously in the form of Francophobia before and during the nineteenth century, Germanophobia in the twentieth century and outbursts of Russophobia across the entire period. Dislike of foreigners from the continent, as one experienced politician on the national and European stage summed up the condition, meant that long after the end of the Second World War the British could still hear the distant wail of air-raid sirens in the night and catch the whiff of the garlic breath of duplicity and cowardice (Patten 2005).[16] Unsurprisingly, one Cabinet minister on the eve of Britain's first application to join the EEC in 1961 warned Macmillan that there was no sure hope of carrying the British people into the

EEC on the back of the advice of pro-EEC economic pundits and enthusiasts who 'would be no match for the ghosts of Louis XIV and Napoleon, the Kaiser and Hitler ... '[17] In similar vein, the Queen Mother expressed a widespread prejudice of her generation when she reportedly commented on the EC/EU in the early 1990s: 'It will never work, you know ... It will never work with all those Huns, wops and dagos'.[18] Her doubts about the future viability of the EC/EU have been widely shared by official and public opinion in the country since the launching of the Schuman Plan in 1950 down to present-day scepticism about the survival of the euro zone.

The sense of apartness or 'island of the mind' condition represents an element of continuity in Britain's relationship with the process of European integration since 1945. During this same period, however, 'Europe' as the hostile 'other' has emerged as an even more important element in definitions of British identity or Britishness. This development is all the more pronounced as some of the long-standing symbols of that identity like monarchy, empire and Protestantism no longer occupy their centre-stage position of sixty years ago and as some studies point to a gradual long-term process of declining British identity.[19] Particular attitudes towards the EC/EU at any given time have reflected changes, most notably in the manufacture of British identity. 'Europe' as associated with the EC/EU has arguably accounted for many of the demons in British mythology about the outside world in the past sixty years and has certainly carried a load of negative connotations that arise out of a number of different factors and perform a variety of functions. Projections of the EC/EU as the hostile 'other' were, and in some quarters still are, regarded as a principal means of buttressing the UK state. Besides which, the British decision to seek EC membership has long served as a painful reminder of the country's reduced power and status in the world, most obviously associated with the withdrawal from empire and relative economic decline.

The sense of separateness or otherness from Europe was a constant feature of a widespread British view of mainland Europe in the twentieth century that was often grounded in a Victorian understanding of English history and of the rise and development of empire. It found expression, for example, in the widely read books of three historians in the second quarter of the century: Trevelyan, Fisher and Bryant. The last was a particular favourite of Prime Ministers Churchill, Attlee and Wilson, but all three of them provided, according to one study of the subject, the mental baggage of a generation or more of post-1945 politicians and civil servants with their emphasis on the sense of the separateness of Britain from mainland Europe. The 'strange island, anchored off the continent' (Trevelyan 1946: 11) had for a long time enjoyed a high degree of stability and continuity with a unique flexibility in the slow and steady growth of its institutions and of its concept of sovereignty. Furthermore, so it was claimed, Britain had only found its true destiny when it turned away from mainland Europe with its war-torn history, constantly turbulent politics, and changing political systems and borders. Few political leaders better enshrined the powerful historical myth of separateness from mainland Europe than Hugh Gaitskell, leader of the Labour Party, when he opposed the first British application for EEC membership on the grounds that 'It means the end of a thousand years of history ... ' and that the British people 'will not throw away the tremendous heritage of history' (Bell 1996; Ash 2001: 6; Williams 1979). In this same vein and at the end of the First World War John Maynard Keynes commented: 'England still stands outside Europe. Europe's voiceless tremors do not reach her. Europe is apart and England is not of her flesh and blood' (Keynes 1920: 1). Seventy years later Margaret Thatcher was to declare 'in my lifetime all our problems have come from mainland Europe and all the solutions have come from the English-speaking nations of the world ... '[20]

Such observations reflect the importance of a longstanding feature of British policy towards the politics and international relations of mainland Europe. Any form of engagement should be strictly limited and primarily designed to maintain a balance of power. What had to be resisted at all costs was the domination of the European continent by a single power or what used to be referred to as a 'universal monarch'. The strategy of limited involvement and fear of costly continental entanglements has changed little in the last hundred years (N. Johnson 2004: 7). In some respects, the EC/EU was simply the latest version of that 'single power'. Thatcher, for example, referred to Brussels and the EU bureaucracy as the 'Belgian Empire'. Other British politicians over the years have frequently viewed the EC/EU as either a tool for creating a France-dominated Europe or more often as a useful disguise for the revival of German power in Europe. In so doing, they have often reflected a set of ambiguous attitudes towards the EC/EU. Such attitudes are often rooted in a combination of arrogance or superiority and an acute sense of weakness and insecurity, whether centred on anxiety about the preservation of national independence and sovereignty or suspicions about proposals originating in other EU capitals and fears about being hoodwinked by smarter operators there. The interminable haggling about terms of entry to the EEC, about the signing of EU treaties, and about opt-outs and 'red lines' accompanying the evolution of Britain's membership of the EC/EU, all highlight how far alignment with rather than outright resistance to this 'single power' has proved a disagreeable necessity. A semi-detached, associate or country membership mentality has often been in evidence, frequently perpetuating the illusion that British strength is defined by standing apart and by resorting to the language of boycotts and showdowns.

A fairly constant feature of British policy has involved a more or less covert attempt to slow down the pace of integration whether by prioritizing the enlargement of the EC/EU or by involvement in shaping outcomes without any commitment to participation. To a greater or lesser extent ever since the Schuman Plan of 1950, British governments have approached the process of European integration with a view to maximizing their influence in any negotiations while minimizing their commitment to the outcome. Ideally, therefore, they have preferred to remain in the slow lane to integration, while attempting to direct traffic in the fast lane. They have recognized that efforts to obstruct plans for further integration or to reduce the possibility of a multi-speed Europe were best mounted from within rather than outside the inner councils of the EC/EU. That said, it is important to note that a recurring feature and important factor in the evolution of the EC/EU has been Britain's absence from the early workings of key schemes such as the Schuman Plan, the Rome Treaties and the euro zone. This absence has helped to ensure, if unintentionally on the British side, the successful launching of such projects. It has also had the effect of walling off British governments from the strong sense of collective experience and identity generated by such projects. In each case, moreover, the initial British reaction to any initiative invariably consisted of a mixture of disbelief and disdain for what was often regarded as euro-rhetoric and window dressing or what Thatcher described as 'airy fairy nonsense' in her reference to enthusiasm for European political integration. In a similar manner to the sceptical reactions of British governments in the 1950s to the common market plans of the Six, Thatcher in the later 1980s dismissed the likelihood of an economic and monetary union, believing or hoping that the project would come to nothing.

Continuity and change are also evident in the various aspects of British foreign policy-making in the European context. Strategic indecision, lack of vision, and a preference for a reactive rather than proactive stance are often cited as among the hallmarks of British policy towards the EC/EU. Some of these features were and are the inevitable consequence of having to respond to events outside Britain. Others are in accord with those definitions of British foreign policy associated with Lord Salisbury, prime minister and foreign secretary for much of the later nineteenth century. Salisbury's preference in foreign affairs was 'to float lazily downstream occasionally putting out a diplomatic boat-hook to avoid collisions' while at the same time recognizing that: 'Whatever happens will be for the worse, and therefore it is in our interest that as little should happen as possible'. The pragmatic approach, the imperturbable diplomatic style and the piecemeal treatment of issues as they arise and on their merits, all tend to emphasize, as one classic study of British foreign policy notes, the external event rather than the goal or purpose which the UK government wishes to pursue – easily construed as an example of 'ad hoc indirection'. Furthermore, such characteristics are less indicative of a positive, creative effort to alter or shape the external environment than of a preference for the static, the secure and the comfortable. (Cecil 1921: 130; Roberts 1999: 84; Vital 1968: 99, 110; Trewin 2008: 358). It often appears that British governments marginalize themselves in EC/EU policy areas when they prove more effective in blocking ideas emanating from other member states than in putting forward their own ideas (Wall 2008: 77).

An authoritative, insider's account of British foreign-policy-making in recent decades identifies several underlying flaws: an inflated notion of Britain's capacity and influence, a failure to adjust to reality, an overweening trust in pragmatism and reaction to events as they occur, an inability to plan ahead and set clear objectives, and a disinclination to define publicly an international role for Britain and persuade public opinion of its merits (Coles 2000: 33).[21] Each of these features crops up time and again in British policy towards the EC/EU. For example, Whitehall's response to some of the major developments in the history of the EC/EU, especially its underestimation of the drive towards European integration, often demonstrated a failure to adjust to reality, an unwillingness to learn from the past or at least to probe unexamined assumptions, and an inflated sense of Britain's capacity and influence as the leading player in Europe often cited as the main objective. A strong element of panic set in when the EC/EU developed at a pace beyond British expectations, as when Macmillan in 1960 unsuccessfully pressed the EEC states to delay the acceleration of their tariff-cutting programme or when Blair in 1997 toyed with the idea of a quick phone call to Chancellor Kohl of Germany to see if he would be agreeable to postponing the launch of the euro (Peston 2006: 200). The common representation of EC/EU business as a series of one-off episodes rather than a dynamic process has signified a pragmatic, reacting to events approach. This handling of matters has combined with an inability or unwillingness to formulate and enunciate a set of clear objectives based on a long-term strategy or a developed vision of the EU's future.[22] Negotiating positions hammered out in a tightly organized and centralized Whitehall framework have afforded uniformity of view on a particular issue across departments (Wall 2008: 190). This decision-making system, however, has limited the degree of flexibility during the course of negotiations, and has often indicated defensive policy ambitions rather than a positive, proactive European strategy (Menon 2004: 41).

Another related and significant feature of Britain's involvement in the EC/EU lies in the contrast between the routine conduct of business in Brussels and the deeply adversarial nature of the British political system. To be sure, there is a difference of perspective in this regard between senior British officials, who are permanently or regularly involved in EC/EU matters, and government ministers who are on day trips to Brussels and who are concerned with the management of the media as well as the substance of official proceedings. Julian Bullard, the British ambassador to Bonn in 1987, for example, reportedly pleaded for more thought to be given to the style of British policy in Europe, noting that the plain speaking of the House of Commons did not translate well into Continental languages, especially in countries that lived by coalition and compromise (Wall 2008: 76). There is much evidence to support the case that the dynamics, method and character of the EC/EU policy-making process, especially in the form of coalition-building and variable sum politics, do not fit into the binary conception of politics dominant at Westminster (Bogdanor 1994: 4). Among other things, the Westminster system ultimately rests on a view of politics as a zero sum game of winners and losers rather than on the idea of a positive or variable sum set of outcomes. The winner-takes-all culture is as evident at the ballot box in elections for the UK parliament as in the workings of parliamentary politics. Over the years, this condition has often resulted in popular representations of British involvement in EC/EU business as aggressive, uncooperative and confrontational diplomacy. This was the case, for example, during the premiership of Wilson and Major, but most notably so during the Thatcher premiership of the 1980s when, according to one report, her insistence that the word 'compromise' should never appear in any briefing paper meant that the Foreign and Commonwealth Office had to find ways of couching their strategic suggestions round the unfailing notion of battle and victory (Trewin 2008: 547). With the possible exception of Thatcher – for whom victory was all – the 'Battle of Britain' rhetoric of heroic stands, no surrender and glorious victories, has reflected the need to impress both the parliamentary opposition, eager to exploit any suggestion of government weakness in Brussels, and a public either neutral or hostile to the EC/EU. Such an approach has invariably conveyed the false impression that any EC/EU transaction can be reduced to a simple choice with no middle way between the idea of cooperation between sovereign states and a federal Europe.[23]

This approach has invariably meant that Britain's relationship with the EC/EU has rarely demonstrated smooth, linear progression. In fact, it has taken the form of an unpredictable trajectory governed by political and diplomatic twists and turns and often subject to vacillation, unexpected decisions and unintended consequences. The period 1945–73 witnessed first a negative and then a confused response to the origins of the EEC that was followed by a major reversal of policy towards the idea of EEC membership with a protracted controversy over the merits of membership. In the period since 1973, participation in the EC/EU has invariably attracted a high degree of equivocation among policymakers and public alike. Governments in both periods frequently demonstrated a hesitant approach to the EC/EU or 'procrastination on principle' as John Major described his preferred approach to new plans for Europe (Major 1999: 273). Furthermore, the disinclination to define publicly an international role for Britain has partly arisen out of ambiguity about Britain's relationship with the EC/EU and partly out of a wide variety of official definitions of Britain's role and status in the world (Coles 2000: 178). These tendencies were often allied to an unfortunate penchant for bad timing whenever government decided to advance further in the field of European integration. For example, British entry into the EC occurred at a time when the virtually uninterrupted and so-called Golden Age of growth in the Western international economy since the early postwar years was coming to an end. In the subsequent recession-hit 1970s, Britain enjoyed little of the trade-led economic growth from EC membership enjoyed by the original members of the Six. British moves in the area of monetary integration were equally ill-timed. This was first evident in 1972 when the Heath government joined the so-called 'snake in the tunnel' which was designed to limit the fluctuations between the currencies of the EC member states but which collapsed shortly afterwards under the strain of global monetary instability. Then again in 1990, belatedly and reluctantly, the Thatcher government decided to place sterling in the ERM of the EMS in what proved to be a short-lived, disastrous measure 'for the wrong reasons, at the wrong time and at the wrong rate' (Denman 1996: 267).

The often tortuous course of British policy and diplomacy in this context is typified and partly explained by the way in which governments over the past thirty years, especially on coming to power, have offered strong professions of support for the EC/EU and for a major British role in the organization. However, their resolve has subsequently weakened and they have beaten a retreat to a more sceptical view of the matter by the end of their period in office (Forster 2002), frequently leaving themselves isolated in EU circles. Thatcher, for example, played a leading role in the creation of the SEA. In doing so, she made a British contribution to the history of the EU that was second only to that of Heath, her sworn political enemy. She also claimed at the time of the introduction of the SEA that Britain was leading the way in the EC. Yet she subsequently recoiled in horror before some of its consequences, notably the emergence of economic and monetary union. By the end of her period of office she was virtually ignored by her EU peers. Thatcher's successor, John Major, came to power in 1990 with a pledge to put Britain 'at the very heart of Europe'. By the end of his period of office in 1997, however, Europe was at the heart of the bitter divisions within the Conservative Party and his government was effectively sidelined in EU affairs.

The incoming Blair government in 1997 followed a similar path in that Blair himself, together with FCO ministers, immediately promised 'constructive engagement' (Robin Cook) with the EU which was viewed as 'an opportunity not a threat' (Douglas Henderson). The new government's decision to sign up to the Social Chapter of the Maastricht Treaty was taken as indicative of an encouraging attitude towards the EU. A year later Blair declared a sea-change in the British approach to Europe away 'from self-imposed isolation to full-hearted cooperation' and significantly influenced the EU policy agenda, notably in launching the UK–France St. Malo initiative on European defence (1998) and the 'Lisbon Agenda' (2000) on economic reform.[24] These initiatives together with some strongly pro-EU speeches in this period aimed to 'normalize' relations between Britain and the rest of the EU. Thereafter, however, the initial enthusiasm to open a new, positive phase in Britain's EU stance began to wane. A more cautious tone took hold with diminishing evidence of any strategic attempt to shape a coherent pro-EU Labour government. It seemed to be the case that, as the europhile Mandelson commented, apart from Blair, 'nobody was talking about Europe' (Trewin 2008: 634). Philip Gould, Blair's pollster and political analyst, advised that many more ministers than Blair should talk about Europe as part of their daily lives, but he also warned that if Blair got too far out in front of public opinion on Europe he would lose the people and the issue (Trewin 2008: 602). The possibility of a strong and sustained pro-EU campaign was all the more unlikely as a succession of nine individuals held the post of Europe minister in the FCO during Blair's premiership.

Far more importantly, the British commitment of military forces to the US-led invasion of Iraq (March 2003) aroused strong opposition in the country and also among government critics of the war in some of the EU states, notably France and Germany. Blair's personal authority was seriously and permanently damaged. Any possibility of realizing his ambition of giving Britain leadership in Europe and of finally reconciling the British with their European destiny fell by the wayside with the haemorrhaging of his political capital. A major policy reversal (April 2004) to hold a referendum on the proposed EU Constitutional Treaty was directly due to Blair's weakened domestic standing (Wall 2008: 189; Cook 2003: 168). This decision signified for many what Denis MacShane, a former Europe minister in the Foreign and Commonwealth Office in Blair's government, described as 'game over for any serious Labour leadership on or in Europe'.[25] In June 2005 after the failure to reach agreement over the EU budget and the British rebate at the Brussels European Council, the eurosceptic *Daily Telegraph* commented: 'It happens, sooner or later, to all British prime ministers. They begin with hopeful talk about putting Britain at the heart of Europe. They end up iso-lated'.[26] Meanwhile, the possibility of British entry into the euro zone slid into abeyance, while the promised national debate on its merits failed to materialize, particularly as the invasion of Iraq overshadowed the issue of Britain's EU policy. This outcome did not distress most Labour government ministers who, as MacShane acidly observed, had in any case spent most of their formative years ranting against the EC/EU and all its works, including Blair himself in the early 1980s.

Part of the reason for the persistent tendency of governments to retreat from their initial resolve lies in the often finely balanced calculations sur-rounding the cost of exclusion from and the price of inclusion in the EC/EU. As often as not, the national debate over EC/EU membership has focused on a preoccupation with the largely measurable price of membership rather than with the more speculative political cost of staying out of the EC before 1973 or out of particular EU projects like the euro zone. Unlike the original member states of the EEC, Britain had no overriding, fundamental or com-pelling argument for making European integration its top foreign policy priority. At least the case for making it such over the past sixty years was never entirely clear and convincing. During his period of office as the Eur-opean Commission's trade commissioner, Mandelson commented that 'there was never a knockdown argument as to why Britain had to take the bold and uncertain leap of joining [the EEC]'.[27] This much is evident, for example, in the long-standing, marked differences between Whitehall departments about the nature and extent of British involvement in the process of European inte-gration.

The contrast between the Foreign Office (FCO – Foreign and Common-wealth Office since 1968) and the Treasury, for long the two key departments in the making of European policy, is a case in point. Both departments were broadly in agreement about European policy until the first application for

EEC membership, disagreeing only over tactical responses to the emergence of the EEC. Since 1960, however, the FCO position has undergone a greater degree of change than that of the Treasury. During the 1960s the FCO convinced itself that there was no alternative to EEC membership. It has subsequently highlighted the political advantages of involvement in the formation, if not full membership, of any new EC/EU project. The emphases of individual foreign secretaries, among other things, have influenced the extent to which EC/EU membership has received a high profile, more obviously so, for example, during the foreign secretaryship of George Brown, Geoffrey Howe, Douglas Hurd and Robin Cook than in the case of Selwyn Lloyd, David Owen and Jack Straw. The Treasury, however, has consistently adopted a cautious, sceptical stance ever since the first attempt to secure EEC membership.[28] Indeed, it has been the most eurosceptic department in Whitehall. In the late 1940s it intransigently opposed the idea of participating in a west European customs union. In the early 1970s at the time of the Heath application for EEC membership, it warned that EEC plans for an economic and monetary union could lead to a European federal state and that Britain could be left with less control over its own affairs than the individual states in the USA. Several considerations have influenced this Treasury position, besides its short-termist perspective and ready use of any economic arguments to oppose further involvement in the process of European integration. Concern about the impact of EC/EU membership on Britain's interests beyond Europe has loomed large. The cost of membership has also figured as a key consideration whether in relation to the country's general economic performance or with reference to particular difficulties such as the British contribution to the EC/EU budget. In the past ten years or so, moreover, the Treasury's euroscepticism with Gordon Brown as Chancellor of the Exchequer for much of this period has played an influential role in maintaining Britain's exclusion from the euro zone and in designing the five tests that had to be satisfied before entry to the euro zone. The Treasury's negative assessment in 2003 of the case for entering the euro zone was aptly summarized by *The Economist* as 'Five Tests and a Funeral' (Cook 2003: 169). Such divisions at the heart of government have underlined the lack of agreed strategy or vision about the longer-term direction and management of change within the EC/EU context. This feature has often hobbled ministers from making the case for a particular policy such as entering the euro zone. It has also lent weight to the view that the absence of a single overarching concept, design or 'Idea of Britain' to inform more detailed objectives and diplomatic activity has prevented clear and credible policies on Britain's role in Europe and has also avoided the need for hard choices (Coles 2000: 43–47).

While British governments have sought to avoid visionary thinking about the EC/EU and thereby reinforced the mainland European parentage of the organization, they have nonetheless followed a broadly consistent line in terms of British preferences. There are certain long-standing features of the British engagement with the EC/EU that can be traced back to the very beginnings of the post-war debate about European integration in the late 1940s: the emphasis on minimal goals and on 'negative' integration (the removal of existing restrictions on economic, commercial and financial transactions between EC/EU states) as opposed to 'positive' integration (the introduction of new common policies); the quest for unconditional and ideally free rider access to the economic benefits of EC/EU membership; the preoccupation with reconciling Britain's European and extra-European interests and commitments; the prioritizing of enlargement over further integration; the projection of European integration as primarily an economic rather than a political phenomenon; support for intergovernmental cooperation; antipathy towards the idea of a federal Europe with the spectre of a European federal superstate often invoked by government ministers to assuage public opinion (Wall 2008: 208); considerable distaste for an open-ended commitment to the goal of 'ever closer union' on the EC/EU masthead; deep suspicion of any European rhetoric that suggests an irreversible journey to an unknown destination; an aversion to a tight, little inward-looking Europe; and a pronounced preference for viewing EU membership as a fall back or a minimal, defensive position rather than as a base camp for an advance towards further integration.

Another persistent and striking feature of British involvement in the EC/EU has concerned the perception of European integration as a two-edged sword holding out both a threat and an opportunity. At a very general level, for example, the anti-marketeers of yesteryear and their eurosceptic successors have focused on the threat posed to national sovereignty and independence. Meanwhile, pro-marketeer or europhile opinion has viewed membership as an opportunity to undertake a much-needed process of modernization, the leading exponents of this view being George Brown in the 1960s, Heath in the 1970s and Blair at the turn of the century. Likewise, the projection of the EC/EU as a threat or as an opportunity has figured as a persistent feature of the priorities of, and the conflict between, the political parties. For example, in the early post-war decades a large body of Labour Party opinion viewed the EEC as endangering the party's stand on national economic planning and controls. Similarly, Thatcher in her Bruges speech of 1988 portrayed the prospect of a European super-state as a threat to her declared domestic programme of rolling back the frontiers of the state. In the case of both major parties, and most notably when in opposition, the EC/EU has often been viewed as an opportunity to make political capital out of the government's handling of EC/EU affairs. Shortly after becoming Chancellor of the Exchequer in 1997, Gordon Brown reportedly commented that the key was to change the nature of British perception and to make the British think of Europe 'as an opportunity, as a way of finding a new role for Britain in the world' (Trewin 2008: 538). For much of the period since 1997, however, the sense of threat has overshadowed the idea of opportunity to the point where, as one well-informed commentator has put it, even in Whitehall it is quite hard to find any real sense that Europe is an opportunity rather than a threat

(Stephens 2005). According to one recent insider's account, there is also an instinctive dislike of EU legislation across Whitehall departments, where the common response to a proposed piece of EU legislation is 'No unless' as compared with the 'yes if' response of most of the other EU states (Wall 2008: 200).

Northern Ireland, Scotland and Wales offer a detailed example of how the EC/EU has represented both a threat and an opportunity. On the one hand, European integration has meant that decision-making power was further removed both politically and physically. Each of these territories with its own Secretary of State in the UK Cabinet could potentially exercise influence at the heart of government. After Britain's accession to the EC, however, they had to rely on other government departments to represent their interests in Brussels. As a result, their access to decision-makers was less direct in a formal sense. Conversely, European integration has offered them the prospect of a new political arena with which they could engage. Initially, this tended to be restricted to lobbying, but by the 1990s they had entered that arena as actors in their own right. Equally, as the decade progressed, the EU recognized that its regions and territories were the building blocks of the EU. The member states were not the only means through which the EU could engage with citizens. While the EU was keen to provide its territories with a greater voice, it remained too centralized as far as legislation was concerned. That became an issue for the newly devolved governments in the UK. They had apparently secured greater autonomy over a range of domestic matters, but in a good number of instances those matters had an EU dimension and EU law took precedence. It was therefore incumbent on the devolved governments to call for greater decentralization within the EU and that they did, both in relation to the proposed Constitutional Treaty and the Lisbon Treaty. Whether the proposals set out in the Lisbon Treaty really do enhance the autonomy of the devolved governments is not yet known. The same applies to the devolved legislatures. In the meantime the quasi-devolution aspects of the CFP such as the creation of Regional Advisory Councils and the decentralization of fisheries management is indicative of the realization in Brussels that 'one size does not fit all'. It remains to be seen, however, whether further decentralization is on the horizon.

A preoccupation with asserting a global leadership role for Britain, initially based on empire and subsequently on a post-imperial nostalgia, has figured as a key element in the making of British foreign policy. This emphasis, in turn, has had an enduring influence on British policy and attitudes towards the EC/EU, not least as a world outlook has led in practice to less concern or respect for Europe.[29] The memory of empire fed into and underpinned the assertion of a leadership role in the world. Britain's claim to a special place in the wider world was further reinforced by what was represented as the smooth transition from Empire to Commonwealth. The quest for post-imperial European and global leadership remained in being even when there appeared to be an attempt to escape from Britain's imperial past. While treating empire as clearly belonging to Britain's past, for example, Blair nonetheless declared in rhetoric easily mistaken for imperial fantasy that: 'We are a leader of nations, or we are nothing' and that Britain's frontiers 'reach out to Indonesia' (Deighton 2002: 109).[30] None of his predecessors in Downing Street publicly disputed this proposition. In 1954 Oliver Franks, a leading British official at the time, succinctly summarized the deeply ingrained, long-standing view of the British political establishment: 'Britain is going to continue to be what she has been, a Great Power'.[31] At this same time Eden warned his Cabinet colleagues that once the prestige of a country started to slide 'there is no knowing where it will stop'.[32]

A mixture of motives and considerations accounted for such views at any particular time including concerns about national and personal prestige and purpose, and the influence of history, tradition and inertia. In addition, there has been the enduring ambition to project Britain as the joint world policeman with the USA or at least as a house prefect of the international system. Even when objective conditions clearly underlined Britain's relative decline in the international system, there remained a keen determination to lay claim to a global leadership role, as if bombastic assertions were designed to obscure from the public the scale of the retreat. Towards the end of the period 1947–70 that witnessed the decline of the empire, for example, Harold Wilson as prime minister still insisted that Britain's frontiers extended to the Himalayas and this at a time (1965) when the Commonwealth member states of India and Pakistan made use of Soviet rather than British mediation in their conflict over Kashmir. At the same time, leading Cabinet supporters of British membership of the EEC like Brown (Foreign Secretary) and Stewart (Secretary of State for Economic Affairs) argued that EEC membership was essential to keep up Britain's international status and place at the 'top table'. A similar frame of mind was evident much later when Douglas Hurd, as a former foreign secretary, portrayed Britain as 'punching above its weight' on the international scene. At the same time, Garel-Jones, an FCO minister, was said to have argued against the case for adopting a totally EC-oriented role by asserting that 'History has dealt us a more important role' (Trewin 2008: 367). Such imagery suggested that if Britain stopped punching above its weight it would be no different from the continental Europeans. British political leaders since the 1960s are commonly charged with having failed to inform the British public about the loss of sovereignty arising out of EC/EU membership. Arguably a more substantive and valid criticism in this context has concerned the failure of nerve of these leaders to educate the public about the full nature and extent of Britain's reduced power and status in the wider world. Far from facing up to the challenge of coping with the retreat from past glory and the language of empire, politicians have often preferred to seek refuge in some of the overstated trappings and posturings of 'great power' status. All the baggage of Britain 'punching above its weight', as one commentator has observed, was the 'diplomatic version of distressed gentlefolk keeping up appearances, making ourselves ridiculous and obnoxious to our real equals, the other Europeans'.[33]

Since 1945, British political leaders have laid claim to a global role akin to the mission statement of John Wesley, the founder of Methodism, that: 'The world is my parish'. Like Wesley they have also often taken it upon themselves to preach to the world in accordance with the Miltonic advice: 'Let England not forget her precedence of teaching nations how to live', easily mistaken by outsiders as a form of sanctimonious interventionism and moralising delivered in a hectoring tone of voice. The subject matter of the sermonizing has ranged far and wide from the benefits of Atlantic cooperation to the moral value of the Commonwealth. However, it has particularly concentrated on Europe and European integration, lending weight to the view that throughout the period since 1945 British political leaders have travelled across the Atlantic to learn and across the English Channel to preach (Wallace 2005). The preaching to European audiences has extended, for example, from the benefits of 'socialism in one country' in the late 1940s to the strengthening of the democratic credentials of the EEC through admitting Britain with its 'mother of parliaments' in the 1960s and 1970s. More recently, mainland European audiences have been treated to lectures by British political leaders on the dogma and superior merits of unfettered 'Anglo-Saxon' free market capitalism in the form of economic liberalization and deregulated markets, at least until the events of October 2008 in the financial markets suggested otherwise. As Chancellor of the Exchequer in the period 1997–2007, for example, Gordon Brown was particularly renowned for lecturing his fellow EU finance ministers on why they should follow his model of economic reforms and his example of prudent management of public finances, as compared with the deficiencies, for example, of the German social market economic model. Predictably, therefore, when Brown abandoned fiscal prudence for deficit financing in 2008 he drew sharp criticism and a measure of Schadenfreude from the German finance minister, Peer Steinbrück, who claimed that the Brown government had adopted a strategy of 'crass Keynesianism'. Sermon texts used throughout the period since 1945 have focused on the general theme that only Britain knows what is good for Europe and have included such matters as the benefits of the British model of European cooperation, the inadequacies of mainland European models of integration, the weaknesses of the euro zone and the necessary, seemingly unachievable, changes to facilitate British entry, and the importance and uniqueness of Britain's self-styled role as the bridge between Europe and the USA.

All governments since 1945, with the possible exception of the Heath government of 1970–74, have upheld the view that Europe could not be separated from the global dimensions of British foreign policy. Furthermore, they have insisted that the European continent did not represent the major, exclusive area of British strategic interest. Any form of regional or European cooperation was at best a subordinate and diminutive piece in the global jigsaw and at worst an impediment to what British policymakers viewed as the higher priorities of global cooperation or interdependence. This latter emphasis in the early decades after the Second World War was often referred to as the 'one world (or collective) approach'.[34] It found expression in support for the liberalization of international trade and payments and the lifting of restrictions on inconvertible currencies. These aims were combined with marked opposition to any exclusively European arrangement on such matters. This emphasis, therefore, partly accounted for Britain's refusal to consider tariffs in a purely European setting during the 1950s, thereby excluding itself from the origins of the EEC. It was also evident in the process of seeking and then adjusting to EEC membership in the 1960s and 1970s. During this period, the EEC of the Six was often dubbed 'Little Europe' and, most notably among opponents of EEC membership, this description was intended to convey the impression of the EEC as a very restricted, regional entity: 'Out of Europe and into the World' was the message of one of the anti-marketeer 'no' slogans in the 1975 referendum (Malmborg and Stråth 2002: 16).

In more recent decades many of the features of the 'one world approach' have found their way into the concept of globalization. However defined, globalization has often overshadowed European integration in some parts of British political discourse about the external environment, occasionally reducing the EU to a redundant or anachronistic feature. Set against this background, the EU has figured in British circles not as an end in itself but as a means for achieving global goals. The labelling may have changed but the global perspective has remained more or less intact over the years: it was the theme of a speech by Harold Macmillan on a visit to Boston in the US in 1961 and also by Gordon Brown, albeit featuring different issues, on a visit to the same place in 2008. Significantly, the Brown government's current initiative is entitled Global Europe and is designed, in accordance with long-standing British preferences, to encourage the EU to spend less time on its structures, institutions and laws and more time on its global role,[35] a 'globalized context which we are best placed to oversee/supervise' according to an earlier report of Brown's views on the subject (Trewin 2008: 812).

The global character of British interest in the external environment has acted as a major factor in shaping policy and attitudes towards the EC/EU. Most obviously, it has prompted British political leaders since 1945 to insist, as Bevin expressed the matter to a US politician in 1947, that Britain was not 'just another European country' and that its principal overseas interests lay beyond Europe.[36] This view diverted attention away from occupying a full role in the EC/EU before and after Britain's accession. It also perpetuated in the domestic context an inflated impression of Britain's standing on the international stage in view of the country's limited military and economic strength. The resources and effort poured into upholding the image of Britain as a world power have arguably worked against the process of full adaptation to the EC/EU. As a result, it is argued, Britain has often punched below its weight in the EU for lack of sustained political engagement (Deighton 2002; Wallace 2005).

The determination to occupy a position of leadership on the wider inter-national stage has also served to reinforce particular impressions of the EC/EU. One enduring impression of EC/EU membership over the years is that of a subsidiary, bolted-on extra or imposition belonging to the external envir-onment rather than a widely acknowledged, integral feature of British national life. The relationship between Britain's global position and policy towards the EC/EU has, of course, undergone a transformation, most notably in the form of EEC membership that ranks among the small number of fun-damental changes executed by British governments since 1945. This develop-ment reflected among other things an acute sense of national decline. EEC membership was viewed as a principal means of buttressing the claim to global leadership. In some quarters, the possibility of British leadership of the EEC was mocked as a substitute for empire on the basis of a delusion.[37] At the same time, Britain's self-styled important role in world affairs placed it apart from and in front of other major European powers. In this respect EEC membership was a case of change but within a deeply laid continuity, at one and the same time avoiding unqualified commitment to the process of Eur-opean integration and maintaining the pretence that EEC membership was vital but would change nothing. Certainly, the view of Britain as apart from and superior to the continental European powers was regarded as a piece of fiction by these powers. Nevertheless, it served the purpose of conveying to a domestic audience a particular image of Britain as occupying a pivotal role in international affairs, whether in the form of the Churchillian 'three circles' doctrine of the early post-Second World War decades or more recently by the claims of both Blair and Brown that Britain was best placed to bring Europe and the US together.

Such claims highlight a central feature of the external environment for British policymakers since 1945, the so-called 'special relationship' between Britain and the USA that has variously influenced the nature and extent of British involvement in the EC/EU. This relationship has attracted markedly different judgements that are beyond the scope of this study. Here, the emphasis is on British assessments of this relationship in the European con-text and most particularly on some of the changing and enduring implications of this relationship for British policy towards the EC/EU.[38]

Several key axioms of British policy towards the USA have had a long-standing bearing on policy and attitudes towards the EC/EU. First, British governments since 1945, with the exception of the Heath government of 1970–74, have strongly upheld the view that Britain's main bilateral relation-ship in the world is with the USA. They have also acted on the understanding that that there should be no repetition of the disastrous impact of the Suez crisis of 1956 on relations between London and Washington, and that this relationship should be maintained whatever the cost. They have also stressed the importance of the Atlantic Alliance as the principal forum for the conduct of relations between the Western states. This heavily 'Atlanticist' complexion of British foreign policy has involved a keen determination to safeguard the

British position as the foremost ally and principal cheerleader of the USA in Europe. It has entailed a systematic attempt to ensure that any EC/EU proposals in the defence and security field have not conflicted with or undermined NATO. No other NATO member state since 1950 has matched Britain's unwavering support for the organization. A prominent position within NATO as the most faithful US ally has served a number of functions other than the explicitly defence and security ones. Most notably, it has enabled the British government to maintain the idea of the 'special relationship', to keep up appearances on the world stage and the capacity 'to punch above its weight', and to project a triumphalist representation of British foreign policy. Furthermore, Britain's standing in NATO via the 'special relationship', it can be argued, has increased its sense of superiority over its mainland European allies and has prolonged British delusions of grandeur (Marsh and Baylis 2006: 187). Britain's credentials in this regard have rarely passed unnoticed or unquestioned on the continent. Thus, for example, de Gaulle feared that Britain as an EEC member state would act as an American Trojan horse. This view was endorsed much later by Gerhard Schröder, the former German Chancellor. Schröder maintained that Britain's 'special relationship' with the USA not only weighed on its European-focused future but meant that Britain more than any other European state was prepared to anticipate American wishes and turn them into European political issues. In British government circles, the advantages of a close relationship with the USA in terms of financial, intelligence, military and defence support have invariably counted for more than any gains from the EC/EU relationship. In effect, the defence and security advantages of the former have outweighed the economic welfare benefits of the latter, and the Ministry of Defence, in particular, has rarely missed an opportunity to highlight the adverse consequences of displeasing Washington. Among other things, the USA has demanded less than the EC/EU in terms of the *overt* loss of formal national sovereignty and independence.[39] Furthermore, just as the USA in the 1940s was viewed as the future and Europe as the past so the economic model that has dominated British policy-making in recent decades has owed far more to the form of free market, deregulated capitalism of the American type than to any mainland European model with its normally greater emphasis on state intervention in the economy, welfare provision and regulation.

Second, British governments since 1945, again with the exception of the Heath government of 1970–74, have emphasized what they regarded as Britain's unique and invaluable role as a bridge or intermediary between Europe and the USA. The well-worn bridge metaphor had its post-war origins in Britain's leading role in enlisting US economic and security support in the late 1940s. It has been employed ever since by British Prime Ministers from Macmillan to Brown with the occasional extra gloss as applied by Blair 'Call it a bridge, a two lane motorway, a pivot or call it a damn high wire ... ' (Wallace 2005). The self-appointed function of the British government in such a position was, as Blair put it, to keep its sights firmly on both sides of the

Atlantic, though as one French diplomat unhelpfully pointed out the problem with being a bridge is that you get walked over. In fact, the 'bridge' has generally carried only one-way traffic from Washington to Europe, while the idea that the British government might seek to take the lead in achieving a common EU view before taking that view to Washington was never entertained under Blair's premiership (Wall 2008:215; Trewin 2008: 555). Unsurprisingly in this respect, the idea of acting as a bridge between the US and Europe also meant, among other things, that British governments came to know and care more about the workings of the US system of government than those of any mainland European country. Thus, for example, Churchill's comment that 'No lover ever studied every whim of his mistress as I did those of President Roosevelt' had its parallel in the instruction issued to the new British ambassador to the US on taking up his appointment in 1997 to 'get up the arse of the White House and stay there'.[40] In both cases, it occasionally seemed that some of the principals in London acted as if the USA could be regarded less as a foreign country and more as part of the Anglo-Saxon world. Furthermore, it was often assumed that Washington would somehow on the basis of mutual understanding, goodwill and sentimentality about the 'special relationship' take British interests into account in its policies. Meanwhile, the preoccupation of the British media with US politics has offered a longstanding and striking contrast to its negligible interest in and coverage of the politics of other EU states.

Third, British governments, most markedly so in the case of the Macmillan, Callaghan and Blair administrations, have steadfastly resisted the idea of being forced to choose between the USA and Europe, always publicly regarding this as a false choice. In seeking to maintain a balance between the European and transatlantic dimensions of British policy and diplomacy, British political leaders have invariably insisted that a special relationship with Washington could be combined with close relations with the EC/EU powers. Some of the problems of attempting or failing to do so, however, have to a greater or lesser extent featured ever since the 1940s. As one Foreign Office paper of 1958 put it, maintaining a special relationship with Washington could be at the expense of building close relations with European states, yet only through close relations with and a leadership role in Europe could Britain bring influence to bear in Washington. More than forty years later a similar point was made by a German foreign ministry spokesman when he argued that successive British governments had laid themselves open to a 'double self-mutilating whammy'; they had failed to recognize that a country that does not matter in Europe will never be taken seriously by Washington and they had actively invested in their special relationship with the US a positive reason not to be involved in Europe (Trewin 2008: 727). Successive British political leaders have given little credence to such views. They have often underestimated the extent to which their emphasis on the special relationship has weakened relations with major mainland European neighbours and overestimated the amount of weight and influence that Britain on its own can bring to bear on Washington.[41] The difficulties of maintaining a balance between the European and transatlantic dimensions of British policy have proved all the greater because of the British emphasis on the 'special relationship'. In a major foreign policy speech in November 2008, Gordon Brown claimed that the 'special relationship' in future would increasingly be one between Europe and the US, rather than just Britain and the US.[42] It remains to be seen, however, whether this signifies a major change in British percep-tions of relations with Washington or is a mere rhetorical flourish.

Finally, the UK/USA 'special relationship', as prioritized and treasured by British governments, has provided an opportunity to avoid full commitment to the EU. It has also deprived Britain of any European alternative to the role of America's adjutant, giving rise to the view that the 'special relationship' for much of the period since Churchill coined the expression and first cast it in cosy propaganda has amounted to a 'misguided sentimental investment' that has paid few dividends for Britain (Charmley 2004, 1995: 360–61). In addi-tion, the 'special relationship' has also served to obscure the nature and extent of Britain's declining role in world affairs, this being the key change in UK/USA relations since 1945 as the imbalance of power in favour of the USA in 1945 has become ever greater. Shadowing Washington, as one historian has commented, has allowed British policymakers who still hunger for the big international stage some continued admission, though now far removed from Attlee's aspirational comment on Britain and the USA as being 'equal in counsel if not in power'.[43] A further more debatable aspect of the 'special relationship' turns on Britain's client status and the master and vassal rela-tionship between Washington and London, causing Blair to comment that 'Britain has got to be a partner, not a poodle' but aptly summed up for some observers by President Bush's humiliating greeting for Blair at an interna-tional conference in July 2006: 'Yo Blair' (Trewin 2008: 790).[44] There is sub-stance to the view that much emphasis on the adverse impact of EU membership on British national independence in British political circles has deliberately attempted to deflect attention away from the major, if largely unnoticed, challenges to British independence from US influence.[45] The 'spe-cial relationship' in this case has served as a grandiose term for Britain's subordination to the US with little or no payback from Washington.

The next section considers the theme of continuity and change in the domestic or internal context. It examines government management of the question of EC/EU membership in the public arena and also considers the operation and significance of a number of factors in shaping policy and attitudes. Particular attention is paid to some of the key constraints on government, notably in the form of parliamentary politics, the political parties, the pressure groups, the press and public opinion.

Government management of EC/EU membership has attracted changing assessments, but in many other respects the degree of continuity is striking. For example, it is possible to take a more favourable view of earlier British policy in the light of the perceived failings and weaknesses of the EU in recent years. Highly critical assessments of the handling of the question of EEC membership by British governments in the 1950s and 1960s have often given way to a greater understanding of and sympathy for the circumstances and problems facing such governments. In effect, the benefit of hindsight and the recent shortcomings of the EU strengthen the case for defending the British failure to participate in the making of the EEC or at the very least for recognising that the process of decision-making consisted of finely balanced arguments, divided opinions and difficult judgements. At a relatively early stage in Britain's EEC membership, there emerged a greater appreciation of such judgements. On the tenth anniversary of British entry into the EEC, for example, *The Economist* was forced to concede as a long-standing supporter of EEC membership that Harold Wilson, whose pocket calculator approach to the issue of EEC membership had earlier attracted strong criticism in its columns, had after all correctly emphasized the importance of the terms of membership in arriving at a decision on membership.[46]

The failure to build a strong and sustained pro-EC/EU platform has figured as a constant feature of most government management of the issue in the past fifty years. One indicator of this trend is evident in the declining amount of government expenditure on promoting information about the EC/EU. The budget of a recent Europe minister in the FCO, for example, was actually less in nominal and real terms than the amount of government expenditure on the referendum campaign of 1975, and this at a time during the second Blair administration when in the first instance a national debate on British entry into the euro zone was launched and subsequently a referendum was promised on the EU's Constitutional Treaty.[47]

Few, if any, Prime Ministers have taken on and followed through a large-scale and systematic attempt to win the argument on Europe. Heath and Wilson did so for specific purposes, the former to secure EEC membership and the latter to maintain membership but doing so with a low-key role reflecting, among other things, his difficulties over divisions in the Labour Party. Other leaders like Macmillan and Blair made keynote speeches on the EC/EU, but significantly these were often to overseas rather than domestic audiences and each failed to maintain any momentum in the face of cabinet, party, press and other constraints. In Blair's case, moreover, even if he had made a greater effort to reconcile the British public with the EU he would still have fallen foul of the overwhelming body of eurosceptic press opinion.[48] The failings of the Blair government in this respect lend substance to the view that the delivery of a speech strongly defending British membership of the EC/EU was a task best left to a junior minister 'on the occasional wet night in Dudley' (Stephens 2005).[49] Such handling of the matter was unlikely to change the terms of the British debate about the EU. Equally importantly, government presentations in support of British membership of the EC/EU have often oversimplified the issue. They have created the impression that the entire business was really a matter of judgement for the political elite rather than for the electorate, a case of government management of public ignorance and expectations. Governments have also demonstrated a marked preference for keeping apart the political and economic aspects of European integration and for emphasizing the economic rather than the political aspects of EC/EU membership. This aspect of government management was evident, for example, in the continued use of the expression 'Common Market' long after Britain had joined the EEC, understandably so as EEC membership was sold to the public as a beneficial economic project. This emphasis has also been equally evident in the past ten years in the Labour government's primarily economic tests for determining whether Britain should join the euro zone, all of which leaves a confusing picture of the role and identity of the EC/EU in the public mind.

A recurring feature of government management of EC/EU membership is best summed up in what one of Harold Wilson's biographers described as his three main objectives in the referendum of 1975, these being to keep his party in power and in one piece and Britain in Europe (Pimlott 1992: 659). Since Macmillan's first application for EEC membership, the engagement of British governments with the EC/EU has involved a form of three-dimensional chess requiring the simultaneous pursuit of negotiations at the EC/EU level, the construction of parliamentary majorities, and the management of public opinion. In the Wilson governments of 1974–76, as in the Major governments of 1990–97, the appearance of divisions over the EC/EU left the damaging public impression of a disunited, quarrelsome party. For this reason alone, British political leaders from Macmillan and Wilson to Major and Blair fought shy of promoting a popular debate about the EC/EU. They invariably feared that the issue would be used as a pawn in party politics to expose deep divisions within their own parties with fatal electoral consequences. At the same time, however, they sought to preserve British membership of the EC/EU. To a greater or lesser extent, it has always proved difficult to square this circle. No anti-EC/EU government, in fact, has yet come to power. Anti-EC/EU opposition parties, however, have been in evidence, most notably the Labour Party in the early 1960s and again in the early 1980s. More recently, the post-1997 Conservative Party has emphasized its eurosceptical credentials while attempting to shed the image of a party divided over Europe by marginalizing pro-EU enthusiasts in its ranks. The party has avoided any sustained narrative and positive strategy about EU membership. It has promised to hold a referendum on the Lisbon Treaty if returned to power at the next general election and if the treaty has not entered EU law, though the party's position is currently unclear in the event of the treaty entering into force before the party returns to power. David Cameron, the Conservative Party leader, has expressed occasional support for the long-running and often rejected idea of British membership of a North Atlantic Free Trade Area or market, while William Hague, the Shadow Foreign Secretary, has declared that a Cameron government would never join the euro.[50]

In their handling of the question of British membership of the EC/EU, British prime ministers have also been concerned to ensure that the issue has not undermined their own authority or been dangerously exploited by their senior ministerial colleagues to advance their leadership ambitions. Personal rivalry and conflict in the upper echelons of government has figured as an endemic, if immeasurable, feature of Britain's relationship with the process of European integration. For example, relations between Macmillan and Butler following the outcome of the contest for the premiership in 1957 always remained strained, and Butler's doubts about the wisdom of the first application for EEC membership were a source of anxiety to Macmillan. While in Opposition between 1970 and 1974, Wilson as Labour Party leader was clearly determined to ensure that Callaghan, who was one of the major contenders for his post and who lurked like a pike in the shadows (in the words of Roy Jenkins), did not seek to advance his leadership claims by exploiting the rising tide of Labour Party opposition to EC membership. Thatcher's premiership and its ending witnessed a rather different form of personal animosity in the shape of a hitherto loyal and mild-mannered senior minister, Geoffrey Howe, whose resignation from the government speech triggered a set of events that eventually led to Thatcher's resignation.[51] Finally, in this respect, British policy towards the EC/EU was one aspect of the personal conflict between Blair and Brown throughout the period 1997–2007. Blair feared that Brown could be in a very strong position if he split from himself over Europe and in particular over the question of British entry into the euro zone (Trewin 2008: 634)

Another recurring feature of Britain's EC/EU membership concerns the relationship between domestic crises and the value of the EC/EU as a panacea or external support system for the British economy. Discredited or failed national policies together with a loss of confidence by government in its economic management have regularly produced circumstances in which the EC/EU has figured as a lifeboat in turbulent domestic and international economic conditions. The perceived value of EC/EU membership has increased as part of 'a reactive series of manoeuvres to a growing sense of crisis within British politics' (Buller 2000: 167), though not without disastrous consequences whether in joining the EC on the brink of an economic recession in 1973 or entering the ERM in 1990. As a general rule, government and public have viewed the EC/EU more favourably as domestic economic conditions have worsened and less favourably as the British economy has performed well. Fears about the relative economic decline of Britain in the 1960s and 1970s served to reinforce the view of the EC/EU as a necessary protective or modernizing force for the British economy. Both the first and second applications for EEC membership in part reflected the failure of domestic policies and the seeming absence of any alternative to membership. Similarly, the Thatcher governments of the 1980s deepened British involvement in the EEC through signing the Single European Act and entering the Exchange Rate Mechanism in 1990 and did so against the background of their failed monetary and counter inflationary policies. The uninterrupted growth of the British economy since 1992 especially in contrast with the sluggish economic performance of France and Germany, however, suggested that the better the British economy performed the less attractive the EU looked and the less need there was for Britain to become more closely integrated with the rest of the EU. As the global financial system seized up in August 2007 and as growth came to an end in 2008 in the face of a major financial and banking crisis and against the background of worsening global economic conditions, however, it seemed that the lifeboat metaphor was being recycled. This was most evident when Brown reiterated part of the earlier rationale for EEC membership in a period of global uncertainty.[52] In these circumstances, there were also faint, indirect intimations of a more receptive attitude to the idea of joining the euro zone in certain British political circles, especially as sterling was increasingly squeezed between the world's two major currency blocs of the dollar and the euro and also proved more vulnerable to bank runs than these global reserve currencies.

Modernization has appeared on the obverse side of the coin marked the relative decline of Britain and has remained as a more or less persistent feature of government management of EC/EU membership in the domestic context. Membership has represented both an escape route from the failings of domestic government and an opportunity to modernize the British economy. In many respects EC/EU membership was represented as offering an automatic, neutral 'invisible' hand which would sift through and solve Britain's economic problems (Buller, 2000:166). In the 1960s and 1970s membership was often viewed as a means of rejuvenating British industry in the face of the perceived failure of government intervention and exhortation as well as the limitations of 'muddling through'. In later years, the scale of government expenditure and facilities in the leading EU states emerged as models for British imitation whether in terms of transport infrastructure or the level of expenditure on public health. The completion of a high-speed link to the channel tunnel on the British side some fifteen years after this provision was made on the French side, however, indicated the gap between British and mainland European provisions in the modernizing process, at least in this sector. It also highlighted the considerable differences in the levels of public debt for public investment between Britain and the core economies of mainland Europe. In 2007, public debt as a percentage of GDP in Britain's case (43.6 per cent) was significantly lower than the average for all EU states (58 per cent) and even lower than that of France (63.9 per cent) or Germany (64.9 per cent).[53] There are, besides, other characteristics of the British economy that distinguish it from the core economies of the EU and that have remained in being irrespective of the party in power in recent decades. The most notable of such features are lower levels of welfare spending, lower levels of worker protection, more liberal markets and openness to the global economy, and a larger stake in and dependence on certain economic sectors such as financial services (Fella 2002: 225). In the economic, monetary and financial crises of 2007–8, moreover, it often seemed that the British economy was following a trajectory more akin to that of the US economy than to that of the major continental European economies. While the former experienced an economic recession superimposed on a financial and banking crisis, the opposite was more clearly the case in most of the continental EU economies.

A major and largely unchanging feature of British policy and attitudes on the EC/EU concerns the vexed issue of sovereignty, the contrasting features of constitutional rules and practices as between Britain and mainland Europe, and relations between the executive and the legislature in the handling of EC/EU business. There is no disputing that EC/EU membership has undermined the concept of parliamentary sovereignty far more than any other domestic development since the emergence of a parliamentary monarchy and of the undivided sovereignty of Parliament in the late seventeenth century. The crossing of the Rubicon in this respect was the European Communities Act of 1972, by which the legislative powers of Parliament were qualified by the commitment to implement EEC laws. Very different views of sovereignty, however, have had an enduring bearing on the question of EC/EU membership. Theoretical sovereignty as formal or symbolic control exists at one end of a spectrum of opinion, at the other end of which lies the idea of real sovereignty with an emphasis on losing or pooling sovereignty in the EC/EU in order to increase the degree of power and control a member state can bring to bear in shaping its environment. Heath, Blair and, to a lesser extent, Macmillan upheld the latter position. There is ample scope for differences of view here, not least over whether the loss of national sovereignty and of exclusively national decision-making is outweighed by the advantages of EC/EU membership, and also about the relationship between power and sovereignty and the validity of the view that 'A man in the desert is sovereign. He is also powerless' (Michael Heseltine).[54] Furthermore, there are different views as to what counts as a loss of sovereignty in a wider meaning of that term, whether for example the fact that 20 per cent of British firms have become foreign-owned in recent years amounts to 'an extraordinary loss of British sovereignty' and whether the real threat to British sovereignty has long been the USA.[55]

The sovereignty issue affects all EC/EU member states. A pronounced antipathy towards the mainland European tradition of written constitutions, however, is a distinctive feature that British governments have brought to their handling of the basic, underlying constitutional rules and procedures of the EU. The British preference for an uncodified or unwritten constitution with scope for evolutionary change looms large in this context. So, too, does the development of informal procedures and the penchant for piecemeal institutional changes (and for one definition of the British constitution as simply 'what happens' according to the legal theorist John Griffith).[56] All such features stand in marked contrast to the emphasis on the importance of constitutional arrangements and on institutionalizing political and economic integration throughout the history of the EC/EU (Bogdanor 2005).

This contrast points to two very different ways of doing politics. As noted above, the democratic element in the history of the EC/EU has always been overshadowed by a top-down, bureaucratic and corporatist approach to politics dominated by politicians, bureaucrats and technocrats within the individual states and within the Commission. In British circles, the Commission in particular has often attracted venomous criticism as an unelected body variously regarded as unaccountable, interfering and dictatorial. The EC/EU system seems far removed from the workings of British parliamentary government with its *formal* emphasis on representative democracy and ministerial accountability.[57] These arrangements are often grounded in a longstanding belief that there is no reason for Britain to manufacture a written constitution or to undertake major constitutional experiments when so much of its political system has stood the test of time with occasional reform of the worst abuses. Significantly, even after more than thirty years of EC/EU membership there is still no inclination on the British side to imagine that anything useful can be learnt from the EU or from its member states in the field of political practices and constitutional procedures; the introduction of a system of proportional representation for European parliamentary elections was the first notable exception in this respect.[58] The Blair government's handling of domestic constitutional reform did not even make a gesture towards learning from mainland European experience. In addition, the Blair governments also failed, like their predecessors, to understand that there was no prospect 'of reforming the institutions of the EU in the image of the British constitution' (G. Johnson 2004: 307). In a similar manner, the incoming Brown government published a Green Paper 'The Governance of Britain' that made no reference at all to the EU. It thus failed to take account of the fact that Britain's governance was inextricably bound up with the governance of the EU, an omission that 'almost baffles belief' according to one leading commentator (Marquand 2008).

'The Governance of Britain' Green Paper raises one issue dealing with relations between the executive and the legislature, in the form of proposals for strengthening parliamentary scrutiny of the executive, that touches on another enduring feature of Britain's EU policy-making. It is a commonplace to note that parliament long since became subordinate to the executive.[59] Certainly, throughout the period of British membership of the EC/EU, the dominant position of the executive over the legislature has prevailed in all aspects of EU policy-making. This condition simply became more pronounced during the Blair premiership as Blair showed little or no interest in parliamentary procedures and frequently bypassed the institution. There may be differences of opinion over how effectively parliament has scrutinized proposed EC/EU legislation. The House of Lords has often emerged with greater credit than the House of Commons in this regard, if only because the latter conveys the impression of being a point-scoring debating society or as Douglas Hurd, a former Foreign Secretary, commented 'the Continentals can't understand why our procedures allow so much time for bloody-mindedness' (Trewin 2008: 363). A widespread and deep knowledge of EU economic and commercial affairs, moreover, has rarely characterized some parliamentary proceedings. Bryan Gould, a former Labour government minister and a trained economist, concluded that the level of parliamentary ignorance about economics was at times 'quite astonishing' (Gould 1995: 115), while in the EU context Chris Patten claimed that many MPs did not know the difference between EMU and ecu (Trewin 2008: 331). According to Robin Cook, former Leader of the House of Commons, debates in the Commons on the EU tended to take the form of grand theatre on such matters as the principle of membership or the general structure of the EU, with far less detailed consideration of issues and of 'attention to the nitty gritty'.[60] But the fact of the matter is that parliament is excluded from the formulation of EU legislative proposals. EU decisions are ultimately taken by government, i.e. the executive acting in the ministerial councils of the EU. Government defence of parliamentary sovereignty has in many respects served as a smokescreen of gestures to parliament and public, behind which the executive has maintained and reinforced its power and autonomy in EU policy-making. Meanwhile, the power of parliament has been substantially undermined and has drained away either to the EU institutions or to the government (G. Johnson 2004: 110).[61]

Continuity and change are also evident in the attitudes of the political parties towards the EC/EU. The absence of any long-term national consensus concerning the value and purposes of European integration has figured as a more or less permanent feature of the British political landscape for almost fifty years. Competition between the major parties and the changing balance of forces within these parties have invariably put at risk any axiomatic assumptions about the issue. A broad consensus between the Conservative and Labour Parties existed only in the period 1945–60 when British aloofness from the origins of the EEC commanded widespread support. Since 1960, however, EC/EU membership has proved a major political battleground between the Conservative and Labour Parties, except for occasional periods of ceasefire when the leadership of both parties has preferred not to talk about the subject. The recent parliamentary debate on the Treaty of Lisbon is a case in point. Treatment of the EU as a temporary no-go area in British politics has often reflected the importance of concealing party divisions for electoral considerations. Party opinion on the EC/EU has rarely, if at all, conformed to the larger Left/Right division in British politics; as often as not the left wing of the Labour Party has shared similar positions to the right wing of the Conservative Party on EC/EU membership, though for markedly different ideological and other reasons.

The issue of EC/EU membership has also served a number of latent functions in terms of inter- and intra-party conflict, most notably as a safety valve for deflecting attention away from party weaknesses and for minimizing the degree of dissent within a party on other matters, as a means of destabilizing an opposing political party, and as a bogeyman for governments and parties under pressure on other fronts. Conflicts over Europe have exacted a heavy cost in British politics, whether in contributing to the downfall of political leaders like Thatcher and Major or in causing upheavals and divisions within governments. Whereas in the 1960s and 1970s the Conservatives were regarded as the 'pro-European' party, the bulk of the Labour Party treated EC membership as anathema and eventually supported withdrawal from the EC in the early 1980s. By the 1990s these roles had reversed, after each party had moved in opposite directions in the intervening period for a variety of reasons, some of which had little or nothing to do with EC/EU affairs. The Liberal/ Liberal Democrat Party has consistently supported EC/EU membership and European integration ever since it was the first party in the late 1950s to press for British membership of the EEC. This position has recently changed, however, as deep splits emerged in the party over the Lisbon Treaty which forced the party leader, Nick Clegg, into the humiliating position of abstaining in the Commons vote on the treaty.[62]

While the major parties have undergone internal convulsions and dramatic changes in their attitudes towards EC/EU, public opinion has proved far more constant. To a large extent the outcome of the referendum of 1975 set the pattern for the next thirty years. There is little dispute that the referendum verdict was unequivocal but also unenthusiastic and that support for EEC membership was wide but did not run deep (Butler and Kitzinger 1976: 280). Majority opinion was largely persuaded by the possible economic benefits of EEC membership. At the same time there was no wish to become even more closely integrated with the EEC. Subsequent and recent polls largely confirm similar preferences. For example, a January 2008 *Guardian/ICM* poll on the attitudes of the British public towards the EU concluded that there was clear if unenthusiastic support for continued EU membership and no appetite for deeper engagement. Meanwhile, an *Ipsos Mori* survey, charting the most important issues facing Britain, reported that only between 2 per cent and 7 per cent of voters cited Europe among their concerns, far behind their main concerns about crime, immigration, health, defence and the economy.[63] This lack of public interest is often combined with another unchanging aspect of public attitudes towards the EU in the form of a high degree of ignorance about the purposes and workings of the EU. Prejudice has often filled the gap between public knowledge of and interest in the subject. This characteristic remains as evident today as thirty years ago. In the referendum campaign of 1975, there was massive exposure to the arguments on both sides. However, Roy Hattersley, who was then a junior minister at the FCO, expressed doubt as to whether 'ten per cent [of the public] voted on the merits of the issue or even according to their reaction to the question on the ballot paper. They put a cross against their prejudices … ' (Hattersley 1995: 158). Little has changed even in quarters that might be expected to demonstrate a greater degree of interest in and knowledge of European activities. For example, one former Europe minister in the FCO claimed that the poor level of policy discussion and debate in political parties was most evident on Europe (MacShane 2005: 13–14). Meanwhile, the Bologna Accord, which aims to harmonize different European higher education systems by creating a single system of degrees by 2010, has aroused strong student protests on the continent but has attracted little interest in Britain university circles according to one leading academic.[64]

The difference of attitude between the political parties and the public in this regard has a bearing on the course and outcome of the general debate about Europe as conducted by the pro- and anti-marketeers of yesteryear and their europhile and eurosceptic descendants. The steely conviction and attention to minutiae of the zealots on both sides of the argument about EC/EU membership have often been far-removed from mainstream public opinion, with its limited inclination to view EC/EU membership as a great issue of principle. The chasm between the two sides over time has remained as wide as ever. Conflicting assessments of the detailed advantages and disadvantages of EC/EU membership are ultimately based on value judgements about the organization, about whether it represents opportunity or threat, a silver bullet or a poisoned chalice. More profoundly, there are differences about whether Britain's separation from mainland Europe through its global and particularly imperial experience is to be understood as either a transient historical phenomenon or as a defining feature of the British experience with Britishness and Europeanism forever remaining an excluded or conflict-ridden combination (Bogdanor 2005: p. 699). At the same time, the contest between the major political parties over ownership of the concept of Britishness invariably involves attempts to limit or eliminate any reference to Europe.

Another important element of continuity concerns some of the major features of each body of fundamentalist opinion. For example, the pro-marketeers and europhiles have failed to build a lasting mass base of support for EC/EU membership. Their public image as an élitist group has rarely struck a popular note. They have objected to government by referendum on European issues, opposing the idea of a referendum in 1975, again at the time of the Maastricht Treaty and more recently on the abortive Constitutional Treaty. Jacques Delors, a former president of the EC Commission, once famously warned: 'You can't fall in love with a Single Market!' Raymond Aron, a fellow Frenchman and political philosopher, earlier (1954) claimed that the European idea lacked the characteristics of messianic ideologies and concrete patriotism and was the creation of intellectuals, this accounting for 'its genuine appeal to the mind and its feeble echo in the heart' (Haas 1958: 29). So much has proved to be the case in Britain where the campaign of the pro-marketeers and europhiles has elicited no strong emotional commitment to their cause. Their message has failed to offer a feel-good narrative about Britain and the EC/EU, often relying on public opinion which, whatever its suspicions of or opposition to the EU, has tended to believe that further involvement in the EU was inevitable. In fact, the europhile case has often come under attack for comprising unappealing arguments about EC/EU membership as the main or sole solution to Britain's problems. Speculating about how best to 'get inside the British head and make it more excited' about EU membership, Robin Cook, the former foreign secretary, was in no doubt what was unlikely to inspire the public; 'You must be joking' was his considered response to the view that the public would be captivated by any announcement that the Blair government's five tests for entry to the euro zone had been satisfactorily met (Trewin 2008: 738). Pro-EC/EU opinion has also attracted criticism for failing to instil into the population at large any sense of a common European culture. The essentially negative, if valid, case presented by government and europhiles alike, that Britain would be worse off outside the EC/EU, has rarely aroused popular support (Wall 2008: 210). Besides the argument based on the absence of any alternatives to EC/EU membership, the pro-markeeters and europhiles have also often invited criticism for a persistent unwillingness to explain the precise impact of membership on national sovereignty.[65]

Unlike their opponents, the anti-marketeers and eurosceptics have exploited a rich seam of opinion inclined to view Britain's EU ties in terms of injured national sovereignty, lost independence and outraged national identity. A sympathetic press has not hesitated to project the EU as the hostile 'other' across the English Channel. It has drawn heavily on military metaphors of surrender and defeat in defence of British sovereignty and independence, and it has often depicted the EC/EU as an imposition from above masterminded by wily foreigners. Eurosceptic opinion has made major advances in the past twenty years, so much so that it is very much in the ascendant while the once dominant pro-marketeer force, that swept all before it in the 1960s and 1970s, has become a weak europhile rump. The latter has lacked the cutting edge of eurosceptic presentations. These have easily placed responsibility for all manner of ills at the door of the EU and have exploited popular opposition to British entry into the euro zone (Trewin 2008: 448). A paradoxical feature of the rising tide of eurosceptic opinion, however, is that it has not, as yet, managed to translate the large reservoir of public support for its views into electoral gains with the prospect of an incoming government seriously challenging the status quo of Britain's EU membership. There is, in effect, little evidence of a public preference for disconnecting from the recent past and returning to some pre-EEC 'golden age', if only for fear of sliding into an uninviting form of isolation. William Hague, as the Conservative Party leader in the 2001 general election, called on voters to follow him in saving Britain from the European dragon, but he later admitted that 'No-one came' (Stephens 2005).

The press and other media represent a key, if immeasurable, factor in influencing public opinion, in acting as a constraint on government and political parties alike, and in contributing to the often feverish political atmosphere surrounding Britain's EU membership. There is not the space here to cover the debate on the precise influence of the press in this particular field and on whether, for example, it shapes or reflects opinion at large and whether politicians, rightly or wrongly, believe that newspapers influence public opinion. What is less debatable is the character of much British press coverage of EU matters. One of the most detailed studies of the subject concludes that 'the majority of the reading public is indeed insulted by the quality of the press performance with regard to European issues'. Tabloid discourse especially, according to this study, is assertive, engages in crude stereotyping and xenophobic outbursts, distorts issues, omits information, and is heavy with ideological force (Anderson and Weymouth 1999: 185).[66]

Certainly, a large section of the press has so persistently conveyed the view that there is no villain like the EU and no better negative headlines than the 'Britain isolated in the EU' or 'Government makes underhand concessions to EU' that europhobic is often a more accurate label for this mentality than eurosceptic. Factual accuracy and balanced reporting have rarely impeded a preference for distortion, misrepresentation, fiction and a generally infantilized approach to EU matters. Much press comment has invariably portrayed the EU as a behemoth, whereas its weaknesses rather than strengths are in fact all too evident whether in its lack of resources or its limitations in projecting a common foreign and security policy within the system of international power politics. Furthermore, the myths about the EU in the form of scare stories, rumours and half-truths as peddled through the British press are legion. For example, the Euromyths website section of the London office of the EU Commission includes the following newspaper reports in recent years: that the EU was changing the definition of an island; that 21-gun salutes had to be muffled; that combine harvesters were banned from use in wet conditions; that Brussels intended to put a speed limit on playground roundabouts; that warning signs would soon be required for mountains telling climbers that they were high up; that women had to hand in their used sex toys; and finally, as if to give a new dimension to the cleavage between Britain and Brussels, that the EU had declared 'a crackpot war on busty barmaids by trying to ban them from wearing low-top tops'.[67] At the same time a preoccupation with the domestic angle on any EU story has often meant that the British press has relegated a major item to the sidelines. Alastair Campbell, Blair's press officer, reportedly noted that following one informal meeting between EU leaders when the key piece of news by all accounts concerned a Franco-German disagreement, the British press was running around like headless chickens asking where was the story: 'i.e. where was the Britain-versus-the-rest story'. This was but one example in Campbell's view of how far the domestic press provided inferior coverage and analysis of Britain's EU policy as compared with the mainland European press (Trewin 2008: 594).

The strength of eurosceptic/europhobic press attacks on the EU and on Britain's EU policies, however, does not wholly rely on myths, falsehoods and public vilification. Such attacks invariably launch into the subject by setting a particular issue or government measure in the context of a version of British history that resonates with its readership and is able to command all of the best tunes and lines. As one recent study argues, the historical stories used by such press sources are more familiar to the British public and more persuasive as a result (Daddow: 2007). A typical example of the genre was the approach of the *Sun* to the idea of British membership of the euro zone in 1998 and to the signing of the Treaty of Lisbon by Brown in 2007. the *Sun* reached for one of the most iconic figures of twentieth century British public life and some of the most memorable political oratory of the century when it expressed unflinching opposition to the euro and promised '*We will fight, fight, fight. And even if we lose, we hope people will use the words of one of the greatest of our statesmen, Winston Churchill, and say ... This was their finest hour*'. On the day Brown signed the Lisbon Treaty, moreover, the *Sun* reproduced his signature with the simple caption 'Surrender signature', and it headlined the government's refusal to hold a referendum on the subject by deliberately misquoting Churchill, 'Never have so few decided so much for so many'.[68] The europhile case has clearly lacked this kind of 'history' on its side. It has invariably proved unable to utilize such potent images, events and memories in order to penetrate the clutter of the modern media with a set of powerful symbolic messages. Instead, popular qualms about EU membership, together with an often aphasic grasp of the mainsprings of European integration, have flourished in the absence of a sense of shared history between Britain and the other major EU states. In consequence, mainstream British political culture has encountered difficulties in coming to terms with the historical foundations, language and rhythm of European integration.

British press attitudes towards the EC/EU have undergone a striking change in the past thirty years. At the time of the referendum of 1975, for example, the press overwhelmingly supported EC membership with a fairly simple, compelling narrative. This press consensus included even the *Daily Express* and the *Sunday Express* which in the early 1960s under the influence of their proprietor, Beaverbrook, had taken a staunchly anti-EEC line.[69] In recent years, however, the reverse is very much the case. With very few exceptions, the press has become more solidly eurosceptic than at any time over the past fifty years, strongly so in the case of the foreign-owned press of the Murdoch and (as was) Black stables, and The Telegraph Group under the ownership of the British Barclay brothers. The press is also much more vituperative in its coverage of EU activities, markedly so in the case of the *Sun* and the *Daily Mail* with the latter often viewed as the 'benchmark audience' in government circles (Trewin 2008: 734). Is it therefore more influential? Some evidence would suggest so. Beaverbrook in the 1950s and 1960s, for example, never exercised the influence over Macmillan that Murdoch is alleged to have brought to bear over the Blair governments, particularly in pressing the case against British membership of the euro zone. Lance Price, Blair's former spin doctor, has claimed that when he worked at Downing Street Murdoch seemed like the '24th member of the Cabinet'. Price maintained that Murdoch might not even have had to lean on Blair to ensure that no British government minister said anything positive about the euro, as anticipatory compliance was Murdoch's most powerful weapon.[70] Shortly before he left office, Blair likened the British media to a feral beast. In doing so, it seems unlikely that he overlooked the way in which a eurosceptic media had greatly constrained his attempts to normalize Britain's EU membership. At his final EU Council press conference as Prime Minister, for example, he was invited to address the criticism that he had never managed to win the argument for Europe with British voters. On discovering that the hostile questioner was from the europhobic *Daily Telegraph,* Blair ruefully commented 'Well thank you for your help in winning this argument over the years!'[71]

Other evidence certainly suggests that the combination of a hostile media and parliamentary criticism has severely restricted the freedom of manoeuvre of British governments in the conduct of EU business in far more direct and constraining ways than was the case thirty years ago. A study of senior officials closely involved in Britain's EU negotiations over the past thirty years, for example, concluded that the signals given by London in its EU policies have ranged from the confused to the downright hostile. Furthermore, successive British governments faced such venomous criticism at home in their dealings with EU matters that this increasingly tended to leave the country looking isolated and out of step with other EU states (Menon 2004: 45).[72] These conditions also meant that government was reluctant to take pride in Britain's contribution to the EU, causing José Manuel Barroso, President of the European Commission, to comment. 'You will never persuade people to support an organization which you pretend does not exist'. At the same time in October 2006, Barroso posed the question: 'Does the United Kingdom want to continue to drive from the centre; or return to sulking from the periphery?'[73]

This book has attempted to chart and to explain the tortuous course of British policy and attitudes towards the EC/EU. It has examined the deep-seated ambivalence and divided opinions that have long characterized the British approach to the process of European integration since 1945. Clearly, no single event can sum up or epitomize major developments. One event, however, came close to doing so. It occurred on December 13 2007 when Gordon Brown signed the Treaty of Lisbon against the background noise of a largely hostile British press. He did so away from the public gaze, on his own, and after the other EU leaders had collectively signed the treaty and dined together. Brown's behaviour was ridiculed by Britain's EU supporters and critics alike. In many ways, however, his handling of the episode fairly represented Britain's troublesome relationship with the process of European integration since 1945. He appeared as the reluctant latecomer to the dinner party, and he was primarily concerned about the impact of his actions on the domestic audience rather than on his EU counterparts. He subsequently mounted a dogged defence of the treaty in its passage through parliament, largely on the basis of economic arguments and with little regard for any other strategic or visionary considerations. The parliamentary debate on the treaty itself all too clearly reflected, according to one political commentator, 'This country's half-hopes and half-fears about the EU, our mistrust and dither, our flirtation and sabre-rattling ... '[74] This was precisely the condition that Brown himself had strongly criticized in the mid-1990s when he had claimed that Britain could not afford 'a government which sees us hovering half in and half out [of the EU] for ever. The case must be made for full participation in Europe's future' (Peston 2006: 188). The case remains to be made. Meanwhile, the signing of the Lisbon Treaty episode offered a cameo sketch of some of the enduring features of British handling of EC/EU matters over the years. In particular, it suggested that far from occupying the centre of the European Union field Britain preferred to remain on the sidelines.

Chronological Table

1945	May	End of the Second World War in Europe (May 8).
	July	Labour Party under Clement Attlee won the general election.
	July/August	Potsdam conference of American, Soviet and British leaders.
1947	January	Merging of British and American occupation zones in Germany (Bizonia).
	March	UK/France Treaty of Dunkirk signed.
		Announcement of the Truman doctrine.
	June	Announcement of the Marshall Plan
	October	General Agreement on Tariffs and Trade (GATT) signed.
1948	March	Brussels Treaty signed by UK, France and the Benelux states.
	April	Organisation for European Economic Co-operation (OEEC) established to administer the European Recovery Programme (Marshall Plan).
	May	Congress of Europe at The Hague.
	June	Berlin blockade began.
1949	April	North Atlantic Treaty signed.
	May	Statute of the Council of Europe signed by ten states.
1950	May	Announcement of the Schuman Plan.
	June	Outbreak of the Korean War.
	October	Announcement of the Pleven Plan for a European army.
1951	April	European Coal and Steel Community (ECSC) Treaty of Paris signed by Belgium, France, Italy, Luxembourg, The Netherlands and West Germany.
	July	ECSC began to function.
	October	Conservative Party under Winston Churchill won the general election.
1952	May	European Defence Community (EDC) Treaty signed by the six ECSC states.

1954	August	French National Assembly rejected the EDC Treaty.
	October	Signature of the Paris Agreements and the formation of the Western European Union.
	December	Treaty of Association between UK and ECSC.
1955	April	Anthony Eden succeeded Churchill as prime minister.
	June	Messina conference of the six ECSC states.
	July	Spaak committee convened to consider plans for further European integration.
1956	March	Spaak Report on the creation of a common market.
	Oct./Nov.	Suez crisis.
	November	Announcement of British plan for a free trade area (FTA).
1957	January	Harold Macmillan succeeded Eden as prime minister.
	March	Treaties of Rome signed establishing the European Economic Community (EEC) and the European Atomic Energy Community (EAEC).
	October	Formation of the Maudling Committee under the aegis of the OEEC to consider the plan for an FTA.
1958	January	Treaties of Rome came into operation.
	December	France blocked further discussion of the FTA plan.
1959	January	First EEC tariff reductions and increases in import quotas.
1960	January	European Free Trade Association (EFTA) Convention signed in Stockholm by Austria, Denmark, Norway, Portugal, Sweden, Switzerland and the UK.
	May	Failure of Four-Power summit in Paris.
	December	OEEC reorganized into the Organisation for Economic Co-operation and Development (OECD).
1961	August	First UK application to join the EEC.
1962	January	Agreement on the main features of the EEC's Common Agricultural Policy (CAP).
	December	Kennedy/Macmillan meeting at Nassau and the Polaris agreement.
1963	January	De Gaulle vetoed UK membership of the EEC.
	October	Alec Douglas-Home succeeded Macmillan as prime minister.
1964	October	Labour Party under Harold Wilson won the general election.
1965	April	Merger Treaty of the European Communities (EC) signed. It entered into force on 1 July 1967.
	July	France began a boycott of EC institutions.
1966	January	Luxembourg Agreement ended French boycott of EC institutions.
	March	Labour Party won the general election.
	May/July	EEC negotiated an agreement on the CAP.

1967	May	Second UK application for EC membership.
	November	De Gaulle vetoed UK membership of EC.
1968	July	Completion of the EEC customs union.
1969	April	De Gaulle resigned as President of the Fifth French Republic.
	December	The Hague summit of EC leaders agreed in principle to enlarge the EC and to devise a plan for economic and monetary union.
1970	April	EC agreement on new arrangements for financing the budget through automatic revenue ('own resources').
	June	Conservative Party won the general election under Edward Heath.
		EC opened membership negotiations with Denmark, Ireland, Norway and the UK.
	October	Publication of the Werner Report on Economic and Monetary Union and the Davignon Report on European Political Co-operation.
1971	March	EC Council of Ministers agreed to embark on the first of three stages towards economic and monetary union by 1980.
1972	January	Conclusion of EC membership negotiations and signature of Treaties of Accession by Denmark, Ireland, Norway and the UK.
	October	UK parliament voted in favour of the principle of UK membership of the EC.
		Paris summit of EC leaders reaffirmed the goal of achieving economic and monetarry union by 1980.
1973	January	Accession of Denmark, Ireland and the UK to the EC.
1974	March	Labour government under Wilson returned to power after general election with a commitment to renegotiate the terms of entry to the EC.
	December	Paris summit of EC leaders agreed to establish the EC.
1975	March	Conclusion of the UK's renegotiation of the terms of entry to the EC.
	June	UK referendum resulted in a majority for the renegotiated terms of entry and continued membership of the EC.
	December	Rome European Council meeting agreed to hold direct elections to the European Parliament.
1976	April	James Callaghan succeeded Wilson as prime minister.
1977	November	Direct elections to the European Parliament postponed until 1979 due to UK failure to meet the original deadline.
1978	July	Franco-German proposal for a European Monetary System (EMS) announced at the Bremen European Council meeting.

	December	Formal announcement of UK decision not to participate in the Exchange Rate Mechanism (ERM) of the EMS.
1979	March	EMS began to function.
	May	Conservative Party under Margaret Thatcher won the general election.
	June	First direct elections to the European Parliament.
1980	May	EC Council of Ministers agreed to reduce UK contribution to EC budget for two years.
1981	January	Accession of Greece to the EC.
	November	Genscher-Colombo Plan.
1982	January	Common Fisheries Policy agreement.
1983	June	Conservative Party under Thatcher won the general election.
		Stuttgart European Council meeting adopted the Solemn Declaration on European Union.
1984	January	Free trade area established between the EC and the EFTA.
	June	Fontainebleau European Council meeting agreed a formula for reducing the UK contribution to the EC budget. British paper entitled 'Europe – the Future'.
1985	January	Jacques Delors appointed President of the Commission.
	June	Milan European Council meeting agreed in principle to establish a Single Market by the end of December 1992 and to convene an intergovernmental conference (IGC) on EC reform.
	December	Luxembourg European Council meeting agreed on the principles of the Single European Act.
1986	January	Accession of Spain and Portugal to the EC.
	February	Single European Act signed in Luxembourg.
1987	June	Conservative Party under Thatcher won the general election.
	July	Single European Act came into force.
1988	June	Hanover European Council meeting instructed a committee chaired by Jacques Delors to consider plans for the achievement of Economic and Monetary Union (EMU).
	September	Thatcher's speech at the College of Europe in Bruges.
1989	January	Delors reappointed President of the Commission.
	April	Delors Report on a three-stage progression towards the achievement of EMU.
	June	Madrid European Council meeting agreed to begin first stage of EMU on July 1 1990.
	December	At the Strasbourg European Council meeting all EC states except UK approved the Charter of Basic Social Rights for Workers (Social Charter) and also agreed to establish an IGC on EMU at the end of 1990.

1990	June	Dublin European Council meeting agreed to convene an IGC on Political Union.
	July	First stage of EMU came into effect.
	October	UK entered the ERM of the EMS.
		Rome European Council meeting agreed to implement the second stage of the Delors Plan for EMU by 1994.
	November	John Major succeeded Thatcher as Conservative Party leader and prime minister.
	December	The two IGCs on EMU and Political Union opened in Rome.
1991	December	Maastricht European Council meeting agreed the Treaty on European Union (Maastricht Treaty). UK government secured opt-outs covering the Social Chapter and the third and final stage of EMU.
1992	February	Treaty on European Union signed in Maastricht.
	May	Conservative Party under Major won the general election. EC and EFTA signed a treaty establishing the European Economic Area (EEA).
	June	Danish voters rejected the Treaty on European Union in a referendum.
	September	UK withdrew from the ERM.
1993	January	Single Market came into effect.
	February	EC opened negotiations with Austria, Finland and Sweden (and Norway – April 1993) on their applications for membership.
	May	Danish voters approved the Treaty on European Union after Denmark obtained opt-outs from the Treaty.
	July	UK ratified the Treaty on European Union.
	November	Treaty on European Union formally came into effect.
1994	January	Second stage of EMU came into effect with the establishment of the European Monetary Institute (EMI) in Frankfurt.
	July	Tony Blair elected leader of the Labour Party.
1995	June	Cannes European Council meeting recognised that the introduction of a single currency by 1997 was unrealistic.
1996	March	IGC convened to review the Treaty on European Union.
	December	Dublin European Council meeting agreed a single currency stability pact.
1997	May	Labour Party under Blair won the general election and announced its intention to accept the European Social Chapter.
	June	Amsterdam European Council meeting agreed the Treaty of Amsterdam following the IGC review of the Treaty on European Union.

		William Hague elected leader of the Conservative Party.
	October	Gordon Brown, Chancellor of the Exchequer, specified five economic tests for UK entry into the euro and indicated that the UK would not be ready for entry before the end of the current parliament.
	December	Luxembourg European Council meeting invited the Czech Republic, Estonia, Hungary, Poland, Slovenia and Cyprus to start membership talks in March 1998 with a view to entry to the EU early in the next century.
1998	January	UK's six-month presidency of the EU began.
	May	11 of the 15 EU states agreed to proceed to the third and final stage of EMU (scheduled for January 1 1999) with provision for the establishment of a European Central Bank, the fixing of exchange rates and the introduction of a single currency – the euro. Denmark, Sweden and the UK had previously obtained opt outs from this timetable, while Greece was deemed to have failed to qualify.
	June	End of UK's presidency of the EU.
		European Central Bank established.
1999	January	The euro was launched in 11 countries (Greece joined in 2001).
2001	February	Treaty of Nice signed
	March	Swiss rejected EU membership at a referendum.
	June	Irish rejected Treaty of Nice in a referendum.
2002	January	Euro notes and coins distributed in 12 countries.
	October	Irish voted in favour of the Treaty of Nice at a second referendum.
2003	February	Treaty of Nice came into effect.
	March	The EU was involved in peace making operations in the Balkans – as a result of its Foreign and Security Policy. The EU Agreed to create an area of Freedom, Security and Justice for all of its citizens by 2010.
2004	May	Eight countries from Central and Eastern Europe joined the EU (Czech Replublic, Estonia, Latvia, Lithuania, Hungary, Poland, Slovenia and Slovakia). Cyprus and Malta also joined.
	October	Twenty-five countries signed a Treaty establishing a European Constitution.
2005	May	French voters rejected the Constitutional Treaty in a referendum.
	June	Netherlands voted no on the Constitutional Treaty.
	July	UK began the Presidency of the EU.
2007	July	ECOFIN Council approved the adoption by Malta and Cyprus of the euro from January 1 2008.

Representatives of the Member states met in Brussels for the formal opening of the IGC on the Draft Reform Treaty.

	December	Treaty of Lisbon signed.
2008	June	Irish rejected the Lisbon Treaty in a referendum (53.4% against).

Appendix
Structures and Procedures in the European Union

The institutions and decision-making procedures of the EU have evolved over time. In part this was because of the need for greater democratic oversight and control. In addition as integration proceeded apace both in relation to enlargement of the EU and with regard to new areas of policy additional procedures came into play. In its early days, democratic oversight was limited in part because the European Coal and Steel Community was primarily a technocratic and functionalist project, albeit that it possessed supranational authority. However, the actual decision-making can be primarily supranational (e.g. in relation to the Single Market), or intergovernmental (e.g. defence) or a mix of the two (e.g. regional development). More particularly there is no single locus of power in the EU, instead power is shared amongst the various political actors and the extent to which they can influence decision-making can be dependent on what stage the policy process has reached.

As far as the EU is concerned the institutional structure is far from straightforward, not least because the function of the various actors has changed to a lesser or greater degree over time. The European Commission is responsible for drawing up the draft budget, formulating policy, overseeing its implementation (albeit that this is usually undertaken by the member states) and, in so doing, it is also the 'guardian of the treaties'. Consequently, if a member state fails to implement a policy, in the final resort the Commission might bring the matter to the European Court of Justice (ECJ). The Commission also negotiates international agreements, although the final decision rests with the member states in the Council. The ECJ has a number of functions including resolving disputes, for example between the member states and the EU, the member states themselves or individuals and the EU. Under the Single European Act the Court of First Instance was established in 1989. It was intended to deal with more minor disputes, especially if they involved disputes between staff in the EU and their institutions.

The European Parliament's role was modest at first and it was originally called the 'Common Assembly' under the ECSC. It was renamed as the European Parliament (EP) in 1962 and it was not directly elected until 1979. Initially, where the treaties so allowed it was only informed or consulted and, as far as the latter was concerned, there was little certainty that the Council of Ministers or the European Commission would pay much attention to its views. That changed slightly following the SEA, with the introduction of the 'co-operation procedure'. Under this procedure if the EP objected to a proposal on a second reading the proposal could only be adopted by the Council of Ministers by unanimity. The EU acquired more substantive power under the Treaty on European Union. Where the treaty so-allowed it now had co-decision with the Council of Ministers – in effect this amounted to a veto. Co-decision increased following the Treaty of Amsterdam in 1997 and the Treaty of Nice three years later. One of the reasons why co-decision increased was the enlargement of the EU. As it became larger unanimity was no longer tenable (except in areas of policy that remained inherently inter-governmental) but the actual weighting of votes amongst the constituent members became a potentially divisive issue during the Nice negotiations (for further reading on this refer to Gowland *et al.* 2006: 329).

The Council of Ministers meets in a range of functional formats (e.g. an Agricultural Council). The relevant ministers from the member states stand at its apex, beneath which lie Corepeur who comprise the permanent representatives of the member states and the working groups. Essentially, the Council adopts or rejects the Commission's proposals. The European Council is not an institution as such but it does have a pivotal role to play within the EU. Formed in 1974, it has something of a strategic role with regard to structural funding or enlargement. The governments of the member states not only are represented in the Council they also implement EU policy and depending on the relevant proposal they might have a measure of discretion over this. At first, decision-making within the Council was by unanimity – in effect each state possessed a veto but that risked bringing policy-making to a stand still. Consequently there were moves to introduce a more collective form of decision-making whereby if there was a majority in favour then the proposal would be adopted by the Council. However, this was by no means welcomed by all member states and it led to France withdrawing its participation in the Council until the so-called Luxembourg Compromise was agreed in 1966. Effectively, it was a device which allowed a member state to refuse to accept a proposal if it believed that the latter would have an adverse affect on its national interest. The Compromise was somewhat ephemeral inasmuch as it lay outside the bounds of the Treaties. The SEA and the treaties which followed heralded greater use of Qualified Majority Voting in the Council of Ministers, whereby the distribution of votes amongst each member states varies.

There are two consultative bodies – these are the Committee of the Regions (CoR) and the Economic and Social Committee (ECOSOC). Where the treaties so allow, one or both are consulted but formally they possess little authority over EU decision-making. ECOSOC is the older of the two and is designed to incorporate civil actors such as employers, unions and consumer interests into the policy process. The CoR was a by-product of the TEU, following pressure from territorial actors in Germany and Belgium for a greater involvement on the part of the EU's regions. Although much was made of the CoR at its inception, it faced a number of hurdles not least that its representatives were drawn from widely differing entities. For example a Minister President of a German Land could be sitting beside a councillor from Dundee. The dilemma, however, related not so much to the status of the individuals concerned but that a Landtag and an urban council might have differing needs in relation to the EU and its policies.

Notes

Introduction

1 *Official Journal of the European Union*, Vol. 50, C306/157.
2 Peter Lilley. Source: *http://news.bbc.co.uk/1/hi/uk*. The transfer of powers from the UK Parliament to the EU prompted Lilley, a British MP and former Conservative government minister, to introduce an MP's (Pay and Responsibilities) Bill in June 2008. The bill proposed to cut the pay of MPs to reflect their reduced legislative responsibility in the wake of the expected ratification of the Lisbon Treaty by the UK Parliament. Lilley conceded that his bill was unlikely to become law and that his main intention was to demonstrate the extent to which legislative authority had drained away from Parliament to the EU. At the time of writing, the future of Britain's opt-out from the EU's working time directive is under threat as a result of a vote by the European Parliament (December 2008) that all such opt-outs from the working time directive should be abolished.
3 *http://euobserver.com/9/2703*.
4 See, for example, the *Observer*, Will Hutton, October 5 2008 and November 16 2008 and the *Guardian*, Philip Whyte and Simon Tilford, October 14 2008.
5 The *Sun*, December 11 2008.
6 *Daily Mail*, January 1 2009.
7 *http://news.uk.msn.com/uk/article*.
8 House of Commons European Scrutiny Committee, *Democracy and Accountability in the EU and the Role of National Parliaments*, 33rd Report, 2001–2, HC 152, para 20.
9 *The EU: What's in it for me? http://ec.europa.eu/unitedkingdom/*.
10 *New Dictionary of National Biography*, Oxford: Oxford University Press, 2004–5.
11 See, for example, his speech on November 23 2001 at Birmingham University, *www.phoenix-tv.net/ubirmingham/eriscript.htm*.
12 BBC News Online Magazine May 25 2004.
13 Similarly, it is incorrect to refer to Britain and the EU from Thatcher to Blair, as the sub-title of a recent book does.
14 Eurostat (2008) *Key figures on Europe – 2007/08 edition*.
15 National Archives (hereafter NA), Foreign and Commonwealth Office (hereafter FCO), *The Reform Treaty: The British Approach to the EU Intergovernmental Conference, July 2007*. *Hansard*, 23 June 2008 (figures quoted by Prime Minister Gordon Brown in the House of Commons).
16 For an introductory guide to the institutions of the EU, see Peterson and Shackleton 2002. See also Cini 2003. For theories of European integration, see Rosamond 2000.

17 There were one or two exceptions to this, such as when a minister from the Scottish Executive represented the UK on the Education Council from time to time, but essentially the matters at hand were 'low politics'.

1 Limited liability, 1945–55

1 For this view see, for example, Milward 2002.
2 *Documents on British Policy Overseas* [hereafter DBPO], Series II, no. 52, London: HMSO. NA., CAB 128/17, CM (50) 29th Conclusions, May 8 1950.
3 For a review of some of the different assessments of Bevin's concept of Western Union, see Melissen and Zeeman 1987; Croft 1994; Kent 1993.
4 NA, FO [Foreign Office] 371/73045, memorandum by Bevin, January 12 1948.
5 NA, FO 371/38523; Reynolds 1991: 177–78.
6 Note, for example, the advice of Anthony Eden as Foreign Secretary in the Churchill government of 1951–55, 'the more gradually and inconspicuously we can transfer the real burdens from our own to American shoulders, the less damage we shall do to our position and influence in the world'. NA., CAB 129/53, C(52)202.
7 For the historiography of the UK–USA 'special relationship' see Élie 2005.
8 For the view that the USA wanted a compliant, non-imperial Britain as part of a European federation, see Charmley 1995.
9 NA., FO 371/67674, Cooper to Bevin, October 16 1947. For a strong presentation of the Foreign Office view see especially NA., FO 371/71766, Foreign Office paper on a west European customs union. For Treasury and Board of Trade views immediately prior to the Western Union initiative see, for example, NA., CAB 134/215, EPC 47 6th meeting, November 7 1947. See also NA., BT [Board of Trade] 11/352, Note by the Board of Trade, June 26 1947.
10 See also Ward (ed.) 2001. For the importance of imperial memories and British attitudes towards European integration since 1945, see Deighton 2002.
11 For an official description of the 'one world' approach see NA., CAB 21/3323.
12 NA, CAB 134/219 E.P.C. (48) 78, September 7 1948.
13 NA, FO 371/77999, Hall-Patch to Berthoud, April 4 and 16 1949.
14 NA, CAB 134/221, EPC (49) 6, January 25 1949. See also NA, CAB 128/16, CM (49) 62, October 27 1949.
15 See, for example, NA, FO 371/85842, Makins, minutes of a meeting with Monnet, May 16 1950.
16 For some of the initial reactions to the plan in Whitehall see, for example, NA., FO 371/85841, Stevens' memorandum on the French proposal to establish a Franco-German Coal and Steel Authority, May 10 1950. See also NA., FO 371/85843, Jebb to Strang, May 11 1950.
17 For Monnet's talks with British officals in 1949 see, for example, NA., FO 371/77933, Note of four conversations between Plowden and Monnet, March 3–7 1949, and NA, T[Treasury] 229/207, Hitchman, April 11 1949. See also K. Jones 1994: 160–61, and Hennessy 1992: 378–81.
18 For this view see, for example, NA., FO 371/62555, Stevens, December 22 1947.
19 See, for example, NA., FO 371/85844, Franks to Foreign Office, May 29 1950.
20 The first meeting of ministers following the Schuman announcement concluded that 'much time would elapse before substantial progress could be made with this proposal in France or Germany': NA., CAB 130/60, GEN 322/1st meeting, May 11 1950.
21 See NA., FO 371/85844, Foreign Office to Ankara, June 4 1950.
22 NA., FO 371/85852, Rickett to Jay, Note of a meeting of ministers, June 21 1950.
23 NA., FO 371/85847, Harvey, 6 June 1950. See also NA., FO 371/85850, Harvey to Younger.

24 For detailed treatment of this subject, see Milward 1984.
25 See NA., CAB 134/293, FG (WP) (50) 38, Working Party on proposed Franco-German Coal and Steel Authority.
26 For a near contemporary exposition of this view see, for example, Nutting 1960. For a more recent critical assessment of the Labour Government's response to the plan see Dell 1995. For a collection of essays on the failings of the British political system in this field see, for example, Broad and Preston (eds) 2001.
27 For an extract from the minutes of this Cabinet meeting, see Gowland and Turner (eds) 2000a: 24–25.
28 *DBPO* Series II, Volume 1, No. 75, Strang to Younger, June 2 1950.
29 On the case for some form of association between Britain and the Six, see Lord 1994.
30 *Parliamentary Debates (Hansard) House of Commons Official Report* [hereafter H.C.Deb], vol. 542, col. 603.
31 NA., FO 371/116040, Jebb to Macmillan, 15 June 1955. See also, for example, NA., FO 371/116040, Ellis-Rees to the Foreign Office.
32 For a detailed account of British policy towards the issue of West German rearmament, see Dockrill 1991.
33 See, for example, NA., CAB 134/1030, no. 19, Ellis-Rees to Macmillan, October 11 1955.
34 NA., CAB 134/1226, E.P. (55) 11th meeting, November 11 1955.
35 NA., T 234/195, June 28 1956.
36 For group think, see Janis 1982.
37 For the Trend Report, see NA., CAB 134/1030, M.A.C. (55), 'The United Kingdom and a European Common Market', October 24 1955.
38 For a detailed discussion of the Foreign Office and particular obstacles to policy changes, see K. Johnson 1983, and Kane 1996.
39 NA., C.M. 19 (55) – The Cabinet Secretaries' notebook – meeting held on June 30 1955.

2 Agonizing reappraisal, 1956–72

1 NA., FO 371/116048, The Brussels conference on European integration.
2 NA., T 236/6018, minute of a Treasury meeting, April 24 1956.
3 NA., FO 371/122034, Thorneycroft to Butler, August 23 1956. See also NA, BT 11/5514. A Foreign Office paper summarized the problem, 'we dare not combat growing integration of W.[Western] Europe, we dare not remain isolated. General rule – if you can't beat it, join it. But it is axiom of British policy, that we can't do that either' (NA., FO 371/143697, undated paper entitled 'The U.K. and Western European Organisations').
4 In September 1956 Macmillan argued against any attempt to work for the breakdown of the Messina initiative on the grounds that this would not serve Britain's long-term interest and would 'Balkanise Europe' – Source: NA., CAB 195/15, Cabinet Secretaries' notebooks, September 14 1956.
5 For the history and politics of the EEC/EU see Gowland *et al.* (eds) 2006.
6 NA., FO 371/146268, memorandum by A. Rumb, September 15 1959.
7 See, for example, Monnet 1978, Spaak 1971, Marjolin 1989.
8 For historical treatment supporting this view see, for example, Lamb 1987.
9 See NA., T 234/100, Macmillan to Bridges, February 1 1956 – paper entitled European Integration. See also NA., T 234/183, brief for discussions with Professor Erhard, February 14 1956, and NA., CAB 13/1373, minutes of a meeting of the Cabinet Atlantic (Official) Committee, March 5 1956.
10 For a classic exposition of this view see Camps 1964.
11 NA., T 236/6018, Macmillan to Eden, undated.

12 NA., T 234/358, Clarke to Gore-Booth, January 8 1959. Cabinet divisions, for example, were evident in discussions of commercial policy in September 1956. Amory, Macmillan and Thorneycroft emphasized the importance of Plan G in creating a more competitive British economy. Butler, however, doubted the wisdom of the plan, feared that it would be unpopular with the Conservative Party and raised the problem of safeguarding sterling's role as a world currency within a regional trade bloc. Source: NA., CAB 195/15 Cabinet Secretaries' notebooks, September 18 1956.

13 NA., T 234/100, Macmillan to Bridges, February 1 1956, See also NA., BT 11/5520. For one of the best analyses of the Commonwealth in British policymaking towards the EEC in this period, see Alexander (2000). For the relative value of UK trade with the Commonwealth and with Western Europe at this time see Gowland and Turner 2000a: 73.

14 For this view see, for example, Ellison 2000 and Schaad 1998.

15 NA., T 236/6018, memo by D. F. Hubback, October 25 1955.

16 NA., FO 371/122033, August 9 1956. See also NA., BT 11/5520, Butler to Eden, August 15 1956.

17 NA., FO 371/150154, European Economic Integration papers by Figgures and Clarke. NA, T 234/720, Bretherton to Clarke, February 3 1960.

18 Macmillan 1972: 64. NA., FO 371/145774, Steel to the Foreign Office, 31 March 1959. See also Huth 1995.

19 NA., PREM 11/1138, paper by Eden, December 1956. For a comparative study of Eden and Macmillan in this field, see Ruane and Ellison 2004.

20 For detailed treatment of this episode, see Kane 1996.

21 NA., PREM 11/2315, Macmillan to the Chancellor of the Exchequer and the Foreign Secretary, June 24 1958.

22 NA., PREM 11/2827, Butler to Macmillan, March 24 1959.

23 *The Economist*, July 22 1961. *The Times*, July 31 1961.

24 For the most detailed review of the historiography, see Daddow 2004. See also Kaiser 2002 and Clemens 2004 for contrasting treatment of the origins of the first application.

25 See, for example, NA., FO 371/142597, Steel to the Foreign Office, October 28 1959.

26 *The Economist*, May 28 1960.

27 *FRUS 1958–1960*, Volume VII, No. 113, memorandum of conversation, March 28, 1960. See also NA., PREM 11/2532 'The Prime Minister's Alleged remarks about 6s and 7s', and NA., FO 371/150269, Steel to the Foreign Office, March 31 1960.

28 See NA., FO 371/150160, NA., FO 371/150163, NA., FO 371/150168, NA., T 172/2142.

29 NA., FO 371/150290, memo of a conversation between Hallstein and Gore-Booth, July 28 1960.

30 *The Economist*, June 11 1960.

31 See, for example, Evans 1981. See also NA., FO 371/156453, Dean to Hoyer Millar, July 17 1961.

32 NA., PREM 11/3325, 'Memorandum by the Prime Minister'.

33 NA., FO 371/150363, paper by L. G. Holliday on 'United Kingdom Relations with the Six', July 6 1960.

34 NA., CAB 134/1821, F. P. (60) 1, 24th February 1960, 'Future Policy Study 1960–70'.

35 For Enoch Powell's critique of Macmillan and Europe, see *The Spectator*, January 10 1987.

36 NA., BT 11/5563, memo by W. Hughes, June 13 1960. In the period 1958–60, British exports to the EEC increased from 13.2 per cent to 14.5 per cent, while

British exports to the Commonwealth declined from 41.2 per cent to 38.5 per cent of total British exports (Source: NA., PREM 11/3563, UK Exports and Imports).

37 See, for example, Ashton 2007. At the same time there were some gloomy assessments of the historical impact of the British Empire as well as the beginnings of a long decline in popular and academic interest in the Empire and Commonwealth until recent years. Richard Turnbull, one of the last governors of Aden, claimed that when the empire finally collapsed it would leave behind it only two monuments: the game of Association Football and the expression 'Fuck off', Weight 2002.

38 NA., FO 371/143705, 'Future Policy Study': memo by P. Dean, August 15 1959. Evidently, some leaders in Washington were impressed by British strengths in this field. Richard Nixon, for example, is to be heard ruminating on one of the infamous Nixon tapes: 'Wouldn't it be great if the British were strong enough to play a bigger role in the world. They're so goddamn intelligent'. Quoted by Timothy Garton Ash in the *Guardian*, December 11 2008.

39 NA., CAB 134/1852 E. Q. (60) 27, 'The Six and the Seven: Long Term Arrangements', May 1960.

40 NA., CAB 134/1821, European Economic Association Committee, May 9 1961. For the best detailed analysis of the attitudes of British business towards European integration in this period, see Rollings 2007.

41 NA., PREM 11/3270, Bishop to Macmillan, February 24 1961.

42 NA., T 236/6553, 'The effects of membership of the Common Market on the U. K. balance of payments', May 15 1961.

43 *The Times*, May 8 1961.

44 NA., CAB 134/1852 E. Q. (60) 27, 'The Six and the Seven: Long Term Arrangements', May 1960.

45 Quoted in Greenwood 2004.

46 *The Economist*, August 5 1961. [USA] National Security files, 1961–63, Box 1700489, August 7 1961, memo for the President from George Ball. the *Guardian*, August 1 1961. Macmillan's low key announcement was in marked contrast to his performance immediately afterwards with the Lobby where, according to his press officer Harold Evans, in a post-prandial afterglow he swung the chairman's gavel perilously backwards and forwards, talked about the First World War trenches and how they enabled you to stay calm, said he could still do the 18th hole at St Andrews in four, and that he was now going to let off 300 or 400 cartridges – on which cue he suddenly got up and left, Evans 1981: 156. The episode seemingly confirmed Harold Wilson's view that Macmillan's role as a *poseur* was always a pose.

47 See, for example, NA, FO 371/158176, record of a conversation between Gladwyn and Monnet, May 8 1961.

48 For the presentational aspects of the announcement, see for example NA., PREM 11/3554, Eccles to Macmillan, April 24 1961.

49 NA., CAB 134/1853, Cabinet Economic Steering Committee (Europe) Committee, 1960.

50 For an illuminating treatment of this theme, see Kaiser 2002.

51 NA., FO 371/152119, 'British Cultural Diplomacy'.

52 NA., PREM 11/2679, Chequers meeting on European political and economic questions, November 29 1959. NA., PREM 11/3132, Lloyd to Macmillan, December 31 1959.

53 NA., PREM 11/2531, Eccles to Macmillan, July 14 1958.

54 See also NA., CAB 128/34, CC (60) 32nd Conclusions, May 20 1960.

55 See, for example, NA., PREM 11/3644, Macmillan to Menzies.

56 *FRUS*, Volume XIII, West Europe and Canada, No. 383, Telegram from the Embassy in the UK to the Department of State, July 17 1961.

57 NA., PREM 11/3554, Watkinson to Macmillan, April 24 1961.
58 NA., CAB 134/1821, European Economic Association Committee, May 17 1961.
59 NA., CAB 134/1853.
60 NA., PREM 11/4415, 'Public Opinion and the Common Market', September 18 1962.
61 For the view that party advantage did enter into Conservative thinking about the EEC application, see Beloff 1973: 172 and Butler and King 1965: 79.
62 NA., PREM 11/3133, April 22 1960, 'The Six and the Seven'.
63 NA., BT 11/5563, Comment on E. S. (E) (60) 11, G. H. Andrew, May 9 1960.
64 See, for example, NA., PREM 11/3133, Macmillan memo on talks with de Gaulle, March 14 1960. See also Horne 1989: 257.
65 For detailed treatment of the relationship between Britain's first EEC application and UK–USA relations, see Kaiser 1996.
66 Macmillan placed such high value on UK–USA relations that he was responsible for suppressing details of the unprecedented disaster at the Windscale nuclear plant (October 10 1957) for fear that any publicity about the incident might jeopardise US nuclear assistance to Britain. (Source: BBC 2, 8 October, 2007.)
67 NA., PREM 11/2986, Foreign Office paper on 'The Future of Anglo-American Relations', January 5 1960.
68 For recent assessments of relations between Macmillan and de Gaulle, see Warner 2002 and Mangold 2006.
69 *FRUS*, 1961–63, Vol. XIII, 1109–10.
70 Bishop, one of Macmillan's advisors, was to the fore in regarding Britain's nuclear weapons as a wasting asset that could be used to gain French support for Britain's EEC application. See his anonymous memo to Macmillan 'Thoughts on policy towards Western Europe', NA. PREM 11/2985.
71 NA., PREM 11/3325, Macmillan to the Foreign Secretary, January 11 1961.
72 For a particularly illuminating view of UK–USA relations and the EEC membership issue at this time see NA., FO 371/158162, minute of a meeting of Ball, Heath and Lee, March 30 1961.
73 For some of the most recent assessments of the Wilson government and European integration, see Daddow (ed.) 2003.
74 *FRUS*, 1964–68 Vol. XIII, No. 265, Memorandum of Conversation, July 27 1966.
75 For example, 26.5 per cent of Australia's exports in 1959–60 went to Britain, but by 1971–72 the figure had fallen to 9.2 per cent. Source: Benvenuti 2005.
76 In a memo to Brown, Gore-Booth, the most senior official at the Foreign Office, commented 'we have now stated ... the abandonment of our claim to be a world power ... ', NA., FCO 46/42, Gore-Booth to Brown, January 18 1968.
77 NA., CAB 128/42, minutes of a Cabinet meeting on April 30 1967.
78 NA., PREM 13/1476, record of a meeting at the Elysée Palace, January 25 1967. De Gaulle also ordered all US military forces out of France, causing one diplomat to ask 'does that include the ones under the ground?'
79 For a summary of the arguments put forward at this Cabinet meeting, see NA., PREM 13/909, Trend to Wilson, October 28 1966. Trend, the Cabinet Secretary, indicated the major difficulties that Britain would have to overcome before it might eventually join the EEC, but he added 'what alternative is open to us?'
80 NA., PREM 13/2108, Wilson to Brown, April 20 1967. Wilson reported that ministers who were previously anti- or floating had taken the view to 'have a bash' and, if excluded from the EEC, not to whine but to create a Dunkirk-type robust British dynamic.
81 NA., PREM 13/1521, Wilson to Brown, June 21 1967.
82 *FRUS*, 1964–68, Vol. XIII, No. 280, telegram from Rusk to the Department of State, December 13 1967.

83 *FRUS*, 1964–68, Vol. XIII, No. 291, telegram from Wilson to Johnson, January 15 1968.
84 NA., PREM 13/2110, Chalfont to Wilson, January 17 1968. For the Soames affair, see Pine 2004.
85 NA., PREM 15/369, 'Options for British external policy if our application for membership of the Communities fails', undated.
86 *The Spectator*, October 10 1970. Roberts 2006.
87 For an insider or Whitehall account of the negotiations, see O'Neill 2000.
88 Quoted by P. Hennessy in the *Independent*, December 17 1990.
89 See, for example, NA., FCO 7/1427, memo by Audland, January 31 1969.
90 See, for example, NA., PREM 15/375, record of a meeting between Heath and the British ambassador in Washington, June 18 1971.
91 *Encounter*, 1963.
92 See, for example, NA., FCO 30/771, record of conversation between the Chancellor of the Duchy of Lancaster and the French Minister of Foreign Affairs, November 9 1970, at which the former said that 'the essentials of the negotiations could be settled as a result of Anglo/French cooperation and initiative'.
93 For an assessment of the likely success of the British application by the British embassy in Paris and of French attitudes to the main negotiating issues, see NA., PREM 15/371, Soames to Greenhill, April 21 1971. For discussion of the main factors relating to a possible Heath–Pompidou meeting, see NA., PREM 15/370, Note of a meeting on April 23 1971 attended by Heath, Home and Rippon.
94 For ministerial fears about the impact of Britain's EC membership on the balance of payments and unemployment, see, for example, NA., PREM 15/3777, Carr to Heath, July 1 1971.
95 *The Times*, October 14 1971.
96 H.C.Deb., Vol. 818, cols 32–33, May 24 1971. See also Cmd 4715 (July 1971) *The United Kingdom and the European Communities*, and Heath 1998: 210–11.
97 *The Times*, January 2 1973. A fairly accurate snapshot impression of public attitudes towards Britain's entry into the EC was captured in a special Church of Scotland prayer to mark the event. It included the following verse, 'Our God, We are now in the Common Market. Some of us feel that this has been a mistake. Some of us believe that this will bring opportunities for good. Most of us just don't know' (Gowland 1973). Representative of the last category was a woman in Liverpool who, when asked by a Conservative Party official about her views on the Common Market, replied, 'Where are they building it, luv?' quoted in Weight 2002: 485.
98 NA., PREM 15/371, Hurd to Heath, April 22 1971, record of a meeting between Rippon and the French ambassador.
99 NA., PREM 15/372, paper by M. Wolff entitled 'Europe: Parliament and Public Opinion', May 10 1971.

3 Adjustment to Membership, 1973–84

1 This is the central thesis advanced by Roy Denman. Denman's experience with the EC dated from 1960, when he was involved in trade negotiations with officials from the European Commission. He was a member of the team which negotiated British entry to the EC and thereafter became successively Head of the European Secretariat in the Cabinet Office (1975–77), Director General for External Relations with the European Commission (1977–82) and EC Ambassador to Washington (1982–89).
2 Hugo Young discusses this difficulty in adjusting to a new role in Europe with particular reference to Foreign Office officials, writing 'Trained in Anglo-Americanism,

pickled in the heritage of Commonwealth, they were slow to remake themselves as Europeans. Many of the senior people never really did'. See Young, 1998: 176.

3　George 1990: 64–65, 99–104.

4　A speech at Ardglass in Northern Ireland on July 31 1976.

5　Stephens 1996: 2–3. See also Blair 2002: 52–54 and Young 2000: 192–94.

6　Callaghan made a specific and highly critical reference to the unfortunate experience of the 'snake' in his statement to the Commons explaining the government's decision not to enter the ERM: *H. C. Deb.*, Vol. 959, Col. 1426, December 6 1978.

7　OECD (1970–80) *Main Economic Indicators*.

8　The Heath government's unduly optimistic predictions about the impact of EC membership on the British economy were largely based on the assumption that Britain's experience would replicate that of the original Six. See Cmd 4715 (July 1971), *The United Kingdom and the European Community*. It is worth noting that the Treasury dissented from the White Paper's conclusions. Douglas Allen, the Permanent Secretary, was deeply sceptical about the net economic benefits of entry. See Young, *This Blessed Plot*, 1998, p. 225.

9　On the tenth anniversary of British entry to the EC, *The Economist* published a balanced assessment of the economic consequences: *The Economist*, December 25 1982–87 January 1983, pp. 61–62.

10　Roy Jenkins, Home Secretary in the third Wilson government, was a forceful exponent of this argument. See, for example, the speech which he made to a Britain in Europe rally in Edinburgh on May 14 1975.

11　See, for example, the pamphlet issued by the Labour Common Market Safeguards Committee on the first anniversary of the June 1975 referendum: *The Common Market: Promises and Reality*. See also the speech made by Anthony Wedgwood Benn, the then Trade and Industry Secretary in the third Wilson government, at the Coventry Police Hall on May 16 1975.

12　*Let Us Work Together–Labour's Way Out of the Crisis*, Labour Party general election manifesto, February 1974.

13　It must be pointed out, though, that food prices figured prominently in the 1975 referendum campaigns.

14　Cmd. 4715 (July 1971), *The United Kingdom and the European Communities*.

15　Heath 1998: 372; George 1991: 57, 66–69. Urwin 1995: 151. Schmidt, the West German Chancellor, was deeply sceptical about the value of the ERDF. For his attitude, see Bulmer and Paterson 1987: 202.

16　See, for example, the extremely critical verdicts, from very different standpoints, by the pro-marketeer Labour MP John P. Mackintosh and the Labour anti-marketeer Douglas Jay: *H. C. Deb.*, Vol. 888, Cols 411–13, March 11 1975; Vol. 889, Cols 858–61, April 7 1975.

17　The decision to hold a referendum by the following June at the latest was announced to the Commons on January 23 1975: *H. C. Deb.*, Vol. 884, Cols 1745–50. The detailed arrangements for the conduct of the referendum were set out in Cmd. 5925 (February 1975), *Referendum on United Kingdom Membership of the European Community*.

18　Benn's efforts to secure support for the idea of a referendum can be traced in his diaries: See Benn 1996: 214, 236–37, 254–57. See also Jenkins 1992: 341–48; Goodheart 1976: 44–59; Kitzinger 1992: 392; Ziegler 1993: 381–87.

19　The two most detailed studies of the 1975 referendum are Butler and Kitzinger: 1976 and Goodheart: 1976.

20　Details of the expenditure by both sides were set out in a White Paper: Cmd. 6251 (October 1975), *Referendum on UK Membership of the European Community: Accounts of Campaigning Organisations*.

21 The only press organs to back the 'no' campaign were the *Morning Star, Tribune,* the *Scottish Daily News* (a recently created co-operative), the *Dundee Courier and Advertiser* and the *Spectator.* Business sentiment was overwhelmingly favourable to Britain staying in the EC, as was revealed in a survey published by the *Times* on April 9 1975. This was especially the case with big companies. See 'British Industry and Europe', *A Report by the CBI Europe Committee,* March 1975.

22 See Pimlott 1992: 659.

23 National Executive Committee of the British Labour Party, *European Election Manifesto, 1979.*

24 *The New Hope for Britain,* Labour Party general election manifesto, 1983.

25 See, for example, Owen 1991: 66–67.

26 Jenkins 1992: 424.

27 According to the authors of the most detailed study of the referendum, the verdict 'was unequivocal but it was also unenthusiastic. Support for membership was wide but it did not run deep' (Butler and Kitzinger 1976: 280).

28 For the terms of the Lib–Lab pact see Steel 1989: 129–30.

29 Callaghan admitted that he 'could not travel fast' in EC affairs because of opposition within the Labour Party: Callaghan 1987: 493.

30 Callaghan 1987: 399.

31 For a detailed account and analysis of the 1976 IMF crisis, see Burk and Cairncross 1992.

32 Callaghan stressed his concern about lack of economic convergence in his statement to the Commons explaining the government's position on the EMS: *H. C. Deb.,* Vol. 959, Cols 1421–26, December 6 1978. See also Callaghan 1987: 493; Morgan 1997: 614–16.

33 Dell 1995.

34 See Thatcher 1995: 334–35. See also Jenkins 1992: 402; Beloff 1973: 81.

35 Cited in Wall 2008: 177.

36 For Thatcher's prejudices about the Foreign Office, see Gilmour 1992: 226–27; Wall 2008; H. Young 1998: 314–18.

37 Gilmour 1992: 235; Jenkins 1992: 498–99; Thatcher 1995: 80–82; Wall 2008: 7.

38 Thatcher 1995: 336–38. See also Wall 2008: 30.

39 For information on the Anglo-French discussions, see Wall 2008: 31, 34.

40 See G. Howe 1994: 401–2; Thatcher 1995: 542–44; H. Young 1998: 322–24; Urwin 1995: 188.

4 Trench warfare, 1985–97

1 The celebrated 'game, set and match' was uttered by a spokesperson rather than Major himself. It nevertheless accurately reflected his own views. See Hogg and Hill 1995: 157; n.7, Seldon 1998: 248 and H. Young 1998: 432.

2 *The Economist,* September 25 1993.

3 Out of office, Thatcher appeared to disown this decision and spoke as if it had not been made by her government. Certainly, at the time of the debate over the Maastricht Treaty she criticized the policy of maintaining the pound within the ERM. See, for example, the *Independent,* June 29 1992.

4 'Europe – The Future', *Journal of Common Market Studies,* 1984: 74–81. See also Howe 1994: 407–9.

5 Interviews in BBC 2 television documentary *The Poisoned Chalice,* part 3.

6 Interviews with Powell, Butler and Williamson in BBC 2 television documentary, *The Poisoned Chalice,* part 3. H. Young 1998: 336.

7 The *Independent,* October 22 1988.

8 The Jimmy Young Show, BBC Radio 2, July 27 1988.

9 The *Independent,* September 9 1988.

10 Wall 2008: 79. Wall also notes that Thatcher's first guiding principle as set out in the speech – 'willing and active cooperation between sovereign independent states is the best way to build a successful European Community' – was taken almost word for word by Blair as his defining vision when he delivered a speech in Oxford in February 2006.

11 *Parliamentary Debates (Hansard) House of Commons Official Report* [hereafter *H. C. Deb.*], 959, col. 1424, December 6 1978.

12 For an account of Thatcher's increasingly desperate rearguard action against ERM entry see Stephens 1996: chs 3–7.

13 *Financial Times*, October 18 1989. Walters continued to campaign against placing sterling in the ERM and not only predicted doom when this happened in 1990 but also developed his arguments in a book *Sterling in Danger* (1990).

14 *The Spectator*, July 12 1990.

15 Ridley's interviewer, Dominic Lawson, wrote in *The Spectator* article: 'Mr Ridley's confidence in expressing his views on the German threat must owe something to the knowledge that they are not significantly different from those of the Prime Minister'. See also G. Howe 1994: 632–33; Urban 1996: 153; Stephens 1996: 102; Trewin 2008: 300.

16 *H. C. Deb.*, vol. 178, col. 873, October 30 1990; G. Howe 1994: 643–44.

17 *H. C. Deb.*, vol. 180, cols. 461–65, November 13 1990; G. Howe 1994: 665–67.

18 *The Times*, March 12 1991.

19 Inflation stood at 10.9 per cent and 1.8 million were unemployed (J.W. Young 2000: 150).

20 Although written some time after the Conservatives were in office, the following passages by John Redwood, a cabinet minister in Major's government and a notable eurosceptic, reflect the position of those who opposed EMU.

> 'If you want a democratic country it needs its own currency. One people, one governing system, one central bank, one currency: these go together'(Redwood 2001: 87).

And:

> 'The optimum area for any single currency is the area that represents a political nation. Single currencies go well with single markets where those markets are unified by a common language and a common outlook' (Redwood 2001: 93).

William Hague, who led the party after Major's resignation, was also deeply critical of EMU. Again this passage post-dates Major's period in office but it does reflect the tenor of the eurosceptics' concerns.

> On 1 January 1999 eleven West European countries will take a momentous step. They will adopt a single currency between them and accept the authority of a single central bank. But momentous though this step will be, it will create as many problems as it solves. And the most important is the danger that the single currency will lead to an increasingly centralised Europe. I therefore believe that Europe should not press on towards an unacceptable degree of political union just to make the single currency succeed. I fear that a single currency could push us beyond the limits to Union.

William Hague in a speech to the INSEAD Business School, May 19 1998, cited in Anderson and Weymouth, 1999, 205.

21 For example in a YouGov Survey for the TaxPayers' Alliance and Global Vision in January 2009, 64 per cent were opposed to the UK joining the euro and 24 per cent were in favour (*The Herald*, January 12 2009 p. 12).

22 Although this extract post-dates Maastricht by some time, it is indicative of the strength of opinion on the matter by the *Sun* newspaper, with one of the highest circulations in the UK:

> ... It is clear that the Tory Party could never take Britain into a single currency. There are barely a handful of MPs who favour the closer political and economic integration it would require. ... The national interest is about more than whether we are just better off. Our sovereignty, heritage and way of life matter too. (the *Sun*, Leader, April 14 1997 cited in Anderson and Weymouth 1999: 86)

23 Major, *H.C. Deb.*, vol. 201, col. 276, 18 December 1991.

24 In effect it could be regarded as both a principle (decisions being taken at the lowest level where appropriate) and procedural device. For a fuller analysis of this see Scott *et al.* 1994.

25　European Union rests on the principle of subsidiarity, as is made clear in articles A and B of title I of the Treaty of European Union. This principle contributes to the respect for the national identities of Member States and safeguards their powers. It aims at decisions within the European Union being taken as closely as possible to the citizen. (European Council, 1992 DOC/92/08 Annex 1 to part A, Edinburgh December11–12 1992, p 6).

26 The Report stated:

> The Treaty on European Union simply makes a distinction between exclusive and shared competence without specifying the limits. In the new areas, the Treaty carefully establishes case by case a dividing line between matters that may be covered by Community measures in a given area and matters that must be left to the Member States.

The Report then explained the principle's 'consequences':

> – Community competence is not the rule but rather an exception to national competence; in other words, the Community must have powers specifically conferred on it;
> – far from having an effect of freezing Community action, the dynamic of the subsidiarity principle should make it possible to expand it if required, or limit or even abandon it when action at Community level can no longer be warranted;
> – the regulatory role of subsidiarity, for which need-for-action is the criterion, applies to shared competence only; it cannot be used as a pretext for challenging measures in areas such as the internal market where the Community has a clearly defined and undeniable obligation to act.

European Commission, 1993, COM (93) 545 final, Commission, Brussels, November 24 1993, pp. 1–2.

27 See, for example, Duff *et al.* (eds), 1994: 53–56.

28 Just seven Conservative MPs voted against the Government's Bill, with three abstentions.

29 Seldon 1998: 285–86.

30 Their numbers included: Margaret Thatcher, Norman Tebbit, Nicholas Ridley, William Cash, Tony Benn and Paddy Ashdown (the then leader of the Liberal Democrats).
31 Stephens 1996: 205.
32 See Blair 2002: 165, Table 8.2.
33 BBC TV, 1999, The Major Years, 2nd programme.
34 Ibid.
35 'What I did not want as Foreign Secretary was for us to kick over the table, as we left it, because then the chances of actually getting back into reasonable co-operation with countries whose co-operation we desperately needed would be nil'. Douglas Hurd, BBC TV, 1999, The Major Years, 2nd programme.
36 Ibid.
37 Ibid.
38 Ibid.
39 The cost was between £1.8bn. and £3bn. (Blair 2002: 170).
40 BBC TV, 1999, The Major Years, 2nd programme.
41 'Of course divisions like this in any party have a very profound effect and it had a profound effect on us. We lost very heavily in the 1997 election'. John Major, BBC TV, 1999, The Major Years, 2nd programme.
42 For further analysis of Westminster and the Maastricht Treaty see Baker *et al.* 1994: 37–59.
43 BBC TV, 1999, The Major Years, 2nd programme.
44 Ibid.
45 Teddy Taylor MP, BBC TV, 1999, The Major Years, 2nd programme. See also Hugo Young (1998, *This Blessed Plot: Britain and Europe from Churchill to Blair*, London: Papermac) cited in Geddes 2004: 194–95 in which five categories of eurosceptics are highlighted – Irreconcilables, Constitutionalists, Free marketeers, Nationalists and 'Wets'.
46 The *Sunday Times*, David Smith, April 7 1996; the *Independent*, Donald Macin-tyre, April 3 and 4 1996.
47 They joined in 1995.
48 J.W. Young 2000: 165.
49 Gowland and Turner 2000b: 291.
50 *The Times*, October 11 1995.
51 *The Times*, October 12 1994.
52 Gowland and Turner 2000b: 295.
53 Cmd. 3181 (March 1996), A Partnership of Nations: the British Approach to the Intergovernmental Conference 1996. M. Rifkind provided details of the UK's position in a Commons statement on March 121996. H.C.Deb., vol. 273, cols 785–89.
54 Cmd. 3181 (March 1996), A Partnership of Nations: the British Approach to the Intergovernmental Conference 1996.
55 Gowland and Turner 2000b: 310.
56 Ibid.
57 For a fuller discussion on this see Gowland and Turner 2000b: 310–21.
58 *The Times*, June 19 1996.
59 The *Independent*, May 30 1996.

5 Northern Ireland, Scotland and Wales in the European Community/Union, 1973–98

1 The term 'territorial' refers to stateless nations such as Scotland or a region such as the North West of England. On occasion the terms sub-state and regions are used in its place.

2 It could be claimed that as they are territorial branches of the UK government they are not subordinate as such. However, as far as EU affairs were concerned, the departments in London acted as the 'lead' and ministers from those departments represented UK interests in the Council of the EU.

3 In this context, the usage of the term 'political dependency' stems from the premise that supreme political authority resided in London, albeit that this was less tenable across a swathe of policies in the aftermath of accession to the EU.

4 The term 'lead department' refers to those departments in London which were responsible for representing UK interests in the EU. For example the Department of Trade and Industry was the lead for the EU's structural funds.

5 HMSO 1973: Cmd. 5460, vol. I.

6 HMSO 1973: Cmd. 5460-I, vol. II, *Memorandum of Dissent*, by Lord Crowther-Hunt and Professor A.T. Peacock, 48, Para. 112.

7 HMSO 1975: Cmd. 6348, 18, Para. 87.

8 Ibid. Para. 89.

9 Butler, D. and Kitzinger, U., 'The 1975 Referendum', London: Macmillan, 1978 cited in M. Keating and B. Jones, (1995) 'The UK Experience', in B. Jones and M. Keating (eds) *The European Union and the Regions*, Oxford: Clarendon Press, p. 95.

10 Those government papers that are available indicate that these areas of policy were matters of concern in the period prior to UK accession.

11 They were: Baden-Wurttemberg, Catalonia, Lombardy and Rhone-Alpes (B.J. Jones 1997: 66).

12 Responding to a question from a Member of the Legislative Assembly in 2001, an official commented:

> Before devolution, an EU steering group that was run by the Department of Finance and Personnel was responsible for wider EU issues. However, the pressure of the structural funds meant that all that body's time was spent in dealing with structural funds. Frankly, there was no wider debate on EU issues. (Mr Haire, an official at the Office of the First Minister and Deputy First Minister giving oral testimony to the Committee of the Centre, the Northern Ireland Assembly. Minutes of Evidence, Wednesday December 5 2001, Col. 13.)

13 The same applied to English local government.

14 This related to the deregulation of financial markets.

15 Keating and Jones made the following observation, for example:

> (...) In 1981 the rapid decline in the Welsh steel industry, as required by the Davignon Plan, brought into existence the South Wales Standing Conference, which encompassed MPs and MEPs, local authorities, the Wales Trades Union Congress, the Confederation of British Industry Wales and other community organizations. Little was expected of Mrs Thatcher's government and, apart from the presentation of its report and recommendations to the Welsh Office, the Standing Conference concentrated its efforts on the EC Commission. (Keating and Jones 1995: 103)

16 He said:

> As many of you will know, I was one of the founder members of NICE and, as a director of that organisation, was involved in developing its role during the era of direct rule. Throughout that time there was a pervasive feeling, across all the political parties, that we were not as well served as we might

have been by the United Kingdom representation in Brussels, or by the direct rule Administration, in expressing our interests in Europe. That is why a number of members of the Ulster Unionist Party, the DUP, and SDLP and the Alliance Party undertook the establishment of NICE. We worked through the 90s to develop and refine its approach to European matters. It played a very important role. (Mr Haughy, the Junior Minister and the Office of the First Minister and Deputy First Minister, giving oral testimony to the Committee of the Centre, the Northern Ireland Assembly, Minutes of Evidence, Wednesday February 6 2002, col. 862.)

17 He explained:

No one is more frustrated or disappointed than I am by the fact that difficulty arose when NICE was, for resource and other reasons, reaching the point where it had to make quick decisions. We had a direct rule Administration, which had a cumbersome and rather old-fashioned method of policy-making and doing business. That all came at the wrong time and direct rule. Ministers were not as acutely aware as you and I, and our colleagues were of the need to act quickly and to build on the work of NICE'. (Ibid. Col. 885)

18 The Royal Society of Edinburgh, 2004: 5, Para. 26.

19 The co-ordinating procedures for European policy within Whitehall are based around a traditional cabinet committee structure, whose origins can be traced back to 1961–63. The structure has three tiers of formal committees: the Cabinet Sub-Committee on European issues (E)DOP; very senior officials EQ(O*); formerly EQ(S); and EQ(O). EQ(O)L is a specialist sub-committee comprising the lawyers' network radiating out through Whitehall from COLA [Cabinet Office Legal Advisors (UK)]. In addition, the Friday meeting was developed after accession as a forum for the main affected Departments in Whitehall to review the major short-to medium-term issues of European policy. Beyond these more or less formal meetings, there existed all manner of opportunities for *ad hoc* meetings, sometimes chaired by the COES [Cabinet Office European Secretariat (UK)], as well as numerous informal contacts. For the Scottish and Welsh Office, participation in the formal meetings was assured, should personnel and time be available, and if business perceived to be of relevance were on the agenda. (Bulmer *et al.* 2002: 22)

20 According to Bulmer *et al.*, the territorial Secretaries of State were members of the Ministerial Sub-Committee on European issues both prior to and after devolution in 1999 (Bulmer *et al.* 2002: 21).
21 See, for example, Scott *et al.* (1994).
22 Kennedy *et al.* observed:

It could be argued, however, that a very broad *policy* response to EU membership has been developed, de facto, by civil servants and others. Departmental officials have, in their negotiation of development plans and programmes with European Commission officials, played a key role in the formulation of policy in Northern Ireland. Deciding priorities over a wide range of public sector activities, and over large amounts of public expenditure has, it would seem, been left largely to the NI civil service and the European Commission with a minimum of input from any political or democratic master at either regional or national level.

Greater consultation and the partnership principle have modified this position, and brought in other actors, including the voluntary sector and some elected representatives at the local level, but the key inputs remain those of the civil service and the European Commission. There is still little real accountability, given the limited parliamentary scrutiny of Northern Ireland affairs, and very little transparency. This does not imply any criticism of the civil service; it is in some ways the inevitable result of direct rule which has left political direction of the province's affairs in the hands of central government ministers with no party or constituency base in the region. (Kennedy *et al.* 1998: 11)

23 Kennedy *et al.* claimed:

In any event, it is not clear what channels would be open to Mr Murphy, as a junior minister to have a regular input into European policy formation at UK level, nor the extent to which Mr Murphy or the Secretary of State would feel able or willing to push a Northern Ireland line at variance with the general consensus of their government or party. (Ibid.: 12)

24 Bulmer *et al.* suggested that there was the perception amongst the members of the Welsh European Centre (WEC) that it lacked efficacy. They observed:

Secondly, there had been a history of indifference to hostile relations between the Welsh Office and the WEC membership. The grassroots' promotional organisations in Wales, including those participating in the WEC, had come to view the Welsh Office as at best insufficiently pro-active in working for Welsh interests and at worst as the servant of a Wales-hostile Conservative central government' (Bulmer *et al.* 2002:149).

6 The Blair governments and European integration 1997–2007

1 For the 'sleaze' factor, see Seldon 1997: 713–17.
2 See Gowland and Turner 2000b: 230–43. See also Wall 2008: 161.
3 Cited in Peston 2006: 181.
4 Wall 2008: 161.
5 Scott 2004: Derek Scott was Blair's economic adviser from 1994–2003. See also Peston 2006: 181.
6 Routledge 1998: 273–74, 282–83. A MORI poll published in *The Times* of April 17 1997 put support for staying in the EU at only 40 per cent – the same figure as that for withdrawing.
7 The *Sun,* March 17 and April 22 1997. See also Peston 2006: 196.
8 Jacques Santer and Helmut Kohl were among those who gave an enthusiastic welcome to the Blair government: the *Independent,* Sarah Helm, May 4 1997.
9 The *Independent,* Sarah Helm, May 6 1997: Donald Macintyre and Imre Karacs, May 8 1997; Imre Karacs May 10 1997.
10 Simon, the chairman of BP, was given special responsibility for the single market: Seldon *et al.* 2005: 317. See also the *Financial Times,* Simon Kuper, May 7 1997; the *Independent,* Diana Coyle, May 5 1997; Sarah Helm, May 8 1997; Chris Goldmark, May 8 1997.
11 Alexandre Lamfalussy, the President of the European Monetary Institute, the precursor of the European Central Bank, described Brown's decision as 'music to my ears': cited in *The Independent,* Sarah Helm, May 8 1997. Major had always refused to give independence to the Bank of England. See Lamont 1999: 120–21.

12　Peston 2006: 130.

13　The *Independent*, Sarah Helm, May 6 and 7 1997.

14　The *Independent*, Anthony Bevins, June 13 1997.

15　*The Times*, June 12 1997.

16　In December 1999 the EU ordered France to lift the ban on British beef exports, but the government of Lionel Jospin decided to continue it. In the end it required a judgement from the ECJ to compel France to permit imports of British beef. See Price 2006: 175. See also Wall 2008: 157.

17　See R. Taylor, 'New Labour, new capitalism', in Seldon 2007: 218–19.

18　The *Independent*, Sarah Helm, June 6 1997. See also The *Independent*, Anthony Bevins, May 23 1997; Imre Karacs, 7 June.

19　*The Economist*, September 25 1993.

20　Seldon 2007: ix. See also Scott 2004: 201, 220–21; Bogdanor, 'Social Democracy', in Seldon 2007: 164–65.

21　A concession to the British and Irish viewpoint was contained in the draft text of May 6 1997 on the pooling of justice and immigration policy: The *Independent*, Sarah Helm, May 7 1997.

22　Wall 2008: 174–75.

23　*H.C.Deb.* vol. 296, cols. 313–18, June 18 1997; The *Independent*, Anthony Bevins, November 1 1997.

24　The *Independent*, Sarah Helm, July 15 and 17 1997. See also Duff, *Reforming the European Union*, pp. 107–8.

25　The *Independent*, Imre Karacs, July 25 1997; Katherine Butler, June 16 1998; *H.C.Deb* vol. 314, col. 368, June 18 1998.

26　*The Independent on Sunday*, editorial, June 13 1997; Katherine Butler, July 9 and 17 1997.

27　*The Independent*, Nicholas Schoon, July 10 1997; *The Times*, Charles Bremner and Michael Hornsby, March 19 1998.

28　For a time in the summer of 1997 the possibility of a postponement of the euro launch was under serious consideration in various EU capitals, including Berlin. See Scott 2004: 215–16. See also Peston 2006: 199–200; Seldon *et al.* 2005: 319.

29　K. Clarke, Foreword to Duff 1998: 9–17.

30　See, for example, Riddell 2006: 135. See also Wall 2008: 169; Seldon *et al.* 2005: 327.

31　Cited in Seldon *et al.* 2005: 318.

32　Routledge 1998: 10.

33　In an end-of-year interview in which he spoke of the problems of sustaining long-term economic convergence, he expressed the view that 'it would have been risky for the UK to join in the first wave': *Financial Times*, Richard Adams, December 31 1997. See also his evidence to the Treasury Select Committee on January 29 and April 2 1998: The *Independent*, business section, January 30 and April 3 1998.

34　The *Independent*, Colin Brown; Colin Brown and Nigel Cope, both October 29 1997.

35　Peston 2006: 179, 189–90, 202. See also Seldon *et al.* 2005: 318.

36　*Financial Times*, 'Secrets of ERM debacle revealed', James Blitz and Cathy Newman, 10 February 2005. See also the *Guardian*, 'Tories cry foul over secret papers', Ashley Seager, Larry Elliot and Julian Glover, February 10 2005.

37　Lack of preparation for joining the euro was particularly marked amongst small and medium sized companies. See *Getting Ready for the Euro*, First Report, HM Treasury, July 1998.

38　In late September 1997 a deputation of 17 prominent industrialists pressed Blair to give a firm government commitment to the euro as a way of bringing sterling down to a level which would be less harmful to exports: The *Independent*, business section, September 24 1997.

39 The *Independent*, Michael Harrison, July 27 1997.
40 The *Independent*, Rupert Cornwell, October 7 1997. For a useful analysis of public attitudes on the euro see P. Kellner, 'EMU and public opinion', in Duff 1998: 117–37.
41 For an analysis of the eurosceptic press' hostility to the euro and the Blair government's tactics for dealing with the problem see P. Riddell, 'EMU and the press', in Duff 1998: 105–16. See also O. Daddow, 'Playing Games with History: Tony Blair's European Policy in the Press', *BJPIR*, 2007, vol. 9, 582–98.
42 The editor-in-chief of the *Daily Mail*, Paul Dacre, was rabidly opposed to British membership of the single currency.
43 Price 2006: xii. Price also writes that it seemed like 'no big decision could ever be made inside No. 10' without account being taken of Murdoch's likely reaction. Price's diaries are full of references to contacts with Murdoch and of attempts by No. 10 to keep them secret.
44 Peston: 2006: 195.
45 Scott 2004: 213.
46 Seldon *et al.*: 2008: 294.
47 Peston 2006: 197–98, 200–201.
48 A number of detailed accounts have been written of the crisis precipitated by Peston's *Financial Times* article. See for example, Bower 2007: 248–52; Peston 2006: 203–14; Routledge 1998: 324–26. See also Scott 2004: 216–17.
49 *H.C.Deb.*, vol. 299, cols. 585–88, October 27 1997.
50 The *Independent*, Anthony Bevins, Katherine Butler and John Lichfield, November 6 1997; Katherine Butler, November 17 1997.
51 The *Independent*, Rupert Cornwell, November 7 1997: Katherine Butler, November 17 and 18, December 2 1997.
52 Lionel Jospin, the French premier, was amongst those who made cutting observations to the effect that Britain could not belong to a club if it did not pay its fees. See the *Financial Times*, interview with Jospin, December 9 1997.
53 For the decisions taken about enlargement at the Luxembourg European Council of December 12 1997, see Avery and Cameron 1998: 135–39.
54 For an account of Blair's much-criticised efforts at mediation in the row between France, Germany and the Netherlands over the appointment of the first head of the ECB, see Gowland and Turner 2000b: 360–63.
55 The *Independent*, Katherine Butler, June 5 1998.
56 For critical comments by Hague and Howard, see *H.C.Deb.*, vol. 313, cols 1236, June 11 1998; vol. 314, col. 370, June 18 1998.
57 Cited in Sinclair, 'The Treasury and economic policy', in Seldon 2007: 192.
58 The *Independent*, Michael Harrison and the business section, November 11 1997.
59 For Blair's statement in full, see *The Times,* February 24 1999.
60 In his diary entry of February 26 1999, Lance Price noted: 'The Sun went gaga, the Mail, Telegraph and Times were all opposed and, with the exception of the Express, the so-called pro-European papers were typically timid'. See Price 2006: 80.
61 *The Times*, 'The Commons', February 24 1999.
62 The *Independent*, Anthony Bevins, June 14 1997. Hague's warnings about the single currency became increasingly apocalyptic, with his comparison of the risks of membership to those of being trapped 'in a burning building with no exits'. See The *Independent*, Anthony Bevins, May 21 1998.
63 *The Independent on Sunday*, Stephen Castle, January 18 1998; *Independent*, Colin Brown, January 22 1998; Fran Abrams, February 14 1998.
64 See, for example, Price 2006: 152, 160.
65 Polly Toynbee, 'We Europeans must lead the charge for reform', *Guardian*, September 17 2003.

66 See Bower 2007: 247. After being close political associates Brown and Cook had become bitter rivals.
67 For details of this particular incident, see Cook 2003: 170; Price 2006: 230.
68 See, for example, Price 2006: 222, 237, 249, 276.
69 For information on the Granita deal and its significance for relations between Blair and Brown, see Bower 2007: 141–45, 147, 230, 265, 377, 199, 382–83; Peston 2006: 76, 98, 115, 150, 178–79, 288, 326–29; Riddell 2006: 16, 70.
70 See the *Financial Times,* editorial, 'Initiating growth', September 18 2003.
71 Scott 2004: 218.
72 Price 2006: 299. See also Peston: 2006: 222; Seldon, 2007: 204–5.
73 Scott 2004: 223–25. See also Peston 2006: 228–40.
74 Blair is said to have used a number of intermediaries to put this proposal to Brown, including John Prescott, Clare Short, the International Development Secretary, and Anje Hunter, Blair's special assistant. See Peston 2006: 228–29, 330–32.
75 The full text of Brown's statement is to be found in the *Financial Times* of June 10 2003.
76 *The Times,* 'Parliamentary sketch', Ben MacIntyre, June 10 2003.
77 *Financial Times,* Ed Crooks and James Blitz, 'Euro row to go on as Brown puts off a decision', June 9 2003.
78 Ibid.
79 *The Guardian,* Polly Toynbee, September 17 2003.
80 the *Guardian,* Ian Black and Patrick Wintour, September 15 2003; Patrick Wintour, September 16 2003; Polly Toynbee, September 17 2003; *The Independent,* editorial, 17 September 2003.
81 Wall 2008; 172; Seldon *et al.* 2005: 392–406.
82 For details see Wall 2008 172–75.
83 For a brief analysis of Anglo-American relations during the Blair years, see Riddell 2006. A fuller account is to be found in Riddell 2003.
84 Cited in Riddell 2006: 139.
85 *The Guardian,* John Harris, November 30 2006; *The Times,* Tom Baldwin and Philip Webster, November 30 2006.
86 *The Times,* Tom Baldwin and Philip Webster, November 30 2006.
87 For an interesting analysis of these developments from a French perspective, see *L'Express,* Bernard Guetta. 'En Europe, les lignes bougent', December 15–22 2005; François Geoffrey, 'LEurope à la calculette', 15–22 December 2005.
88 Cmd. 5934, *A Constitutional Treaty for the EU: The British Approach to the European Union Intergovernmental Conference 2003,* foreword by Tony Blair, p. 3. For the similar response from Jack Straw, the Foreign Secretary, see the *Guardian,* September 9 2003.
89 For the government's attitude to the draft constitution, see the *Guardian,* September 9 2003. This contains the full text of Straw's Commons statement on the draft. See also Cmd. 5934, *A Constitutional Treaty for the EU: The British Approach to the European Union Intergovernmental Conference 2003.*
90 *The Daily Telegraph,* editorial, September 10 2003; *Daily Mail,* editorial, September 10 2003; *Sun,* editorial, September 10 2003; *The Times,* editorial, September 10 2003; *Guardian,* Michael White, Patrick Wintour, and Ian Black, September 10 2003.
91 The *Guardian,* April 21 2004.
92 *The Financial Times,* leader, April 20 2004.
93 The *Sun,* leading article, April 20 2004.
94 The *Guardian,* Nicholas Watt, April 19 2004; Martin Kettle, April 20 2004; *Financial Times,* Christopher Adams and James Blitz, April 20 1920.
95 the *Guardian,* April 20 2004.

96 *Guardian*, April 21 2004.
97 See, for example, the *Sun*, 'non, non, non', May 30 2005.
98 *Guardian*, May 30 2005
99 *The Times,* Rory Watson, November 17 2004; the *Guardian*, David Gow, November 18 2004.
100 *Guardian,* Nicholas Watt, January 21 2005
101 *Guardian*, Jon Henley, Patrick Wintour and Nicholas Watt, May 30 2005.
102 By December 2005 a poll revealed that only 1 per cent of respondents wanted Chirac to stand for re-election: *L'Express*, Denis Jambar, 'Monsieur 1%', December 15–22 2005. For another devastating critique of the Chirac presidency in 2005, see *L'Express*, Christophe Barbier, January 5 2006.
103 *The Courier and Advertiser*, July 2 2005.
104 Barroso's reaction to the British proposals to reduce regional funding was to warn Blair against behaving like the sheriff of Nottingham by taking from the poor to give to the rich: *The Guardian,* Nicholas Watt and Michael White, December 1 2005.
105 *Guardian*, Bruno Waterfield, January 24 2006.
106 *The Financial Times*, December 4 and 5 2005; the *Sun*, editorial, December 17 2005.
107 *The Courier and Advertiser*, January 18 2007.
108 *The Daily Mail*, April 20 2007; the *Sun*, April 20 2007.
109 *Sun*, George Pascoe-Watson, June 25 2007.
110 *Sun*, editorial, June 26 2007.
111 P. Stephens, 'Commentary', in Seldon 1997: 644.

7 The European Union and Constitutional change in the United Kingdom since 1999

1 *Monitor*, Constitution Unit Bulletin, Issue 29, January 2005, p.1.
2 The term 'primary legislation' refers to 'framework' areas of policy such as health and transport.
3 For instance, there is reference to the EU in the Belfast Agreement both in relation to the North/South Ministerial Council and the British–Irish Council. As far as the former is concerned under paragraph 3 (iii), it states: [The Council shall meet] 'in an appropriate format to consider institutional or cross-sectoral matters (including in relation to the EU) and to resolve disagreement'. Paragraph 17 also refers to 'the Council considering the European Union dimension of relevant matters' and ensuring that 'the views of the Council are taken into account and represented appropriately at relevant EU meetings' (*The Agreement* 1998: 11–13). Under paragraph 5, on the British–Irish Council, reference is made to 'approaches to the EU' as 'suitable issues for early discussion' (ibid.: 14).
4 The issue of ministerial attendance at the Council is rather ambiguous. There have been a few occasions when territorial ministers have acted as lead in the Council, but to-date this has occurred in areas of 'low politics' (e.g. education). It could also be argued that when they do lead for the UK, de facto they are UK ministers not territorial ones. There have been a number of times when they have attended the Council as part of the UK delegation. But they do not have the automatic entitlement to be present. They require the consent of the lead department.
5 The Scottish Executive's European Strategy, Scottish Executive External Relations Division, January 2004.
6 For a fuller discussion on this, see Bulmer *et al.* 2002 and Winetrobe 1999.
7 For a fuller analysis on this, refer to: House of Lords, 2003, HL Paper 28, Select Committee on the Constitution, Devolution: inter-institutional relations in the United Kingdom (especially para 1, p. 5).
8 Gray 2001: 38.

9 For an explanation of the term 'dual polity' refer to Chapter 5.
10 The Government of Wales Bill was passed at Westminster during July 2006. This heralds the inception of so-called 'Assembly measures'. However, it remains to be seen the extent to which the Assembly enjoys greater autonomy even though it formally becomes a legislature with a legal identity separate from that of the Assembly Government from May 2007.
11 Executive devolution for Wales and legislative devolution for Scotland and Northern Ireland.
12 'The Union, particularly when new members join, will become too large to run from Brussels; what is needed is for national, regional and local government to take on greater responsibility in EU affairs ... This process should also link together the different level (*sic*) of government, involve checks and balances needed for democratic decision making, and encourage people to participate more widely'. (The European Commission, June 1 2000, 'EU Governance Under Review', *The Week in Europe*, London.)
13 See the White Paper on the Scottish Parliament: HMSO (1997), Cm3658, *Scotland's Parliament*, 5.1.
14 See, for example, Wright 2005, with regard to Scotland, and Jones 2002 and 2003 for Wales. See also the Scottish Executive's European Strategy dated 2004. Its aims included the following:

> 'To position Scotland as one of the leading legislative regions in the European Union, with a thriving and dynamic economy.
> To bring effective influence to bear on the UK Government, EU Member States, regions and institutions on EU policy issues affecting Scotland'.

It would therefore concentrate on:

> 'Promoting Scottish interests in Europe.
> Enhancing the profile of Scotland in Europe'.
> Maximising our influence with the UK Government on EU issues.
> (The Scottish Executive's European Strategy, Scottish Executive External Relations Division, January 2004)

15 'The Executive's Brussels office in Scotland House is a crucial asset. It will present Scottish views directly to the EU institutions and provide crucial and early intelligence to secure Scotland's interests. Specifically, it will seek to influence EU decision-making on dossiers of importance to Scotland, working in collaboration with Departments and UKRep, and advise on opportunities for being more proactive in Brussels by, for example, suggesting policy initiatives where Scotland has innovative ideas to offer. The SEEUO will report to Ministers on EU intelligence and the delivery of the Executive's European strategy in Brussels, and liaise with secondees from the Executive working in the EU institutions'. (ibid.)

16 *Devolution Monitor Report*, Spring 2005, North Seaton, Closure of the Wales European Centre. The author observed:

> 'Whilst this move will create a single voice for Wales in Europe, some have indicated concern over the number of lobbyists left in Brussels to promote Welsh interests following the closure'.

17 That is to say this information is available on the relevant websites.

18 Since the Assembly was a corporate body, formally there was no distinction between the political leaders of the administration and the assembly members – though that began to change – as Osmond observed:

> 'The core difficulty is the Assembly's creation as a corporate body – a "single legal personality" as the Counsel General, Winston Roddick, has it – in which its legislative and executive functions are combined rather than separated, as is normal in parliamentary institutions. The constitutional history of the Assembly's opening period was dominated by an emphatic rejection of this mode of operation. Instead, the assembly moved as far as it possibly could in the direction of separating its administrative and legislative roles' (Osmond 2003: 19).

19 That is not to say that the situation for Wales has been straightforward – see, for example, B.J. Jones 2002 and Wright 2004.

20 E.g. para-military weapons and the Royal Ulster Constabulary.

21 In some respects this line of argument is open to challenge. The author suggested that this was one of the by-products of devolution to some senior Scottish civil servants who remained silent. A possible explanation for their reticence was that Scotland was governed by a coalition at the time and officials therefore had the added complication of dealing with ministers from two political parties. However, in using the term 'strategic leadership' the author is suggesting that policy-making was dealt with more strategically than hitherto. In part because there were more ministers to provide political leadership. In addition because they were drawn from a body which was directly elected by the people of each territory, unlike UK ministers, who were appointed by the Prime Minister in London, whose party might not enjoy electoral support in one or more of the territories.

22 See, for example, Kiiver 2006: 5.

23 There have been a few occasions when territorial ministers have led for the UK but de facto at that moment in time they are UK ministers.

24 The author saw part of a copy of what purported to be this report but he elected to use the material cited in the *The Herald*, as this was in the public domain, given the First Minister's subsequent comments – see main text relating to end note 23. The papers the author saw had no official reference details and so could not be verified.

25 *The Herald*, October 22 2007, p. 2

26 *The Herald*, January 23 2007, p. 6.

27 The author wishes to point out that this term was derived from Professor C. Jeffery who used it in a different context.

28 He warned: 'We need to make sure that the drive to devolve power within Member States is not negated by a drift towards centralized decision making within the EU' (Jack McConnell, Speech in Brussels on June 6 2002).

29 He observed: 'I do not believe that the European Court of Justice could play this role. I cannot see it as an effective – or – credible subsidiarity watchdog' (Ibid.).

30 This phrase is derived from an article in *Agenda*, by Desmond Clifford, Spring 2004, p. 48. This author points out that the wording herein differs in context from that of the Agenda article.

31 It was rejected by referendums in France and the Netherlands.

32 Article 8 of the Protocol on the application of the principles of subsidiarity and proportionality stated: 'In accordance with the rules laid down in the said Article, the Committee of the Regions may also bring such actions against European legislative acts for the adoption of which the Constitution provides that it be consulted'. This provision was retained under the protocol in the Lisbon Treaty (2007).

33 EU legislation must be proportional in terms of the administrative and economic costs of implementation versus outcome.
34 Scotland and Wales are both nations in their own right. The term 'national parliaments' has been used herein because this was the terminology adopted in the Constitution for Europe.
35 Article 3 stated:

> 'For the purposes of this Protocol, "draft European legislative acts" shall mean proposals from the Commission, initiatives from a group of Member States, initiatives from the European Parliament, requests from the Court of Justice, recommendations from the European Central Bank and requests from the European Investment Bank for the adoption of a European legislative act'.

36 HL Paper 101, 2005, para 76, p. 20.
37 ibid, para 120, 121 and 126, p. 28
38 ibid., 2005, para 109, p. 38.
39 ibid., para 202, p. 39.
40 ibid., paras 206 and 207, p. 39.
41 ibid., para 209, p. 40.
42 'The UK Government recognises that the devolved administrations will have an interest in European policy making in relation to devolved matters and issues which impact on devolved matters or which will have a distinctive impact of importance to devolved administrations. The UK Government intend to involve the devolved administrations as fully as possible in discussion about the formulation and implementation of such policy. The devolved administrations are entitled to produce assessments of subsidiarity compliance in their own right, and the Government would fully expect them to do so. The devolved legislatures could subject these statements to scrutiny but they would not be able to hold the UK Government to account through such an assessment. Relations with the European Union remain the responsibility of the UK Government and the UK Parliament. The devolved legislatures might, however, wish to contribute directly to the formation of a view from the UK Parliament under the monitoring mechanism on the subsidiarity implications of a proposal through transmitting their own views on the proposal to the UK Parliament'. (HL 101, 2005, Memorandum by Her Majesty's Government, para 14, p. 62)
43 We have also considered how the devolved assemblies could have an input in the process. It would not be possible to wait for representations from them. Instead, we have proposed that (i) that when our staff encounter a document to which objection may be made on the grounds of subsidiarity, they alert the devolved assemblies so that the assemblies have as much opportunity as possible to make their views known, and (ii) that we will indicate to the devolved assemblies that if they identify subsidiarity problems which we have missed, we will be willing to rescind clearance (if necessary) and initiate the procedure for objecting on subsidiarity grounds. The European affairs committees in the Scottish Parliament and the National Assembly for Wales have welcomed these proposals'. (HL 101, 2005, Memorandum by the House of Commons European Scrutiny Committee to the House's Modernisation Committee, para 34, p. 65)
44 Interview 23/05/05.
45 Geoff Hoon, minister for Europe, 'What now for the European Union?' A speech given in Edinburgh on 19/03/07, Foreign and Commonwealth Office Website.
46 For instance, a YouGov poll of Novemeber 23 2006, gave the SNP 49 seats at Holyrood and Labour 36. (http://www.alba.org.uk/polls/yougovindependence. html – accessed 13/02/07.)

47 Margo MacDonald is the sole independent MSP, although she was once a member of the SNP.
48 In Wales Labour secured 26 seats, the Lib Dems 6, Plaid Cymru 15, the Conservatives 12 and others 1 (Monitor, special supplement, the Constitution Unit issue 36, May 2007)
49 Monitor, May 2007, the Constitution Unit Newsletter, Issue 36, May 2007, p. 2.
50 Under 'Amendments to the Treaty on European Union and to the Treaty Establishing the European Community', Article 2 (3) para 4, Treaty of Lisbon.
51 ibid. Article 3a (2).
52 The relevant institutions are The Presidents of the European Parliament, the Council and the Commission, Article 6, Protocol on the Application of the Principles of Subsidiarity and Proportionality, Treaty of Lisbon, 2007.

53 'Scotland will today effectively take control of efforts to protect cod stocks in its own waters under a landmark devolution deal with the European Union. Late last year the Scottish Government was given the right to tailor its own policies for conserving the fish in the North Sea and Atlantic. The deal comes into force today with the backing of the World Wild Life Fund and the Scottish Fishermen's Federation, long-time foes on the future of the nation's marine resources. Under the new deal skippers who help protect stocks will be rewarded with extra days at sea and those who do not will be expected to stay longer in port. Richard Lochhead, the Minister for Rural Affairs and the Environment, yesterday announced the launch of the scheme, called Conservation Credits.

(...) Under the scheme, fisheries experts will set aside areas where cod are spawning or wherever there are large numbers of young fish. Skippers will be expected to steer clear of these zones, usually for 21 days. (...) Aside from avoiding no-catch zones, skippers will also have to agree to technical measures to save young fish including new nets. Fishing leaders admit they have to live up to the scheme or face the return of the big stick without the carrot. (.) The EU formally approved the Conservation Credit scheme on Friday (although reported in *The Herald* the previous December)'. (*The Herald,* February 4 2008, p. 8)

54 Interview May 23 2005.

8 Continuity and Change since 1945

1 For an assessment of the EU policies of the incoming Blair government in 1997, see, for example, Fella 2002.
2 House of Commons European Scrutiny Committee, *Democracy and Accountability in the EU and the Role of National Parliaments,* 33rd Report, 2001–2, HC 152, para 20 – extract from a presentation by Robin Cook, Leader of the House of Commons.
3 *The Times,* April 29 1978.
4 Shortly after the signing of this treaty, Adenauer stressed his understanding of its meaning and also his distaste for the idea of British membership of the EEC, 'Look, what is Europe? First and foremost, France and us. And things are going pretty well. If the British make a third, there's no certainty that they'll continue to do so'. Quoted in Bell 1997: 202.
5 The *Guardian,* Chris Patten, September 19 2008.
6 In November 2007, the European Court of Auditors failed to sign off the EU's accounts for the 13th consecutive year, citing as the main reason weak internal

controls at the Commission and in the member states: *http://www.euractiv.com/en/pa/eu-accounts*. In June 2008, Giles Chichester, the leader of the British Conservative Party in the European Parliament, reportedly quit his post after admitting breaking the rules on expenses to the tune of £500,000. He described the incident as a 'whoops-a-daisy' moment: the *Guardian*, June 6 2008. This was but one of many incidents involving the use of parliamentary expenses that have convinced some observers that the main beneficiaries of the activities of the European Parliament, as in the case of the UK Parliament, are its own members.

7   For this view, see Siedentop 2001.

8   See, for example, Milward 1984 and Moravcsik 1998.

9   See, for example, Dinan 2004 and Dyson and Featherstone 1999.

10 Quoted in Gowland *et al.* (eds) 2006: 343. For an introduction to theories of political integration and the EU, see pp. 343–362 in this book.

11 Speech by Peter Mandelson at Hull University on September 7 2007 on 'The EU and globalisation'. For a study of Blair's presentation of the case for British membership of the EU, see Daddow 2007.

12 Eurobarometer,   *http://Europa.eu.int/comm.publicopinion/cf/waveoutput.en.cfm*; *http://ec.europa.eu/publicopinion/archives/eb*. *Guardian*, March 8 2008.

13 For a discussion of the meaning of the word 'Europe' in British usage, see Ludlow 2002: 122. See also, Daddow 2007 and Spiering 1997.

14 the *Guardian*, January 1 1973.

15 For a study of Britain's long and deep involvement in European politics and for the view that Britain's security has depended on maintaining its ramparts in Europe, see Simms 2007.

16 Williams and Searle satirised British images of other leading peoples in a set of schoolboy verdicts: 'a) the Russians are roters [*sic*] b) Americans are swank pots c) the French are slack d) the Germans are unspeakable e) the rest are as bad if not worse than the above', Williams and Searle 1973. For the view that the image of the xenophobic Englishman was well-established by the eighteenth century, see Langford, 2000.

17 NA., PREM 11/3554, Eccles to Macmillan, April 24 1961. Two years later, the poet W. H. Auden wrote 'If I shut my eyes and say the word *Europe* to myself, the various images which it conjures up have one thing in common; they could not be conjured up by the word *England*', Auden 1963: 53.

18 The *Guardian*, November 10 2008.

19 See, for example, National Centre for Social Research, *British Social Attitudes*, January 2007.

20 *The Times*, 6 October 1999.

21 Coles retired from the posts of Permanent Under-Secretary at the Foreign and Commonwealth Office and Head of the Diplomatic Service in 1997.

22 In the late 1980s as the single market took shape, the British ambassador to Bonn commented that the British government lacked vision in its EC policy and did not seem to be interested in any particular objective except the single market 'in which Smarties can be sold in the same packet everywhere from Copenhagen to Constancia' (Walls 2008: 76).

23 In his resignation speech of November 13 1990, Geoffrey Howe expressed the matter as follows: 'We must at all costs avoid presenting ourselves yet again with an over-simplified choice, a false antithesis, a bogus dilemma, between one alternative, starkly labelled "co-operation between independent foreign states", and a second, equally crudely labelled alternative, "centralised federal super-state"', *H. C. Deb.*, vol. 180, 461–65 *passim*, November 13 1990.

24 The *Independent*, May 6 and 8 1999. *Dundee Courier and Advertiser*, July 1 1998.

25 *Guardian*, April 26 2008.

26 *Daily Telegraph*, June 19 2005. According to Hugo Young's notes of a conversation with Chris Patten, as early as 1999 Patten thought that Blair might be going through the stage common to all British prime ministers, starting with every intention of making progress on Europe but 'then getting turned off ... and thoroughly pissed off'. Two years later, Patten concluded that Blair was a ditherer and an uncommitted leader on Europe, while Brown attended EU finance ministers' meetings only when it suited him to do some 'Eurobashing'. In a note to himself on Blair, Young commented in July 2000 that 'the genius who is looked up to by so many European leaders is turning out to be a bit thin'. Source: Trewin 2008: 602, 661, 722–23.

27 The *Guardian*, January 18 2007. For this view, see also Coles 2000: 43–44.

28 When Roy Jenkins, Chancellor of the Exchequer (1967–70), wanted to deliver a speech about the benefits of EEC membership, he was informed that the Treasury did not have a single civil servant capable of drafting a text.

29 For the relationship between the claim to global leadership and British policy towards the EC/EU, see especially Deighton 2002.

30 The *Guardian*, September 29 2003 and January 17 2007.

31 *The Times*, November 8 1954.

32 NA., CAB 129/53, C(52)202.

33 *Guardian*, Polly Toynbee, July 16 2004. The cost of 'keeping up appearances' in the view of some commentators can be too high. For example, two items in the government's current defence expenditure – the Royal Navy's two planned aircraft carriers and the American-built Joint Strike Fighters to fly off them and the Trident nuclear missile system – will each cost over £20 billion, *Guardian*, Max Hastings, December 8 2008.

34 For a description of the 'one world approach', see, for example, NA., CAB 21/3323.

35 Keesings Contemporary Archives 1961: 18053–54, *Guardian*, April 19 2008.

36 *Foreign Relations of the United States,* 1947, vol. III, 271.

37 See, for example, Powell in 'The Commmentary' in Brivati and Jones (eds) 1993.

38 For contrasting assessments of the 'special relationship' and its benefits to Britain, see, for example, Marsh and Baylis 2006 and Wallace 2005.

39 It has been argued, however, that on occasions such as British involvement in the US-led invasion of Iraq, Britain ceased to be sovereign in the conduct of its relations with Washington and made the sort of sacrifice of national independence never required in the EU. *Guardian*, December 6 2008, Review of *The Hugo Young* Papers by Chris Patten.

40 The *Independent on Sunday*, November 13 2005.

41 NA., FO 371/132330, Foreign Office paper on Anglo-American relations, January 27 1958. This paper concluded that:

> 'we cannot afford to build up a position as the First Lieutenant of the United States if this is done at too great an expense to our position. As the leader of Europe we should be an invaluable ally to the United States. Isolated from Europe, our value, and therefore our influence, would fall away disastrously'.

42 The *Guardian,* November 11 2008.

43 NA., FO 800/517/US/50/57, Attlee to Bevin, December 10 1950.

44 The *Guardian,* July 18 2006.

45 The *Guardian*, Linda Colley, November 23 2007. NA., FO 800/517/US/50/57, Attlee to Bevin, December 10 1950.

46 *The Economist*, December 25 1982–January 7 1983, pp. 61–62.

47 The *Guardian*, April 26 2006.

48 For the difficulties involved in altering deeply entrenched eurosceptical opinions in the British press and for Blair's failings in this respect, see Daddow 2007.

49 Blair's European speeches impressed mainland European audiences, though German sources close to Chancellor Merkel claimed that Blair 'never stuck his neck out for Europe' and all the political risks he took were towards Washington, and never Europe, the *Guardian*, February 20 2008. For government reluctance to take on the eurosceptic press, see, for example, Trewin 2008: 577–78.

50 In January 2008 David Cameron, the Conservative Party leader, called for a 'true single market' between the EU and North America, *Guardian*, January 23 2008. *Daily Mail*, January 1 2009.

51 Howe's speech was colourfully described by one writer as 'the anger of the Sex Pistols conveyed in the voice of Eeyore', O'Farrell 1998.

52 'I have no doubt that in this time of global uncertainty we should not be forever throwing into question, as some would, the stability of Britain's relationships with the EU'. Gordon Brown quoted in the *Guardian*, February 22 2008.

53 CIA, *The World Factbook*, 2007.

54 The *Guardian*, October 21 2004.

55 The *Guardian*, Will Hutton, June 25 2007. the *Guardian*, Linda Colley, November 23 2007.

56 Quoted by Simon Jenkins in the *Guardian* November 25 2005.

57 For this view, see Johnson 2004.

58 Proportional representation has since become more common in some UK domestic elections and is now used in a variety of forms for the election of the Northern Ireland Assembly, the Scottish Parliament, the Welsh Assembly, the London Assembly and the London mayor.

59 For example, Richard Crossman, Leader of the House of Commons in the period 1966–68, commented that 'The Executive rules supreme in Britain and has minimum trouble from the legislature', Crossman 1976: 130.

60 House of Commons European Scrutiny Committee, *Democracy and Accountability in the EU and the Role of National Parliaments*, 33rd Report, 2001–2.

61 See also, Turpin 2001. For critical comment on the House of Commons scrutiny of EU business, see House of Commons European Scrutiny Committee, *Democracy and Accountability in the EU and the Role of National Parliaments*, 33rd Report, 2001–2.

62 One in five of the Liberal MPs rebelled against Clegg's instruction to abstain from the referendum vote, and three of his front bench team resigned. At the party's annual conference in September 2008, Clegg acknowledged that the party's long-standing support for the EC/EU enjoyed little public support and that British entry into the euro zone was not 'realistic' at present – www.Telegraph.co.uk, September 15 2008. At the same time, Charles Kennedy, Clegg's predecessor, warned against 'pandering' to euroscepticism and feared that the EU was slipping down the party's agenda –www. guardian.co.uk, September 16 2008. Vincent Cable, the party's Treasury spokesman, maintained that it would be 'pointless' to hold a referendum on the euro as it was obvious that it could not be won' *Guardian*, 19 December 2008.

63 The *Guardian*, January 26 2008. *The Times*, March 5 2008.

64 The *Guardian*, Frank Furedi, June 17 2008.

65 For the view that the pro-marketeers failed to educate the British public and instead mounted a propaganda campaign to manufacture consent for EEC membership, see Mullen and Burkitt 2005.

66 The *Guardian*, June 12 2007.

67 European Commission website: The EU and the UK.

68 The *Sun*, June 24 1998. Some of Churchill's other sayings are cited less often in the eurosceptical press, such as his hopes for 'a Europe where men and women of

every country will think as much of being Europeans as of belonging to their native land and wherever they go in this wide domain will feel truly "Here I am at home"' – Quoted Sampson 1968: 4. the *Sun*, December 13 2007.

69 Only an ill-assorted group, comprising the Communist *Morning Star*, *Tribune*, the *Scottish Daily News*, the *Dundee Courier and Advertiser* and the *Spectator*, opposed EEC membership.

70 The *Guardian*, July 1 2006. See also Cook 2003: 170.

71 *http://www.number10.gov.uk/Page12094.*

72 Michael Palliser, British ambassador to the EC in the period 1973–75 and later head of the Diplomatic Service, commented on Britain's EU policy in 1993 'The danger of the present stance is that once again we are seen to be only negative. We refuse to take a single initiative. We are seen as hostile ... People just don't trust us. Therefore our line is mistrusted, because it is seen as proceeding from congenital lack of enthusiasm', Trewin 2008: 397.

73 *http://europa.eu/rapid/pressReleasesAction.*

74 *The Times*, Matthew Parris, March 8 2008. Brown's widely acknowledged lack of concern for EU sensitivities was reflected in the comment of one of his aides 'Brown hates going to Brussels. He hates the way you have to be nice to prime ministers of obscure countries and remember their names. He is frustrated that he cannot just bang his fist and get his way', *Sunday Times*, June 8 2008.

Bibliography

Alexander, P. (2000) 'The Commonwealth and European Integration: Competing Commitments for Britain, 1956–67', unpublished thesis, Cambridge University.
——. (2003) 'From Imperial Power to Regional Power: Commonwealth Crises and the Second Application', in Daddow, O. J. (ed.) *Harold Wilson and European Integration: Britain's Second Application to Join the EEC*, London: Frank Cass Publishers.
Anderson, P.J and Weymouth A. (1999) *Insulting the Public? The British Press and the European Union*, Harlow: Longman.
Anderson, B. (1992) *John Major*, London: Headline.
Arter, D. (2004) *The Scottish Parliament. A Scandinavian Style Assembly?* London: Frank Cass.
Ash, T. G. (2001) 'Is Britain European?', *International Affairs*, January, 77, 1, 1–13.
Ashton, S. R. (2007) 'British Government Perspectives on the Commonwealth, 1964–71: An Asset or a Liability?', *The Journal of Imperial and Commonwealth History*, Vol. 35, No.1.
Auden, W. H. (1963) 'Going into Europe', *Encounter,* Vol, 112, No. 53.
Avery, G. and Cameron, F. (1998) *The Enlargement of the European Union*, Sheffield: Sheffield Academic Press.
Baker, D., Gamble, A. and Ludlam, S. (1994) 'The Parliamentary Siege of Maastricht 1993: Conservative Divisions and British Ratification', *Parliamentary Affairs*, 47(1) pp. 35-59.
Ball, G. W. (1982) *The Past has Another Pattern: memoirs*, New York: Norton.
Ball, S. and Seldon, A. (eds) (1996) *The Heath Government 1970–74: A Reappraisal*, London: Longman.
BBC TV, 1999, The Major Years, 2nd programme.
Beetham, R. (ed.) (2001) *The Euro Debate: Persuading the People*, London: Federal Trust.
Bell, P. (1996) 'A Historical Cast of Mind: Some Eminent English Historians and Attitudes to Continental Europe in the middle of the Twentieth Century', *Journal of European Integration History*, Vol. 2, No. 2.
Bell, P. M. H. (1997) *France and Britain 1940–1994: The Long Separation*, London and New York: Longman.
Beloff, N. (1973) *Transit of Britain*, London: Collins.
Benn, T. (1988) *Out of the wilderness: diaries 1963–7*, London: Arrow Books.
——. (1996) *The Benn Diaries: Selected, Abridged and Introduced by Ruth Winstone*, London: Arrow Books.

Benvenuti, A. (2005) 'Dealing with an expanding European Community: Australia's attitude towards the EC's 1st Enlargement', *Journal of European Integration History*, Vol. II, No. 2.

Bill, J. A. (1997) *George Ball: Behind the Scenes in US Foreign Policy*, London: Yale University Press.

Blair, A. (2002) Saving the Pound? Britain's Road to Monetary Union, Harlow: Pearson.

Bloemen, E. (1995) 'A problem to every solution: The Six and the Free Trade Area', in T. B. Olsen (ed.) *Interdependence versus Integration: Denmark, Scandinavia and Western Europe 1945–1960*, Odense: Odense University Press.

Blunkett, D, (2006) *The Blunkett Tapes*, London: Bloomsbury.

Bobbit, P. (2008) *Terror and Consent: The Wars for the Twenty First Century*, London: Allen Lane.

Boehm, L. M. (2004) 'Our man in Paris: The British Embassy in Paris and the Second UK Application to Join the EEC, 1966–67', *Journal of European Integration History*, Vol. 10, No. 2.

Bogdanor, V. (1994) 'Britain and the European Community' in J. Jowell and D. Oliver (eds) *The Changing Constitution*, 3rd edition, Oxford: Clarendon Press.

——. (2005) 'Footfalls echoing in the memory. Britain and Europe: the historical perspective', *International Affairs*, Vol. 81, No. 4.

Börzel, T. A. (2002) *States and Regions in the European Union. Institutional Adaptation in Germany and Spain*, Cambridge: Cambridge University Press.

Bourne, A. K. (2000) *The EU's 16th Member State in Taxation Matters? The Basque Taxation Regime, the Challenge and the Defence*, UACES Research Workshop, 'Regionalism and the EU: Comparative and Interdisciplinary Challenges', Queens University of Belfast, 21–22 June 2000.

——. (2002) *European Integration and the Politics of Accommodation in Nationally-Diverse societies: The European Union, Practices of 'Shared Sovereignty' and the Prospects for Consensual Politics in the Basque Country*, ECPR Workshop, Turin, March 22–27 2002.

——. (2003) The Impact of European Integration on Regional Power, *Journal of Common Market Studies*, Vol. 41, No. 4, pp. 597–620.

Bower, T. (2007) *Gordon Brown Prime Minister*, London: Harper Perennial.

Brandt, W. (1978) *People and Politics: the years 1960–1975*, London: Collins.

Brivati, B. and Jones, H. (eds) (1993) *What Difference did the War Make?*, Leicester: Leicester University Press.

Broad, R. and Preston, V. (eds) (2001) *Moored to the Continent? Britain and European Integration*, London: Institute of Historical Research.

Buller, J. (2000) *National Statecraft and European Integration: The Conservative Government and the European Union, 1979–1997*, London and New York: Pinter.

Bullock, A. (1985) *Ernest Bevin: Foreign Secretary 1945–1951*, Oxford: Oxford University Press.

Bulmer, S. and Paterson, W. (1987) *The Federal Republic of Germany and the European Community*, London: Unwin Hyman.

——. Burch, M., Carter, C., Hogwood, P. and Scott, A. (2002) *British Devolution and European Policy-Making. Transforming Britain into Multi-Level Governance*, Basingstoke: Palgrave.

Bulpitt, J. (1983) *Territory and Power in the United Kingdom*, Manchester: Manchester University Press.

Burk, K. and Cairncross, A. (1992) *'Goodbye Great Britain': The 1976 IMF Crisis*, New Haven and London: Yale University Press.

Butler, D. and King, A. (1965) *The British General Election of 1964*, London: Macmillan.

Butler, D. and Kitzinger, U. (1976) *The 1975 Referendum*, London: Macmillan.

Cairncross, A. (ed.) (1982) *Anglo-American Economic Collaboration in War and Peace 1942–1949 by Sir Richard Clarke*, Oxford: Clarendon Press.

Butt P. (1992) 'British pressure groups and the European Community' in S. George (ed.) *Britain and the European Community*, Oxford: Clarendon Press.

Callaghan, J. (1987) *Time and Chance*, London: Collins.

Campbell, J. (1993) *Edward Heath: a biography*, London: Jonathan Cape.

Camps, M. (1964) *Britain and the European Community 1955–1963*, London: Oxford University Press.

Castle, B. (1993) *Fighting all the way*, London: Macmillan.

Cecil, G. (1921) *Life of the Marquis of Salisbury*, Vol. II, London: Hodder and Stoughton.

Charlton, M. (1983) *The price of victory*, London: BBC.

Charmley, J. (1995) *Churchill's Grand Alliance: The Anglo-American relationship 1940–57*, London: Hodder and Stoughton.

——. (2004) 'Splendid Isolation to Finest Hour: Britain as a Global Power, 1900–1950' in *Contemporary British History*, Vol. 18, No. 3, Autumn.

Clemens, G. (2004) 'A History of Failures and Miscalculations? Britain's Relationship to the European Communities in the Postwar Era (1945–73)', *Contemporary European History*, Vol. 13, No. 2.

CIA, *The World Factbook*, 2007 (available at *http://www.cia.gov/cia/publications/factbook/goes*).

Cini, M. (ed.) (2003) *European Union Politics*, Oxford: Oxford University Press.

Clifford, D. (2004) 'How Devolution Changed European Policy', *Agenda*, Spring 2004, pp. 47–49, Cardiff: Institute of Welsh Affairs.

Coles, J. (2000) *Making Foreign Policy*, London: John Murray.

Colman, J. (2004) 'The London Ambassadorship of David K. E. Bruce during the Wilson–Johnson Years, 1964–68', *Diplomacy and Statecraft*, Vol. 15.

Cook, R. (2003) *The Point of Departure*, London: Simon & Schuster.

COSAC (2005) *Report on the Results of COSAC's Pilot Project on the 3rd Railway Package to Test the Subsidiarity Early Warning System*, May 2005.

Croft, S. (1994) *The End of Superpower: British Foreign Office Conceptions of a Changing World, 1945–51*, Aldershot: Dartmouth.

Crossman, R. (1976) *The diaries of a Cabinet Minister, vol. 2: Lord President of the Council and Leader of the House of Commons 1966–68*, London: Hamilton Cape.

Daddow, O. J. (ed.) (2003) *Harold Wilson and European Integration: Britain's Second Application to Join the EEC*, London: Frank Cass Publishers.

——. (2004) *Britain and Europe since 1945: Historiographical perspectives on integration*, Manchester: Manchester University Press.

——. (2007) 'Playing Games with History. Tony Blair's European Policy in the Press' in *British Journal of Politics and International Relations*, Vol. 9.

Daily Telegraph

Day, R. (1989) *Grand Inquisitor: Memoirs*, London: Weidenfeld and Nicolson.

Deighton, A. (2002) 'The past in the present: British imperial memories and the European question', in J-W. Muller (ed.) *Memory and Power in Post-War Europe*, Cambridge: Cambridge University Press.

Dell, E. (1995) *The Schuman Plan and the British Abdication of Leadership in Europe*, Oxford: Oxford University Press.

Denman, R. (1996) *Missed chances: Britain and Europe in the Twentieth Century*, London: Cassell.

Dinan, D. (2004) *Europe Recast: A History of European Union*, London: Palgrave Macmillan.

Dockrill, S. (1991) *Britain's policy for West German rearmament, 1950–1955*, Cambridge: Cambridge University Press.

Documents on British Policy Overseas Series II, (1986) Vol. 1, London: HMSO.

Dorey, P. (ed.) (2006) *The Labour Governments 1964–1970*, London: Routledge.

Duff, A., Pinder, J. and Pryce, R. (eds) (1994) *Maastricht and Beyond*, London: Routledge.

Dundee Courier and Advertiser

Dutton, D. (ed.) (1995) *Statecraft and Diplomacy in the Twentieth Century*, Liverpool: Liverpool University Press.

Dyson, K. and Featherstone, K. (1999) *The Road to Maastricht: Negotiating Economic and Monetary Union*, Oxford: Oxford University Press.

Élie, J. B. (2005) 'Many times doomed but still alive: an attempt to understand the continuity of the special relationship', *Journal of Transatlantic Studies*, Vol. 3, No. 15.

Ellison, J. R. V. (2000) *Threatening Europe: Britain and the Creation of the European Community 1955–58*, Basingstoke: Macmillan.

Encounter

Eurobarometer, *http://ec.europa.eu/publicopinion/archives/eb.* website accessed 1st December 2008

Eurobarometer, *http://Europa.eu.int/comm/publicopinion/cf/waveoutput.en.cfm.* website accessed 1st December 2008

European Commission, *The EU: What's in it for me, http://ec.europa.eu/unitedkingdom/* Website accessed 1st December 2008

Eurostat (2007/08) *http://www.europa.eu.int/comm./eurostat/.*

Evans, H. (1981) *Downing Street Diary: The Macmillan Years 1957–1963*, London: Hodder & Stoughton.

Foreign Relations of the United States, (1995) Vols. VII and XIII, U.S. Department of State: Washington.

Fella, S. (2002) *New Labour and the European Union: Political strategy, policy transition and the Amsterdam Treaty negotiation*, Aldershot: Ashgate.

Financial Times

Fisher, H. A. L. (1935) *A History of Europe*, London: Eyre and Spottiswoode.

Foreign and Commonwealth Office, *The Reform Treaty: The British Approach to the EU Intergovernmental Conference* July 2007.

Forster, A. (2002) *Euroscepicism in Contemporary British Politics. Opposition to Europe in the British Conservative and Labour Parties since 1945*, London: Routledge.

—— and Blair, A. (2002) *The making of Britain's European Foreign Policy*, Harlow: Longman.

Geddes, A. (2004) *The European Union and British Politics*, Basingstoke: Palgrave Macmillan.

George, S. (1990) *An Awkward partner: Britain in the European Community*, 1st edn, Oxford: Oxford University Press.

——. (ed.) (1992) *Britain and the European Community*, Oxford: Clarendon Press.

——. (1998) *An Awkward Partner. Britain in the European Community*, 3rd edn, Oxford: Oxford University Press.

Gerstenlauer, H. (1985), German Länder in the European Community in M. Keating and B. Jones (eds), *Regions in the European Community*, Oxford: Clarendon Press.

——. (1995) German Länder and the European Community, in B. Jones and M. Keating (eds) *The European Union and the Regions*, Oxford: Clarendon Press.

Giddings, P. and Drewry, G. (ed.)(2004) *Britain in the European Union: law, policy and parliament*, Basingstoke: Palgrave Macmillan.

Gilmour, (1992) *Dancing with Dogma*, London: Simon & Schuster.

Goodheart, P. (1976) *Full-hearted Consent: the Story of the Referendum Campaign*, London: Davis–Poynter.

Gould, B. (1995) *Goodbye to All That*, London: Macmillan.

Gowland, D. (1973) *Common Market or Community?* Luton: Luton Industrial College publications.

Gowland, D. and Turner, A. (eds) (2000a) *Britain and European Integration 1945–1998: A documentary history*, London: Routledge.

——. (2000b) *Reluctant Europeans: Britain and European Integration, 1945–1998*, Harlow: Longman.

Gowland, D., Dunphy, R. and Lythe, C. (2006) *The European Mosaic: Contemporary Politics, Economics and Culture*, Harlow: Pearson Education.

Grant, C. (1994) *Delors: Inside the House that Jacques Built*, London: Nicholas Brealey.

Gray, J. (2001) Welsh Europeans in Whitehall and Brussels, *Agenda* Winter 2000/2001, Cardiff: Institute for Welsh Affairs.

Griffiths, R. T. (1995) 'The United Kingdom and the Free Trade Area: A Post Mortem', in T. B. Olsen (ed.) *Interdependence versus Integration: Denmark, Scandinavia and Western Europe 1945–1960*, Odense: Odense University Press.

Haas, E. B. (1958) *The Uniting of Europe*, Stanford: Stanford University Press.

Hassan, G. and Warhurst, C. (eds) (1999) *A Modernisers Guide to Scotland. A Different Future*, Edinburgh: Centre for Scottish Public Policy and the Big Issue.

Hattersley, R. (1995) *Who Goes Home? Scenes from a Political Life*, London: Warner Books.

Heath, E. (1998) *The course of my life: my autobiography*, London: Hodder & Stoughton.

Heggie, G. (2006) 'The Scottish Parliament and the EU Constitution. Moving beyond the Principle of Partnership?', in P. Kiiver (ed.) *National and Regional Parliaments in the European Constitution Order*, Groningen: Europa Law.

Hennessy, P. (1992) *Never again: Britain 1945–51*, London: Jonathan Cape.

Hogg, S. and Hill, J. (1995) *Too close to call*, London: Warner Books.

Holt, A. (2005) 'Lord Home and Anglo-American relations, 1961–63', *Diplomacy and Statecraft*, Vol. 16.

HMSO (1973) Cm 5460, *Royal Commission on the Constitution 1969–73 Volume 1 Report*, London.

——. (1973) Cm 5460-I, *Royal Commission on the Constitution 1969–1973, Volume II, Memorandum of Dissent*, by Lord Crowther-Hunt and Professor A.T. Peacock.

——. (1975) Cm. 6348, *Our changing democracy. Devolution to Scotland and Wales*, London.

Hooghe, L. (1995) 'Belgian Federalism and the European Community', in B. Jones and M. Keating (eds) *The European Union and the Regions*, Oxford: Clarendon Press.

Horne, A. (1988) *Macmillan, Volume 1 (1894–1956)*, London: Macmillan.

——. (1989) *Macmillan, Volume 2 (1957–1986)*, London: Macmillan.

House of Commons European Scrutiny Committee (2001–2), 'Democracy and Accountability in the EU and the Role of National Parliaments', 33rd Report.

House of Lords, European Union Committee, 14th Report of Session 2004–5, *Strengthening National Parliamentary Scrutiny of the EU – the Constitution's Subsidiarity Warning Mechanism*, HL Paper 101, April 14 2005.

Howe, G. (1994) *Conflict of Loyalty*, London: Macmillan.

Howe, S. (1993) *Anticolonialism in British Politics: The Left and the End of Empire 1918–1964*, Oxford: Clarendon Press.

http://www.euractiv.com/en/pa/eu-accounts.

http://www.number10.gov.uk/Page12094.

http://europa.eu/rapid/pressReleasesAction.

Huth, S. (1995) 'Anglo-German relations 1958–59: The postwar turning point', *Diplomacy and Statecraft*, Vol. 6, No. 3.

Janis, I. L. (1982) *Groupthink: Psychological Studies of Policy Decisions and Fiascoes*, Boston: Houghton Mifflin College Div.

Jeffery, C. (1997a) 'Conclusions: Sub-National Authorities and "European Domestic Policy"', in C. Jeffery (ed.) *The Regional Dimension of the European Union. Towards a Third Level in Europe?* London: Cass.

——. (1997b) Farewell the Third Level? The German Länder and the European Policy Process, in C. Jeffery (ed.) *The Regional Dimension of the European Union. Towards a Third Level in Europe?*, London: Cass.

——. (1997c) Regional Information Offices in Brussels and Multi-Level Governance in the EU: a UK–German Comparison, in C. Jeffery (ed.) *The Regional Dimension of the European Union. Towards a Third Level in Europe?*, London: Cass.

——. (2005) Devolution and the European Union: Trajectories and Futures, in A. Trench (ed.) *The Dynamics of Devolution: The State of the Nations*, Thorverton: Imprint Academic.

Jenkins, R. (1992) *A Life at the Centre*, London: Pan Books.

John, P. (1997) 'Europeanization in a Centralizing State: Multi-level Governance in the UK', in C. Jeffery (ed.) *The Regional Dimension of the European Union. Towards a Third Level in Europe?* London: Cass.

Johnson, G. (2004) 'Introduction: The Foreign Office and British Diplomacy in the Twentieth Century', in G. Johnson (ed.) 'The Foreign Office and British Diplomacy in the Twentieth Century' in *Contemporary British History* (special issue), Vol. 18, No. 3, Autumn.

Johnson, K. (1983) 'The National Interest and the Foreign Policy process; the British decision on EEC membership, 1955–61', unpublished thesis, Cambridge University.

Johnson, N. (2004) *Reshaping the British Constitution*, Basingstoke: Palgrave Macmillan.

Jones, B. and Keating, M. (eds) (1995) *The European Union and the Regions*, Oxford: Clarendon Press.

Jones, B. J. (2002) 'Wales in Europe. Developing a Relationship', in J.B. Jones and J. Osmond (eds) *Building a Civic Culture. Institutional Change, Policy Development and Political Dynamics in the Assembly for Wales*, Cardiff: Institute of Welsh Affairs and the Welsh Governance Centre.

——(2003) 'Wales in the European Union: Refining a Relationship', in. Magone, J.M (ed.) *Regional Institutions and Governance in the European Union*, Connecticut: Praeger.

——. (1997) 'Welsh Politics and Changing British and European Contexts', in Bradbury, J. and Mawson, J. (eds) *British Regionalism and Devolution. The Challenges of State Reform and European Integration*, London: Jessica Kingsley.

Jones, K. (1994) *An Economist among Mandarins: A Biography of Robert Hall (1901–1988)*, Cambridge: Cambridge University Press.

Jones, M. (2003) 'Anglo-American Relations after Suez, the Rise and Decline of the Working Group Experiment and the French challenge to NATO, 1957–59', *Diplomacy and Statecraft*, Vol. 1.

Journal of Common Market Studies, Oford: Blackwell.

Kaiser, W. (1996) *Using Europe, Abusing the Europeans: Britain and European Integration, 1945–1963*, Basingstoke: Palgrave Macmillan.

—— and Staerck, G. (eds) (2000) *British foreign policy, 1955–64: contracting options*, Basingstoke: Macmillan.

——. (2002) 'A never-ending story: Britain in Europe', *British Journal of Politics and International Relations*, Vol. 4, No. 1.

Kane, E. (1996) 'Tilting to Europe? British policy towards developments in European integration 1955–58', unpublished thesis, Oxford University.

Keesing's Contemporary Archives, London: Chadwyck-Healey.

Keating, M. (2001) *Plurinational Democracy. Stateless Nations in a Post-Sovereignty Era*, Oxford: Oxford University Press.

Keating, M. and Jones, B.J. (eds) (1985) *Regions in the European Community*, Oxford: Clarendon Press.

—— and Jones, B. (1995) 'The UK Experience', in Jones, B. and M. Keating (eds), *The European Union and the Regions*, Oxford: Clarendon Press.

—— and Waters, N. (1985) 'Scotland in the European Community', in M. Keating and B. Jones (eds) (1985) *Regions in the European Community*, Oxford; Clarendon Press.

Kennedy, D., Gorecki, P., Nutall, G., Sweeney, B. and Wilson, R. (1998) *Post-Agreement Northern Ireland and the European Union*, European Liaison – Institute of European Studies, Belfast: Queen's University of Belfast.

Kent, J. (1993) *British Imperial Strategy and the Origins of the Cold War*, Leicester: Leicester University Press.

Kerremans, B. and Beyers, J. (1997) 'Belgian Sub-National Entities in the European Union: Second or Third level Players?', in C. Jeffery (ed.) *The Regional Dimension of the European Union. Towards a Third level in Europe?*, London: Cass.

Kerremans, B. (2000) 'Determining a European Policy in a Multi-Level Setting: The Case of Specialized Co-ordination in Belgium', *Regional and Federal Studies*, 10: 36–61.

Keynes, J. M. (1920) *The Economic Consequences of the Peace*, New York: Harcourt, Brace and Howe.

Kiiver, P. (2006) Introduction, in P. Kiiver (ed.) *National and Regional Parliaments in the European Constitution Order*, Groningen: Europa Law.

Knudsen, A-C. L. (2005) 'The Politics of Financing the Community and the Fate of the First British Membership Application', *Journal of European Integration History*, Vol. II, No. 2.

Koestler, A. (ed.) (1963) *Suicide of a Nation? An Enquiry into the State of Britain*, London: Vintage.

L'Express

Lamb, R. (1987) *The failure of the Eden government*, London: Sidgwick & Jackson.

Lamont, N. (1999) *In Office*, London: Little, Brown.

Langford, P. (2000) *Englishness identified: manners and character 1650–1850*, Oxford: Oxford University Press.

Lawson, N. (1992) *The View From No. 11*, London: Bantam Press.

Lee. S. (2007), *Best for Britain? The Politics and legacy of Gordon Brown*, Oxford: Oneworld Publications.

Lord, C. (1994) '"With but not of": Britain and the Schuman Plan, a Reinterpretation', *Journal of European Integration History*, Vol. 4, No. 2.

Ludlow, P. (2002) 'Us or Them? The meaning of Europe in British Political Discourse' in M. Malmborg and B. Stråth (eds) *The Meaning of Europe: Variety and contention within and among Nations*, Oxford and New York: Berg.

Ludlow, N. Piers (2003) 'A Waning Force: The Treasury and British European Policy, 1955–63', *Contemporary British History*, Vol. 17, No. 4.

——. (2005) 'A Welcome Change: The European Commission and the Challenge of Enlargement, 1958–73', *Journal of European Integration History*, Vol. II, No. 2.

Macmillan, H. (1972) *Pointing the way, 1959–1961*, London: Macmillan.

——. (1973) *At the end of the day, 1961–1963*, London: Macmillan.

MacCormick, N. (1999) *Questioning Sovereignty*, Oxford: Oxford University Press.

MacShane, D. (2005) *Britain's Voice in Europe*, London: The Foreign Policy Centre.

Major, J. (1999) *The Autobiography*, London: HarperCollins.

Manchester Guardian/The Guardian.

Malmborg, M. and Stråth, B. (eds) (2002) *The Meaning of Europe; Variety and contention within and among the Nations*, Oxford and New York: Berg.

Mangold, P. (2006) *The almost impossible ally: Harold Macmillan and Charles de Gaulle*, London: I. B. Tauris.

Marjolin, R. (1989) *Architect of European Unity: Memoirs 1911–1986*, London: Weidenfeld and Nicolson.

Marks, G. (1993) 'Structural Policy and Multilevel Governance in the EC', in A.W. Cafruny and R.G. Rosenthal (eds) *The State of the European Community. Vol 2 The Maastricht Debates and Beyond*, Boulder: Lynne Rienner.

Marquand, D. 'England and Europe: the two E's that lie in wait for Brown's Britishness', 1 February 2008, *http://www.opendemocracy.net/ourkingdom/articles/browns_britishness.*

Marsh, S. and Baylis, J. (2006) 'The Anglo-American "Special Relationship": the Lazarus of international relations', *Diplomacy and Statecraft*, 17.

Mazey, S. and Mitchell, J. (1993), 'Europe of the Regions: Territorial Interests and European Integration. The Scottish Experience', in S. Mazey and J. Richardson (eds) *Lobbying in The European Community*, Oxford: Oxford University Press.

McGowan, L. and Murphy, M. (2000) *Coming to terms with Europe and EU Integration: the Handling of European Policy-making within the Devolved Institutions of Northern Ireland*, paper presented at the UACES workshop on Regionalism and the EU: Comparative and Interdisciplinary Perspectives, Queen's University Belfast, June 21–22 2000.

Melissen, J. and Zeeman, B. (1987) 'Britain and Western Europe 1945–51: opportunities lost?', *International Affairs*, Vol. 63.

Menon, A. (ed.) (2004) *Britain and European Integration: Views from Within*, Oxford: Blackwell.

Milward, A. S. (1984) *The Reconstruction of Western Europe 1945–51*, London: Methuen.

——. (2002) *The Rise and Fall of a National Strategy 1945–1963 (The United Kingdom and the European Community)* Vol. 1, London: Frank Cass.

Mitchell, J. (1997) 'Scotland, the Union State and the International Environment', in M. Keating and J. Loughlin (eds) *The Political Economy of Regionalism*, London: Cass.
——. (2003) *Governing Scotland*, Basingstoke: Palgrave.
Monnet, J. (1978) *Memoirs*, London: Collins.
Moravcsik, A. (1998) *The Choice for Europe: Social Purpose and State Power from Messina to Maastricht*, London: University College London Press.
Morgan, K., *Callaghan: a life* (1997), Oxford: Oxford University Press.
Mullen, A. and Burkitt, B. (2005) 'Spinning Europe: Pro-European Propaganda Campaigns in Britain, 1962–75', *The Political Quarterly*, Vol. 76, No. 1 January–March.
Muller, J-W. (ed.) (2002) *Memory and Power in Post-War Europe*, Cambridge: Cambridge University Press.
Murkens, J.E. (2001) *Scotland's place in Europe*, London: The Constitution Unit.
Murray, G. (2000) 'New Relations Between Scotland and Ireland', in A. Wright (ed.) *Scotland: the Challenge of Devolution*, Aldershot: Ashgate.
National Centre for Social Research (2007) *British Social Attitudes*, January.
New Dictionary of National Biography (2004–5), Oxford: Oxford University Press.
Naughtie, J. (2002) *Rivals: The Intimate Story of a Political Marriage*, London: Fourth Estate.
Northern Ireland Assembly, Committee of the Centre (2002) *Inquiry into the Approach of the Northern Ireland Assembly and the Devolved Government on European Union Issues*, Report and Proceedings of the Committee Relating to the Report, Session 2001/2002, Second Report, Belfast: the Stationery Office.
Nutting, A. (1960) *Europe will not wait*, London: Hollis & Carter.
O' Farrell, J. (1998) *Things Can Only Get Better: Eighteen Miserable Years in the Life of a Labour Supporter, 1979–1997*, London: Doubleday.
Olsen, T. B. (1995) *Interdependence and Integration: Denmark, Scandinavia and Western Europe 1945–1960*, Odense: Odense University Press.
Olsen, J. P. (c. 2002), *Four Faces of Europeanization*, Arena Seminar, the University of Oslo, Undated.
O'Neill, C. (2000) *Britain's entry into the European Community: report by Sir Con O'Neill on the negotiations of 1970–1972 edited by Hannay, D.*, London: Whitehall History Publishing in association with Frank Cass.
Osmond, J. (2000) 'A Constitutional Convention by Other Means', in Hazell, R. (ed.) *The State and the Nations. The First Year of Devolution in the United Kingdom*, Thorverton: Imprint Academic.
——. (2003) 'From Corporate Body to Virtual Parliament', in R. Hazell (ed.) *The State of the Nations 2003*, Thorverton: Imprint Academic.
Owen, D. (1991) *Time to Declare*, London: Michael Joseph.
Park, J. (1997) 'Wasted Opportunities? The 1950s Rearmament Programme and the Failure of British Economic Policy', *Journal of Contemporary History*, Vol. 32, No. 3.
Parliamentary Debates (Hansard) House of Commons Official Report, London: Chadwyck-Healey.
Parr, H. (2005) 'A Question of Leadership: July 1966 and Harold Wilson's European Decision', *Contemporary British History*, Vol. 19, No. 4.
Parris, M. (2002) *Chance Witness: An Outsider's Life in Politics*, London: Penguin.
Patten, C. (1998) *East and West*, London: Pan Books.
——. (2005) *Not Quite the Diplomat*, London: Allen Lane.
Peston, R. (2006) *Brown's Britain*, London: Short Books.

Peterson, J. and Shackleton, M. (eds.) (2002) *The Institutions of the European Union*, Oxford: Oxford University Press.

Pickering, J. (2002) 'Politics and Black Tuesday: Shifting Power in the Cabinet and the Decision to Withdraw from East of Suez, November 1967–January 1968', *Twentieth Century British History*, Vol. 13, No. 2.

Pilkington, C. (2001) *Britain in the European Union today*, 2nd edn, Manchester: Manchester University Press.

Pimlott, B. (1992) *Harold Wilson*, London: HarperCollins.

Pine, M. (2004) 'British Personal Diplomacy and Public Policy: The Soames Affair', *Journal of European Integration History*, Vol. 4, No. 2.

Price, L. (2006) *The Spin Doctor's Diary: Inside Number 10 with New Labour*, London: Hodder & Stoughton Books.

Raunio, T. and Wright, A. (2006) 'Holyrood and Europe: An Incremental Response to Deparliamentarisation', *Journal of Regional and Federal Studies*, Vol. 16, No. 3, September 2006.

Rawnsley, A. (2001) *Servants of the People: The Inside Story of New Labour*, London: Penguin Books.

Redwood, J. (2001) 'Sovereignty and Democracy,' in M. Rosenbaum (ed.) *Britain and Europe. The Choices we Face*, Oxford: Oxford University Press.

RegLeg (2004), *Declaration of Edinburgh*, Adopted by the 5th Conference of Presidents of Regions with Legislative Powers, November 30 2004.

Reynolds, D. (1991) *Britannia Overruled: British Policy and World Power in the 20th Century*, Harlow: Longman.

Rhodes, R.A.W. (1974) 'Regional Policy and a "Europe of Regions": a Critical Assessment', *Regional Studies*, 8: 105–14.

Riddell, P. (1991) *The Thatcher Era and its Legacy*, Oxford: Blackwell.

——. (2003) *Hug Them Close: Blair, Clinton, Bush and the 'Special Relationship'*, London: Politico's.

——. (2006) *The Unfulfilled Prime Minister: Tony Blair's quest for a legacy*, London: Politico's.

Roberts, A. (1999) *Salisbury: Victorian Titan*, London: Weidenfeld and Nicolson.

——. (2006) *A History of the English-speaking Peoples since 1900*, London: Weidenfeld and Nicolson.

Rollings, N. (2007) *British Business in the Formative Years of European Integration, 1945–1973*, Cambridge: Cambridge University Press.

Rosamond, B. (2000) *Theories of European Integration*, Houndsmill: Palgrave.

Routledge, P. (1998) *Gordon Brown: The Biography* London: Pocket Books.

Roy, R. (2000) 'The Battle for the Pound: The Political Economy of Anglo-American Relations 1964–68', unpublished thesis, London School of Economics.

Royal Society of Edinburgh (2004) *Inquiry into the Future of the Scottish Fishing Industry*, Edinburgh.

Ruane, K. and Ellison, J. (2004) 'Managing the Americans: Anthony Eden, Harold Macmillan and the Pursuit of "Power-by-Proxy" in the 1950s', *Contemporary British History*, Vol. 18, No. 3.

Sampson, A. (1968) *The New Europeans*, London: Hodder and Stoughton.

Sandbrook, D. (2005) *Never had it so good: a history of Britain from Suez to the Beatles*, London: Little, Brown.

Sanders, D. (1990) *Losing an Empire, Finding a Role: British Foreign Policy since 1945*, Basingstoke: Macmillan.

Schaad, M. (1998) 'Plan G – A "Counterblast"? British Policy towards the Messina Countries, 1956', *Contemporary European History*, Vol. 7, 1998.

Schieren, S. (2001) Independence in Europe: Scotland's Choice?, in *Scottish Affairs*, No. 31, Spring 2000, pp. 111–27.

Scott, A., Peterson, J., and Millar, D. (1994) 'Subsidiarity: A "Europe of the Regions" v. the British Constitution', in the *Journal of Common Market Studies*, Vol. 32, No. 1, March 1994, pp. 47–67.

Scott, D. (2004) *Off Whitehall: A View from Downing Street by Tony Blair's Adviser*, London: I. B. Tauris & Co. Ltd.

Scottish Office (1991a) *The Scottish Office and the European Community: A Review*, European Funds Division and the Central Research Unit.

——. (1991b) *The Scottish Office and the European Community: Implementation Plan for the Review Recommendations*, European Co-ordination Division September 1991.

Seldon, A. (1997) *Major: A Political Life*, London: Weidenfield & Nicolson.

——. (1998) *Major: A Political Life*, London: Phoenix.

——, Snowdon, P. and Collings, D. (2008) *Blair Unbound*, London: Pocket Books.

——, Ballinger, C., Collings, D. and Snowdon, P. (2005) *Blair*, London: The Free Press.

——. (ed.) (2007) *Blair's Britain 1997–2007*, Cambridge: Cambridge University Press.

Siedentop, L. (2001) *Democracy in Europe*, London: Penguin Books.

Sillars, J. (1986) *The Case for Optimism*, Edinburgh: Polygon.

——. (1989) 'Independence in Europe, SNP, Edinburgh', in L. Paterson *A Diverse Assembly*, Edinburgh University Press, Edinburgh.

Simms, B. (2007) *Three Victories and a Defeat*, London: Allen Lane.

Smith, J. (2003) 'An Incremental Odyssey: The Structural Europeanization of Government Bureaucracy', *Scottish Affairs*, 44: 132–56.

Spaak, P-H. (1971) *The continuing battle: memoirs of a European, 1936–1966*, London: Weidenfeld and Nicolson.

Spiering, M. (1997) 'Why the British are not Europeans', *Europa*, Vol. 2, No. 1.

Steel, D. (1989) *Against Goliath: The David Steel Story*, London: Weidenfield and Niholson.

Stephens, P. (1996) *Politics and the Pound: The Conservatives' Struggle with Sterling*, Basingstoke, Macmillan.

——. (2005) 'Britain and Europe: An Unforgettable Past and an Unavoidable Future' in *The Political Quarterly*, Vol. 7, No. 1, January–March.

Tebbitt, N. (1989) *Upwardly Mobile*, London: Weidenfeld and Nicolson.

Thatcher, M. (1993) *The Downing Street Years*, London: HarperCollins.

——. (1995) *The Path to Power*, London: HarperCollins.

The Agreement (1998) The Government of the United Kingdom of Great Britain and Northern Ireland and the Government of Ireland.

The Economist

The Herald.

The Independent.

The Independent on Sunday.

The Observer.

The Spectator.

Sun.

The Times.

The Sunday Times.

Tratt, J. (1996) *The Macmillan government and Europe: a study in the process of policy development*, Basingstoke, Macmillan.

Treaty Establishing a Constitution for Europe, 2005, European Communities, Luxembourg.

Treaty of Lisbon, amending the Treaty on European Union and the Treaty Establishing the European Community, 2007, Official Journal of the European Union, C 306, Vol. 50, 17 December 2007.

Trench, A. (2003) 'Intergovernmental Relations', in R. Hazell (ed.) *The State of the Nations 2003*, Thorverton: Imprint Academic.

Trevelyan, G. M. (1946) *English Social History*, London: Longman.

Trewin, I. (ed.) (2008) *The Hugo Young Papers: Thirty Years of British Politics – Off the Record*, London: Allen Lane.

Tugendhat, C. (1986), *Making Sense of Europe*, London: Viking.

Turpin, C. (2001) 'The Constitutional Impact of British Membership of the European Union', in R. Broad and V. Preston (eds) *Moored to the Continent? Britain and European Integration*, London: Institute of Historical Research.

Urban, G. (1996) *Diplomacy and Disillusion at the Court of Margaret Thatcher: An Insider's View*, London: I. B. Tauris.

Urwin, D. W. (1995) *The Community of Europe: A History of European Integration since 1945*, Harlow: Pearson Education.

Vital, D. (1968) *The making of British foreign policy*, London: Allen and Unwin.

Wall, S. (2008) *A Stranger in Europe: Britain and the EU from Thatcher to Blair*, Oxford: Oxford University Press.

Wallace, W. (2005) 'The collapse of British foreign policy' in *International Affairs*, Vol. 81, No. 1, January.

Walters, A. A. (1990) *Sterling in danger: the economic consequences of pegged exchange rates*, London: Fontana Paperbacks.

Ward, S. (ed.) (2001) *British culture and the end of empire*, Manchester: Manchester University Press.

Warner, G. (2002) 'Review article on Why the General said No', *International Affairs*, Vol. 78, No. 4.

Warner, G. (ed.) (2005) *In the Midst of Events: The Foreign Office diaries and papers of Kenneth Younger February 1950–October 1951*, London: Routledge.

Weight, R. (2002) *Patriots: National Identity in Britain 1940–2000*, Basingstoke: Macmillan.

White, R. (1995) '"Through a glass darkly" The Foreign Office investigation of French federalism, January-May 1930', in D. Dutton (ed.) *Statecraft and Diplomacy in the Twentieth Century*, Liverpool: Liverpool University Press.

Wilford, R. and Wilson, R. (2000) 'A "Bare Knuckle Ride": Northern Ireland', in R. Hazell (ed.) *The State and the Nations. The First Year of Devolution in the United Kingdom*, Thorverton: Imprint Academic.

——. and Wilson, R. (2008) Northern Ireland, *Monitor*, Issue 38, London: The Constitution Unit.

Williams, P. (1979) *Hugh Gaitskell: A Political Biography*, London: Jonathan Cape.

Wilson, H. (1970) *Final Term: The Labour Government 1974–76*, London: Weidenfeld & Nicolson and Michael Joseph.

Winetrobe, B. (1999) *Scottish Parliament*, SPICe, Research Paper 99/12.

Wright, A. (1995) 'The Europeanization of the Scottish Office', in S. Hardy *et al.* (eds) *Region Building*, pp. 81–85, the Regional Studies Association, London.

——. (1996) 'Scottish Fishermen and the EU: A choice between two Unions?', *Scottish Affairs*, 14: 27–41.

——. (2000a) Scotland and the EU: All Bark and no Bite?, in A. Wright (ed.) *Scotland: the Challenge of Devolution*, Aldershot: Ashgate.

——. (2000b) 'The Europeanization of Scotland. A Driver for Autonomy', in M. Graves and G. Girrard (eds) *Europe United, the United Kingdom Disunited?* Brest: University of Brest.

——. (2000c) '*2002 Review of CFP*', *Scottish Affairs*, No. 32: 59–78.

——. (2003) 'The Internationalisation of Scottish Politics. Who Governs Scotland?', in Magone, J. (ed.) *Regional Institutions and Governance in the European Union*, Westport: Praeger.

——. (2004) 'Devolution, Westminster and the EU', in P. Giddens and G. Drewry (eds) *Britain in the European Union: Law, Policy and Parliament*, Basingstoke: Palgrave,

——. (2005) *Who Governs Scotland?* London: Routledge.

Young, H. (1990), *One of Us: a biography of Margaret Thatcher*, London: Pan Books.

——. (1998) *This Blessed Plot: Britain and Europe from Churchill to Blair*, London: Papermac.

Young, J. W. (1996) 'The Heath Government and British entry into the European Community', in S. Ball and A. Seldon (eds) *The Heath Government 1970–74: A Reappraisal*, London: Longman.

——. (2000) *Britain and European Unity 1945–1999*, 2nd edn, Basingstoke: Macmillan.

Ziegler, P. (1993) *Harold Wilson The Authorised Life*, London: Weidenfeld & Nicolson.

Index